# The Business of Sports

Sports has evolved into a profitable, complicated, and multi-dimensional business, as broad and complex as any. This unique volume explores the business aspect of sports with an orientation to those topics that are most relevant to journalists. It provides journalists with the foundation for understanding the various parts of the sports business. Moving beyond sports writing, this text offers a distinct perspective on professional, college, and international sports organizations—structure, governance, labor issues, and other business factors within the sports community.

Additions to this second edition include:

- Updates throughout, including disciplinary policies throughout the major sports leagues;
- Expanded discussion of intellectual property issues and merchandising;
- New sections on ethical issues in sports, aimed at journalists.

Written clearly and compellingly, *The Business of Sports* includes cases (historical, current, and hypothetical) to illustrate how business concerns play a role in the reporting of sports.

**Mark Conrad** is Associate Professor and Chair of the Legal and Ethical Studies Area at Fordham University's School of Business Administration, where he teaches Sports Law, Media Law, and other law classes. He also teaches at Columbia University's graduate program in Sports Management. Professor Conrad has published in academic, legal, and general circulation publications, including *The New York Times*, *Wall Street Journal*, *Sports Business Journal*, and the *New York Law Journal*. He is a frequent blogger for Sports Law Blog. Professor Conrad received his J.D. from New York Law School, and he holds an M.S. from Columbia University's Graduate School of Journalism.

# COMMUNICATION SERIES
Jennings Bryant/Dolf Zillmann, General Editors

Selected titles include:

**Real Feature Writing, 2nd Edition**
*Aamidor*

**Professional Feature Writing, 5th Edition**
*Garrison*

**The Handbook of Sports and Media**
*Raney/Bryant*

**The Essentials of Sports Reporting and Writing**
*Reinardy/Wanta*

# The Business of Sports

A Primer for Journalists

2nd Edition

**Mark Conrad**

First edition published 2006
by Lawrence Erlbaum Associates Inc.

This edition published 2011
by Routledge
270 Madison Ave, New York, NY 10016

Simultaneously published in the UK
by Routledge
2 Park Square, Milton Park, Abingdon, Oxon OX14 4RN

*Routledge is an imprint of the Taylor & Francis Group, an informa business*

© 2006 Lawrence Erlbaum Associates, Inc., 2011 Routledge, Taylor and Francis

Typeset in Sabon by Prepress Projects Ltd, Perth, UK
Printed and bound in the United States of America on acid-free paper by Edwards Brothers, Inc.

*Library of Congress Cataloging in Publication Data*
Conrad, Mark, 1958–
The business of sports : a primer for journalists / Mark Conrad. — 2nd ed.
p. cm.
Includes index.
1. Sports—Economic aspects. 2. Sports administration. 3. Sports journalism. I. Title.
GV716.C665 2010
796.068—dc22
2010026433

ISBN 13: 978-0-415-87652-0 (hbk)
ISBN 13: 978-0-415-87653-7 (pbk)
ISBN 13: 978-0-203-83530-2 (ebk)

To Kaz and Josh, the stars of my home team, and to my parents, who brought me into the big leagues

# Contents in Brief

# Detailed Table of Contents

# Preface to the First Edition

Professional and amateur sports occupy a prominent place in society, as a dynamic and visible entertainment business with worldwide reach. The numbers of spectators, viewers, and participants run into the billions. Millions of people either read the sports pages of a newspaper, buy a sports-oriented magazine, watch the sports segment of a newscast, subscribe to a cable service offering sports programming, or listen to or call in to a "sports talk" radio station.

At one time, sports coverage was quite simply scores, standings, and star performances. However, the continuing popularity and increased complexity of the sports landscape require that sports journalists possess a background on issues more fundamental than mere knowledge of the game. The sports industry is a multi-billion-dollar business that involves many unique and complicated issues—issues that often beg to be discussed and analyzed in an objective and systematic way. Think of the amount of coverage the labor controversies receive, for example. Other issues also abound, including contract rights, free agency, amateur eligibility, drug testing, franchise relocation, stadium construction, and athlete and spectator injuries. There are also the questions of intellectual property rights, racial and gender discrimination, and the use and power of agents and financial advisors. Even seemingly arcane matters such as league governance, calculation of team revenues, salary cap restraints, and taxation of athletes' salaries result in greater discussion and coverage.

Many seasoned journalists do an excellent job covering the business of sports. But others—not only writers and broadcasters, but also many sports talk hosts—do not. Misstatements of facts, improbable assumptions, and other evidence of a lack of understanding occur all too frequently. For students of journalism and communications (and younger practitioners of the craft), this text is a primer to the business of sports and provides a guide to give students and newly minted sports writers, producers, and broadcasters a basic knowledge of the sports business.

This text covers many facets of the business. I focus on what I think constitute the main issues of importance to young journalists: professional, amateur, and international sports structure and governance, contract and labor issues, and stadium economics. Agents, intellectual property, testing for performance-enhancing drugs, personal injury, and media issues are also covered, although in shorter chapters. Some readers may be surprised at the paucity of discussion of criminal activity by athletes. Since most criminal cases against athletes involve actions outside of the athletic activity, the issues are no different for an athlete than for a nonathlete. The trials of O. J. Simpson and the charges against Kobe Bryant do not directly bear on the sports business, and there are many sources for learning about the criminal justice system.

Many readers will notice that a great deal of the subject matter is complex and very detailed. Topics such as salary caps and stadium revenues are difficult by nature, but are crucial to a knowledge of the business of sports.

I wish to thank all who contributed to this book—my graduate assistants Hannah Amoah, Benjamin Berlin, Jacob Preiserwicz, Paul Rudewick, Lisa Brubaker, Alyona Teeter, Anide Jean, Hanna Minkin, Jeffrey Franco, Jeff Li, Parandzem Gharibian, and Samuel I. Mok. I also want to thank my colleagues Priti Doshi, Esq.; Marianne Reilly, Associate Athletic Director, Fordham University; and Bob Pockrass, Associate Editor of *NASCAR Scene* for all their help. Finally I want to express my gratitude to Acquisitions Editor Linda Bathgate and Senior Production Editor Marianna Vertullo for their patience, encouragement, and guidance. Similar thanks go to Kirsten Kite, who went beyond the call of duty in creating the indices that appear in the book.

# Preface to the Second Edition

Often second editions of academic texts do not require much content change from that of the prior editions. However, the changes in the sports business landscape over the last half-decade necessitated considerable revisions in this text. Professional sports leagues have new owners and in some cases, new commissioners. Franchise values continue to increase, despite the economic downturn of the late 2000s. Collective bargaining agreements that were freshly minted in 2006 expire in 2011, with the possibility of labor unrest in any or all of the four major league sports. Drug testing (better termed testing for performance-enhancing drugs [PEDs]) became a cause célèbre in the halls of Congress, which resulted in greater testing regimens, but a feeling that the authorities must play catch-up with the pharmacologists who, in the laboratory trenches, develop new forms of performance-enhancing drugs and their masking agents. Sports endorsement contracts have become even more sophisticated. Salaries for in-demand coaches continue their spiral. Intellectual property issues involving dissemination of team logos and player names into newer technological formats provide fascinating property issues, but bedevil the courts, which have to apply more traditional laws to new electronic media.

The 2008 and 2010 Olympics are now history. The NCAA continues to face pressure to ease some of its bedrock amateurism rules. Sports injuries receive greater attention in the wake of the high-profile cases of former NFL players disabled by the effects of concussions received during their playing days. The increasing utilization of social media, such as Twitter, and blogging limits privacy as never before, but expands and changes the scope of intellectual property rights.

All this necessitated a new edition of the book. More comprehensive and more up to date, the second edition of *The Business of Sports: A Primer for Journalists* includes more discussion about international sports (including a description of the "promotion/relegation" system found in much of world soccer), labor agreements, and the interconnection between sports leagues and antitrust law. New media—including creations such as Twitter—that did not exist in 2005 and the increased prevalence of Internet streaming of sports events are covered. A major change is an enhanced treatment of ethical issues in sports. Found in almost every chapter, the goal of the "ethical issues" segment is to alert readers of the ethical consequences of a policy or rule, or lack thereof. Ethical issues often pose not answers but questions, which result in debate and discussion.

Finally, on a more technical matter, many of the references found in the first edition were websites that no longer exist. Those found to be inaccessible were eliminated and replaced by updated websites.

During my one-year-plus time in revamping the old text into the new edition, I have been assisted by two of my graduate assistants. Thanks go to Patrick Harrington, an undergraduate student at Fordham University's College of Business, who displayed a keen sensitivity for proofreading and identified some inconsistencies in the text. Yao Huang deserves major league kudos for his hard work in this endeavor. Yao was absolutely indispensable in fact checking, perusing the various collective bargaining agreements, and updating references. Without him, this project would not be done.

# Introduction
## What Makes Sports a Unique Business?

In 2008–09 almost 137 million people attended Major League Baseball, National Basketball Association (NBA), National Hockey League (NHL), National Football League (NFL), and Major League Soccer contests. Another 75 million attended college football, basketball, and hockey games. Such numbers define sports as a premier entertainment business. Evolving over the last century from a mom-and-pop-style business into a dynamic economic juggernaut of high revenues, lucrative compensation, and high visibility, professional and amateur sports are watched, debated, invested in, and broadcast. For anyone seeking to cover sports, its business structure is just as salient as the runs, touchdowns, and baskets made on the field.

Yet the sports business defies easy categorization. Unlike manufacturing, it does not focus on the production of goods. Unlike real estate, it does not relate only to the buying and selling of land. Unlike accounting or law, it does not involve licensed professionals charging fees for advice. But an industry it is, evolving into multifaceted enterprises with tentacles reaching far beyond its original objective.

The sports business displays similarities to the entertainment industry. At first glance one may wince at this characterization, but sports have greater similarity to film, theater, and music than to manufacturing goods or to real estate. Like these entertainment forums, sports provide a form of leisure, not a necessity for survival—a diversion, albeit a passionate one. People pay to attend sports exhibitions by choice, not by governmental fiat.

With sports, as in other aspects of entertainment, the focus is on the *person*, not the property. Professional athletes (and some would argue collegiate athletes as well) engage in personal services. Star athletes, like star performers, command tremendous public recognition with their on- and off-the-field exploits, often covered by media thirsty for every angle of their lives. Athletes are frequently public figures, which means that the media have a de facto license to report on their athletic and nonathletic activities. And they are often far better known than the owners who pay them.

As in the case of entertainers, agents represent professional athletes. Although differences exist, their basic role is the same: negotiating employment contracts and marketing their clients. As shown later in this book, agents not only do the face-to-face negotiations, but also have to sell the image of the athlete to the public, much like an agent representing a film or music star. Additionally, both athletes and entertainers work under the rules of their unions. For example, film actors often have to operate under the rules negotiated by the Screen Actors' Guild and Hollywood studios. Similarly, football players have to operate under the agreements negotiated between the NFL Players Association (NFLPA) and the NFL.

In the amateur world, fame (but not fortune) greets the top National Collegiate Athletic Association (NCAA) athletes in football and in men's and, increasingly, women's basketball. Better known than the valedictorians of their classes, these top players bring considerable publicity and revenues to the institutions they attend in terms of ticket sales, broadcast revenues, and merchandising. Note the term *revenues*, not profits. In most collegiate athletic programs, costs outpace revenue, and therefore the programs lose money.

As for entertainers, athletes' careers and fortunes ride a roller-coaster of highs and lows. A famous star makes three bad films, diminishing or possibly ending his or her career. An athlete in the midst of his second disappointing season will incur the wrath of the fans and may be released on completion of his contract (or during the contract, as is often the case of the NFL). On the other hand, an unsung third-string player may lead teammates to a championship and be forever immortalized.

Unlike entertainers, who have received compensation for their work for centuries, athletes traditionally embraced the ideal of "amateurism." In the nineteenth century, sports activities were largely the domain of wealthy men who participated in polo, yachting, and tennis (Thorne, Wright, & Jones, 2001). The twentieth century brought viability to "professionals" in sports, and the result has been a dramatic increase in the economic effects of sports exhibitions, which by the end of the century generated nearly $400 billion annually in the United States through corporate sponsorship, stadium construction, licensing, apparel, equipment, media investments, and spectator expenditures (Thorne, Wright, & Jones, 2001, citing Burton, 1999; Hunter & Mayo, 1999). Amateur sporting events such as the NCAA tournaments and college bowl games also have been revenue raisers.

Contrary to the pieties of certain sports writers of yore, sports have been a business longer than some care to admit. Today, the industry is simply a bigger one. The increased popularity and complexities of the sports universe have resulted in the expansion of the sports business to include issues such as intellectual property, stadium construction, and business governance. Revenue streams have diversified. For example, until the advent of modern broadcasting, gate receipts were virtually the only revenue stream for sports. In the last eighty years, revenues from radio, then television, then cable, and now satellite and Internet have brought billions of dollars to the pockets of team owners, athletes, colleges, conferences, and amateur organizations. Sports marketing has therefore evolved into an important specialty, as merchandise sales, sponsorships, and naming rights command an important base in producing revenues and branding the sport.

The ownership of sports franchises has changed greatly. In the early twentieth century, owners of baseball teams often had a reputation of being "penny-ante" businessmen just one stop on the right side of the law (Fetter, 2003). Today, some of the largest corporations and wealthiest individuals own franchises, which are often a crown jewel of their financial portfolios. And some of the players achieve wealth matching or exceeding the level of successful corporate chief executive officers.

All of these considerations result in a complex economic and regulatory structure, with a vast array of rules and a full slate of constituencies that have to be satisfied. Leagues, team owners, coaches, players, colleges, amateur athletic associations, unions, agents, and the Olympic personnel are just some of the players in the business of sports.

Until recently, all too many sports writers focused on the hits, runs, touchdowns, and personalities of the players. Today, to be an effective sports writer, one has to know the business behind the scores.

## What Makes Sports a Unique Industry?

Today, professional and amateur sports in North America have unique attributes. Although we discuss these characteristics in more detail in the following chapters, a short summary follows here.

### A Cartel Structure

At the outset, those wishing to understand the professional team sports structure will realize the uniqueness in its organization and operation as compared with most other businesses. In a market-driven economy, the goal of a typical business is to achieve success by direct competition with others. Whether the business is automobiles or appliances, most consumers choose to buy a product from a number of firms manufacturing or selling that item, and their decision to purchase is based on factors such as needs, quality, brand reputation, and/or price. The same can be said for choosing service professionals. One may choose a physician or a lawyer from a number of practitioners, based on references, training, professional manner, and insurance coverage.

This traditional competitive structure is not found in professional sports leagues and amateur organizations. First and foremost, the competition is limited not by circumstance, but by intention. Almost every sports organization's structure restricts free and open competition. In the professional sphere, the leagues limit the number of competitors by awarding exclusive franchises in different markets. With a few exceptions, one team occupies that particular market. In doing so, leagues create a limited market and operate as a cartel. In certain respects, this is analogous to the Organization of the Petroleum Exporting Countries (OPEC). In both cases, membership is limited and the product is controlled. OPEC countries may control and have controlled the production levels of oil in attempts to dominate the market. Sports leagues regulate which teams may compete, where they can compete, the number of players on a team, and the sharing of certain revenues.

This does not mean that no competition exists. There is direct and often intense competition among the teams in a given league, even resulting in rancor between the owners of those teams. In a competitive atmosphere, the desired goal (and the hope of fans) is for that team to win a championship. If they have the resources and the will, owners will acquire expensive free-agent players to increase their chances of success. Think of the Boston Red Sox and the New York Yankees.

Yet, on another level, these teams cooperate in very important matters, such as labor issues, broadcasting, merchandising, and revenue sharing. The result is a hybrid identity. The team sells itself as both a local franchise and a representative of the league. As shown later, differences exist among the major leagues regarding the sharing of revenues and salary controls, but the basic organizational plan remains similar. This competition versus cooperation dichotomy is explained in more detail in chapter 1.

Many of the controversies that have bedeviled sports leagues involve the balance of power between the central office and the team owners. Centralized league control of independent franchises has existed in its present form for over ninety years. Major League Baseball created the position of commissioner to run the league's affairs. As the chief executive officer of baseball, the commissioner was empowered to set league policy, control discipline, and, in more recent years, spearhead labor negotiations with the players. Other leagues replicated this system.

This interplay of a centralized authority with the independently owned teams that compete against each other in that collective has created tension between the players, team owners, and the league commissioners. The courts have had a role in these disputes because the unique nature of professional sports league structure has raised antitrust law concerns. (A notable exception, however, is Major League Baseball, which has been exempt from antitrust laws.)

The specter of antitrust lurks through much of the legal regime of professional and amateur sports. Courts have been asked to determine the anticompetitive impact of league and organization decisions for the last half-century. As will be discussed in later chapters, these antitrust challenges involve complex legal applications and, at times, inconsistent legal conclusions.

Because of the often extensive and expensive litigation, an alternative known as a "single-entity" league was created over the last decade and a half. We discuss this in more detail later in chapter 1. Simply put, in a pure single-entity league, no independent owners exist. Rather, the league owns and operates the teams in a single corporation. There may be some advantages in this schema, particularly in salary control, but there are structural disadvantages as well. For reasons discussed in chapter 1, the allure of single-entity leagues has diminished, as these leagues either folded outright or were transformed into a more traditional league or a hybrid.

Another alternative is the approach that has governed many non-U.S. professional soccer leagues. This system, known as "promotion and relegation," also discussed in chapter 1, creates a system in which teams are promoted to higher divisions or demoted to lower levels of competition based on success (Ziegler, 2009). Promotion and relegation leagues result in more fluidity and fewer antitrust issues, but the system may weaken the marketability and economic value of individual teams. Therefore, this approach has not caught on in the United States.

On the amateur and international levels, the cartel structure also exists. There are exclusive bodies—both national and international—that govern various team and individual sports. The International Skating Union regulates competitive figure skating, and U.S. Figure Skating is its domestic affiliate. The International Association of Athletics Federations (IAAF) and USA Track & Field do the same with track and field competitions. And, of course, the NCAA is the body that legislates, adjudicates, and enforces the rules for collegiate sports for most four-year colleges in the United States. The NCAA has de facto control of collegiate athletics and produces a tome-like manual of bylaws to ensure that college athletes conform to the organization's definition of *amateur*. The enforcement powers of these organizations are considerable, although in recent years some of their decisions have been successfully challenged in the courts.

Members of these international and amateur organizations, whether they are colleges, affiliates, or athletes, must abide by the often complex rules promulgated by their central governing bodies. They must submit to the rules and regulations of the NCAA, or, in the case of noncollegiate but traditionally amateur sports, the national governing bodies and the international governing organizations. A figure skater performs under the rules of U.S. Figure Skating, which is under the jurisdiction of its international parent, the International Skating Union.

Often, bureaucratic power struggles erupt. Tensions may occur between individual schools and the NCAA, or between international organizations and their national counterparts, over eligibility and drug-testing issues.

Until recently, dispute mechanisms were scattershot or nonexistent. These issues are discussed in detail in chapters 3 and 4.

### Key Centralized Operations

By agreement, sports organizations and leagues have centralized control over certain important facets of their business. These powers focus on franchising and income-producing possibilities.

*Exclusive Franchising Authority.* In the professional leagues, in order to admit new franchises, an affirmative vote of the other team owners is needed. Usually, a high percentage (known in corporate law parlance as a maxi-majority) of owners in the league must approve any new franchises. For example, in Major League Baseball, that requirement is a three-quarter-majority vote (Major League Baseball Constitution, Article 2, sec. 2). The commissioner and the owners (or an appointed committee) screen the applications, utilizing a "due diligence" standard in scrutinizing the finances and investigating the backgrounds of the applicant(s) to ensure they display proper "good character" before approving the new franchise (NHL Bylaws, secs. 35.1, 37).

*Marketing and Licensing Control.* Each of the professional leagues (often with the players' unions' approval and participation) has created separate divisions to control the licensing of its intellectual property, which include trademarks, copyrighted materials, and the likenesses of its athletes. As is explained in chapter 12, although differences exist, the basic agreement is that sales revenues from items containing league and team logos and players' names and likenesses are divided among all the teams and the players. Such rights amount to billions of dollars in the league's coffers. Similar powers exist in the NCAA, but they are not as encompassing. Member schools and athletic conferences do retain rights involving licensing and merchandising.

Often, the leagues, as representatives of their teams, conclude agreements with vendors to license the names of their member teams to apparel and shoe firms and companies making collectables, such as trading cards and bobblehead dolls.

*Broadcasting.* In professional sports, the determination and division of broadcasting rights varies from league to league, but all of the major leagues have the power to negotiate exclusive broadcasting, cablecasting, and satellite rights, and, increasingly, Internet video streaming and mobile phone agreements. The scope and amount of these rights differ considerably. In Major League Baseball, local broadcasting and cable rights are independently negotiated and are not shared by other teams. This results in considerable disparity in revenue streams, as major market teams such as the New York Yankees receive far more revenue than the Pittsburgh Pirates. Major League Baseball's "national rights," such as a game of the week and the postseason competition, are part of the national package. With minor exceptions, the teams share those revenues equally. In contrast, the NFL's broadcasting and cable agreements give the league far more control. The result has been less dominance by large-market franchises. The NBA and, until recently, the NHL followed a system similar to baseball's.

Amateur sports organizations also negotiate broadcasting agreements with various broadcasters and cablecasters. However, the type and scope of these agreements vary. The NCAA contracts to broadcast its championship games in every sport except the highest division of football, which, for legal reasons, is controlled by the athletic conferences. For example, the NCAA has a contract with CBS and Turner Broadcasting to broadcast men's basketball tournament games. Conferences such as the Southeastern Conference negotiate such rights on behalf of the member schools. Rarely, an "independent" (non-conference-based) school such as Notre Dame concludes its own broadcasting arrangement (in this case with NBC).

International sports organizations, such as the International Olympic Committee (IOC), negotiate television contracts with broadcasters all over the world. Similar powers, albeit less ubiquitous, exist in international governing bodies of particular sports to broadcast world championship events. The IOC selected NBC as its exclusive broadcaster in the United States. As a longstanding rightsholder for the Summer and Winter Games, NBC will broadcast and video stream the 2012 Games in London. These contracts include considerable rights fees, given the elite nature of the Olympics. Such sums (over $800 million for the 2010 Vancouver Winter Games) give considerable financial heft to the Olympics movement.

*Close Relationships with Government.* Nearly every professional sports team is privately owned. Yet, despite the private ownership, franchises become an extension of their communities. Often the team and even the league may negotiate with cities and counties for help in the building of new sports facilities. In many cases, such entities have created considerable financial incentives to prevent teams from relocating.

During the stadium-building boom of the 1990s and early 2000s, this largess by governments cut across party lines. Politicians who considered themselves fiscal conservatives and were loath to increase spending nonetheless supported significant public expenditures—through authorization of bonds and even tax increases—to help pay for the construction of new stadiums and arenas (Malkin, 2001; Keating, 1997). Additionally, funds for highway access and other "indirect" support were approved. And, as we see in chapter 8, favorable lease terms between the stadium owner (in many cases a local or county government or a governmental authority) are frequently negotiated. While the use of governmental support for new sports facilities has been controversial, the recent economic downturn has resulted in more public scrutiny and, in many cases, criticism of such deals as expensive and not resulting in meaningful economic development for the given community (Bagli, 2008).

*Restrictions on Player Salaries and Movement.* Every sports league, including minor leagues, has significant salary controls in place. Although there is no question that elite professional athletes from the major sports leagues command high salaries, the salary structure and right to seek similar employment from another team are far more restricted than those found in most industries. It is a myth that all professional athletes have the freedom to work for whatever team they wish. In fact, only a small class of "free agents" fit into this category. In fact, many athletes are restricted from signing contracts with rival teams once their obligations terminate, owing to their relative lack of seniority. These restrictions derive from the terms of the collective bargaining agreements negotiated between the leagues and the players' unions.

Until the mid-1970s, player restrictions were so absolute that the athletes were virtually indentured servants of their teams. The only way they could join another team in the league was by a trade, a breach of contract, or a contractual release by the team. Not surprisingly, that "reserve" system artificially reduced salaries. However, as explained later in chapter 6, the players' associations agreed to keep some of these restrictions in place.

*Tax Advantages.* Ownership of a sports team has certain tax benefits that are not found in other businesses. When one purchases a sports franchise, the Internal Revenue Service allows the new owner to assign a part of the purchase price to player contracts and then depreciate them. Bill Veeck conceived this rule when he was in the process of selling the Cleveland Indians to a group headed by his friend (and the great ballplayer) Hank Greenberg in 1950. Quirk and Fort (1997) provide the following example. If someone buys an NFL team for $200 million, the new owner can assign 50 percent of that amount to existing player contracts and then can depreciate those contracts over five years (at $20 million/ year). Let's assume that team revenue is $100 million per year and that costs, exclusive of the contract depreciation, are $90 million. On the one hand, this seems like a minor bookkeeping technique, because no actual cash is expended. But it has an effect on the team's bottom line in an important way. Based on what was just said, say the team has a profit of $10 million for a year. When one adds that $20 million depreciation, there turns out to be a loss of $10 million per year, saving the owner significant amounts of federal tax. Commentators noted that the advantageous tax policies "resulted in the 'puzzling phenomenon' of skyrocketing franchise values coinciding with sustained tax losses" (Weiler & Roberts, 2004). The use of tax-free bonds to finance stadiums has also been criticized. For example, the New York Yankees received over $1 billion in tax-exempt bonds issued by New York City (Holo & Talansky, 2008). More discussion follows in chapter 8.

*Exclusive Right to Rent or Own Stadiums or Arenas.* As noted earlier, a boom in stadium and arena construction occurred over the last two decades. Municipalities and counties would assist in funding a facility in the hope of either keeping an existing team or luring a franchise from out of town. The stakes were high. If a team cannot own or lease the stadium on favorable terms, this can severely hurt the team's balance sheet.

The negotiation of stadium agreements is one function that is retained by a particular franchise. Sometimes the franchise will own the stadium outright, such as in the case of the Washington Redskins. More often, the team will sign an agreement to have exclusive rights to use the stadium for a period of time. These agreements are often very specific, with the team often receiving a percentage of parking fees, advertisements, and concessions. We discuss the terms of a stadium deal in chapter 8.

*Quasi-public Nature.* Despite private ownership, sports franchises take on the character of their area and become part of the community. The effect on the community psyche from a team's departure to a new city can be profound. Some say that Brooklyn never recovered from the day the Dodgers moved to Los Angeles—and that was over half a century ago!

Although it is true that a major employer in a town or small city may take on a similar persona, there is a significant difference. For decades, Kodak, in Rochester, New York, employed a large number of workers and dominated the economic and civic landscape of the community (Eaton, 2000). A professional sports team does not. Employees include the players (many of whom do not live in the area in the off-season), managerial and coaching staff, front-office staff, and stadium or arena personnel (such as security guards and vendors). Based on the numbers, a sports franchise hardly qualifies as the dominant business in the area.

*Finally . . . Fan Loyalty.* The factors just discussed derive from an overlooked aspect of the sports business: the loyalty of the fan. The sports fan is an odd consumer, often fiercely loyal and unbusinesslike. Once a person becomes bonded with a particular sports team—professional or collegiate—the connection often becomes extremely powerful and very long term. And the brand loyalty of the team transcends its success.

Let's take this example. If a consumer purchased a product that turned out to be of lower quality than he or she expected, most likely that person would abandon allegiance to that firm and would purchase the product made by a rival company. Imagine that consumer, after purchasing a poorly made car requiring many unsuccessful repairs, buying a new car of the same brand! Not very likely. But, in sports, many fans will continue to support their poorly performing teams. Look at fans of such teams as the Chicago Cubs. The team has not won a league pennant since 1945 or a World Series since 1908. Why would these souls spend their hard-earned dollars year after year to subsidize a team that has been less than top quality? Despite unpopular strikes and lockouts, fans have often come back to root for their teams. Talk of fan unions and of boycotts of particular sports and teams has generally come to nothing.

Psychologists have studied the reasons for fan loyalty. Dan Wann, a psychologist at Murray State University, found a number of reasons for being a sports fan. They include:

- Entertainment: watching a game is a form of leisure.
- Escape: You can't yell at your boss. You shouldn't yell at your spouse. You can, and will, yell at the team you root for.
- "Eustress": The pleasurable combination of euphoria and stress, alternating between the euphoria felt when a player homers in the first inning, and the stress resulting when that same player strikes out later in the game.
- Aesthetic: You appreciate the grace and precision of a well-turned double play.
- Family: Going with family members to a game is a bonding experience.
- Self-esteem: Your team wins, therefore you win.
- Group affiliation: The other fans at the ballpark also want the team to win, validating your own affinity for the team.

(King, 2004)

The dissemination of sports through traditional and new media has created a greater following among existing fans and a potential base for more enthusiasts. At one time, the only way one could view a sporting event was by attending the event in person. Gate attendance was the predominant source of revenue. With the advent and utilization of radio, then television, cable, satellite, and Internet, greater opportunities to follow the team or athlete allow more people to become fans, with the ability to view the event from a more comfortable venue.

Team loyalty continues even if a fan moves to a different part of the country because of the availability of information and broadcasts about the team. It also results in greater revenue to the team, its athletes (assuming they are professionals), and the particular league or organization.

This leads to a unique, often (but not always) profitable industry, a fascinating business—and a great venue for aspiring journalists. I hope that the following chapters prove this point.

## References

Bagli, C. (2008, November 3). As stadiums' costs swell, benefits in question. *New York Times*, p. A29.

Burton, R. (1999, December 19). From heart to stern: the shaping of an industry over a century. *New York Times*, sec. 8, p. 11.

Eaton, L. (2000, June 6). A city, once smug, is redefined; company town becomes a town of tiny companies. *New York Times*. Retrieved August 21, 2009, from http://www.nytimes.com/2000/06/06/nyregion/a-city-once-smug-is-redefined-company-town-becomes-a-town-of-tiny-companies.html?pagewanted=1

Fetter, H. (2003). *Taking on the Yankees: Winning and losing in the business of baseball*. New York: W. W. Norton, pp. 28–29.

Holo, R., & Talansky, J., (2008). Taxing the business of sports. *Fla. Tax Rev. 9*, 161, n. 174.

Hunter, R., & Mayo, A. (1999, July–September). The business of sport. *The Mid-Atlantic Journal of Business, 35*, 75–76.

Keating, R. J. (1997, March–April). We wuz robbed!: The subsidized stadium scam. *Policy Review* (Heritage Foundation), *82*, 54–57.

King, B. (2004, March 1). What makes fans tick? *Street and Smith's Sportsbusiness Journal*, p. 25.

Malkin, M. (2001, April 4). Bush's baseball tax fetish. *Capitalism Magazine*. Retrieved June 14, 2005, from http://www.capmag.com/article.asp?id=446

Major League Baseball Constitution, Article 2, sec. 2 (2000).

NHL Bylaws, Sections 35.1, 37.

Quirk, J., & Fort, R. D. (1997). *Paydirt: The business of professional team sports*. Princeton, NJ: Princeton University Press, p. 104.

Thorne, D., Wright, L. B., & Jones, S. A. (2001). The impact of sports marketing relationships and antitrust issues in the United States. *Journal of Public Policy & Marketing, 20*(1), 73.

Weiler, P., & Roberts, G. (2004). *Sports and the law* (3rd ed.). St. Paul, MN: West, p. 632.

Ziegler, M. (2009). Outside U.S., Pads would face relegation. *San Diego Times-Union*. Retrieved July 20, 2009, from http://www3.signonsandiego.com/stories/2009/jul/19/1s19relegate23335-outside-us-pads-would-face-releg/?uniontrib

# 1   The Structure of Professional Team Sports

Professional sports governance centers on leagues that evolved over the last century. Ubiquitous and complex, leagues govern their sports and create an organizational decision-making structure, providing governance on issues as varied as player and owner discipline, revenue control, and expansion and relocation of league franchises. Because of the importance of these issues, a working knowledge of the structure and power of professional sports organizations is imperative for any journalist covering this industry.

A few basic points: All professional sports leagues and their member teams are private entities and operate with a considerable degree of autonomy. Their internal rules and regulations are generally immune from governmental scrutiny. Because the leagues and, particularly, their teams (with a few exceptions) do not sell shares on a public stock exchange, no public release of financial records and no standardized auditing procedures are required under the U.S. securities laws. Hence, journalists should exhibit a healthy skepticism of claims of losses made by teams, because it is difficult to have independent verification of that information.

Furthermore, team owners have considerable latitude in running their business. There is no requirement that a team owner must put the best product on the field, and examples exist of unsuccessful yet profitable teams. The National Hockey League's (NHL's) New York Rangers went through a dry period of no Stanley Cup championship from 1941 to 1994 and no championship since then. However, while the team has languished in performance, it has ranked highly on the balance sheet. According to *Forbes Magazine*, in 2009 the Rangers ranked as the second most valuable NHL franchise ($416 million) and had an operating income of $27.7 million, also second best in the NHL. Their income surpasses that of the 2009 Stanley Cup champions, the Pittsburgh Penguins (which ranked eleventh) (Forbes.com, 2009).

League membership rules and requirements constitute the most important check on a team owner's powers. As pointed out in the Introduction, sports leagues possess many unique attributes, characteristics quite different from other types of businesses and even from amateur sports organizations. (Their attributes and complexities are discussed in chapter 3 and 4.)

## The Professional Leagues

Traditional professional sports leagues, such as Major League Baseball, the National Football League (NFL), the National Basketball Association (NBA), and the NHL, have both cooperative and competitive characteristics. Unique in their organization and operation as compared with most other businesses, these leagues lack a pure free-market competitive structure. Each restricts free and open competition in a number of ways. The leagues have the inherent power to limit the number of competitors by awarding exclusive franchises in different markets. With a few exceptions, it's one team to a market. Therefore each league operates as a cartel, much like the Organization of the Petroleum Exporting Countries (OPEC), as membership is limited and the product controlled. OPEC countries have controlled the production levels of oil in attempts to control the market. Sports leagues control the numbers of teams, their locations, and the numbers of players on a team. They also mandate the sharing of certain revenues, league-wide merchandising, and a unified negotiation strategy with players' unions. Thus, cooperation exists—as a condition of membership in the league.

League control of independently owned franchises has existed in its present form for over ninety years. In 1920, Major League Baseball became the first "modern" league, with the creation of the office of the commissioner to run the league's affairs. As the chief executive officer (CEO) of baseball, the commissioner was empowered to set league policy, control discipline, and, in more recent years, to spearhead labor negotiations with the players.

This does not mean that there is no competition between the teams in the league. On one level, direct competition exists. Some team rivalries are quite intense, even resulting in rancor between the owners of those teams. In a competitive atmosphere, the desired goal (and the hope of its fans) is for a team to win a championship. With the resources and the desire, owners will acquire expensive free-agent players and/or highly successful coaches and general managers to increase their chances of success.

The result is a hybrid identity. The team sells itself as both a local franchise and a representative of the league. Differences exist among the major leagues regarding the sharing of revenues and salary controls, as shown later, but the basic organization remains similar among the major leagues.

The system is hardly perfect. Many of the controversies that have bedeviled sports leagues involve the balance of power between the central office and the team owners. This interplay of centralized authorities with autonomous teams that compete against each other in that collective has created tension among the players, team owners, and the league commissioners. The courts have had a role in many of these disputes because the nature of the league structure has raised antitrust law concerns, except in the case of Major League Baseball, which has been exempt from application of antitrust law.

Because of the often extensive and expensive litigation, some new leagues created an alternative approach known as a "single entity." This is discussed in more detail later in this chapter. Simply put, in a pure single-entity league, no independent owners exist. Rather, the league owns and operates the teams in a single for-profit corporation. Such leagues' record of success has been mixed.

## A Short Summary of the Four Major Leagues

Each of the four major professional leagues is operated as a not-for-profit organization. Of course, the teams themselves are profit-making businesses, but Major League Baseball, the NFL, the NBA, and the NHL cannot accumulate capital; rather, they have to distribute any profits among their teams.

### National Football League

The NFL, established in 1920, is an unincorporated association, rather than a standard *for-profit* business (NFL Constitution and Bylaws, Article VI). Its sources of management authority derive from an executive committee composed of one representative (often the owner) of each club and the commissioner, elected by the executive committee. The commissioner (presently Roger Goodell) possesses disciplinary powers, dispute resolution authority, and decision-making authority, including the power to appoint other officers and committees (NFL Constitution, secs. 3.1–3.9). The commissioner has executive power unless the collective bargaining agreement with the NFL Players' Association renders specific powers to other authorities. Other powers include suspension and banishment for life from involvement in the NFL. Notably, the commissioner possesses considerable power to impose disciplinary action and render disciplinary punishment. Although the executive committee has more general decision-making powers, the commissioner wields considerable influence in the decisions of the committee.

Presently, the NFL commissioner is the only major league CEO that has the power to settle disputes between players and teams. Instead of an independent third party (as required under other leagues' collective bargaining agreements), the commissioner retains that authority and his decision cannot be appealed (NFL Constitution, Article VIII(b)(3)).

The creation or sale of a franchise requires a positive vote of three-quarters of the owners (NFL Constitution, sec. 3.2). The NFL permits ownership of teams by corporations, individuals, or partnerships, but limits the "home territory" of a team to a seventy-five-mile radius, with certain limited exceptions, such as the New York Metropolitan area and the San Francisco Bay Area (which each have two teams). Presently, the NFL contains thirty-two teams.

The NFL has the most centralized operations of any traditional league. Notably, it splits $3 billion a season in network and cable television money, a revenue-sharing arrangement far greater than other leagues. The idea came in the early 1960s from the Cleveland Browns' then owner Art Modell, who convinced the owners George Halas (Chicago Bears), Dan Reeves (Los Angeles Rams), and Jack Mara (New York Giants) to join a proposed revenue-sharing plan and give up the ability to independently negotiate TV rights. The shared television rights ensured competitive balance and helped the league immensely.

The revenue sharing also applies to gate receipts. Currently, 40 percent of the gate receipts from NFL games go into a pool that is eventually divided equally among the teams. Before 2002, the NFL had earmarked the 40 percent of gate revenues for the visiting team. However, unshared revenues from luxury box seating, stadium naming rights, and stadium signage have created greater economic disparity among the member teams. Franchises with new stadiums tend to receive more of such income than older venues. Mike Brown, the owner of the Cincinnati Bengals, said the revenue gap between NFL teams in big and small cities grew from $10 million in the late 1990s to more than $100 million by 2007 (Curnutte, 2007).

At present, the NFL is probably the premier sports league. In an ESPN survey in 2010, 67 percent of Americans consider themselves to be fans of professional football, highest among the eleven sports tested (Demographic trends among major sports, 2010). Revenue reached $6 billion in 2009 (Plunkett Research, 2009). Attendance rose 5 percent from 1999 to 2008, which represents over 17.4 million fans attending NFL games at nearly 90 percent of stadium capacity (*Street and Smith's Sportsbusiness Journal*, 2008) Corporate sponsors pay huge fees to associate with the NFL. For example, in 2004, Gatorade signed an eight-year deal with the league, worth $500 million (Markiewicz, 2004). Visa is paying $400 million over six years. And those are just two of the NFL's official sponsors (Rodack, 2004). For the money, sponsors are able to use NFL team, Super Bowl, and Pro Bowl logos in their marketing activities, and they have the right to do promotions surrounding key events.

Under former commissioner Paul Tagliabue, who assumed the position in 1989, the NFL entered an era of sustained labor peace. Present commissioner Goodell, selected in 2006, has been confronted with the possibility of labor unrest, as the present collective bargaining agreement expires in 2011.

Goodell has taken a greater interest in disciplinary issues. Shortly after assuming his position, Goodell enacted and enforced a players' "personal conduct" policy in light of a number of highly publicized transgressions involving NFL players. Under this policy, the commissioner has the power to suspend indefinitely any player who engages in violent or criminal behavior. That means that a player may be sanctioned even if he is not convicted of a crime (Edelman, 2009). As one commentator noted: "Goodell has definitely defined himself as being a bigger sheriff than any other previous commissioner" (*Sports Business Daily*, 2009).

### National Basketball Association and National Hockey League

Like the NFL, the NBA and NHL are unincorporated, not-for-profit associations with centralized offices and commissioners. They share considerable similarities.

Like the NFL, membership in these leagues is limited. Each entity or person seeking an NBA or NHL franchise or wishing to buy an existing team must be approved by the affirmative vote of no fewer than three-fourths of the members. A three-fourths majority is also required to transfer a membership to another entity. The commissioners of both leagues—David Stern in the NBA and Gary Bettman for the NHL—have similar powers to the NFL's Goodell. However, some limitations exist. In the NBA, for example, the commissioner's disciplinary actions for off-the-court conduct are reviewable by a neutral arbitrator (NBA CBA, Article XXXI, sec. 8).

Presently, the NBA is far more popular than the NHL. The thirty-team league flourished in an era of superstars, such as Michael Jordan, Larry Bird, Erwin "Magic" Johnson, and Shaquille O'Neal. But another reason for the success in the 1990s was its commissioner, David Stern. In 2004, one commentator remarked that, in leading the NBA, "[David] Stern has single-handedly done more as commissioner of the NBA over a [then] 20-year tenure than any other top executive in sports history" (Rovell, 2004). Stern took over a league with declining attendance, few recognizable stars, and red ink, as seventeen of the twenty-three teams reported financial losses. Fan apathy had grown rampant. Many believed that the league was too Black, and drug use was common (Allen, 2004).

Stern pioneered the salary cap, aggressively marketed the league, and licensed its product brilliantly. During his tenure, franchise values increased from $15 million in 1984 to as high as $613 million in 2009 (Van Riper, 2009). Gross revenues from licensed products increased from a mere $10 million in 1984 to over $3.3 billion twenty-five years later. Overall annual league revenues increased from $118 million to more than $3.8 billion in 2008 (Badenhausen, Ozanian, & Settimi, 2008), and U.S. television rights will average $930 million annually, which is up 21 percent from the prior broadcasting deal (Wolfly, 2007). An ESPN poll in

2010 showed that about 49 percent of U.S. sports fans were NBA fans (Demographic trends among U.S. sports fans, 2010).

With less power to impose sanctions on noncourt events, Stern has been known as a powerful manager who has not hesitated to impose disciplinary sanctions for in-game conduct that he feels is detrimental to his sport. Despite arbitration appeals, he suspended Gilbert Arenas of the Washington Wizards indefinitely, without pay, for bringing guns into the Verizon Center (Futterman, 2010). Previously, he suspended Indiana Pacers players Ron Artest (season-long), Stephen Jackson (thirty games), and Jermaine O'Neal (twenty-five games) for participation in a melée during a game with Detroit Pistons on the Pistons' home arena. This melée between the players and fans received considerable coverage and the severity of the penalties resulted in players' union protests (McCallum, 2004). Stern made light of his powers, saying the vote on the penalties was "unanimous . . . 1–0."

The NHL, on the other hand, has had more difficulty increasing its popularity. Traditionally a Canadian sport, which operated with just six franchises until 1967, it has expanded rapidly over the last twenty years, resulting in a present total of thirty teams. Franchises moved or were awarded to a number of untraditional Sunbelt markets, such as Dallas and Phoenix. Some relocations angered Canadian fans as teams from Quebec and Winnipeg moved to U.S. cities. Questions have been raised about the economic viability of some of the league's franchises, notably the Phoenix Coyotes, which filed for bankruptcy in 2008 on account of undercapitalization, poor management, and low attendance (Ozanian & Badenhausen, 2008a). U.S. fan interest in the NHL, as noted on the ESPN poll noted earlier, is about 34 percent (Demographic trends among U.S. sports fans, 2010).

Gary Bettman has been commissioner since February 1993. A protégé of David Stern, Bettman came to the NHL from the NBA. Much of his tenure has been marked by sluggish television ratings in the United States, a lack of marketable superstars, and a relative lack of success of franchises in key cities such as New York, Chicago, and Los Angeles. Nevertheless, game attendance has rivaled the NBA in many cities, and the top NHL franchise, the Toronto Maple Leafs, has been valued at about $400 million (Van Riper, 2009).

Yet Bettman achieved success in controlling player salaries. For much of the 1990s and early 2000s, salaries have increased faster than revenues, and most analysts have concluded that, league-wide, the NHL teams are losing money. For 2003–04, the team losses ranged from $96 million (Ozanian, 2004) to $224 million (Snavely, 2005), the latter figure claimed by the league.

Labor–management tensions over salaries resulted in a league-imposed lockout, resulting in the cancellation of the entire 2004–05 season. In

July 2005, the NHL and the National Hockey League Players' Association (NHLPA) agreed to a new collective bargaining agreement, which imposed significant salary controls. This cap, coupled with the rise of young stars such as Washington Capitals' Alexander Ovechkin and Pittsburgh Penguins' Sidney Crosby and Evgeni Malkin, has increased the league's exposure, attendance and revenues (Ozanian & Badenhausen, 2008a).

## Major League Baseball

Thirty teams, sixteen in the National League and fourteen in the American League, make up Major League Baseball. Unlike the other sports, Major League Baseball's roots derive from a merger of two independent entities, the National League and the American League, in 1903. For decades, its governing document (known as the Major League Agreement) was akin to articles of confederation, rather than a unitary constitution. Before the mid-1990s, each of the leagues had its own president and staff. In a shift toward centralization, the league presidents were eliminated and instead there is now a vice-president and an executive council.

The present governing document, the Major League Baseball Constitution, dates from 2000. It gives the commissioner "executive responsibility" for labor relations and maintains the power to take actions deemed detrimental to the sport.

Like their counterparts in other leagues, baseball owners retain significant voting rights in league matters. To approve an expansion, a three-fourths majority of all member clubs in the league seeking expansion and a majority of clubs in the non-expanding league are required. The same ratios are required for the movement of a team. The owners also define the appropriate "home territory" for a particular team. For example, the Los Angeles Dodgers' and the Los Angeles Angels' territory includes Orange, Ventura, and Los Angeles Counties.

Bud Selig, an owner of the Milwaukee Brewers, became acting commissioner in 1992 (and commissioner in 1998) after the forced resignation of Fay Vincent. Selig is the first commissioner with a direct ownership interest (although his daughter runs the affairs of the Brewers). His term has been extended to 2012.

Selig's early tenure was marked by labor disputes, culminating in a 1994 strike that resulted in the cancellation of the postseason. In more recent years, he stewarded an era of greater popularity of the game, better organization, and labor peace. With the opening of many new ballparks, coupled with a sophisticated new media division, revenue streams have increased under Selig's tenure (Isidore, 2007). However, some of that success has been tarnished by the lax standards in policing the use of performance-enhancing substances, which may have helped players increase their prowess and resulted in the breaking of some long-cherished records, such as the single-season and career home run records (Wilbon,

2004). As of 2010, 58 percent of U.S. sports fans are devotees of baseball (Demographic trends among U.S. sports fans, 2010).

In part thanks to its longstanding exemption from antitrust laws, Major League Baseball teams exercise control over affiliated minor league teams in a manner which could be illegal if done by other sports (Weiler & Roberts, 2004, p. 172). Major League Baseball teams negotiate affiliation agreements with such teams, which serve as feeders for talented players going to the Major League Baseball club. Yet the minor leagues have constitutions and bylaws that delegate decision-making authority to a board of directors and the minor league's president. Some decisions, however, require ratification by Major League Baseball. For example, all proposed franchise sales and transfers of minor league teams must be registered with the commissioner, who in certain instances can reject a sale or transfer if it is deemed "not in the best interests of baseball." The commissioner must approve a proposed franchise relocation. The commissioner also must approve any grant of protected territory to a minor league club (Rosner & Shropshire, 2004).

Minor League Baseball attendance remained strong in 2009. The fifteen leagues and 176 clubs drew 41,644,518 patrons in 10,269 openings. The average crowd of 4055 was only 2.9 percent, or 119 fans a game, lower than the prior year, when the total attendance of 43.2 million fans broke the all-time attendance record (minorleaguebaseball.com, 2009).

## The Major Stakeholders in a Traditional League Structure

### *The Commissioner*

The scandal caused by a number of Chicago White Sox players accepting bribes to "throw" the 1919 World Series was the single event that led to the creation of an all-powerful commissioner to run baseball. As many fans know, eight players from the Chicago White Sox were accused, but never convicted, of accepting money to "throw" the World Series. As a morality tale, the story of players such as "Shoeless Joe Jackson" betraying the fans has been retold countless times.

However, the "Black Sox" scandal was not the only reason for a drastic change of governance. At the time, baseball was run by a three-member commission, consisting of the presidents of the National League and American League and a third party, usually a team owner. In reality, the American League president, Byron Bancroft "Ban" Johnson, exercised the most power. The tripartite system was widely disliked, and many found this scandal an excuse to end the system and replace it with a more centralized authority.

In November 1920, Kenesaw Mountain Landis, a federal judge who ruled in favor of what is now known as Major League Baseball in an antitrust case a few years earlier, was unanimously selected as commissioner by the owners. Shortly afterward, a charter setting forth the commissioner's authority was drafted. On January 12, 1921, Landis told a meeting of club owners that he had agreed to accept the position upon the clear understanding that the owners had sought "an authority . . . outside of your own business, and that a part of that authority would be a control over whatever and whoever had to do with baseball" (Finley v. Kuhn, 1978). Empowered to investigate "any act, transaction or practice suspected to be detrimental to the best interests of baseball," Landis (and future commissioners) had authority to summon persons, order the production of documents, and "determine, after investigation, what preventive, remedial or punitive action is appropriate in the premises, and to take such action either against Major Leagues, Major League Clubs or individuals, as the case may be" (MLB Constitution, Article 1, sec. 2).

This "best interests of the sport" clause has been a bedrock section of the NFL, NBA, and NHL league constitutions as well. The terms used vary slightly, however. In the NFL, the commissioner has the disciplinary authority to protect "the integrity of the sport" (NFL Constitution, Article 8, sec. 8.3). The NBA gives the commissioner the authority to "expel, suspend or fine any club official, employer or player for conduct detrimental or prejudicial to the Association" (NBA Constitution, Article 35), while in the NHL's document conduct "dishonorable, prejudicial to, or against the welfare of the League" deserves sanction (NHL Constitution and Bylaws, sec. 17). In these leagues, such decisions can be appealed to the Board of Governors, a committee consisting of some or all team owners, something rarely done (Weiler & Roberts, 2004, p. 32). On paper, it gives the commissioner the right to be a judge, jury, and in some cases appeals court, in investigating alleged transgressions among owners, players, officials, and administrators.

Before the rise of players' unions and collective bargaining agreements, the commissioner's power was almost limitless. One court decision described Landis's mandate as that of a "plenipotentate" (Milwaukee American Ass'n v. Landis, 1931), and during Landis's term (1920–44) he indeed ruled with an iron hand. He meted out discipline, sometimes ruthlessly, to maintain what he considered the integrity of the sport. That meant fining, suspending, and even banning players and owners for transgressions, which included gambling and other criminal activity. He even suspended Babe Ruth for the first six weeks of the 1922 season when Ruth violated the prohibition of "barnstorming" (Ambrose, 2008). More recently, however, the unilateral power of the commissioners to punish players has been limited, primarily because of mandatory grievance arbitration procedures found in collective bargaining agreements of some, but not all, of the major leagues. What makes these provisions noteworthy is not only the right of a player to take certain disciplinary matters to an independent arbitrator, but the standard—known as "just cause"—that the arbitrator uses to determine whether the punishment is justified. "Just cause" is a fairly high standard, which requires that substantial evidence exists for the commissioner's determination and that the resulting penalty is reasonable under the circumstances. In effect, "just cause" results in giving the arbitrator the power to provide an independent check on the commissioner's power (Enterprise Wire Co. v. Enterprise Independent Union, 1966).

Even with these limitations, the disciplinary power of a commissioner is not to be taken for granted. For infractions and violations of policy during competition, the commissioner (or someone in the commissioner's office) can impose fines and suspensions. Although limited by labor agreements, the commissioner still can mete out punishment, although the precise level of punishment varies among the leagues. In Major League Baseball, the fines are imposed by either Selig or Major League Baseball's vice-president of on-field operations. For teams, the fines range to a maximum of $2 million (MLB Constitution, Article 1, sec. 3). Regarding player discipline, Major League Baseball and the NBA have a grievance arbitration system in effect whereby a neutral party adjudicates the dispute if the player appeals the ruling. However, under collective bargaining rules, Stern, as noted earlier, has sole discretion over penalties for on-court behavior, and his actions cannot be appealed to a neutral party (NBA CBA, Article 31, sec. 8). In the NFL, as noted earlier, Goodell's power is broader, as he can suspend players without pay for a period he deems appropriate and also can fine them up to $500,000 in cases involving conduct detrimental to the league (NFL Constitution, Article 8, sec. 8.13). Only employees of the league hear appeals (NFL–NFLPA CBA, Article 11, sec. 1).

Because the owners elect commissioners, the commissioners frequently (although not always) serve as representatives of ownership interests. Often commissioners will work as part of an owners' management committee. This committee may consist of representatives of all the teams or a smaller group. Although the commissioner has the disciplinary authority and often the final say on governance matters, the owners' committee will often control decisions involving franchise relocation or the granting of new franchises. In those matters, the commissioner will take a back seat. Depending on the league, the management committee may control labor negotiations (as is the case in Major League Baseball) or the commissioner may spearhead them (as in the NBA).

Yet fans and even unseasoned journalists think that the commissioner is a lackey of the owners. That view is simplistic and inaccurate. The commissioner's role is more than just a cheerleader or shill for the owners since that person is the face of the league and must convince the public that he or she acts in the league's best interests—which sometimes may be counter to owners' parochial interests. Each of the major league commissioners can and has fined and suspended owners. In 1990, the Yankees' George Steinbrenner was suspended for two years by commissioner Fay Vincent for paying a known gambler $40,000 for information about the Yankees' player Dave Winfield (Weiler & Roberts, 2004, p. 33).

Typically, the commissioner runs a central "operations" office, which may include such duties as scheduling, hiring officials, marketing the league, controlling the intellectual property of the teams, negotiating nationwide broadcast and cablecasting agreements, dealing with minor leagues (the case in baseball), engaging in political lobbying, and interacting with other sports leagues or international sports governing bodies, particularly regarding Olympic eligibility (Cozzillio et al., 2007).

Commissioners are well paid for their services. In 2009, baseball's Bud Selig received compensation of over $18 million per year; the NFL's Roger Goodell was paid $10.9 million, the NBA's David Stern $10 million, and the NHL's Gary Bettman $7.1 million (Mickle, 2009).

In short, establishing policy, marketing the sport, and building cohesion among the owners and players rank as the principal duties of a commissioner.

### The Teams

The teams (known officially as "franchises") that constitute a league are its backbone. Particular markets are awarded franchises based on a vote of league owners through an application process. Also, in rare situations, teams can be dissolved or folded either by the team terminating operations outright or by two teams merging their operations. An example of the latter occurred in 1978 when the NHL's Cleveland Barons ceased operations and merged with the then-Minnesota North Stars (Ohio History Central, n.d.).

Traditional league sports franchises are classified as joint venturers which unite under the umbrella of the league. Although the amounts differ in each league, certain revenues are shared, while others are kept by the team. Examples of unshared revenues include fees from local broadcasting rights (more limited in the NFL than in the other traditional leagues), parking, concessions, club seating, and luxury boxes. Given the autonomy of the traditional league structure, individual teams employ their own personnel—athletes and management—who are paid by that team, rather than by the league itself. Team responsibilities include negotiating stadium leases and local television and radio broadcast rights, engaging in local marketing efforts, selling individual and season tickets, and leasing luxury box seating. Teams also provide their own marketing and promotional personnel.

Since teams are individually owned in the traditional leagues, they can be bought and sold (with league approval). Despite the economic ups and downs, team values have increased consistently over the last thirty years. In 2009, the Montreal Canadiens sold for over $500 million (Canadian), a record price in the NHL, despite not winning a championship in almost two decades; the Chicago Cubs sold for $900 million, a Major League Baseball record; and the St. Louis Rams, in an outdated building, with a poor team and facing the NFL's unstable labor future, still found a buyer willing to value the club at $750 million (Kaplan, 2010).

Most significantly, teams are in charge of the product they put on display. The team administrators—which include the owners, general managers, and coaching staffs—craft a group of athletes in the hopes of on-field performance success. As we will see, in a "single entity" league, many of these functions are controlled not by the individual team, but rather by the league itself.

In addition to the league commissioner, teams have the right to suspend, fine, and even terminate players for breach of contract or for conduct detrimental to the team. The punishment may apply to petty offenses. A player for the Cleveland Browns was fined $1701 (the maximum allowed under the collective bargaining agreement) because he failed to pay for a $3 bottle of water he'd consumed at a hotel while the team was on the road (Cooper, 2009).

### The Owners

Each league has its own system of selecting team owners. Individuals, corporations, limited partnerships, and limited liability companies constitute ownership in most traditional sports leagues. In the past, most owners were individuals; more recently, corporations have acquired ownership interests. A number of franchises remain family businesses. However, a league may impose restrictions; the NFL prohibits publicly traded corporations from ownership and also bars its team owners from owning a professional sports team in a different city. Other limitations include a minimum percentage of an NFL team that a lead owner (or general partner) needs (Kaplan, 2009).

Some individual owners bear the mark of longevity—Connie Mack with the Philadelphia Phillies (1901–54) and George Hallas of the Chicago Bears (1920–83) come to mind. Others have been family dynasties, such as the Griffithses (Washington Senators, Minnesota Twins, 1919–84) and the Maras (New York Giants, 1925–present). Certain individuals, such as the late New York Yankees' owner George Steinbrenner, have been hands-on managers, whereas others have been less conspicuous. More recently, corporate ownership has existed, as Cablevision (New York Knicks and Rangers) and Disney (Anaheim Angels) have purchased and owned franchises. Even celebrities have taken the ownership route. In past years, Bing Crosby owned small portions of two baseball teams, and Bob Hope once owned 11 percent of the Los Angeles Rams and a part of the Cleveland Indians (Downey, 2003). In 2004, Jon Bon Jovi became a part-owner of the Philadelphia Soul of the now defunct Arena Football League.

Often, a managing partner–limited partner relationship exists among many sports franchises. Limited partners usually invest a sum of money, hoping for a profitable return, but do not take an active part in the management of the team. But these investors often invest for the joy (or ego) or having an ownership stake in a major or minor league professional team, as well as for the profit potential. In some cases, limited partners get experience seeing the operations of a franchise, leading them to become managing partners of a team in the future. John Henry, a principal owner of the Boston Red Sox, once owned a small piece of the New York Yankees (Nethery, 2004).

### Players

The one group that traditionally has had little influence in professional sports governance is the players. As employees, they occupy positions not as management, but as paid workers performing services for their teams. Until thirty-five years ago, they had little leverage in the negotiation of their contracts, primarily on account of onerous rules such as baseball's reserve clause that depressed wages.

Since that time, the players have made significant improvements in their compensation and have been active in asserting their rights through the labor–management negotiations. The number of strikes and lockouts and resulting favorable agreements with management attest to their power. Yet, even today, the player's role in the management and operations of the league remains minimal.

### Players' Associations

The major reason for the players' growing influence has been the presence of players' associations. Such worker unions, organized under the nation's labor laws, give these athletes to power to elect representatives to collectively bargain with team owners. As will be discussed in chapter 6, players' unions have resulted in significant wage increases and the development of various forms of free agency to give players the right to choose the team of their liking. They have also spawned bidding wars for highly prized free agents. Additionally, grievance arbitration procedures have restricted the potential for arbitrary decision making on the part of the commissioner.

### Agents

Before player unionization, when athletes had little bargaining leverage, the need for an agent representation was minimal. However, with the dawn of free agency and salary arbitration, athletes sought agent representation in their contract negotiations, endorsements, and financial management. The major league players' associations require agents to register with the unions and limit the amount of compensation received to a stipulated percentage; as discussed in chapter 7, agents also serve as the representative of the athlete to the media, and often must attempt to craft the athlete's image in times when the athlete commits some transgression or engages in a controversial act.

### The Media—Old and New

Sports and the media have a symbiotic relationship because they need each other. The media publicize the athlete, team, league, or other organization, and in many cases pay considerable rights fees to broadcast or otherwise distribute sports content. The media gain by obtaining more viewers and listeners, which helps their bottom line. Without the role of the media, the sports business would not attain its scope and power.

Sports media can be divided into "traditional" and "new" media. Traditional media include print, broadcast, and cable and the business model is tried and true. Broadcast and cable pay the bulk of rights fees to teams and the leagues. Additionally, cable sports networks, most notably ESPN, have a specialized twenty-four-hour all-sports niche carrying news and highlights as well as play-by-play content. The role of sports radio has saturated the air waves with constant talk (including second-guessing and criticism) about athletes and teams. Although too scarce, more and more print articles and a few broadcast/cable programs are devoted to the business of sport.

"Newer" media, such as the Internet, are different in that athletes, teams, and leagues have limited control over content. Websites and blogs have contributed to a huge variety—informative, entertaining, outrageous, unfair—of information, keeping sports in the consciousness of millions of fans and adding to the headaches of owners, managers, coaches, and athletes. As is the case with politicians and entertainers, this has resulted in a diminution of an athlete's privacy, discussed in more detail in chapters 9 and 13.

## Cooperation versus Competition

As we noted earlier, the four major professional sports leagues offer a system that features elements of cooperation as well as competition. Because of this hybrid arrangement, professional leagues are a unique business. One court aptly described the conflict by noting:

> [Sports leagues] have problems which no other business has. The ordinary business makes every effort to sell as much of the product or services as it can. In the course of doing this it may and often does put many of its competitors out of business. The ordinary businessman is not troubled by the knowledge that he is doing so well that his competitors are being driven out of business.

Professional teams in a league, however, must not compete too well with each others, in a business way . . . It is unwise for all the teams to compete as hard as they can against each other in a business way. If all the teams should [so] compete, the stronger teams should be likely to drive the weaker ones into financial failure. If this should happen not only would the weaker teams fail, but eventually the whole league, both the weaker and the stronger teams, would fail, because without a league, no team can operate profitably (United States v. NFL, 1953).

This structure has raised an important legal question concerning the antitrust liability of traditional sports leagues. The issue centers on whether they act as "single entities" or as "joint ventures." If leagues determine their policies through a single, concerted decision-making process, then they are unitary bodies, known as single entities, and their policies are immune from the most important antitrust law. If, however, the league is composed of a group of team owners who make policy based on their personal and sometimes competing economic interests, then such decisions are subject to antitrust challenge. The subject of scholarly debate over the last few decades, the U.S. Supreme Court finally answered that question in 2010, concluding that the NFL, despite its centralized decision making, does not confer single entity status. Therefore, the NFL's decisions are subject to section 1 of the Sherman Act, discussed later in the chapter (American Needle v. NFL, 2010).

With this in mind, let's look at the areas of cooperation.

### Salary Structure

No league has an entirely open market in which every player is a free agent with the freedom to jump from one team to another. Every league engages in salary control, and the nature of the restrictions varies from league to league. In the NBA, NFL, and, most recently, NHL, a salary cap structure prohibits "richer" teams from gaining competitive advantage by signing high-caliber players. Major League Baseball, lacking a salary cap system, employs a luxury tax method to control salary growth.

### Equitable Draft

Each of the leagues employs a system for drafting players. Usually the poorest-performing teams have the right to get the best rookie players. That draft pick is an exclusive one for the team. In the NBA and the NHL, the draft replaced a territorial system whereby players living within a stipulated territory became the property of the team that played in that area, a system that produced skewed results. Far more talented young hockey players skated in the province of Quebec than in the Chicago area, giving the Montreal Canadiens greater quality than the

Blackhawks. This could be one reason why the Canadiens won more Stanley Cups—particularly in the 1940s and 1950s—than any other team.

### Sharing of Merchandising Monies

Each of the leagues has a subsidiary involving the sale of league-licensed merchandising. Generally, revenues are shared equally among teams and players. The subject is discussed in more detail in chapter 12.

### Sharing of Gate Receipts

Often the sharing of monies from ticket sales between teams in a given league is limited. The NFL has the most equitable sharing, 60–40 percent, with the home team receiving the larger amount. In Major League Baseball, the American League has an 80 percent–20 percent split. In the National League, it averages 95 percent–5 percent. In the NHL, the home team does not share any of the gate receipts. In the NBA, the home team retains 94 percent of the gate, with the league receiving the other 6 percent (Quirk & Fort, 1997; Easton & Rockerbee, 2002).

### Sharing of Revenues from National Broadcasting and Cable Contracts

The amount of broadcasting revenues shared between teams in a particular league varies. This NFL revenue-sharing model, as noted earlier, was conceived in the early 1960s and became a brilliant success, "beloved worldwide and year after year of strong competitive balance" (Fisher, 2004). The other leagues do share some revenue league-wide, although not to the extent of the NFL. Revenue-sharing systems are discussed in more detail in chapter 6.

### Restrictions on Franchise Relocation

Each of the major leagues has limitations on the movement of franchises. Permission must be given by a vote of the other team owners, often in a so-called "maxi-majority" number, such as two-thirds or 75 percent. Because of legal challenges to team relocations in the 1980s, most team moves have not been seriously contested.

### Rules to Approve Ownership Changes and League Expansion

Each league permits ownership changes and the creation of new franchises only by approval of the existing franchise owners. Criteria may differ, but usually it is a maxi-majority vote (e.g. three-quarters) of the owners.

## Fostering Competition

The traditional league structure also fosters competition among the franchises. The reasons are as follows.

### *Autonomy in Individual Team Operations*

As noted earlier in this chapter, each owner has discretion in operating his or her team. Because teams in each of the traditional leagues earn certain revenues not shared by other teams, the owners have the discretion to use that money for whatever purposes they deem fit. Team owners have the right to hire and fire personnel, usually without league interference, and can acquire players (although within applicable salary constraints and taxes, depending on the league). The teams can market their brand to their particular community in efforts to sell tickets and gain favorable publicity.

### *Competitive Atmosphere*

Even with salary caps or luxury taxes, a team owner has considerable discretion in hiring personnel. The leagues normally do not micromanage the owner in terms of personnel decisions, facility deals, and local broadcasting agreements. Because teams in the traditional leagues do retain control of at least some revenues (the amount varies by league), they can use those monies to find and contract with talented, and in many cases expensive, free-agent players. Often, the team mirrors the spirit of the community it represents, with all the hometown pride and competitive juices aimed against teams from rival cities. Some fierce rivalries exist; probably the best example remains the New York Yankees and the Boston Red Sox.

## Drawbacks

Although the traditional league system remains a mainstay of professional sports, it has drawbacks. They include the following.

### *Disparity of Revenues and Payrolls*

Allowing teams to keep a large portion of their revenue produces franchises with unequal financial resources. At one time, the disparity was relatively minor because gate attendance served as the single most important revenue stream. Since the advent of television, the skew has become greater, as fees paid for broadcast and cable rights vary greatly between large and small markets. As a general rule, owners in lucrative markets have more opportunities to field a successful team than those in smaller, less revenue-friendly areas.

However, a common misperception is that high revenue streams guarantee success. Budding journalists should be careful not to fall into that trap. Examples abound of rich franchises spending money foolishly. The New York Rangers of the NHL serves as a case in point. The team, owned by the media conglomerate Cablevision, had the highest payroll in the NHL from 1998 to 2004, but had losing records and did not make the playoffs during that period (Enquist, 2005). However, a richer team has more leeway and greater ability to absorb high costs than a team that produces smaller revenues.

### The Specter of Antitrust Litigation

Individual owners, players, and players' unions have used antitrust theory to institute lawsuits challenging many league policies and determinations over the last two decades.

Stripped to its essentials, section 1 of the Sherman Anti-Trust Law, the basic statute on the subject, prohibits agreements in interstate commerce between two or more parties that "unreasonably restrain trade." That means that if two or more entities (say, the large automobile manufacturers) get together and agree to limit sales of their cars to specific regions in the United States, that agreement could be an unreasonable and illegal restraint of trade. A key point is what "two or more" means.

Let's examine a hypothetical situation. League X has a franchise, the Alpha Athletes. The franchise wishes to move from Alpha, where it has played for sixty years, to the bustling new community of Beta, 500 miles away. The league requires a three-quarters vote of the owners to permit the move. Only two-thirds approve. If League X is a traditional sports league, the issue becomes whether a Sherman Act violation occurs. If a court concludes that League X is a single organization, or one which has multiple members but a single aggregation of economic power, no violation occurs. But if that court considers League X to be a group of joint venturers, or a confederation of independent businesses, a violation may have occurred, as two or more owners blocked the move. As noted earlier, the U.S. Supreme Court concluded that the NFL does not have the attributes of a single entity and is subject to antitrust litigation under section 1 of the Sherman Act (American Needle v. NFL, 2010). In so ruling, the court rejected the arguments by the league and some scholars that the antitrust liability involving the NFL, NBA, and NHL resulted in the weakening of league power (Roberts, 1984, 1988). Note that Major League Baseball has an antitrust exemption in place due to a 1922 Supreme Court ruling.

Avoidance of the threat of antitrust litigation was the reason the NFL (and the NBA and NHL, which supported the NFL) wanted a single entity immunity. Past antitrust challenges involved different aspects of league decision making, such as prohibitions of team relocations, age restrictions on athletes, and the imposition of labor rules. Most of the rulings in the 1980s and 1990s concluded that traditional leagues are not "single entities" but multiparty joint ventures subject to antitrust law challenges (Los Angeles Memorial Coliseum Commission v. NFL, 1984; Sullivan v. NFL, 1994). However, a few courts differed, concluding that, in certain respects, professional sports leagues may be considered "single entities" immune from antitrust attack (Chicago Professional Sports Ltd. Partnership v. NBA, 1996). Although the leagues emerged victorious in many cases because they were able to prove that the agreement in question was an "unreasonable" restraint, the time and cost of such litigation can be long and prohibitive. The resolution of the antitrust question answers the question of the status of a league and harmonizes the law after a period of judicial inconsistency.

### Labor Issues

Each of the major leagues has suffered through strikes or lockouts with their players' unions over the last twenty years. These actions often resulted in bad publicity, with a decrease in attendance after settlement. For example, Major League Baseball's attendance dropped 20 percent in the season after the 1994 strike (Sandomir, 2002). Traditional leagues cannot simply impose salary caps and other controls on compensation because of collective bargaining rules and, even if no union exists, such acts could run afoul of the antitrust laws. Chapter 6 discusses this subject in detail.

## Alternatives to the Traditional Sports League

### One Alternative: The Single-Entity Model

In the 1990s, newly created sports leagues eschewed the traditional system in favor of a far more centralized one. The concept, known as a "single-entity" league, creates a unitary entity, which, according to its advocates, makes governance easier and negates the threat of antitrust litigation. The single-entity league, if created properly, avoids costly and time-consuming litigation because as a single entity its decisions would be not be subject to antitrust challenges. Basically, this structure is a shield against the use of antitrust lawsuits by owners and players.

In a single-entity league, owners own stock in the league, which would be a for-profit corporation. The principal common feature of all single-entity leagues is one central entity with which all players in the league contract, and which in turn allocates talent to the teams. Such a league consists of investors who buy shares in the league, rather than owning a particular team in the league. These investors, in return for their investment, have the right to operate individual teams and have limited autonomy in running those teams, which includes local promotions and marketing.

In the middle to late 1990s, leagues with single-entity characteristics were popular, the most notable being Major League Soccer (MLS) and the Women's National Basketball Association (WNBA). Other single-entity leagues have included the Major Indoor Lacrosse League, the Continental Basketball Association, and the now-defunct Women's United Soccer Association and American Basketball League (Lebowitz, 1997).

A key advantage is direct and centralized management resulting in quick decisions. For example, in 1996, MLS's Tampa Bay Mutiny franchise encountered problems of financial mismanagement, as the finance director embezzled hundreds of thousands of dollars in ticket sales. MLS fired the offending individual and reorganized the team's front office to prevent these acts from occurring in the future. In a traditional league, the team owner, not the league, would take such action. Although in theory the commissioner of the traditional league could sanction the owner for acts detrimental to the sport, such a determination would be unlikely unless the owner was aware of the misconduct or the mismanagement rose to an egregious level.

Other advantages of a pure single-entity league include the following.

*Unilaterally Imposed Salary Minimums and Maximums.* The league may impose salary caps unless the players unionize and engage in collective bargaining negotiations. In a single-entity league, the directors can decide on salary restraints by fiat and do not have to worry about conflicting ownership interests, such as big-market versus small-market rivalries. If the players organize a union, the negotiations with the players can, theoretically, be smoother, for the same reason.

*"Pure" Sharing of Profits.* As stated earlier in the chapter, no traditional league shares all team profits. On the other hand, a single-entity league shares all profits and expenses equally, regardless of the size of the market.

*Competitive Parity.* Because of the salary structure and the control of player trades, it is less likely that that one or two "rich" teams dominate the sport and skew competitive balance.

*Fewer Problems with Team Relocation.* If a team is not profitable, it affects every owner, and relocation is easier. The league directors can decide to move the team, with little objection from the investor running the team.

*Franchise Expansion Is Easier.* If the league feels that a viable business opportunity exists, it can create a new franchise far more quickly than in a traditional league. No owner is needed, and fees from ticket sales, stadium deals, and broadcast agreements can be drawn into the coffers of the league for all the investors to share.

*More Innovative Agreements with Television Networks, Cable Companies, and Sponsors.* Because these leagues are younger and do not involve individual team ownership, broadcast and cable rights agreements are simpler to negotiate and can be based on different revenue models than the traditional league "rights fee" arrangement. In a single-entity league situation, the league may either buy the time from the network or enter into a co-sponsoring agreement whereby revenues are split in some manner.

*No Antitrust Problems, as the League Is One Business Entity.* This is probably the single biggest reason for the implementation of this model. A pure single-entity league prevents most time-consuming and expensive antitrust litigation.

Yet the existing single-entity leagues have some significant structural problems, which have made it less attractive as a viable alternative to the traditional league. These include:

*Lack of Owner Autonomy to Make Innovative, Locally Oriented Decisions.* Because each investor is a shareholder in the league, the autonomy to make such decisions with regard to team personnel, salary structure, and overall management is severely compromised. All major decisions come from the league office, even if they involve mundane matters that would not occupy the time of a traditional league office. This may stifle creativity and limit the ability of franchises to make decisions based on the particular aspects of their given markets.

*Restrictions on Sale and Relocation.* Owners of teams in traditional leagues have sold or relocated their teams for a potential improvement in business opportunity. A single-entity league can easily block sale of the investors' stock and can prevent the movement of an existing team. Note that it's not as important to the single-entity league for a particular team to "find" a better market, because the value of the investment is dependent on the financial value more of the league as a whole, rather than of a particular team.

*Less Incentive to Improve the Product.* The goal of many owners in a traditional league is to produce a winning team, even a dynasty. In the case of a single-entity league, a dominant team or two may hurt the league, and the investors may take steps to weaken the team by forcing player trades to preserve parity for other teams. That kind of action may anger fans of the dominant team and create a backlash. In such a structure, the owner-investors may not have as much of a "winning attitude."

In part because of the problems just described, none of the present so-called "single-entity" leagues are "pure" single entities. Rather they are hybrids, primarily because of the difficulties in finding investors to support an organization in which their individual rights are limited. When covering these organizations, journalists should ask about the status of the league and not simply rely on statements claiming "single entity." To demonstrate the complexity of the "single-entity" structure, we next examine MLS and the WNBA at the time of their inception, and the subsequent changes in their organization.

*Major League Soccer*

Many writers have referred to MLS as a single-entity league, but that is not entirely accurate. Although it displays many characteristics of such a league, deviations from that model exist. When the league was conceived, its creators sought true single-entity status. It would solicit investors ("investor-operators") to contribute as shareholders in the league, and the league would oversee all policies and would centrally control all earned revenues (Weiler & Roberts, 2004, p. 214). MLS revenues would pay all costs incurred by each team for players, staff, stadium leases, and travel. Any profits would be distributed as dividends to the investor-operators, similar to the way a standard corporation operates.

Under the original proposal, investors would contribute a $5 million fee into a pool with other investors. This pooling arrangement gave the investors minimal control over their contributions. Ultimately, the idea proved unsuccessful in attracting the required amount of capital needed to fund the league. An altered business model resulted, combining elements of a pure single-entity and a more traditional league. As of 2010, there are fifteen owner-investors. Some teams have direct ownership interests, such as the Houston Dynamo (which is 50 percent owned by a group including former boxer Oscar de la Hoya) (MLSnet.com, 2010).

Despite the semi-autonomous nature of the majority of teams, the MLS system does have a very centralized approach. All investors are represented on the MLS management committee, the functional equivalent of a board of directors. The management committee hires, fires, and trades players. It also controls player trades, owns all MLS trademarks and copyrights, executes all stadium leases, and controls all radio broadcast rights, advertising, and sponsorship agreements. The investor-operators, however, are responsible for negotiating local sponsorship and broadcast agreements for their own teams.

How well this system works is a matter of debate. Spectator soccer is a secondary sport in the United States and Canada, and for a long time MLS has, by most standards, lost money (Hannigan, 2004). However, in recent years, some of its franchises have become profitable, in part thanks to rising attendance, use of selected international stars, better television deals, and sponsorship arrangements not seen in other sports. For example, MLS teams started selling ad space on the front of jerseys to go along with the league-wide sponsorship partners who had already been advertising on the back of club jerseys (Weinbach, 2006). Another reason is that MLS has been able to unilaterally impose salary restraints, a course of action upheld by two federal courts, which rejected antitrust challenges to this policy (Fraser v. Major League Soccer, 2000, 2002). More recently, its players have become unionized and salary restrictions are a part of the collective bargaining process. In 2010, the league and players narrowly averted a strike over the issue (Goff, 2010).

Recently, MLS has attracted more favorable publicity because of the star status of some of its top players (Fisher, 2003). As part of his five-year deal with MLS and the Los Angeles Galaxy, David Beckham's contract includes a clause that enables him to operate a team, or part of a team, in MLS as early as the 2012 season (Bell, 2009). As of 2010, about 28 percent of U.S. sports fans displayed interest in MLS (Demographic trends among U.S. sports fans, 2010).

In 2009, per-game attendance ranged from over 9800 for FC Dallas to over 31,000 for the Seattle Sounders. MLS added one team in 2010 (the Philadelphia Union) and two in 2011 (the Vancouver Whitecaps and the Portland Timbers). League officials have said they would like to expand, to twenty teams, perhaps as early as 2012, and it is increasingly likely that Montreal will get the nineteenth team.

### Women's National Basketball Association

The WNBA was formed in 1997. Although not the first women's professional league, nor even the first women's professional basketball league (the defunct American Basketball League has that honor), the eight-team league had the advantage of the publicity and the marketing juggernaut of its venerable brother, the NBA. The WNBA's original business plan tried to use the NBA's large number of season ticket holders to its advantage by trying to sell itself to those ticket holders.

That marketing did not prove successful. The WNBA estimated that a large portion of its fans would come from NBA season ticket holders, but that did not turn out to be the case. Only 10 percent of its fan base came from that source. The fan base centered on women aged eighteen through forty-nine years and their children, particularly their daughters (Heath, 2003)—far different from the male-dominant NBA audience.

The WNBA was originally conceived as a single-entity league. All the twenty-nine NBA teams owned an equal share of the women's league and shared in the WNBA's costs and losses. The league was run by a board of governors representing the investors. Sixteen WNBA teams played in NBA cities and were operated by the NBA teams, arguably an advantage over the teams from non-NBA cities. As in the case of MLS, the advantage was the unitary policy that can result in salary restrictions and centralized control over all operations.

By 2002, the WNBA's board of governors, faced with stagnant or declining attendance and lack of profitability, the folding of two franchises (one of which was in Miami, a city with an NBA team), and the relocation of two more teams (one moving from Orlando to play at a gambling casino in Connecticut), was forced to significantly change the league's structure. As of 2009, the WNBA had thirteen teams, down from a high of sixteen in 2002, seven of which remain owned by NBA teams. Average attendance peaked in 1998 at 10,869; in 2009, it was just over 8000 per game (Women's Basketball Online.com, n.d.).

In what amounted to an admission that the governance system had failed, the board eliminated the single-entity organization and allowed individual owners to buy teams and assume the financial risk. One important reason for the change was the potential value increase of the franchises. If the WNBA became a traditional league, an incentive would exist for an owner to sustain short-term losses to make the team competitive so that team's value would increase. The purchase of the Orlando Miracle by the Mohegan Tribe (which owns a gambling casino in Connecticut) for a league record $10 million confirmed the benefits of individual team ownership.

The WNBA experience illustrates the possibility that the overemphasis on centralized control and the lack of competitive owners may ultimately doom the 1990s experiment with single-entity leagues. Although the traditional league possesses elements of a cartel, the single-entity league displays an idealistic but impractical cooperation model. Also, the creation of a business model for the primary purpose of providing a legal defense against antitrust lawsuits does not result in economic success. What may work as a legal tactic does not result in a positive bottom line. It will be interesting to see how future leagues organize and whether MLS continues its present system.

## United Football League

An alternative to the NFL, the United Football League, commenced operations in 2009. Modest in scope, it has four teams as of 2010 and a modified single entity system, whereby an owner-investor can own 50 percent of a team. Player salaries are restricted. It is difficult to determine the success and viability of this new league, but it has achieved a television deal and cleverly scheduled its games on Friday nights (Fleming, 2009).

## A Second Alternative: Promotion and Relegation

Although issues involving international sports will be covered in chapter 4, soccer (known to most of the world as "football") has produced a very different organizational system than those in either the traditional or single-entity leagues in the United States and Canada. The differences are twofold. First, like other international sports, soccer is governed by international and national governing bodies (FIFA and the FA, the English domestic equivalent), which existed before the birth of professional leagues. So, unlike the NFL, which acts as both governing body and professional league, the European soccer system has both and the league is subservient to the policies crafted by the governing bodies (Szymanski, 2009). Second, these soccer leagues use a "promotion and relegation" system whereby the success of the team is a prerequisite for its level of competition. Successful teams in a "second division" can be promoted to a "first division" while unsuccessful first division teams face demotion to the lower tier. This system creates a fluid system whereby, unlike a traditional U.S. league, no team automatically retains its position in the league irrespective of quality of play. For example, in England, there are four main professional divisions and, over a twenty-year period, 95 percent of teams experienced promotion or relegation (Szymanski, 2009).

Although its adoption in the United States for any sport would be highly unlikely, this system has advantages. First, with teams going up and down the various tiers, poorly performing teams have a strong incentive to produce a better product. Also, such a system would not restrict franchises in the same way as traditional leagues, because a number of teams competing in a given market would be greater. For example, say that in a given city there are teams in each of three divisions. With promotion and relegation, it is possible that more than one team may be in the first division. The number and the identity of the teams in a particular division would be subject to change. This could make the structure essentially antitrust-proof.

However, there are significant economic issues with this arrangement. As inferred from the prior paragraph, the relative ease of promotion or relegation means that different teams are in a particular division from year to year. The league's structure would be more fluid and there would be less control over franchise issues and less exclusivity. Also, the general financial health of particular teams could vary greatly because of uncertainties over which division they occupy in a given season. A team relegated to a lower division would lose significant resale value, as well as prestige.

The venerable system does provide for an intriguing alternative to the league system and journalists should familiarize themselves with it.

---

### Ethical Issue: Leagues' Response to Gambling

Gambling on the outcome of a match by referees, players, coaches, trainers, and other team and league employees undermines the fairness and integrity of the sport competition, resulting in a negative perception by fans of the sport. This hurts not only the career of the person(s) involved, but also the reputation of the league, as gambling calls into question its structure and fairness. Consequently, rules prohibiting gambling in each of the major leagues tend to be strict. A short summary of the sanctions imposed by each of the major leagues follows.

#### NBA

The NBA prohibits betting or wagering on NBA games by referees, players, and other team officials and employees. A ban on betting or wagering is absolute. No one involved in the league may bet on any NBA game no matter if he or she is a participant in that particular game or not. Penalties include fines, suspensions, expulsions, and/or permanent disqualification from further association with the NBA. The commissioner's decision is final and unappealable (NBA Constitution, Article 35(g)).

In particular, the rules involving referees have been broad. The league prohibited referees from gambling in *any* sport, the only major league to do so. The rules go even further: During the season, it barred officials from visiting or attending "any race track, off track betting establishment, casino, or gambling establishment of any kind" (NBA/National Basketball Referees Association CBA, Article 11, sec. 2). However, referees are permitted, during the off-season only, to "visit and place bets at race tracks and attend a show at a hotel/casino" as long as the official "is not present in the gaming area of such hotel/casino" (ibid.).

The disclosure that for at least two seasons the former NBA referee Tim Donaghy bet on games in which he officiated, which may have affected the point spreads in those games, was a major embarrassment for the league. Donaghy ultimately pleaded guilty

---

to charges of conspiracy to commit wire fraud and conspiracy to engage in interstate wagering.

Do you think this rule goes too far? Is there a link between legal gambling in an unrelated sport and the goal of keeping NBA officials free from any taint or conflict in their jobs? A report to the NBA recommended that some of the rules be liberalized. It noted, "Because we believed it unnecessary and unrealistic in this day and age to prohibit a referee from all forms of wagering or going to a casino, we recommended narrowing and clarifying the rules to enumerate specifically the types of gambling activities that are prohibited" (Pedowitz, 2008).

### National Hockey League

Similar to the structure found in the NBA, the power to curb gambling in the NHL rests in the hands of the commissioner. If, in the opinion of the NHL commissioner, based upon such information and reports as he may deem sufficient, a player or referee bets or is interested in any pool or wager on the outcome of any NHL game (no matter whether the person has a connection with such game or not), he can expel or suspend or impose a fine on that person.

The NHL punishes member teams involved in gambling. A team may be suspended or terminated if its officer or employee engages in wagering or "being interested in betting" on any hockey game and/or games. Teams are also required to report any wagering on hockey games and the failure to report that information to the commissioner, or failure to suspend immediately that person, may result in suspension and termination of the team (NHL Constitution, Article 3, sec. 3.9(b)). This standard raises some enforceability questions. The NHL bylaws do not define the term "being interested in betting", but rather vest that power in the commissioner. Could that cause an unfair result? Without any independent determination, does that result in severe punishment to those who may not have actually bet on games?

### National Football League

The NFL explicitly prohibits gambling by players in the standard NFL Player Contract that regulates the "integrity of the game." The clause specifically prohibits a player from accepting a bribe to throw or fix an NFL game, from "failing to report a bribe offer," from "betting on an NFL game," and from "knowingly associating with gamblers or gambling activity." After giving the player the opportunity for a hearing, the commissioner has the right to fine, suspend, and/or terminate the player's contract (NFL Standard Players Contract, sec. 15; NFL CBA, Appendix C). The commissioner also has the power to sanction owners and other employees under the "best interest of the sport" clause (NFL Constitution, sec. 8.3).

### Major League Baseball

Major League Baseball prohibits any player, umpire, club, or league official or employee from betting on baseball games. Two kinds of betting are prohibited: betting on a baseball game in connection with which the bettor has no duty to perform and betting on a baseball game in connection with which the bettor has such a duty. A one-year suspension results for violating in the first category, whereas a ban from the sport sanctions the latter. The rules authorize the commissioner to make a determination of a violation and resulting punishment to preserve "the integrity of, or the maintenance of public confidence in, the game of baseball." As in the other leagues, the commissioner has broad discretion to determine what conduct threatens the integrity of the sport and to remedy gambling-related incidents. Also, a player may be subjected to additional disciplinary action for "just cause" by his club (Major League Baseball Rule 21(d)).

### State and Federal Laws

The regulation of gambling or wagering is highly complex and a detailed treatment is beyond the scope of this volume. However, a few general points merit discussion. Sports betting is generally illegal. In 1992, Congress banned states from being in the bookmaking business, but granted exemptions to Delaware, Nevada, Montana, and Oregon, which permitted sports betting at the time. Delaware posed a special issue because it had allowed only "parlay-style" betting on NFL games—in which two or more games must be bet on at once (28 USC, sec. 3701 et seq.). In order to raise more revenue, the state enacted a law allowing single-game betting (Delaware Sports Lottery Act, 29 Del. Code § 4805). Not surprisingly, the four major sport leagues and NCAA filed suit to prohibit single-game betting. After a trial court denied their request for an injunction, they appealed and the request was granted by a federal appeals court.

That panel ruled against the state of Delaware, concluding that the 1992 law limited the betting exemption to the same type of sports betting they had before the 1992 ban was enacted (Office of the Comm'r of Baseball v. Markell, 2009).

## Information Check

When covering organizational issues involving a professional sports league, a journalist should determine:

1  Is the league a traditional league, a single-entity league, or a hybrid?
2  Who runs the league and what governance powers does that person or group have?
3  Which ownership structure is utilized by a particular team? Corporation? Limited partnership? Sole owner?
4  What rules exist regarding procedures for expansion of franchises? Relocations?
5  How does the league investigate prospective team owners?
6  If the league is a single entity, how is the stock ownership structured? How "pure" is the single entity?
7  What are the backgrounds, terms, and salaries of league officials?
8  Who possesses the disciplinary powers for on- and off-field incidents involving owners, team managers, or players? Is there any right of appeal and, if so, to whom?

## References

Allen, P. (2004, February 10). David or Goliath? Stern turned around a league, but some see him as a dictator. *Seattle Times*, p. C6.

Ambrose, R. (2008). The NFL makes it rain: Through strict enforcement of its conduct policy, the NHL protects its integrity, wealth, and popularity. 34 William Mitchell L. Rev. 1070, 1081.

American Needle v. NFL, 130 S. Ct. 2201 (2010).

Badenhausen, K., Ozanian, M. K., & Settimi, C. (2008, December 8). The business of basketball. Retrieved August 2, 2010, from http://www.forbes.com/2008/12/03/business-basketball-nba-biz-sports-nba08-cz_kb_mo_cs_1203nba_land.html

Bell, J. (2009, September 7). Beckham, M.L.S. and Montreal. *New York Times*, p. B16.

Chicago Professional Sports Limited Partnership v. NBA ("Bulls II)," 95 F.3d 593 (7th Cir. 1996).

Cooper, J. (2009, September 19). Report: Mangini fines player over bottle of water. *NFL Fanhouse*. Retrieved February 21, 2010, from http://nfl.fanhouse. com/2009/09/19/report-mangini-slams-browns-player-for-using-the-minibar/

Cozzillio, M., Levinstein, M., Dimino, J., & Feldman, G. (2007). *Sports law*. Durham, NC: Carolina Academic Press, p. 20.

Curnutte, M. (2007, February 25). Financial gap widening between NFL's haves and have-nots. *USA Today*. Retrieved September 1, 2009, from http://www. usatoday.com/sports/football/nfl/2007-02-25-financial-gap_x.htm

Delaware Sports Lottery Act, 29 Del. Code § 4805.

Demographic trends among U.S. sports fans (2010, April 19). ESPN sports poll. *Street and Smith's Sportsbusiness Journal*, p. 20.

Downey, M. (2003, July 29). Hope's legacy goes beyond making sport. *Chicago Tribune*, p. 1.

Easton, S., & Rockerbee, D. (2002). Revenue sharing, conjectures and scarce talent in a sports league model. Retrieved February 21, 2010, from http://129.3.20.41/ eps/io/papers/0303/0303010.pdf

Edelman, M. (2009) Are commissioner suspensions really any different from illegal group boycotts? Analyzing whether the NFL personal conduct policy illegally restrains trade. 58 Catholic U. L. Rev. 631.

Enquist, E. (2005, July 18) Skating on thin ice; Rangers must win back fans after strike, 7 losing seasons. *Crain's New York Business*, p. 3.

Enterprise Wire Co. v. Enterprise Independent Union (1966). 46 LA 359. (Arbitrator Daugherty).

Finley v. Kuhn, 569 F.2d 527 (7th Cir. 1978).

Fisher, E. (2003, November 30). MLS lures new investors. *Washington Times*, p. C05.

Fisher, E. (2004, February 22). NFL to re-examine successful revenue-sharing plan. *Washington Times*, p. C05.

Fleming, T. (2009, April 21). 4 X 6 = United Football League's premier season. *Tampa Bay Sports Examiner*. Retrieved February 25, 2010, from http://www. examiner.com/x-626-Tampa-Bay-Sports-Examiner~y2009m4d21-4-X-6— United-Football-Leagues-Premier-Season

Forbes.com (2009, November 11). NHL team valuations. Retrieved March 20, 2010, from http://www.forbes.com/lists/2009/31/hockey-values-09_NHL-Team-Valuations_Value.html

Fraser v. Major League Soccer, 97 F. Supp. 2d 130 (D. Mass, 2000), affirmed 284 F.3d 47 (1st Cir. 2002).

Futterman, M. (2010, January 7). Arenas suspension may mark legal feud. *The Wall Street Journal*. Retrieved February 19, 2010, from http://online.wsj.com/ article/SB10001424052748704842604574642501366503922.html

Goff, S. (2010, March 20). MLS, players' union reach deal, avert strike. *The Washington Post*. Retrieved May 10, 2010, from http://voices.washingtonpost. com/soccerinsider/2010/03/mls_players_union_reach_deal_a.html

Hannigan, D. (2004, April 29). Football: Not much Adu leaves America waiting: 14-year-old prodigy has not revolutionized US soccer just yet. *Guardian*, p. 34.

Heath, T. (2003, April 1). WUSA, WNBA's plan: To market, to market; timing, new audiences key to success. *Washington Post*, p. D01.

Isidore, C. (2007, October 25). Baseball close to catching NFL as top money sport. CNNMoney.com. Retrieved February 19, 2010, from http://money.cnn.com/2007/10/25/commentary/sportsbiz/index.htm

Kaplan, D. (2009, October 26). NFL pares ownership rule. *Sports Business Journal*, p. 1.

Kaplan, D. (2010, April 12). Team values tied closer to operating histories. *Street and Smith's Sportsbusiness Daily*, p. 17.

Lebowitz, L. (1997, April 20). Sports Inc. Leagues are forming as "single entities" where decision and profits are shared by all owners. *Ft. Lauderdale Sun-Sentinel*, p. 1F.

Los Angeles Memorial Coliseum Commission v. NFL, 726 F.2d 1381 (9th Cir. 1984).

Major League Baseball Constitution, Article 1, sec. 2 and 3. (2005). Retrieved March 1, 2010, from http://www.law.uh.edu/assignments/summer2009/25691-b.pdf

Markiewicz, D. (2004, February 24). Gatorade pours $500 million into NFL. *Atlanta Journal-Constitution*, p. 2C.

McCallum, J. (2004, November 29). The ugliest game. *Sports Illustrated*, p. 44.

Mickle, T., (2009, July 13) Bettman's NHL compensation hits $7.1 million. *Street and Smith's Sportsbusiness Journal*, p. 3.

Milwaukee American Ass'n v. Landis, 49 F.2d 298 (N.D. Illinois, 1931).

minorleaguebaseball.com (2009, September 22). Baseball attendance tops 41.6 million. Retrieved May 10, 2010, from http://www.minorleaguebaseball.com/gen/articles/printer_friendly/clubs/t483/press/y2009/m09/d22/c7091180.jsp

MLSnet.com (n.d.). Major League Soccer—General Overview. Retrieved February 25, 2010, from http://web.mlsnet.com/about/

NBA CBA (2005). Retrieved August 2, 2010 from http://www.nbpa.org/sites/default/files/ARTICLE%20XXXI.pdf

NBA Constitution and Bylaws, Article 35 (2010). Retrieved April 1, 2010, from http://basketball.about.com/od/history/a/nba-gun-policy.htm

Nethery, R. (2004, September 27–October 3). Limited partnership, unlimited goals—Investors in pro teams spend big for a small piece of the action. *Street & Smith's Sportsbusiness Journal*, p. 19.

NFL Constitution and Bylaws (2006). Retrieved April 1, 2010, from http://static.nfl.com/static/content//public/static/html/careers/pdf/co_.pdf

NFL–NFLPA Collective Bargaining Agreement (2005). Retrieved March 1, 2010, from http://images.nflplayers.com/mediaResources/files/PDFs/General/NFL%20COLLECTIVE%20BARGAINING%20AGREEMENT%202006%20-%202012.pdf

Office of the Comm'r of Baseball v. Markell, 579 F. 3d 293 (3d Cir. 2009).

Ohio History Central (n.d.). Cleveland Barons. Retrieved February 19, 2010, from http://www.ohiohistorycentral.org/entry.php?rec=2434

Ozanian, J. (2004, February 29). Pro hockey is hemorrhaging money. But owning a team is still good business. *Forbes*, p. 124.

Ozanian, J., & Badenhausen, K. (2008a, October 29) The business of hockey. *Forbes.* Retrieved August 15, 2009, from http://www.forbes.com/2008/10/29/ nhl-team-values-biz-sports-nhl08_cz_mo_kb_1029intro.html

Pedowitz, L. (2008, October 1). Report to the board of governors of the National Basketball Association [regarding Tim Donaghy]. Retrieved May 10, 2010, from http://hosted.ap.org/specials/interactives/_documents/100208nba_ pedowitz.pdf

Plunkett Research (2009). Sports Industry Overview. Retrieved September 1, 2009, from http://www.plunkettresearch.com/Industries/Sports/SportsStatistics/ tabid/273/Default.aspx

Quirk, J., & Fort R. (1997). *Paydirt: The business of professional team sports.* Princeton, NJ: Princeton University Press, p. 101.

Roberts, G. R. (1984). Sports leagues and the Sherman Act: The use and abuse of Section 1 to regulate restraints in intra-league rivalry. *UCLA Law Rev., 32,* 219, 241 n. 72.

Roberts, G. R. (1988). The evolving confusion of professional sports antitrust, the rule of reason, and the doctrine of ancillary restraints. *S. Cal Law Rev., 61,* 943, 954 n. 34.

Rodack, J. (2004, August 6). Trade on their name and the NFL will come calling. *Florida Times-Union,* p. B-1.

Rosner, S., & Shropshire, K. (2004) *The business of sports.* Sudbury, MA: Jones & Bartlett, p. 336.

Rovell, D. (2004, January 22). How Stern showed NBA the money. Retrieved March 31, 2010, from http://sports.espn.go.com/nba/columns/story?id=1714434

Sandomir, R. (2002, October 1). Biggest drop for attendance in major leagues since the 1995 season. *New York Times.* Retrieved February 22, 2010, from http://www.nytimes.com/2002/10/01/sports/baseball-biggest-drop-for-atten-dance-in-major-leagues-since-the-1995-season.html?pagewanted=1

Snavely, B. (2005, February 21). Match penalty; labor experts look at where NHL talks went offside. *Crain's Detroit Business,* p. 1.

*Sports Business Daily* (2009). Roger Goodell puts stamp on NFL with personal conduct policy, citing Mortensen, Chris, "Beyond the Lines," ESPN, 7/8/09. Retrieved August 28, 2009 from http://www.sportsbusinessdaily.com/ article/131602

*Sports Business Journal* (2008, December 30). NFL regular-season attendance slightly off from record-setting '07. Retrieved September 4, 2009, from http:// www.sportsbusinessdaily.com/article/126559

Sullivan v. NFL, 34 F.3d 1091 (1st Cir. 1994).

Szymanski, S. (2009) *Playbooks and checkbooks: An introduction to the economics of modern sports.* Princeton, NJ: Princeton University Press, pp. 56–58.

United States v. NFL, 116 F. Supp. 319 (1953).

Van Riper, T. (2009, Jan. 13) The most valuable teams in sports. *Forbes.* Retrieved, August 22, 2009, from http://www.forbes.com/2009/01/13/nfl-cowboys-yan-kees-biz-media-cx_tvr_0113values.html

Weiler, P. C., & Roberts, G. R. (2004). *Sports and the law* (3rd ed.). St. Paul, MN: West.

Weinbach, J. (2006, September 28). Major League Soccer to sell ad space on jerseys. *Pittsburgh Post-Gazette*. Retrieved February 26, 2010, from http://www.post-gazette.com/pg/06271/725842-28.stm

Wilbon, M. (2004, December 4) Tarnished records deserve an asterisk. *The Washington Post*, p. D10.

Wolfly, B. (2007, June 28). NBA remarries partners. *Milwaukee Journal Sentinel*. Retrieved August 22, 2009, from http://www.jsonline.com/sports/brewers/29343174.html

Women's Basketball Online.com (n.d.). WNBA Attendance. Retrieved February 25, 2010, from http://www.womensbasketballonline.com/wnba/wnbattendance.html

# 2 The Structure of Individual Sports

Although the major professional team sports leagues involve similar governance systems, the business operations of individual sports differ greatly among themselves and from the league paradigm. Sometimes secretive, often Byzantine, an individual sport's decision-making structure, compensation, sponsorships, and tournament characteristics are not always easy to determine. The niche interests of these sports, plus the above-mentioned intricacies, may be reasons why individual sports governance does not receive the same amount of coverage as that of the major team sports.

At one time, individual sport competition was limited to amateur athletes. Until the 1960s, professionals were generally prohibited from competing in leading tennis and golf tournaments. At that time, a "professional golfer" meant someone who taught golf in a country club. In the modern era of "open" competition, few, if any, of the top tournaments are closed to professionals.

To gain an understanding of the organizational structure of individual sports, it is crucial to understand the basic characteristics of individual sports competition and the nature of the organizations created to regulate it.

## Tournaments and Tours

In the world of individual sports the central mode of competition is a "tournament" or "event." Although a team-based league such as the National Basketball Association (NBA) schedules and controls all matches, preseason games, and playoff series, individual sports events are often conceived and promoted by independent owners or presenters, with the backing of one or more sponsors. Frequently the event presenters create the event, obtain a venue (if they do not own a facility), and offer prize money to entice individual athletes to compete. The presenter is responsible for the event's ticketing, parking, and security, and receives revenues derived from ticket sales, parking, concessions, sales of licensed products, and, in many cases, broadcasting rights.

Sponsorships are central to event presentation, because the fees paid help defray the costs. Sponsorships vary, and the types of arrangements range from expensive naming rights (involving a specific amount of money to add the rightsholder's name to the event) to more modest promotions such as sponsored entertainment and the right to demonstrate a product during the event. From the point of view of the naming rights-holder (usually a business), the sponsorship offers opportunities to publicize the brand, to communicate with current and future customers, and to generate goodwill. Sponsors utilize a full range of marketing techniques, including advertising, personal selling, sales promotion, and public/community relations.

Generally, sponsorships are divided into two categories: primary (or presenting) sponsors and secondary sponsors. The primary sponsor often makes a long-term financial commitment to the event and sometimes receives a stipulated percentage of the gross revenues. That sponsor will often have "title rights" to the event. An example would be the "Buick Classic" golf tournament. Sometimes the term *primary* is eschewed in favor of *presenting sponsor*, which also receives title rights.

Although primary sponsors play a crucial role, secondary sponsors may also be solicited, especially if the tournament has a track record of success. Sometimes known as "official sponsors," secondary sponsors may be entitled to some (although more modest) percentage of revenues, but more often exposure is key. Although primary or presenting sponsors pay for the "title sponsor" association with the event, the secondary sponsors may not pay fees, but rather provide free lodging, transportation, or clothing. In recent years, the number and types of sponsorship categories has expanded, resulting in more complex deals. Chapter 5 discusses the specifics of a sponsorship agreement in more detail.

This system results in a very diffuse series of events. Unlike a professional team sport, whose events remain under its league's control, most organized individual sports lack direct control from their governing body. Every sport has such a body, such as the National Association for Stock Car Auto Racing (NASCAR) or the Professional Golfers' Association Tour (PGA Tour), and these organizations sanction tournaments, but do not have the degree of control found in the team sports leagues. However, without that sanction from the governing body, an event producer and sponsor may find attracting athletes difficult.

In an attempt to gain more control over events, sports organizations attempt to establish a "tour" or a "series." This is done by NASCAR with its Sprint Cup Series. An integrated succession of events increases the brand identification of the organization and requires producers to pay certain fees to the organization and, more importantly, surrender broadcast rights to the governing organization (in this case, NASCAR). The tour gives the organization more control over eligibility by imposing a ranking system and control over scheduling, so that the tour events are in a certain sequence. Finally, the organization often will choose or approve the officials for the event (Cozzillio & Levinstein, 2007).

## Individual Sports Athletes Are Not Employees

Athletes who compete in tournaments sanctioned by the organization are independent contractors, not employees. That means that participating athletes do not work for NASCAR, the PGA, or the United States Tennis Association (USTA), and, unlike their counterparts in the National Football League (NFL) or the NBA, these individual athletes must absorb the considerable expenses of training, travel, and lodging. In addition, the athlete does not enjoy union benefits because no unionized players' associations exist to bargain for wages and working conditions.

This financial responsibility imposes hardships. Touring costs are high, and a young or lower-ranked athlete must pay those costs (travel, hotel, or equipment) out of his or her own pocket or through a sponsor. On the other hand, top-ranked individual athletes often have endorsement agreements that give them the financial means to travel (with the costs of equipment and clothing paid for by the endorsing company).

The method of compensation differs between team athletes and individual athletes. Team athletes, as employees, are paid based on a contract individually negotiated and (where a union is involved) subject to the collective bargaining agreement between the players' union and the particular league. Whether the team wins or loses, the player receives a paycheck, with taxes deducted. As an independent contractor, the individual athlete receives prize money based on his or her success in the tournament. Fees are generally calculated by the tournament's producer or, in the case of a tour, with input from the sanctioning organization.

The major exception to the success-based payment system is the practice known as *appearance fees*. Defined as a sum of money to entice an athlete to come and play at a tournament, appearance fees have had an "under-the-table" quality. Often unpublicized by the tournament presenter or the sanctioning organization, appearance fees may, in some minds, negate an incentive to win.

On the other hand, valid business reasons exist for a presenter to pay appearance fees. The participation of a top-ranked athlete in a tournament often stimulates public interest, resulting in increased publicity, media exposure, and ticket sales. For example, if a presenter pays $200,000 for an athlete to appear, but that results in a $500,000 increase in revenues, the appearance fee results in a very profitable return. This also lays the groundwork for the continuation of the tournament in the future and the possibility that more top-quality athletes may participate (without the need for appearance fees) (Cozzillio & Levinstein, 2007).

Journalists covering a particular tournament—especially a relatively new event—should ask whether an appearance fee was paid as consideration for a well-known player to participate.

## Scheduling

A team player plays a set schedule of games per season. His or her unexplained and unjustified failure to do so results in a penalty by the team. Individual athletes, on the other hand, make their own schedules. They are not required to play in every tournament in a given season. Although certain sports may require participation in a specified number of matches to maintain ranking, an athlete with enough clout can hold owners and presenters of matches hostage by picking and choosing the events the athlete plays. Although only a very, very few achieve this kind of power, those who do possess a great advantage. Individual athletics bodies often compile this kind of record, and journalists should look to compare the number of events particular athletes participate in.

## Rankings

Instead of standings, individual athletes are ranked. The ranking system quantifies the athlete's success, thereby creating fan interest in a particularly successful athlete. Ranking also serves to retain competitive spirit and to increase athlete winnings in competition and/or endorsement deals. Ranking systems vary from sport to sport but, because individual sports lack a "playoff" structure, ranking is the only way to assess the success of a particular athlete. It is more effective to give that player a number one ranking than just saying that the player is "great" or the "best." Ranking gives the player a "seal of approval" of that success.

High rank has an important effect on endorsement contracts. If an athlete maintains a particularly high ranking, the endorsement agreement often mandates that the athlete receive a bonus or extension of the contract, or both. Additionally, it results in greater demand for that athlete by owners and tournament presenters, with the possibility of large appearance fees (when allowed).

The ranking system, however, is far from perfect, and some of the problems are similar to those of ranking college football teams for late-season bowl games. The Association of Tennis Professionals (ATP; the men's tennis tour), for example, has a ranking system that does not "penalize" a player if he does not play well. A player's ATP ranking is based on the total points he accrued in nineteen tournaments, including the four "Grand Slam" tournaments and eight mandatory top-tier ATP "World Tour Masters 1000" tournaments. In addition, the best four results from a number of other ATP tournaments are included (atpworldtour.com,

2010). The system helps a player who won or placed well in tournaments. Thus, a skewed result occurs, because a top player's early elimination in two of fifteen tournaments played in a given season does not negatively impact his ranking. Significantly, for presenters and sponsors, the ATP's ranking system encourages male players to play more tournaments without threat to their rank and resulting endorsement deals. In professional golf, the PGA Tour and Ladies Professional Golf Association (LPGA) both have the winnings, scores, and positions of major players available at http://www.pgatour.com/r/stats/info/?02395 (PGA Tour) and http://www.lpga.com/player_stats.aspx?mid=4&pid=5 (LPGA). The USTA has the rankings (within the top 500) of each male player available at http://www.usta.com/USTA/Global/Pro_Tennis/USTA_Pro_Circuit/Information/~/media/USTA/Document%20Assets/Pro_Circuit/2009/NationalRankingsTop500/2009USANationalRankingsMen.ashx. Rankings for the top female players are found at http://www.sonyericssonwtatour.com/page/RankingsSingles/0,,12781~0~1~100,00.html. For NASCAR, the source is http://www.nascar.com/kyn/nbtn/ (Nascar.com, 2009).

## Examples of Individual Sports Governing Bodies

Although many such organizations exist, we focus on the organizational structure for three well-known individual sports: automobile racing, tennis, and golf. However, journalists covering other sports in detail should find as much information as possible about the structures of a given sport. The availability of information on the Web makes research easier, but still not simple, especially for lesser-known sports. As you read through the following examples, note the considerable differences in their organizations.

### National Association for Stock Car Auto Racing

The organizational structure of NASCAR, the central organization overseeing stock car racing in the United States, is unique because one family has dominated the organization since its inception in 1947. William Henry Getty "Bill" France, Sr., brought together racing promoters throughout the southeastern region of the United States and created a unified organization in an attempt to "legitimize" the sport, which had a sordid reputation derived from the days of dirt track racing by rum runners. France was a racer and understood the need for an organization to establish rules of competition and meet the needs of drivers, car owners, and track owners (Hangstrom, 1998).

NASCAR has achieved phenomenal success, in large part due to France and other family members who have guided the organization over the last half-century. The sport moved from dirt tracks to paved state-of-the-art racetracks located throughout the United States.

Presently, NASCAR operates on a ten-month season from February through November, sanctioning approximately 1500 races at over 100 tracks across thirty-eight states annually. The competitive divisions of NASCAR are divided into a number of different racing series, including the Sprint Cup Series (the best-known), the Nationwide Series, and the Craftsman Truck Series. NASCAR estimates that there are over 75 million fans of the sport (Nascar.com, 2006).

The Sprint Cup Series currently consists of thirty-six sanctioned points races. At the conclusion of each race, the drivers and teams earn points based on their finishing position, and at the end of the season the driver with the most cumulative points (based on the full season and a final ten-race section called the "Chase for the Championship") is crowned the NASCAR Sprint Cup Series Champion. Purse monies are awarded in each race with additional bonus monies for final point standings (nascar. com, 2010).

NASCAR conducts Sprint Cup races at twenty-two racetracks, each of which is located in the United States. As noted below, two entities (Speedway Motorsports, Inc., and the International Speedway Corporation, or ISC) own and operate eighteen of the twenty-two Sprint Cup speedways. There has been some controversy over the centralized control of race-tracks. NASCAR created the ISC, an affiliated company that owns multiple racetracks, in 1953. Over the years, the ISC has raised funds through public offerings of its shares, which it has used to finance the acquisition and development of additional racing facilities, but the France family retains control and has made all major decisions for the company, As of 2009, 55 percent of all Sprint Cup races are held at racetracks owned at least in part by the ISC. The relationship between NASCAR, the ISC, and other, independent racetracks spawned one unsuccessful lawsuit involving attacking NASCAR's control on antitrust grounds (Kentucky Speedway, LLC v. NASCAR, 2009).

NASCAR expanded the reach of the sport from a regional one to a nationally recognized brand with lucrative television contracts and $2 billion in revenues. In 2003, NASCAR reached its present ten-year, $750 million sponsorship deal with Sprint (then known as Nextel), at that time the most expensive package ever for a U.S. sports property. In addition, NASCAR consolidated a fragmented licensing business to one now worth about $2 billion a year. NASCAR signed an eight-year, $4.48 billion TV deal with Fox, NBC, and Turner (cable), a 40 percent increase from the prior broadcast rights agreement. NASCAR has also been able to receive revenues from racecar advertising requirements. Many of the ads on these vehicles—especially in key sections of the car—are NASCAR approved.

Part of this success came from the changing demographics of NASCAR's audience from a regionally based, White, male, working-class grouping to a more family-based and nationwide one. As of 2010, 45 percent of race fans have an annual income of over $50,000 (NASCAR race fans demographics, 2010). The same could not be said fifty-two years ago, when the fan base primarily consisted of farmers and bootleggers (Cokley, 2001).

When Bill France, Sr., retired in 1972, his son, Bill, Jr., became president. He remained at the helm until 1998. Mike Helton became the first non-family-member president in 2000, and in 2003 Bill France, Jr.'s son Brian became chairman and chief executive officer. NASCAR's five-member board remains solidly under the control of members of the family. This arrangement is unusual, as there are few sports organizations that maintain such family control.

NASCAR utilizes a complicated point system to determine success. The winner of a NASCAR race pockets 180 points. For places 2 through 6, the totals decline in five-point increments. For positions 7 through 11, the points awarded drop four points, then three points for finishers in twelfth place or lower. Similar point totals are awarded to owners. Racing fees and bonuses are based on a complex formula that factors in performance, past performance, and bonuses. More information is found on the NASCAR website (http://www.nascar.com/kyn/nbtn/).

Despite NASCAR's reputation as an economic juggernaut, the economic downturn of 2008–10 hurt NASCAR in terms of sponsorships and attendance, resulting in decreases in race winnings. Also, sponsors dropped out and ticket prices were slashed to prop up attendance. The costs of operating racing teams resulted in mergers, and the economic woes of General Motors and Chrysler added to those difficulties (Paulk, 2010).

## Tennis

In contrast to the centralized power of NASCAR, the structure of tennis is quite the opposite. "Tennis is the only major professional sport in this country that does not have a governing body solely dedicated to the sport," said Arlen Kantarian, then-chief executive of professional tennis at the USTA, as quoted in the *Sports Business Journal* (Kaplan, 2001). One might think the USTA would be that body, but in reality it possesses relatively little power. The USTA owns and runs the U.S. Open, the leading U.S. tennis tournament and one of the four "Grand Slam" events. It also organizes and manages grass-roots tennis programs and oversees the selection of the U.S. team in the Davis and Fed cups. The USTA also runs a "professional circuit" for the development of professional players, allowing these players to gain the experience and ranking points necessary to qualify for the Grand Slams. Finally, the USTA also owns and controls the men's clay court championships and the women's hard court champion-ships (USTA.com, 2009).

The limited powers of the USTA result in a professional tennis structure consisting of a hodgepodge of various organizations with different juris-dictions. Players' groups, tournament owners, and sponsors have more control. Companies such as IMG and Octagon frequently own tourna-ments, and at the same time represent players, as well as sit on the tour boards.

In addition to the USTA, tournament owners, and presenters, separate governing bodies exist that represent men's and women's tennis players. The ATP World Tour is the governing body for men's tennis. It sanctions about seventy events and works to protect the interests of male players. Essentially, it sets rules regarding prize money and tournament qualifica-tion. It also allows representatives of management companies to sit on its board of directors. The ATP World Tour permits and encourages the use of appearance fees, a practice that has drawn criticism. The Sony Ericsson Women's Tennis Association (WTA) is the women's counterpart. Similar to the ATP in structure, the WTA sanctions about sixty events. However, the WTA prohibits appearance fees (Smith, 2000). The six-year, $88 mil-lion sponsorship agreement made in January 2005 is the largest such deal in the history of women's sports. Although the firm dropped its "title sponsorship" the deal was extended to 2013, for a reported $27 million (CBSsports.com, 2010).

In the summer of 2004, sensing the need for more presence in the tennis landscape, the USTA started a six-week tennis season known as the "U.S. Open Series." It includes ten ATP and WTA Tour professional tourna-ments in North America leading up to and linked to the U.S. Open. Players who win the most in the series earn points and arrive at the U.S. Open with a chance to double their prize money and win at least $2 million. (*USA Today*, 2005) To add to the mix, whereas the USTA runs the U.S. Open, other organizations govern the three remaining Grand Slam events: Wimbledon, the French Open, and the Australian Open. However, the organization presenting these events works closely with the International Tennis Federation, the international governing body of the sport.

Tensions have existed between the professional and amateur sides, which may have resulted in executive changes for both the USTA and the WTA. In 2009, Larry Scott, the former head of the WTA, resigned, reportedly after unsuccessfully attempting to merge the WTA and the ATP. Kantarian similarly left the USTA after disagreements surfaced within the organization over whether the focus of the organization should center on professional or recreational tennis, and the head of the ATP was forced out in 2008 under pressure by a number of players (Kaplan, 2009). The present leaders have expressed the hope that more cooperation between the USTA, ATP, and WTA will result.

## Golf

Founded in 1916, the PGA has served as an umbrella organization for the sport. Presently, the PGA works as a trade association, promoting the game to people of all ages and skill levels.

The PGA Tour, once a part of the PGA, but independent since 1968, represents professional male golfers, who play more than 100 "official-money" tournaments. The PGA Tour split from the PGA (now officially known as the PGA of America) in 1968, so that the players could gain more control of their financial benefits and tournament schedule. Although the two organizations work closely together today, the PGA Tour and PGA remain separate entities (Gabriel, 2001). Tour players compete on one of three levels: the PGA Tour is for the very best players, while the Champions Tour and Nationwide Tour are for players not quite on the level of the PGA Tour. Although the PGA of America is less involved in professional competitions, it still sponsors four major golf events—the Ryder Cup, the PGA Championship, the Senior PGA Championship, and the PGA Grand Slam of Golf—and thirty other tournaments for its members.

In 1994, Timothy W. Finchem became the PGA Tour's third commissioner. The next year he undertook a restructuring program designed to strengthen its competitions (which are the PGA Tour's core business), and expand the PGA Tour's international scope. Thanks in part to its present TV deal, the PGA Tour has been enjoying a financial bonanza. TV revenue for 2007 was $367 million, up from $229.8 million in 2002. In 2009, even the 125th-ranked player in terms of tournament winnings earned over $600,000 in official prize money (PGATour.com, 2010).

Over the last decade, the tour has had its superstar, Tiger Woods. For a ten-year period starting in the late 1990s, Woods boosted TV ratings and increased public interest in the game. Tournaments became media events. However, his highly publicized marital problems in 2009 and resulting absence from the tour diminished, at least temporarily, the exposure of the sport (Shipnuck, 2010).

The LPGA serves as the umbrella organization for women's competitive golf. Despite a talented pool of players, the LPGA does not command the popularity or the sponsorship of its male counterpart, and therefore obtains only a fraction of the prize money of the PGA Tour. The group also lacks a comprehensive network television contract and receives a fee only from the tournament sponsors. Most of the LPGA's media deals involve splitting of profits, rather than a predetermined amount upfront (Cassidy, 2001). More recently, the LPGA has been hurt by the economic downturn and some controversial actions by its commissioner at the time. In August 2008, Carolyn Bivens instituted a policy requiring all players to speak English by 2009 or face suspension, without establishing standards for evaluating players' English proficiency, and without indicating if the

LPGA will provide educational resources for those players whose English needs improvement. After widespread criticism, and the possibility of legal action, the policy was reversed (Watanabe & Kim, 2008).

### Information Check

When covering business issues involving individual sports, a journalist should determine:

1  What is the scope of the organization's power over the sport?
2  Is the event in question run by the organization or by independent sponsors?
3  Does the organization permit professionals and/or amateurs to play?
4  What are the eligibility rules?
5  How are rankings calculated?
6  What disciplinary powers does the organization have over its members? Is there a right of appeal?
7  Who owns the broadcast rights to the event?
8  Are there primary and secondary sponsors for the event?
9  What are the sponsors paying?
10 If sponsorships are divided into other product categories what are those categories and what rights do sponsors have?
11 Are appearance fees allowed?

## References

atpworldtour.com, (2010). ATP rankings, frequency asked questions. Retrieved August 10, 2010, from http://www.atpworldtour.com/Rankings/Rankings-FAQ.aspx

Cassidy, H. (2001, January 22). LPGA's Durkin focused on new messaging. *Brandweek*, p. 58.

CBSsports.com (2010, March 7). WTA Tour's new deal with Sony Ericsson drops title. Retrieved May 11, 2010, from http://www.cbssports.com/tennis/story/13025069/wta-tours-new-deal-with-sony-ericsson-drops-title

Cokley, M. A. (2001). In the fast lane to big bucks: The growth of NASCAR. *Sports Law Journal, 8*, 67.

Cozzillio, M., & Levinstein, M. (2007). *Sports law*. Durham, NC: Carolina Academic Press, pp. 46–50.

Gabriel, M. (2001). *The Professional Golfers' Association Tour: A history*. Jefferson, NC: McFarland.

Hangstrom, R. G. (1998). *The NASCAR way: The business that drives the sport*. New York: John Wiley & Sons.

Kaplan, D. (2001, August 27). Can tennis mend its fractured world? *Sports Business Journal*, p. 23.

Kaplan, D. (2009, August 31). New leaders, new style. *Sports Business Journal*, p. 1.

Kentucky Speedway, LLC v. NASCAR, 2009 U.S. App. LEXIS 26974 (6th Cir. 2009).

NASCAR race fan demographics (2010). Retrieved April 12, 2010, from http://www.nascarmedia.com

Nascar.com (2006, December 18). Sirius radio, NASCAR ink five–year partnership. Retrieved May 10, 2010, from http://www.nascar.com/2005/news/headlines/official/02/22/sirius_2007/index.html

Nascar.com (2009). NASCAR rankings. Retrieved November 15, 2009, from http://www.nascar.com/kyn/nbtn/

Nascar.com (2010). How money is distributed. Retrieved August 15, 2010, from http://www.nascar.com/news/features/race.winnings/index.html

Paulk, R. (2010, February 14). NASCAR "turns corner" on the business side. *Pittsburgh Tribune-Review*. Retrieved February 27, 2010, from http://www.pittsburghlive.com/x/pittsburghtrib/sports/racing/s_666055.html

PGATour.com (2010). 2009 PGA Tour money leaders. Retrieved February 27, 2010, from http://www.pgatour.com/r/stats/info/?109

Shipnuck, A. (2010, January 3). What Tiger Woods's "indefinite leave" will cost him—and the PGA Tour. Golf.com. Retrieved February 27, 2010, from http://www.golf.com/golf/tours_news/article/0,28136,1948225,00.html

Smith, D. (2000, November 15). Williams calls for appearance fees. *USA Today*, p. 2C.

*USA Today* (2005). U.S. Open series schedule. Retrieved February 2, 2010, from http://www.usatoday.com/sports/tennis/2005-usopen-series-schedule.htm

USTA.com (2009, January 27). Frequently asked questions about the USTA. Retrieved February 27, 2010, from http://www.usta.com/USTA/Global/About_Us/Organization/Information/1132_FAQ.aspx

Watanabe, T., & Kim, V. (2008, September 6). Putting English on the ball. *Los Angeles Times*. Retrieved February 27, 2010, from http://bx.businessweek.com/business-law/view?url=http%3A%2F%2Fwww.latimes.com%2Fsports%2Fla-me-lpga6–2008sep06%2C0%2C1554284.story

# 3 The Structure of College and High School Sports

Many, if not most, institutions of higher education have sports programs allowing intercollegiate competition. Often, colleges and universities place considerable importance on their sports programs because a school with a successful program gains a number of tangible benefits.

One benefit is the sheer joy of victory. Winning boosts the morale of team members and their school, and a cohesive school spirit and camaraderie often results. Economic benefits may also accrue, as athletic success leads to the branding of the school as a top competitor to a potentially nationwide audience. The resulting national attention raises awareness of a school's educational programs and, ideally, expands the pool of potential applicants.

A frequently cited example is Boston College, a respected Jesuit institution. In 1984, the Boston College quarterback Doug Flutie won the Heisman Trophy and the national championship on a late "Hail Mary" pass. The following year, applications to Boston College increased 25 percent. This result became known as the "Flutie effect." However, some have questioned the existence of the "Flutie effect." A survey of the general public by *The Chronicle of Higher Education* concluded that, among twenty-one goals for colleges, "playing athletics for the entertainment of the community" was the least important. Other goals, such as preparing students to be future leaders and presenting cultural events, were deemed more important. Only 35 percent of respondents said sports were "somewhat" or "very important" for colleges (Scruggs, 2003). However, more recently, a study confirmed the connection, finding that applications increased by 2–8 percent depending on the success of the football and men's basketball teams (Potter, 2008).

Collegiate athletics are revenue generating, but not often profitable, for the schools served. In terms of revenue, the University of Texas attained the top spot in 2008–09, producing over $138 million in revenue. This was followed by Ohio State (just under $120 million), University of Florida ($108 million), and the University of Alabama (just under $104 million) (Staples, 2010).

However, it is a major misconception that most collegiate programs garner profits. Athletics expenses outpaced revenues in schools of what is now known as the Football Bowl Subdivision (formerly known as Division I-A), the top division in the collegiate system, throughout the 1990s and early 2000s, even among conferences that compete in the lucrative Bowl games played to national television audiences. The study noted that only the Southeastern Conference (SEC) schools averaged a profit from 1993 to 2002 (Sylwester, 2004). Of 118 Football Bowl Subdivision programs, 83 percent operated at a deficit in the 2006 fiscal year. In the Football Championship Subdivision (formerly known as Division I-AA) no program made money and the median operating loss that year was almost $9 million (Berkowitz, 2008).

Like their professional counterparts, an umbrella body governs collegiate sports. However, with thousands of schools and dozens of sports, the regulatory structure of collegiate sports is more complex and more controversial. The chief regulator is the National Collegiate Athletic Association (NCAA). Consisting of more than 1000 four-year institutions, the NCAA develops guidelines and standards for athletic eligibility in each of three divisions, known as Divisions I, II, and III. As of 2008, there were 331 Division I schools, 291 Division II schools, and 429 Division III schools. That means that the great majority of four-year institutions are not in the top division, and many do not even offer athletic scholarships.

Many writers, administrators, fans, and athletes have criticized the NCAA's policies. Before any journalist takes out a rapier pen or engages in a verbal attack, that reporter should have at least a working knowledge of the NCAA goals and policies and the scope of its powers.

The NCAA's mission statement notes an idealistic purpose of collegiate athletics. It states: "student athletics is an avocation, balancing their academic, social and athletics experiences." It exhorts student-athletes to perform at the highest level of integrity, to pursue excellence in both academics and athletics, and to encourage diversity and respect philosophical difference and institutional autonomy (NCAA Mission Statement, 2009).

The NCAA exercises jurisdiction over many different college sports, from golf to swimming. The so-called "big-money" sports—football competition from schools of the Football Bowl Subdivision and college basketball (male and female)—are only a small portion of its mandate.

Essentially, the NCAA system creates a social contract: "student-athletes" participate in intercollegiate sports, receive an education, and often (but not always) receive a partial or full scholarship to an institution. In return for these benefits, student-athletes are bound to accept a series of restrictions to maintain their "amateur" status. For many of the 360,000 student-athletes involved, this system works well. For college students talented enough to play a sport on a competitive level, the opportunity to play intercollegiate sports (often with an accompanying scholarship),

under fine coaches and in up-to-date facilities, coupled with the opportunity to receive an education, is a wonderful experience. The difficulty
with the system involves student-athletes at a minority of schools in a very
small number of sports.

## Institutional Control

The NCAA was formed in 1906, as a result of President Theodore
Roosevelt's concern over the high number of injuries and deaths in college football. The NCAA is not a governmental agency, despite the fact
that public universities are part of its membership. The NCAA's nongovernmental status weighs significantly in the organization's procedures and
gives it considerable latitude in enforcement.

The organization seeks to "maintain intercollegiate athletics as an integral part of the education program and the athlete as an integral part of
the student body" (NCAA Division I Manual, 2009, sec. 1.3.1). Its principal goals are to promote intercollegiate athletics, administer national
championships, and maintain integrity and standards of fair play.

Although the NCAA employs personnel to enforce its complex rules, it
is neither a police force nor a district attorney. It mandates that member
institutions report violations, and failure to report results in even greater
punishment based on its internal rules and regulations. This concept,
familiar in academic circles, is known as "institutional control." An NCAA
institution must conduct a self-study to provide university faculty, staff,
and students, as well as the public, with a transparent view of its operations. The period ranges from ten years (Division I) to five years (Divisions
II and III) (NCAA Division I Manual, 2009, sec. 6.3.1; NCAA Division
III self-study guide, 2009–10). The study includes the governance of the
institutions and the roles of the president, athletic director, and compliance officers, and issues of fiscal responsibility, academic rules, and gender
equity. Problems often occur when institutional control breaks down.

A particularly sad example of the breakdown of institutional control
occurred at St. Bonaventure University, a respected institution located
near Buffalo, New York. In 2004, the NCAA placed the school on three-
year probation for violations in the men's basketball program, specifically
concluding that the stiff punishment was justified by the breakdown of
institutional control. The case focused on the eligibility of a particular
men's basketball player who transferred to St. Bonaventure after spending two years at a junior college. The student came to the university after
receiving a "Certificate of Welding," a designation that clearly did not
meet the requirements for academic eligibility under the NCAA's rules.

This violation was serious enough, but the conduct of the then-president
and an assistant men's basketball coach made the situation far worse. The
assistant coach communicated directly with the president (who happened
to be his father) and convinced the president that the student was eligible,

despite advice to the contrary from the athletic director. Compounding the problem, the institution changed the grade of the student-athlete from an incomplete to a "withdrawal" in a particular class taken during the student-athlete's first term at St. Bonaventure so that he remained eligible to travel to "away" games. (The university had a policy denying such travel for those with "incomplete" grades under its institutional policy.) The violation occurred after the president's son asked his father to "request" that the vice-president for academic affairs reconsider his initial decision on a strict withdrawal date deadline.

The result of this hubris was three years of probation (from 2003 to 2006), no postseason competition in either the 2003 NCAA tournament or the Atlantic 10 Tournament (the conference St. Bonaventure belongs to), limitations on recruitment, and developing a new system of governance during the probationary period.

The NCAA found it "extremely troubling that a university president would assert independent interpretive authority with regard to NCAA legislation despite the repeated advice of the Athletic Director. Such lack of judgment . . . [was] at the root of why this case occurred" (Infractions case: St. Bonaventure University, 2004). As a result, the president, the athletic director, and the entire basketball coaching staff resigned. Even though the athletic director objected to the policy, he did not take enough steps to prevent it. That fact marks the core aspect of institutional control: an effective structure must be in place to avoid transgressions and to resolve them effectively when they occur. If the NCAA has to take unilateral action, the severity of the penalties and sanctions increases.

More recently, violations in the men's basketball program at the State University of New York at Binghamton were uncovered. As of early 2010, a committee led by the state's former top judge was investigating accusations that the university violated academic standards to build a competitive men's basketball team. Problems included the arrests of three of the team's players within a three-year period, the dismissal of six players, the resignation of the athletic director, the placement of the basketball coach on paid leave, and accusations that university administrators retaliated against an instructor who said she was pressured to show grading favoritism to athletes (Thomas, 2009).

Obviously, these and other cases merit serious examination and questions about a school's governance system by journalists. For example, what kind of reporting structure exists? What is the role and interrelationship of coaches, athletic directors and the university president? Did the university move into a new or "better" conference or division recently? How much pressure existed from alumni boosters?

The above cases highlight the importance of the role of the athletic director. The athletic director controls the athletic department budget, which often ranges in the tens of millions of dollars annually. Construction of new facilities, fund-raising efforts, Title IX compliance, and a thorough knowledge of NCAA rules are under the aegis of the athletic director and his or her staff. Athletic directors often aid in obtaining sponsorship deals. An ideal athletic director must possess knowledge of finance, marketing, and fund raising. He or she must interact with upper administration such as the president and the board of trustees. The athletic director must possess skills necessary to answer questions posed by the media. Some have even perused Internet chat rooms to quell rumors and criticisms of the athletic program of their particular college or university (Lee, 2004).

## Governance System

The NCAA's governance emanates from an association-wide executive committee, consisting of eleven members from Division I schools and two members each from Division II and III institutions. Composed of college or university presidents, the executive committee is charged with ensuring that each division operates consistently with the basic purposes, fundamental policies, and general principles of the association (NCAA Executive Committee, 2009). In sum, the executive committee is a de facto board of directors.

Additionally, considerable powers are given to committees governing the various divisions. Although committees representing Division II and III schools serve important roles, we focus here on Division I's intradivisional governance system. The Division I Board of Directors has eighteen members. Directly underneath is the Division I Leadership Council, an advisory body to the Division I Board of Directors. It identifies issues important to the future of Division I and offers its expertise in defining appropriate action items. Committees on such policy issues as minority opportunities, ethical conduct, and women's athletics and a student-athlete advisory committee report to the Leadership Council.

The NCAA has a considerable number of committees, cabinets, and task forces governing the wide gamut of activities. Its bureaucratic structure would rival that of any international sports federation or, for that matter, a state or local government. Presently, the NCAA has 125 different committees. A listing is found on the NCAA's website, NCAA.org (NCAA Committees, 2009). Two of the most important are the committees on infractions, independent bodies composed of individuals from NCAA member institutions, and the management council, a day-to-day operating arm of the NCAA, with final approval for all decisions being up to the board of directors. Additionally, each division has its own infractions committee. Other Division I committees include a student-athlete advisory committee, made up of student-athletes "assembled to provide insight on the student-athlete experience," and men's and women's basketball issues committees (NCAA Division I Student Advisory Committee, 2010).

## Divisions

As noted earlier, the NCAA consists of three divisions. The criteria for a school's membership in the appropriate division include the number of sports the school sponsors, the average attendance for home games, and the number of home games played. College football is further subdivided into Football Bowl Subdivision or FBS (formerly Division I-A), Football Championship Subdivision or FCS (formerly Division I-AA), and Division I non-football schools (formerly known as Division I-AAA), which do not compete in college football. The requirements for division membership are intricate, but a basic outline follows.

Division I schools are required to sponsor a minimum of seven men's teams and seven women's teams (or six men's teams and eight women's teams), all of which are required to play 100 percent of the minimum number of contests against Division I opponents—anything over the minimum number of games has to be 50 percent Division I. Men's and women's basketball teams have to play all but two games against Division I teams; men must play one-third of all their contests in the home arena. Division I schools must meet certain financial aid requirements.

Division II schools must sponsor four men's and four women's sports and football teams and men's and women's basketball teams must play at least 50 percent of their games against Division I or II opponents. For sports other than football and basketball there are no scheduling requirements. Division III schools are required to sponsor five men's and five women's sports. There are no financial aid requirements (NCAA Self-Study Guide, 2009–10).

For admission into the Football Bowl Subdivision (the former Division I-A) teams have to meet minimum attendance requirements (average 15,000 people in actual or paid attendance per home game), once in a rolling two-year period (NCAA Division I Manual, 2009, sec. 20.9.1–20.9.7). NCAA Football Championship Subdivision teams do not need to meet minimum attendance requirements. A school must provide an average of 90 percent of the maximum number of football scholarships allowed over a rolling two-year period.

Additionally, each school must play at least five home games each season against another FBS opponent, must sponsor at least sixteen varsity sports, two more than the normal Division I minimum, with a minimum of six men's sports and eight women's sports, and must offer a minimum of 200 athletic scholarships or offer $4 million in athletic financial aid.

Presently, the FBS includes schools from eleven athletic conferences and seven nonaffiliated schools (so-called "independent schools" such as Notre Dame). Schools align themselves into conferences to operate more efficiently. The conference structure provides for cooperative scheduling, negotiation of television contracts, and other similar endeavors. The athletic conference system, not part of the NCAA but an important player in the college sports system, is discussed in detail later in this chapter.

## Enforcement

The most vital cogs in the association's attempts to achieve and maintain integrity are its member schools, which are charged with carrying out NCAA rules (NCAA Division I Manual, 2009, sec. 2.8).

The NCAA manual states that each school "shall monitor its program to assure compliance and to identify and report to the Association instances in which compliance has not been achieved" (NCAA Division I Manual, 2009, sec. 2.8.1). This self-regulation provision means that member institutions are required to report transgressions. If they fail to do so and the transgressions are subsequently discovered, the penalties against the school's athletic program increase in severity. On the other hand, self-reporting of violations will be considered a mitigating factor in determining the penalty (NCAA Division I Manual, 2009, sec. 32.2.1.2). The self-enforcement mechanism varies from school to school, depending on factors such as the mission of the school administration, the determination and aptitude of compliance personnel, and—most of all—the honesty of those they oversee (Gregorian, 2003). Universities often employ compliance officers to ensure that the rules are followed.

The NCAA employs a fifty-three-person "membership services" staff, which works with schools to help interpret rules. The enforcement staff has the power to investigate complaints, based on information received from self-reporting by the school or other methods of information gathering. It has the responsibility to gather "basic information" regarding possible violations and, in doing so, may contact individuals to solicit information. If the enforcement staff has developed "reasonably reliable" information indicating that an institution has been in violation of the association's governing legislation that requires further in-person investigation, the enforcement staff shall provide a written notice of inquiry to the enforcement staff's chief executive officer. If the investigation uncovers significant information concerning a possible major violation, the institution will be notified. To the extent possible, the notice of inquiry also shall contain the following information:

- The involved sport.
- The approximate time period during which the alleged violations occurred.
- The identity of involved individuals.
- An approximate time frame for the investigation.
- A statement indicating that the institution and involved individuals may be represented by legal counsel at all stages of the proceedings.

- A statement requesting that the individuals associated with the institution not discuss the case prior to interviews by the enforcement staff and institution, except for consultation with legal counsel or reasonable campus communications not intended to impede the investigation of the allegations.

Hearings by the infractions committee of the appropriate division (I, II, or III) then occur. The Division I Committee on Infractions currently has ten members, composed of seven individuals from NCAA member institutions and three from the general public. Members have been attorneys, professors, conference commissioners, and athletic department officials (NCAA Committees, n.d.) The infractions committee has the authority to determine what findings (if any) should be made and what (if any) penalties should be imposed upon a member institution. This committee meets up to six times per year and committee members serve three-year terms, for a maximum of nine years (NCAA Committees, n.d.).

The duties of this committee include determining the merits of complaints filed with the NCAA; charging members with the failure to maintain academic or athletics standards required for membership; determining facts related to alleged violations; making findings of violations of NCAA rules; imposing appropriate penalties on member institutions found to be involved in major violations; and carrying out any other duties directly related to the administration of the enforcement program. The NCAA differentiates between "major" and "secondary" violations in assessing punishment. For secondary violations, a hearing is often waived.

Similar to an administrative hearing or arbitration procedure, each side presents its case in front of the entire committee. After the hearing, the committee issues a report summarizing its findings and the recommended penalties (if any) (NCAA Division I Manual, 2009, sec. 32.9.1). The aggrieved party may appeal to an infractions appeals committee. However, this committee does not operate like a court of law. As Michael Rogers, who represented Baylor University in one hearing, stated: "one misconception is that a [committee on infractions hearing] is like a trial we would see in our judicial system." Says Rogers, "It is very different." In an interview in 2010, the chairperson referred to the process as "quasi-judicial" and "in a way like arbitration" and similar to an "administrative hearing" (Dohrmann, 2010).

The most severe penalty is the repeat-violator legislation (so-called "death penalty"), applicable if a major rules violation occurs within five years of another major violation. The second major case does not have to be in the same sport as the earlier case to affect the second sport (NCAA Division I Manual, 2009, sec. 19.5.2.2). The result: termination of the school's program in that sport for two years. In only one instance has the NCAA instituted this punishment to a Division I institution, against Southern Methodist University in 1987.

Other penalties for repeat violators of legislation include:

- Prohibition of some or all outside competition in the sport involved in the last major violation for one or two seasons.
- Prohibition of all coaching staff members in that sport from involvement directly or indirectly in any coaching activities at the institution during that period.
- Elimination of all initial grants-in-aid and recruiting activities in the sport involved in the last major violation in question for a two-year period.
- All institutional staff members serving on the NCAA Presidents Cabinet Council, executive committee, or other committees of the association resign their positions (NCAA Division I Manual, 2009, sec. 19.5.2).

The NCAA is a private organization, not a governmental agency or an organization with direct connections to a governmental agency. In 1988, the U.S. Supreme Court concluded that the NCAA was not a "state actor" and therefore not subject to Constitutional requirements of due process in its enforcement procedures (NCAA v. Tarkanian, 1988). Therefore, it can fashion a system of discipline and enforcement less stringent than that of a government agency. Also, the NCAA does not have to fear lawsuits for alleged violations of fairness and due process.

However, the NCAA is subject to lawsuits involving alleged anticompetitive activities under antitrust laws. In 1984, the U.S. Supreme Court rejected NCAA claims that it was exempted from liability under the Sherman Act, sec. 1, the main antitrust statute, which bars agreements by two or more entities to restrain trade (NCAA v. Board of Regents of the University of Oklahoma, 1984). Another court concluded that the NCAA's policy of limiting compensation for certain part-time coaches violated antitrust laws and the organization had to pay $65 million in a settlement (Law v. NCAA, 1998).

A more recent antitrust case involving the use of a student-athlete's name and likeness may cause even more trouble for the organization. In 2010, a federal judge refused to dismiss a lawsuit by a former UCLA men's basketball player claiming that the NCAA, and by extension its member schools, engaged in antitrust violations involving rules against paying student-athletes for the use of their names and likenesses. Although the court dismissed a portion of the suit, the failure to dismiss all the claims means extra time and expense for the organization (O'Bannon v. NCAA, 2010). It also has the possibility of revealing more of the NCAA's operations as part of the pretrial discovery process (Thamel, 2010).

## The Rules

The substantive rules are contained in the NCAA's *Manuals,* a must-have reference work for journalists, which can be either purchased or downloaded from the NCAA's website (www.ncaa.org). Written like a statutory code, the Division I manual, for example, has thirty-three separate articles and many accompanying sections and subsections.

Like federal or state laws, the manual has its minute details, and many use those as examples when criticizing the NCAA. For example, one clause requires laundry labels on a school uniform to be no more than 2¼ square inches within a four-sided geometrical shape (i.e., rectangle, square, parallelogram) (NCAA Division I Manual, 2009, sec. 12.5.4.1). Criticisms may be valid but, before totally assailing the organization, note that many sections of the bylaws contain important standards applicable to many different sports, not just the "big-time" ones. A journalist who wishes to write an opinion piece attacking the NCAA will have far more credibility if he or she understands the major requirements and the reasons behind them. We summarize some of the key provisions in the Division I manual, as Division I schools are most frequently covered. Because the manual is over 500 pages, the following summary will give readers a basic idea of the key provisions.

### Amateurism

Article 12 of the NCAA's Division I manual discusses the requirement that all student-athletes must be amateurs. The NCAA holds to a traditional definition of amateurism, one that prohibits most forms of compensation for services. The concept dates back to the nineteenth century, when upper-class gentlemen had the time and means to participate in sporting events for the pleasure of doing so. The manual notes that an athlete becomes ineligible to play for his or her school if that athlete "directly or indirectly" receives pay "in any form in that sport" (NCAA Division I Manual, 2009, sec. 12.1.1). The section further prohibits receipt of any compensation from a professional sports organization and even bars playing for a professional team without compensation (NCAA Division I Manual, 2009, sec. 12.2.4). The proscription extends to contracting with an agent or signing a contract with a professional team while playing at school.

The major exception to the no-compensation requirement is the athletic scholarship that some student-athletes receive as consideration for attending the school. But other exceptions exist, although more limited. An individual may receive "actual and necessary" expenses from a professional sports organization to attend an academy, camp, or clinic, provided that no NCAA institution or conference owns or operates the academy, camp, or clinic and no camp participant is above the age of fifteen. Basketball players may accept actual and necessary travel and room-and-board expenses from a professional sports organization to attend that organization's predraft basketball camp (NCAA Division I Manual, 2009, sec. 12.2.1.1.1).

In most cases, a player who seeks to enter a professional league draft loses eligibility (NCAA Division I Manual, 2009, sec. 12.2.4.2). However, there are some important exceptions to this rule. A student-athlete playing basketball may enter the NBA or other professional league draft. If the player is not drafted, he or she may seek to return to intercollegiate participation within thirty days after the draft date. A similar rule is in effect regarding FBS and FCS football. An enrolled student-athlete (as opposed to a prospective student-athlete) in FBS or FCS football may enter the National Football League draft one time during his collegiate career without jeopardizing eligibility in that sport, provided the student-athlete is not drafted by any team in that league and the student-athlete declares his intention to resume intercollegiate participation within seventy-two hours following the National Football League draft declaration date (NCAA Division I Manual, 2009, secs. 12.2.4.2.1 and 12.2.4.2.3).

Many have criticized the strict application of the amateurism rules. One particularly controversial rule states that if a student is a professional athlete in one sport, but wishes to compete as a student-athlete in another sport, he may neither receive an athletic scholarship nor accept any compensation from the professional team or companies seeking endorsement deals (NCAA Division I Manual, 2009, sec. 12.1.2). This situation occurred when Jeremy Bloom, a successful mogul skier, sought student-athlete status to play football at the University of Colorado. As a condition, he was forced to give up endorsement opportunities based on his success as a participant in a very different sport (Bloom, 2003). Another example involved Alan Adair, a third-baseman for the University of Oklahoma who survived brain cancer. He wrote a book about his recovery intended to help others with the disease, only to receive a call from a compliance officer informing him that his college baseball career was over because his name was attached to a "corporate product."

## Ethical Question: Should NCAA Student-Athletes Be Paid?

Some argue that Division I players should be paid outright for their services (Sack, 2008; Gilmore, 2007). On one level, the idea has appeal. Because big-time college athletes—notably those in football and men's and women's basketball—may earn direct or indirect revenues for the school due to fan attendance, more lucrative broadcasting and cable contracts, and the sale of their names and likenesses on merchandise, why should they not receive compensation for their services beyond the scholarship?

However, this idea raises difficult issues. How would "pay" be defined? What monetary limits, if any, should be imposed? What effect would payments have on the often limited budgets of many colleges and universities? Would a pay system create a two-tier system of "profitable" sports versus "unprofitable" sports? Would other sports have to be cut? Would more rules violations occur in an attempt to get talented athletes? Would colleges become de facto minor leagues for the pros? Additionally, a particularly fundamental question involves labor law issues. NCAA member schools would have to comply with state and federal laws regarding issues such as workers' compensation and computation of taxes.

All of these issues pro and con make this question difficult, with both sides making cogent arguments. Journalists should analyze both sides before reaching conclusions.

## Agents

The NCAA and its member schools do not look with favor on sports agent solicitation of student-athletes. Vulnerability to possible exploitation serves as the official reason, but cynics can point to the loss of a talent pool as well. Whatever the motive, the NCAA manual states that "an individual shall be ineligible for participation in an intercollegiate sport if he or she ever has agreed (orally or in writing) to be represented by an agent for the purpose of marketing his or her athletic ability or reputation in that sport." Further, an agency contract not specifically limited in writing to a sport or particular sports shall be deemed applicable to all sports, and the individual shall be ineligible to participate in any sport (NCAA Division I Manual, 2009, sec. 12.3.1). Additionally, "an individual shall be ineligible if he or she *or his or her relatives or friends* [emphasis added] accepts transportation or other benefits from: any person who represents any individual in the marketing of his or her athletic ability, or an agent," even if the agent has indicated that he or she has no interest in representing the student-athlete in the marketing of his or her athletic ability or reputation and does not represent individuals in the student-athlete's sport. This means that a prospective agent or someone working for that agent (known as a "runner") cannot give benefits to a student-athlete (NCAA Division I Manual, 2009, sec. 12.3.1.2).

The NCAA also prohibits student-athletes from using "legal advisors" in contract negotiations with professional teams and forbids these advisors to "make contact" with the pro team that had drafted the athlete (NCAA Division I Manual, 2009, sec. 12.3.2.1). This poses a particular problem in baseball, where college players are frequently drafted. These strict rules limiting an agent's duties have been challenged in Oliver v. NCAA; the NCAA settled for a considerable sum just before trial (Mullen, 2009). This case and the role of agents in general is discussed further in chapter 7.

### Recruiting

*Intricate* and *limiting* characterizes the rules regarding the recruitment of student-athletes by member schools. Intended to equalize recruitment opportunities, the rules prevent wealthier schools, possessing the resources to wine and dine prospective student-athletes, from monopolizing the top talent. However, beneath this noble basis rests the nitty-gritty of the recruiting standards.

These rules cover such issues as restrictions on times and number of trips and places of recruitment. The following serves as an example of the minutiae found in Article 13 of the bylaws. High school prospects cannot be contacted before July 1 following the student's junior year (NCAA Division I Manual, 2009, sec. 13.1.1.1). Similar rules apply to telephone calls made by authorized staff members of the school's athletic department. The frequency of the calls cannot be more than once per week (NCAA Division I Manual, 2009, sec. 13.1.3.1). For FBS and FCS football, the contact may be made in May of the junior year and then again in September of the senior year. Time exceptions also exist for men's and women's basketball (NCAA Division I Manual, 2009, secs. 13.1.3.1.2 and 13.1.3.1.3).

The number of visits to potential recruits by staff members is limited to three in-person, off-campus contacts (except in cases of football and basketball, for which the totals are six and five, respectively) (NCAA Division I Manual, 2009, secs. 13.1.6.2, 13.1.6.3, and 13.1.6.4). No offers or transfers of any financial aid or other benefits to the prospect are allowed, whether directly or indirectly. Specifically prohibited are financial aid, benefits, and arrangements including an employment arrangement for a prospect's relatives, gifts of clothing or equipment, cosigning of loans or providing loans to a prospect's relatives or friends, cash, merchandise, and low-cost housing (NCAA Division I Manual, 2009, sec. 13.2.1). If this occurs, the potential student-athlete will be ineligible until he or she pays that amount back (NCAA Division I Manual, 2009, sec. 13.2.1.2). The institution also suffers sanctions.

Entertainment expenses must be "reasonable" and only for on-campus recruits. A member institution may pay the prospect's actual round-trip transport costs for his or her official visit to its campus, provided a direct route between the prospect's home and the institution's campus is used. Use of a limousine or helicopter for such transportation is prohibited (NCAA Division I Manual, 2009, sec. 13.5.2.1). There is a limitation of one sponsored visit to each school per prospect. However, a prospect may visit a member institution's campus at his or her own expense an unlimited number of times (NCAA Division I Manual, 2009, sec. 13.7.1).

The Division I manual also notes the time periods permissible for recruiting in a given sport (NCAA Division I Manual, 2009, sec. 13.1.4).

### Academic Requirements

In the past, the debate surrounding academic criteria for student-athletes' admission and eligibility has been a battleground between those who feel that standards are too minimal and need tightening and those who feel that increasing standards unfairly discriminates against many of those students who lack skills on account of their socioeconomic circumstances. The claim—rejected by one federal court (Cureton v. NCAA, 1999)— has been that an "adverse impact" results because a higher percentage of African-American student athletes come from backgrounds in which educational opportunities are lacking and therefore have greater difficulties in maintaining the minimums. However, since the present standards, described below, were adopted in 2005, the debate has diminished.

To be eligible to represent an institution in intercollegiate athletics competition, a student-athlete must be enrolled in at least a minimum full-time program of studies, be in "good academic standing," and maintain progress toward a baccalaureate or equivalent degree. Note the lack of a graduation requirement. The rules require only that the student-athlete be "making progress" toward a degree at a prescribed schedule. Note that these standards are minimums. Particular conferences and individual schools often impose higher admission and matriculation standards.

For Division I schools, entering freshmen must have successfully completed a high school core curriculum of at least sixteen academic "core" courses, including:

- Four years of English.
- Three years of math (at the level of Algebra I or higher).
- Two years of natural or physical science.
- One extra year of English, math, or natural or physical science.
- Two years of social science.
- Four years of additional academic courses in any of the above areas or foreign language, computer science, philosophy, or nondoctrinal religion (NCAA Division I Manual, 2009, sec. 14.3.1.1).

Division II schools require completion of fourteen core classes in a similar breakdown, although after 2013 the standards will be raised to those of Division I.

In addition to the core course requirement, the NCAA requires minimum SAT (Scholastic Aptitude Test) or ACT (American College Test) scores. Because of the past debate over the wisdom of these tests and the adverse impact they may have on certain minority group applicants, the NCAA concluded that a sliding scale approach worked best, featuring a combination of high school grade point average and corresponding test scores to give a greater academic picture of an application. The scale in Table 3.1 applies.

Once the student is admitted, the NCAA requires adequate "progress" toward a degree to maintain eligibility. The requirements are back-ended (NCAA Division I Manual, 2009, sec. 14.4.3.2). After two years, a student-athlete must have completed 40 percent of the school's requirements for graduation. At the end of three years, student-athletes must have completed 60 percent, and by the end of four years the figure is 80 percent (NCAA Division I Manual, 2009, sec. 14.4.3.2).

A student-athlete must maintain a grade point average (GPA) that places the individual in good academic standing, as established by the institution. The NCAA requires that the student-athlete maintain a GPA of at least 90 percent of the school's minimum in the sophomore year, 95 percent in the

*Table 3.1* Core GPA/Test Score Index

| Core GPA | SAT | Sum ACT |
| --- | --- | --- |
| 3.550 and above | 400 | 37 |
| 3.500 | 420 | 39 |
| 3.400 | 460 | 42 |
| 3.300 | 500 | 44 |
| 3.200 | 540 | 47 |
| 3.100 | 580 | 49 |
| 3.000 | 620 | 52 |
| 2.900 | 660 | 54 |
| 2.800 | 700 | 57 |
| 2.725 | 730 | 59 |
| 2.600 | 780 | 64 |
| 2.500 | 820 | 68 |
| 2.400 | 860 | 71 |
| 2.300 | 900 | 75 |
| 2.200 | 940 | 79 |
| 2.100 | 970 | 82 |
| 2.000 | 1010 | 86 |

Source: NCAA Division I Bylaws, sec. 14.3.1.1.2.

third year, and 100 percent in the fourth and fifth years (NCAA Division I Manual, 2009, sec. 14.4.3.3.1).

The NCAA also requires disclosure of the graduation rates among student-athletes. Penalties take the form of one lost scholarship for every player who could not return to school owing to academic ineligibility (NCAA Division I Manual, 2009, sec. 30.1.2).

## Transfers

To prevent students from touting their talents around, and to prevent schools from trying to steal away talented athletes from other schools, the NCAA has devised rules that prohibit transfer students from playing on a team for one year (NCAA Division I Manual, 2009, sec. 14.5.1) and limiting transfer of students from two-year (or junior) colleges, with the exception of a student who had maintained a 2.0 GPA with twelve credits per semester (NCAA Division I Manual, 2009, sec. 14.5.4.1). A significant exception occurs where the student transfers from a school after the discontinuance of his or her athletic program. So student X, a member of the men's swim team at a particular Division I school that discontinued intercollegiate swimming, may transfer to another Division I school and need not sit out the year. However, in the case of a popular coach leaving the school after recruiting a student, no waivers are required.

## Financial Aid

Division I schools often offer financial aid, in the name of an athletic scholarship, to student-athletes. Under the NCAA Division I bylaws, "financial aid" includes scholarships, grants, tuition waivers, and loans (NCAA Division I Manual, 2009, sec. 15.02.4.1). The maximum amount allowed (known as "grant-in-aid") covers tuition, fees, room and board, and required course-related books (NCAA Division I Manual, 2009, sec. 15.02.5). If the student receives anything above this amount, the student is ineligible to compete in intercollegiate athletics.

In recent years, the NCAA liberalized the rules regarding earnings from a student-athlete's on- or off-campus employment. Such earnings are exempt, without limitation, and not counted in determining a student-athlete's full grant-in-aid or in the institution's financial aid limitations. This exemption applies only if the student-athlete's compensation is *not* based on the reputation, fame, or following of that athlete and the student-athlete's compensation is at the "going rate" for that locality for similar services (NCAA Division I Manual, 2009, sec. 15.2.7).

Financial aid may be reduced or canceled if the student loses eligibility (NCAA Division I Manual, 2009, sec. 15.3.4.2). The bylaws limit the

number of scholarships available, depending on the sport (NCAA Division
I Manual, 2009, sec. 15.5.3). Additional awards, benefits, and expenses to
student athletes are severely restricted under NCAA rules. These monies,
defined as allowance beyond the NCAA maximum amounts, result in the
student-athlete's ineligibility for intercollegiate competition.

Of particular interest is the prohibition on so-called "extra benefit"
awards. Defined as compensation from the school or representative of
the institution's athletic interests to provide the student-athlete or his or
her relatives or friends with a benefit not expressly authorized by NCAA
legislation (NCAA Division I Manual, 2009, sec. 16.11.1.1), such benefits
include discounts and credits on purchases (such as airline tickets) or services (laundry), telephone cards, credit cards, and entertainment services
such as movie tickets and the use of a car. Even a car ride home with a
coach or staff member is prohibited in most instances (even if the student-
athlete reimburses the costs of gas) (NCAA Division I Manual, 2009, secs.
16.11.2.2.1–16.11.2.2.3).

Student-athletes may not receive cash or cash-equivalent awards, such
as gift certificates, merchandise, or services (NCAA Division I Manual,
2009, sec. 16.1.1.2). One minor exception: As of 2010, a maximum of
$325 can be disbursed for winning a conference and $415 for a national
championship (NCAA Division I Manual, 2009, sec. 16.1.4.2).

Regarding noncash goods, the NCAA permits housing and meal costs
to be paid by the school. Certain preseason practice expenses and meals
incidental to competition are permitted (NCAA Division I Manual, 2009,
sec. 16.5.2). Also, the school covers travel costs for trips to road games.
As of 2010, a per diem award of $20/day is allowed for student-athletes
at NCAA championship tournaments (NCAA Division I Manual, 2009,
sec. 16.8.1.6). Also, a student-athlete may request additional financial aid
(with no obligation to repay such aid) from a fund established pursuant
to a special financial need program approved by the NCAA Management
Council. The institution may provide reasonable local transport in con-
junction with financial assistance approved under this program (NCAA
Division I Manual, 2009, sec. 16.12.2).

*Practice Dates*

The bylaws provide a detailed listing of the prescribed dates and range
of practice sessions for various NCAA sports. Practice dates are limited
to particular times of the year, and violations of such schedules can result
in sanctions for the school. The schedules are found in Article 17 of the
NCAA Division I bylaws.

## The Role of Coaches

Professional athletic coaches have specific goals: to employ strategies and skills to motivate athletes to win games. Collegiate coaches have more varied duties and more constraints under the NCAA system. They must be familiar with the NCAA bylaws, particularly restrictions on practice time and recruiting. Also, they have to build a rapport with the student-athlete, sometimes becoming a confidant, role model, and even surrogate parent. Often these young people, some away from home for the first time, go through a major life transition. College coaches "mold" these student-athletes, and their guidance may help or hinder their maturity.

College coaches also spend a great deal of their time recruiting. The NCAA allows football and basketball coaches to travel a total of forty days over two periods of time during a year. Coaches of other sports may travel to recruit during the whole year, except for specified "dead periods" (interview with Marianne Reilly, assistant athletic coordinator, Fordham University, Bronx, NY, March 15, 2004). Spotting talent, traveling, and interviewing are very important aspects of the job. In professional sports, general managers, not coaches, usually do these tasks.

## A Final Thought

The NCAA policies generate considerable controversy and debate. Many changes and solutions have been proposed to rectify what is wrong about collegiate athletics. Some have proposed paying players a salary (Whiteside, 2004). Others would permit signing endorsement contracts and dealing with agents (Zoppo, 2004). Others opine that colleges should get out of the big-time athletics. Some coaches favor a new rule that calls for lesser penalties when athletes leave school early for financial opportunities in, say, the NBA or NFL and when they transfer to other schools (Blum & Lederman, 2003). Specifically, those coaches favor amending the old rules—which mandate that losses of student athletes who go pro count against a school's graduation record—to a rule that states if athletes leave in good academic standing—for whatever reason—the penalties are much less severe. Some of these ideas may merit consideration.

## Athletic Conferences

In addition to the NCAA, the organizational structure of intercollegiate athletics includes conferences. Conferences serve as "mini-leagues" in which collegiate teams compete. Although there is no mandate that a college or university join a conference (Notre Dame football is one example of an "independent" school), the overwhelming majority of colleges and universities do. Schools gain a variety of benefits from conference membership.

Most conferences have signed television contracts, some quite lucrative, which provide exposure to their member schools. This also creates the potential for more revenues shared through broadcasting and sponsorship agreements. Scheduling is easier with conference membership because of the designated number of competitors. Some larger conferences hold championship tournaments, giving teams more exposure and potentially more revenues, and winning a conference championship usually gives that team the opportunity to compete in the NCAA championship competition. For example, in 2010, thirty-one conferences received revenues from the NCAA basketball tournament. The top ten recipients are listed in Table 3.2. The NCAA also awards the top four teams additional monies (Grimaldi, 2010).

The estimated $167 million given to the conferences represents about one-half of the revenues the NCAA earns on tournaments. Many conferences distribute this money equally to each school. In addition, another one-third goes to directly to the schools, based on the number of scholarships they give, and one-sixth goes to the schools based on the number of sports they play.

The six major conferences and their participating schools are described next.

### Atlantic Coast Conference (ACC)

- Boston College (Eagles)
- Clemson University (Tigers)
- Duke University (Blue Devils)
- Florida State University (Seminoles)
- Georgia Tech University (Yellow Jackets)
- North Carolina State University (Wolfpack)
- University of Maryland (Terrapins)
- University of Miami (Hurricanes)
- University of North Carolina (Tar Heels)
- University of Virginia (Cavaliers)
- Virginia Tech (Hokies)
- Wake Forest University (Demon Deacons)

The Atlantic Coast Conference was founded in 1953, and had seven members until 1978, when Georgia Tech was admitted. With the addition of Florida State in 1991, the ACC expanded to nine members. Since then, Miami and Virginia Tech joined in 2004 and Boston College in 2005.

For football, the conference is split into two divisions: the Atlantic and the Coastal.

*Table 3.2* Major Conference Revenues from NCAA (2010)

| Conference | Amount Received from NCAA Basketball Fund |
| --- | --- |
| Big Ten | $13.2 million (most of any league for third consecutive year) |
| Big 12 | $10.9 million |
| Southeastern Conference | $10.7 million |
| Big East | $10.4 million |
| Pac-10 | $10.0 million |
| Atlantic Coast Conference | $9.8 million |
| Conference USA | $4.9 million |
| Atlantic Ten | $4.4 million |

## Big East Conference

- University of Cincinnati (Bearcats)
- University of Connecticut (Huskies)
- DePaul University (Blue Demons) (excluding football)
- Georgetown University (Hoyas) (excluding football)
- University of Louisville (Cardinals)
- Marquette University (Golden Eagles) (excluding football)
- University of Notre Dame (Fighting Irish) (excluding football)
- University of Pittsburgh (Panthers)
- Providence College (Friars) (excluding football)
- Rutgers University (Scarlet Knights)
- St. John's University (Red Storm) (excluding football)
- Seton Hall University (Pirates)
- Syracuse University (Orange)
- Villanova University (Wildcats) (excluding football)
- West Virginia University (Mountaineers)

Schools in the east and midwest constitute the conference's base. It began in 1978, primarily as a basketball conference. Despite its recent vintage, it has evolved into one of the largest and most competitive conferences. Football was added in 1990, but the presence of that sport created tension between schools that included football and those that did not. That tension resulted in a realignment in 2005, whereby Louisville, Cincinnati, South Florida, Marquette, and DePaul joined the Big East after Virginia Tech, Miami, and Boston College left for the ACC.

## The Big Ten Conference

- University of Illinois (Fighting Illini)

- Indiana University (Hoosiers)
- University of Iowa (Hawkeyes)
- University of Michigan (Wolverines)
- Michigan State University (Spartans)
- University of Minnesota (Golden Gophers)
- Northwestern University (Wildcats)
- Ohio State University (Buckeyes)
- Pennsylvania State University (Nittany Lions)
- Purdue University (Boilermakers)
- University of Wisconsin (Badgers)
- University of Nebraska (Cornhuskers) (as of 2011)

Formed in 1896, this conference predates the establishment of the NCAA and created eligibility rules that became the basis of the NCAA's amateurism standard. This venerable conference's institutions sponsor more than 250 athletic programs (www.BigTen.org).

### The Big 12 Conference

The teams in this conference are divided into two groups, North and South.

### North

- University of Colorado (Buffaloes)
- Iowa State University (Cyclones)
- University of Kansas (Jayhawks)
- Kansas State University (Wildcats)
- University of Missouri (Tigers)
- University of Nebraska (Cornhuskers) (until 2011)

### South

- Baylor University (Bears)
- University of Oklahoma (Sooners)
- Oklahoma State University (Cowboys)
- University of Texas (Longhorns)
- Texas A & M University (Aggies)
- Texas Tech (Red Raiders)

Like the Big East, the Big 12 is a relatively young organization, begun in 1994, when the former Big Eight Conference joined with four Texas schools that had been members of the Southwest Conference, which had just disbanded. Given the large number of member schools, this conference is split into two division and has a championship game.

*Pac-10 Conference*

- University of Arizona (Wildcats)
- Arizona State University (Sun Devils)
- University of California Berkeley (Golden Bears)
- University of Oregon (Ducks)
- Oregon State University (Beavers)
- Stanford University (Cardinals)
- University of California at Los Angeles (Bruins)
- University of Southern California (Trojans)
- University of Washington (Huskies)
- Washington State University (Cougars)

Not surprisingly, the Pac-10 schools reside in the west and northwest. The roots of the Pacific-10 Conference date to 1915. Pac-10 has won more NCAA national championships than any other conference. The top three schools with the most NCAA championships—UCLA, Stanford, and the University of Southern California—belong to the Pac-10.

*Southeastern Conference*

The teams in this twelve-school conference are divided into two groups, the Eastern and Western divisions.

*Eastern Division*

- University of Florida (Gators)
- University of Georgia (Bulldogs)
- University of Kentucky (Wildcats)
- University of South Carolina (Gamecocks)
- University of Tennessee (Volunteers/Lady Volunteers)
- Vanderbilt University (Commodores)

*Western Division*

- University of Alabama (Crimson Tide)
- University of Arkansas (Razorbacks/Lady Razorbacks)
- Auburn University (Tigers)
- Louisiana State University (LSU) (Tigers)
- Mississippi State University (Bulldogs)
- University of Mississippi (Ole Miss) (Rebels)

The SEC, founded in 1933, has had relatively few changes in its roster over the years. As is the case in the Big 12 Conference, a football championship game is needed to determine the conference winner. The SEC is a huge money maker. Starting in 2010, its television contract with CBS and ESPN will bring in over $200 million per year for the next fifteen years (McCarthy & Weiberg, 2009).

In addition to the "big six" conferences listed above, the NCAA Division I includes other major conferences that are not guaranteed bids for a football bowl game. They include the Atlantic-10, Conference USA, Mountain West, Sun Belt Conference, Western Athletic Conference, and Mid American Conference. But, as we will see, conference affiliation plays a major role in determining whether a school can compete in a major bowl game.

## Championships

The NCAA has conducted national championships in various sports since 1921 and currently administers eighty-seven championships in twenty-two sports for its member institutions (NCAA, 2010). The top team in each conference is invited to participate, along with selected other teams. The chosen teams compete against each other in single-game elimination contests until there are two teams left. Those two teams compete for the championship (Hales, 2003).

An exception is in football. Although the NCAA sponsors football championships in its FCS (formerly Division I-AA) and Divisions II and III, it does not control those of the FBS teams. Instead, a longstanding system of independent bowls invites specific teams to play in postseason games. The bowl system has generated considerable controversy and many have sought to change it.

Absent NCAA administration, various standards, such as records and polls (generated by sports writers, selected NCAA head football coaches, and computers), have been used to determine the national champion. This process, influenced by opinions and biases of individual teams and quality of the conferences, has led to legitimate criticisms of inherent subjectivity. A poll or computer ranking creates a "hypothetical" situation and cannot replicate a one-on-one playoff match. In the 1990s, an attempt to make the system more objective resulted in the adoption of the Bowl Championship Series (BCS). There are mixed opinions as to whether the BCS system solves the problem.

### Division I-A College Football Bowl Games—Pre-Bowl Championship Series

The bowl system dates back decades, and over the years different bowl games have been created and disbanded (Sports Fans of America Association, n.d.). Currently there are about twenty-five postseason bowls.

Bowls began as a method to attract tourists to warm-weather climates between Christmas and New Year's Day (Hales, 2003). In more recent years, bowl game administrators have become more market savvy. The major bowls enjoy financial success, which has spawned sponsorship agreements from various businesses. Today, just about every bowl has a sponsor that makes payments to the bowl organization for permission to advertise using bowl logos and other trademarks. Examples are Tostitos for the Fiesta Bowl and Citigroup for the Rose Bowl.

Initially, each bowl negotiated participation agreements with individual teams. Eventually, some of these agreements gave way to multiyear contracts with particular conferences for a specifically ranked team from that conference. For example, the champions of both the Pac-10 and the Big Ten were obligated to participate in the Rose Bowl (McCarthy, 1991). Other bowls chose to remain free to negotiate with any team, which led essentially to a bidding process in which available teams would choose between multiple bowl invitations.

Not surprisingly, this process made it difficult to decide who had won the "national title." Owing to the locked-in contractual obligations, the various bowl games rarely produced a national championship game between the two highest-ranked teams. Most often, the strongest teams were dispersed among multiple bowls, and the mythic national title was often split between two teams. In the history of the independent bowl system, the top two ranked teams met each other in a bowl only nine times. Thus, there has been a consensus "national champion" only seven times in over fifty years of Division I-A football (Hales, 2003).

### The Bowl Championship Series

In the past twenty years, four different systems have been developed in an attempt to create a true national championship game. Such a game would be an economic bonanza, highly marketable to advertisers because of the resulting high television ratings.

The first attempt to organize bowl selection began in 1992 with the advent of the Bowl Coalition. Under this plan, the champions of five major conferences joined with the Fiesta, Cotton, Orange, and Sugar Bowls. The champions of the Southwestern Conference would play in the Cotton Bowl, the SEC in the Sugar Bowl, and the Big Eight in the Orange Bowl, while the Fiesta Bowl received two open bids (Hales, 2003).

The present bowl game arrangement began in 1998 with the creation of the BCS, which consisted of the champions of the six most dominant conferences in Division I-A. The system is intricate: the champions of the ACC, Big East, Big Ten, Big 12, Pac-10, and SEC have automatic berths in one of the participating bowls. The top two teams in the final BCS standings (derived from a computer ranking under management of the BCS) play in the national championship game.

However, this system presents greater difficulties for teams in the other BCS conferences. In order to earn an automatic berth in the top bowl games, the champion of Conference USA, the Mid-American Conference, the Mountain West Conference, the Sun Belt Conference, or the Western Athletic Conference must rank either in the top twelve of the final BCS standings or in the top sixteen of the final BCS standings *and* outrank a team that is champion of a conference that has an annual automatic berth in one of the BCS bowls (Collegefootballpoll.com, 2009).

The BCS system has been lucrative, as it resulted in a $730 million contract with ABC over eight years. As a result, the BCS increased revenue from the four affiliated bowls—Fiesta, Orange, Rose, and Sugar—by 60 percent in the first year. In 2007, Fox became the contract rightsholder, but starting in 2011 the BCS moved to ESPN. Under a four-year contract for a reported $500 million, the cable network will broadcast the Fiesta, Orange, Rose, and Sugar Bowls from 2011 to 2014, in addition to the BCS national championship game.

This system has many detractors because of the perceived unfairness of "have" over "have-not" conferences. The lack of automatic berths for the "nonguaranteed BCS" conferences has a significant effect on the allocation of revenue. Under the funding formula, nearly all the revenue from the BCS bowls goes to the BCS conferences, a major difference from NCAA-run tournaments, which distribute revenue more evenly among all NCAA member schools. The sixty-three BCS schools to date have shared a total of $466 million in revenue from the bowl games, an average of $7.4 million each (Fatsis, 2003). In 2010, the BCS distributed $142.5 million of revenue from its five bowl games, with 81 percent of it—$115.2 million—going to the big six conferences. The majority of the rest—$24 million—went to the others: Mountain West, Western Athletic, Conference USA, Mid-American, and Sun Belt. Notre Dame, as an independent, non-conference-affiliated football team, received $1.5 million. However, if it played in a BCS bowl, it would have received an additional $4.5 million (Smith, 2010).

The disparity of revenues raises legal questions. Some college administrators, such as Tulane University's president Scott Cowen, were distressed at the disparity in the revenues. and considered the idea of suing the BCS and its schools on antitrust grounds. "The BCS schools have essentially banded together to prevent any other school from ever competing against them," said Gary Roberts, then a Tulane sports law professor who informally advised Dr. Cowen (Fatsis, 2003). Members of Congress also expressed concerns. Senator Orrin Hatch (R-UT) called for an investigation of the antitrust implications of the BCS by the Justice Department, which in 2010 considered the request (nbcsports.com, 2010). Sen. Hatch, like a number of others, would advocate a playoff system similar to what is found in other NCAA tournaments but, at the time of writing, no changes in the BCS are planned.

A final issue may be the growth in power of the big six conferences. Some have concluded that these conferences may amass such power as to usurp the NCAA and control the sport of college football (Doyel, 2010), a real possibility given the revenues generated through attendance and television rights.

## High School Interscholastic Sports

In 2005, about 4 million youngsters, or about one in nine students, participated in competitive school athletics. (Darden, 2005). Governance of these competitions also exists, but without an NCAA-like national organization. Rather, the system is more diffuse, with differing governing bodies regulating local, school district, or independent youth league competitions. The organizations tend to be local in nature under a statewide umbrella organization. This system marks a change from the privately controlled (often by the YMCA) system found in the nineteenth century.

Statewide interscholastic associations administer high school sports programs and run state championship tournaments. Committees consisting of coaches, administrators, and parents often set eligibility rules. With laws prohibiting discrimination against students with disabilities, these committees have to draft rules with the goal of inclusion, or face potential lawsuits. What makes this issue problematic is the complexity of enforcement provisions of laws such as the Americans with Disabilities Act. The interplay of laws and regulations and interscholastic athletics becomes important, more than in the case of the NCAA. Unlike the NCAA, which is considered a private organization, most state interscholastic associations are considered "state actors," which means that they can be sued by member schools and by athletes, alleging constitutional violations (Brentwood Academy v. TSSAA, 2001).

Another important issue is liability for injury. The associations (and their local affiliates) have (or should have) drafted risk management procedures to prevent injuries and minimize risk of injury-producing events during competition. Chapter 9 provides more discussion on this issue.

Interscholastic athletes learn teamwork and discipline, but rarely do they see athletic glory. According to the NCAA, fewer than one in thirty-five, or approximately 2.9 percent, of high school senior boys playing interscholastic basketball will go on to play men's basketball at an NCAA member institution. Fewer than one in seventy-five, or approximately 1.3 percent, of NCAA male senior basketball players will get drafted by an NBA team. Therefore, approximately 3 in 10,000, or approximately 0.03 percent, of high school senior boys playing interscholastic basketball will eventually be drafted by an NBA team.

The same can be said of football. About 5.8 percent, or approximately one in seventeen, of all high school senior boys playing interscholastic football will go on to play football at an NCAA member institution. About 2.0 percent, or approximately one in fifty, of NCAA senior football players will get drafted by an NFL team. Approximately 9 in 10,000, or approximately 0.09 percent, of high school senior boys playing interscholastic football will eventually be drafted by an NFL team (Langley, 2006).

## Ethical Issue: Should the Collegiate Sports System Be Changed?

Many in the media, as well as members of the public and members of Congress, have criticized the NCAA and its rules. In particular, changes to the NCAA rules regarding amateurism have been debated for decades. Although the organization has loosened some of the requirements, some seek greater institutional changes. Ideas include paying players a salary for their work, permitting contracts with professional teams while still playing in college, sharing revenues earned from television rights fees and gate receipts, permitting endorsement contracts, and permitting payments to athletes for the use of their names and likenesses. More radical ideas include ending the NCAA control of championships, eliminating and replacing the BCS, and even making collegiate athletics a profit-based enterprise. The underlying basis for these proposals is fairness for the student-athlete. As performers they go on the court or field, are watched by the public, but earn no income. The schools make money, the broadcasters make money, the coaches and staffs make money.

Certainly, the idea has appeal, but all too many seize on the idea of "deregulating" or even eliminating the NCAA as a quick and easy fix to the problems of college sports. A few cautionary words are in order.

Understanding the difficulties and effects of implementing such proposals is necessary to engage in a more sophisticated analysis when writing about proposed changes in NCAA issues. For example, paying players and treating them as employees result in significant costs for the school—in many cases far more than tuition, books, and room and board. As employees, the institutions would have to pay workers' compensation insurance, state and federal taxes, and a negotiated salary. Also, would agents play a direct role in negotiating contracts for star (or potential star) nineteen-year-olds? Another question involves the application of the "pay-for-play" arrangement. Does it apply to *every* collegiate athlete? Just those from certain sports? Just certain players?

Presently, schools award scholarships in many different sports, even those that lack mainstream popularity. A negotiated pay-for-play system contradicts the idea of sharing of scholarship money and puts additional strains on already tight university athletic budgets. Allocating revenues to paying athletes likely leads to Title IX problems if women's teams get less money because some of it goes to male basketball or football players' salaries. Litigation is almost guaranteed.

Permitting athletes to sign professional team contracts while still eligible also has risks. Say star player X of the basketball team enters the NBA draft at the end of his junior year and is chosen. However, the player decides to complete his senior year and play on the college team in order to finish his degree. Injury concerns could limit effectiveness on that team. The same result may occur if the player signs with an agent but continues to play (another reform discussed). The agent may also have qualms about the risk of injury and may hint that the player "go easy."

Another idea is to have a conference realignment based on the revenues a particular school's athletic department generates. The result would be "money conferences." One writer proposed a "for-profit" system that would compete with the NCAA (Staples, 2010). However, such an idea—or other profit-based systems—would greatly affect the mission of collegiate sports as a part of one's educational experience.

The rise of so-called "big-time" programs raises a societal question of whether athletics should be cast further away from the mission of a college or university. Blue-ribbon panels have been convened to make changes in the system, in the hope of preventing college sports from spinning out of control. One commentator concluded that "Chasing after sports revenue and athletic prestige, schools admit more and more athletes, in the process sapping resources from the schools' academic mission and send the message to young people that sports is the best way to get into college" (Just, 2002). The system, according to the authors, leads to students who are balkanized from the rest of the student body and who consistently perform more poorly.

Going even further, should the NCAA be abolished? Could college sports govern themselves? Of all the criticism of the NCAA, few have advocated a laissez-faire system, as it would produce a free-agency free-for-all, whereby the biggest and richest schools could simply attract the best talent and perpetuate a system of haves versus have-nots. Could colleges and universities self-police their programs? Or would it be up to the conferences or even law enforcement to police for transgressions (whatever they are defined to be)?

As noted earlier, the NCAA system comprises many different collegiate sports, most of which do not make the headlines or fill the arenas. At times, the rules may seem intricate, petty, and unfair. But will changes be better? That is at the heart of this dilemma.

James Shulman and William Bowen (2001) researched the academic records of 90,000 students who entered thirty selective schools in 1951, 1976, and 1989, and found that the college sports system has a significant impact on the schools' admissions and the academic performance of their students. They, and many others before and after them, seek changes. The biggest questions for our society are what changes can be accomplished and when and if those changes will occur.

## Information Check

When covering issues involving collegiate sports, a journalist should possess a copy of the NCAA Division I bylaws and, if possible, the equivalents for Divisions II and III. For high school sports, a copy of the organization's rules and regulations would also be helpful. Additionally, some pertinent questions to ask are:

1　What organization or conference governs the particular collegiate or high school sports issue?
2　What violations are alleged?
3　Who reported the violations? The institution or an outside party?
4　How were the student-athletes recruited?
5　What was their educational background and previous academic record?
6　Was institutional control maintained or did it break down? How many knew about the violations?
7　Was a hearing held and who participated in it?
8　Is an appeal available?
9　What is the range of penalties for the violation(s)?
10　What is the total athletic budget and how much of that budget is taken for a particular sport?

# References

Berkowitz, S. (2008, May 16). Few athletics programs in black; most need aid. *USA Today*. Retrieved February 1, 2010, from http://www.usatoday.com/sports/college/2008-05-16-financial-study_N.htm

Bloom, J. (2003, August 1). Show us the money. *New York Times*, p. 21.

Blum, D. E. & Lederman, D. (2003, November 19) NCAA plans new ways to keep score. *USA Today*, p. D1.

Brentwood Academy v. Tennessee Secondary School Athletic Association, 531 U.S. 288 (2001).

Collegefootballpoll.com (2009, April 16). BCS automatic qualification, at-large eligibility and selection procedures, 2007–2010 games. Retrieved March 18, 2010, from http://www.collegefootballpoll.com/bcs_selection_procedures.html

Darden, E. (2005, August). High school sports: slam dunk or air ball? *New York State School Boards Newsletter*, p. 1. Retrieved October 5, 2009, from http://www.tburg.k12.ny.us/citizens_advisory/budget_info/highschool%20sports%20article.pdf

Dohrmann, G. (2010, February 18). An inside look at the NCAA's secretive Committee on Infractions. *Si.com*. Retrieved March 15, 2010, from http://sportsillustrated.cnn.com/2010/writers/george_dohrmann/02/17/usc.coi

Doyel, G. (2010, April 25). While you moan about 96-team tourney, BCS plans its hostile takeover. *CBS Sports.com*. Retrieved April 26, 2010, from http://www.cbssports.com/columns/story/13297254

Fatsis, S. (2003, November 25). In college football, also-rans fight for bigger share of the pot. *Wall Street Journal*, p. A1.

Gilmore, R. (2007, January 17). College football players deserve pay for play. *Espn.com*. Retrieved March 17, 2010, from http://sports.espn.go.com/ncf/columns/story?columnist=gilmore_rod&id=2733624

Gregorian, V. (2003, July 20). The NCAA honor system. *St. Louis Post-Dispatch*, p. D1.

Grimaldi, P. (2010, March 15). NCAA: Win or lose, schools reap rewards from basketball tournament. *Providence Journal*. Retrieved March 18, 2010, from http://www.projo.com/news/content/NCAA_COLLEGES_MONEY_03-15-10_28HNTUS_v33.3c1cb8a.html

Hales, M. (2003). The antitrust issues of NCAA college football within the Bowl championship series. *Sports Law Journal, 10*, 97.

Infractions case: St. Bonaventure University (2004, May 1). *NCAA News*. Retrieved April 1, 2010, from http://web1.ncaa.org/web_files/NCAANewsArchive/2004/Division+I/infractions%2Bcase_%2Bst.html

Just, R. (2002, March 11). Can the next NCAA president reform college sports? *The American Prospect*, p. 15 [citing Robert Brown, an economist at California State University–San Marcos, from a 1990 study].

Langley, C. (2006, May 10). Estimated probability of competing in athletics beyond the high school interscholastic level. *Summit-academy.com*. Retrieved March 18, 2010, from http://www.summit-academy.com/HighSchool/educational%20planning/College%20bound%20athletes/Estimated%20Probability%20of%20Competing%20in%20Athletics.pdf

Law v. NCAA, 134 F.3d 1010 (10th Cir. 1998).

Lee, J. (2004, June). Old school, new school—The role of the athletic director changes with the times. *Street & Smith's Sports Business Journal*, p. 23.

McCarthy, M., & Weiberg, S. (2009, November 13). SEC, Big Ten set the standard for media rights money. *USA Today*. Retrieved March 18, 2010, from http://www.usatoday.com/sports/college/football/2009-11-11-media-rights-money_N.htm

McCarthy, M. J. (1991, April 24). Keeping careful score on sports tie-ins. *Wall Street Journal*, p. B1.

Mullen, J. (2009, October 6). Andy Oliver settles with NCAA prior to scheduled trial. *Sportsbusiness Daily*. Retrieved May 10, 2010, from http://www.sports-businessdaily.com/article/133846

nbcsports.com (2010, January 29). Justice Department may look at legality of BCS. Retrieved March 18, 2010, from http://nbcsports.msnbc.com/id/35151630

NCAA (2010). Areas of Interest—Championships. Retrieved August 20, 2010, from http://www.ncaa.org/wps/portal/ncaahome?WCM_GLOBAL_CONTEXT=/ncaa/NCAA/About%20The%20NCAA/Overview/Human%20Resources/about.html

NCAA Committee on Infractions (n.d.). Retrieved March 15, 2010, from http://web1.ncaa.org/committees/committees_roster.jsp?CommitteeName=1INFRACTION

NCAA Committees (n.d.). Title. Retrieved October 18, 2009, from https://www.ncaa.org/wps/ncaa?key=/ncaa/NCAA/Legislation+and+Governance/Committees/

NCAA Division I Committee on Infractions (n.d.). Retrieved April 5, 2010, from http://www.ncaa.org/wps/portal/ncaahome?WCM_GLOBAL_CONTEXT=/ncaa/ncaa/legislation+and+governance/committees/division+i/infractions/index.html

NCAA Division I Manual (2009). Bylaws, various sections.

NCAA Division I Student Advisory Committee (2010). Retrieved April 10, 2010, from http://www.ncaa.org/wps/portal/ncaahome?WCM_GLOBAL_CONTEXT=/ncaa/ncaa/legislation+and+governance/committees/division+i/saac

NCAA Division III self-study guide (2009–10). Retrieved March 15, 2010, from http://web1.ncaa.org/web_files/AMA/DIII%20Membership/2009–10%20ISSG.pdf

NCAA Executive Committee (2009). Title. Retrieved October 19, 2009, from https://www.ncaa.org/wps/ncaa?key=/ncaa/NCAA/Legislation%20and%20Governance/Committees/Assoc-wide/Executive%20Committee/

NCAA Mission Statement (2009). Retrieved October 18, 2009, from https://www.ncaa.org/wps/ncaa?ContentID=1352

NCAA v. Board of Regents of the University of Oklahoma, 468 U.S. 85 (1984).

NCAA v. Tarkanian, 488 U.S. 179 (1988).

O'Bannon v. NCAA, 2010 U.S. Dist. LEXIS 19170 (N.D.CA).

Potter, D. (2008, March 23). "Flutie Effect" is real. *Seattle Post-Intelligencer*. Retrieved February 27, 2010, from http://www.seattlepi.com/cbasketball/356135_flutie24.html

Sack, A. (2008, March 7). Should college athletes be paid? *The Christian Science Monitor*. Retrieved March 17, 2010, from http://www.csmonitor.com/Commentary/Opinion/2008/0307/p09s01-coop.html

Scruggs, W. (2003, May 3). Sports as the university's "front porch"? The public is skeptical. *Chronicles*, p. 17.

Shulman, J., & Bowen, W. (2001). *The game of life*. Princeton, NJ: Princeton University Press.

Smith, M. (2010, January 25). The BCS' big split. *Street & Smith's Sports Business Journal*, p. 1.

Sports Fans of American Association (n.d.) Extinct college football bowls. Retrieved May 15, 2004, from http://www.sportsfansofamerican.com/inde.htm

Staples, A. (2010, February 17). Time for full-blown conference realignment. *SI.com*. Retrieved February 18, 2010, from http://sportsillustrated.cnn.com/2010/writers/andy_staples/02/16/conference-realignment/1.html

Sylwester, M. (2004, April 16). Athletics expenses gobble up revenues. *USA Today*, p. 19C.

Thamel, P. (2010, February 8). N.C.A.A. fails to stop licensing lawsuit. *New York Times*, p. B14.

Thomas, K. (2009, November 17). SUNY debates the value of Division I sports. *New York Times*, p. B14.

Whiteside, K. (2004, September 1). College athletes want cut of action. *USA Today*, p. 3C.

Zoppo, T. (2004, September 1). Hypocrisy now spelled N-C-A-A. *East Carolinian*, via university wire.

# 4 The International Sports System

Journalists in the United States tend to cover international sports cyclically. Blockbuster events, such as the Olympics, garner huge coverage, whereas other events, such as regional or even international championship tournaments, do not enjoy the public interest that domestic major leagues or college sports do. Unfortunately, the lack of interest means that important controversies and issues arising from international sports are ignored or not adequately reported. When international sports matters such as testing for performance-enhancing drugs are discussed, the flavor of the coverage often takes on a nationalistic tinge (Lenskyj, 1998).

Covering the workings of international athletic organizations is difficult. As private entities that "reside" outside of the United States, they are not subject to any legal requirements to release documents under a Freedom of Information Act-type law. Add to that the often autocratic leadership and relative inexperience in dealing with the press.

In the past, the sheer pettiness and outright corruption exhibited by some of these bodies was startling. Witness this example: Primo Nebioli (an Italian national), then the president of track and field's international federation, arranged with Italian field judges to add almost one-half meter to the long jump of an Italian competitor in the 1987 World Track & Field Championship (which conveniently took place in Rome) so that he could win a bronze medal ahead of an American. This stunt was apparently concocted in retaliation for what the Italians thought was a bad call against the Italian competitors at the prior year's world championship (held in Indianapolis). A videotape inadvertently running evidenced the tampering, and the federation was forced, over the great resistance of its president, to strip the bronze medal from the Italian competitor (Weiler & Roberts, 2004, p. 1067).

In essence, international sports are governed by a system created at an earlier time for a different clientele. Based on the notion that only amateurs compete in international events for the glory of their sport and country, the structure remains quite different from the professional leagues found in the United States. This system—replete with multiple layers of governing organizations and complicated and sometimes arbitrary rules of authority—does not receive adequate journalistic scrutiny. Operating in relative secrecy, these organizations are difficult nuts to crack.

In the last decade, controversies involving international sports governance have become more frequent and more public. Issues of professionalism, substance abuse, and questionable judging have made headlines as allegations of corruption have surfaced. The use of performance-enhancing drugs has been another source of concern. In track and field, for example, the drug-testing issue has frayed the relationships between the domestic affiliate and the international body for the sport.

These events have had some positive effect. In response to unfavorable reports of bribery of Olympic officials and event judges, some international athletic organizations, such as the International Olympic Committee (IOC) and the International Skating Union (ISU), have changed their structure, eligibility rules, and scoring systems in competitions.

The international sports structure differs greatly from the league and collegiate structure. The setup, often perplexing, falls into several categories and levels of power. At the apex sits the IOC, the umbrella organization for the Olympic movement. Under the IOC, each country participating in an Olympic Games competition (known as an "Olympiad") has a national Olympic committee (NOC), the organizing committee for each Olympic Games. In addition, international athletic federations regulate particular sports that compete internationally. Although not directly part of the Olympic organization, they wield considerable power. Finally, there are domestic organizations affiliated with the international federations, known as national governing bodies (NGBs). The jurisdiction and powers of these entities create an interlocking relationship that sometimes becomes tangled.

Let's use the sport of figure skating as an example to illustrate. Although the IOC is the international governing body of the Olympics, the United States Olympic Committee (USOC) is the national Olympic Committee. The International Skating Union is the international federation and U.S. Figure Skating and U.S. Speed Skating are the NGBs. Each organization has its role in regulating the sport, choosing Olympic athletes, and regulating both international and Olympic competition. Often an athlete is subject to rules and regulations of more than one governing organization. As a result, the chain of command may blur, and the individual athlete can be at a loss as to which rules must be followed.

## The International Olympic Committee

### Background

From modest beginnings as a revival of an ancient Greek tradition, the Olympics has become one of the most glamorous events on the world stage and possibly the most prestigious brand in sports (Bitting, 1998).

It is watched by billions of people. Broadcast rights bring substantial sums to the IOC and fees to the host cities. For example, NBC has paid $2.2 billion for the rights to broadcast the 2010 and 2012 Olympics (as of this writing, the broadcast rights for the 2014 and 2016 Games have not been awarded). Hosting the Olympic Games may bring positive publicity to the host city, but often results in considerable costs and controversy. Some cities, such as Montreal, Barcelona, and Sydney, took years to pay the costs of hosting the Games (Merron, 2003; Crouse, 2006), whereas others, such as Salt Lake City, ended up with a small profit (Abrahamson, 2002). The Athens Games were estimated to cost Greek taxpayers over $11 billion (BBC News, 2004), but the 2008 Beijing Olympics, despite a price tag of $42 billion, reportedly earned a slight profit of $16 million (*China Sports Review*, 2009).

The Olympic Games are governed by the IOC, the best-known and most powerful body in international sports. Headquartered in Lausanne, Switzerland, the IOC is a nonprofit, nongovernmental entity that serves as caretaker of the modern Olympics. Founded in 1894 by the French educator Baron Pierre de Coubertin, the IOC's original mandate was to revive the ancient Greek Games. According to IOC rules, the organization grants rights to stage Summer and Winter Games quadrennially. Since 1994, the Summer and Winter Games alternate every two years. For example, the 2010 Winter Games were held in Vancouver, British Columbia, and the 2012 Games will be held in London. Sochi, in Russia, hosts the 2014 Winter Games and Rio de Janeiro, Brazil, the 2016 Summer Games.

The IOC serves three major functions. First, it is an umbrella organization for the various domestic affiliates known as national Olympic committees. Second, it interacts with the international sports federations, which control particular sports and are discussed in more detail later in the chapter. Third, the IOC owns and controls the intellectual property rights, such as copyrights, trademarks, and other intangible properties associated with the Olympic Games. These include such familiar symbols as the five interlocking rings, the Olympic motto ("citius, altius, fortius," which translates to "swifter, higher, stronger"), and the flame (Masteralexis, Barr, & Hums, 1998).

Although the IOC is a nongovernmental organization, the Olympic Charter states that any person or organization involved with the Olympic movement "shall accept the supreme authority of the IOC and shall be bound by its Rules and submit to its jurisdiction," thereby creating a powerful mandate for compliance. The IOC is a United Nations-like organization governing the premier event in international sports competition, but inherently more powerful. The United Nations is a confederation of nation-states that exhibit autonomy and national self-interest in the debates involving political and security questions. The Secretary-General, the U.N.'s equivalent of a chief executive officer, cannot impose his or her values unilaterally. The IOC, on the other hand, has traditionally selected strong-willed individuals to serve as presidents, aided by a compliant board often made up of allies of that president. The president traditionally carries the authority vested in professional league commissioners but is not subject to checks and balances of constituencies such as players' unions (because none exist) or general public scrutiny. One commentator said, "Although the IOC cannot compel governmental compliance, the Olympic Charter reflects current international practice and is thus almost as binding as the law itself" (Ansley, 1995).

### Current Structure

Currently, the 115 active members of the IOC meet at least once a year. The members elect a president for an eight-year term, renewable once for four additional years, and also elect an executive board whose members serve four-year terms. The term of the current president, Jacques Rogge, ended in 2009, but was renewed until 2013. IOC members include fifteen active Olympic athletes elected by their peers at the Olympic Games. Another fifteen members come from international federations, fifteen from the national Olympic committees, and seventy others are individual, non-affiliated members. The mandatory retirement age for IOC members, including the president, is 70.

The executive board, consisting of the IOC President, four Vice-Presidents, and ten other members, is the backbone of IOC governance, akin to a board of directors in a corporation. The board assumes the "ultimate responsibility" for the administration of the IOC by managing the IOC's finances, preparing annual reports, conducting the procedure for acceptance and selection of candidates for the organization of the Olympic Games, and enacting "all regulations necessary" to ensure the proper implementation of the Olympic Charter and the organization of the Olympic Games (Executive Board, International Olympic Committee, n.d.).

### Marketing the Event

The Olympic Games are held in different cities, so a different organization must plan each event. Known as an "Olympic organizing committee," it controls the facility construction, living arrangements, transportation, and media services. The committee must also "sell" the event to the public. If the particular Olympics are successful, then the resulting favorable publicity promotes tourism and leaves that city with new facilities for sports and other functions for future years. In one sense, Olympics preparations become an urban renewal project.

The "selling" of the event is crucial because the host city keeps about 95 percent of the revenue from ticket sales, but obtains little from the lucrative broadcast rights and corporate sponsorships, the major sources of income. Certain cities hosted successful Games—Los Angeles in 1984, Barcelona in 1992, Sydney in 2000, and Salt Lake City in 2002. Others were a financial disaster, such as Montreal's Games in 1976, which almost bankrupted the city and the province of Quebec. The Munich Olympics in 1972 were marred by the murder of eleven Israeli athletes by Palestinian terrorists. Moscow's Games in 1980 were hurt by the boycott by the United States and other nations protesting the Soviet invasion of Afghanistan.

In the post-9/11 environment, host cities have to pay far more for security than in the past. This expense—$1.5 billion in Athens, as compared with $200 million in Sydney—is often paid by the host city. For the Beijing Summer Games, that figure jumped to $6.5 billion, which included 300,000 video cameras and 100,000 antiterrorism squad members (Magnier, 2008). Even with tight security, the fear of possible terrorist incidents could also deter people from attending the Games, therefore hurting the bottom line.

Because of the prestige of the event, the IOC has been highly successful in attracting blue-chip sponsors, who pay large sums to attain the designation of "Olympic sponsor." In 2006 and 2008 it cost between $80 million and $100 million to be an official sponsor of the Turin and Beijing Games (Rein, 2008). The majority of the payments end in the IOC's coffers, although a portion is ultimately dispersed to the host country.

Although several levels exist, the worldwide sponsor role, through the "Olympic Partner" program, is the most important. These sponsors receive exclusive marketing rights and opportunities within their designated product category and can exercise these rights on a worldwide basis (Olympic.org, 2010). These sponsors may develop marketing programs with the IOC, the national Olympic committees, and the Olympic sites organizing committees.

As part of their sponsorship, these companies receive rights to use Olympic trademarks, showcase their products at Olympic locations, and be protected from ambush marketing (a technique whereby competitors attempt to market their products near the official Olympic sites).

## The Scandals

The procedures for selecting host cities for future Olympic Games have received considerable attention in the wake of past scandals involving the selection process. The present IOC structure reflects the changes implemented after a pattern of improper conduct between IOC members and the local organizing committee was revealed in 2002. A Salt Lake City television station received documents outlining a payment made by the

Salt Lake Olympic Organizing Committee (SLOC) to the daughter of an IOC member from Cameroon for her university expenses. Another example of unsavory activity linked to the 2002 bid involved the daughter of an IOC executive board member, a concert pianist of reputedly modest ability, who was hired as a guest artist with the Utah Symphony for a fee of $5000. SLOC bought more than $3750 worth of tickets to watch her perform (Robinson, 2003). Nine members were censured and four others resigned (Longman & Thomas, 1999).

It turned out that the payments before the Salt Lake City Games were not isolated events. Evidence of corruption in the bid for the 1996 Summer Games has also been exposed (Rose, 1999). As a result, in 1999 the IOC voted to ban all-expenses-paid visits to cities bidding for the Olympics. Also, as part of those reforms, the IOC established a new ethics watchdog, made up of three IOC delegates and five independent members (Shipley, 1999). Other changes include the abolishment of visits by IOC members to candidate cities, and, notably for journalists, the release of financial reports on the sources and uses of the Olympic movement's income, an important window into the fiscal policies of the IOC.

Yet, the political intrigue in the selection of host cities continues. Allegations have surfaced that Chinese sports officials agreed to support Jacques Rogge's bid to head the IOC in return for European backing for Beijing's bid (ABC News, 2008) and it has been suggested that Chicago's surprising first-round elimination from the 2016 Summer Games bid was due to poor relations between the IOC and the United States Olympic Committee and the fact that many Europeans voted for Madrid (considered a weaker candidate) in deference to the former IOC head Juan Antonio Samaranch, who, in either a poignant ode or a calculated political gambit (depending on one's point of view), stated: "I am very near the end of my time. I ask you to consider granting my country the honor and the duty of hosting the Olympic and Paralympic Games in 2016" (Futterman, Moffett, & Belkin, 2009).

Despite the controversies and the changes, the IOC's considerable power remains largely intact and is felt by national Olympic committees, international sports federations, and domestic affiliates of those sports federations.

## Professionalism

At one time, only nonprofessionals were eligible to compete in the Olympic Games. An athlete receiving any compensation for athletic competition was ineligible. Jim Thorpe, one of the great all-around athletes of his time, won the gold medal in the decathlon at the 1912 Summer Games in Stockholm. When it was discovered that Thorpe played semiprofessional baseball, the IOC stripped him of his medal (Flatter, 2007).

The strict amateur policy dates from the advent of the modern Olympic Games. In the nineteenth and early twentieth centuries, working-class people did not have the time for or access to sports facilities. The amateurism requirement limited competition to the wealthy, because the average laborer could not afford to train, travel, and compete. The rigid adherence to amateurism later became hypocritical when Communist states used it to great advantage. During the Cold War, athletes from Soviet-bloc countries often had government or military positions, but devoted much if not all of their time to training and competing in athletic events. For example, the hockey players in the Soviet Central Army team worked in the military, but of course never served in any infantry position. The United States and other non-Communist countries accused the Soviets and other Soviet-bloc nations of de facto compensation of their athletes. In response, the Soviets alleged that the United States college system, whereby athletes often received full scholarships, was also a type of compensation.

The IOC relaxed the strict amateur standard in 1986. Presently, professional athletes are permitted to compete under rules stipulated by the particular sport's international federation. Amateurism versus professionalism has not been a controversial Olympic issue since that time.

### Dispute Resolution

Arbitration is the IOC's preferred method of dispute resolution and, since 1994, all Olympic disputes (and many disputes involving international athletic federations) fall under the jurisdiction of the Court of Arbitration for Sport (CAS), an arbitration panel formed by the IOC. When an athlete signs the entry form into the Olympics, he or she consents to the court's jurisdiction to arbitrate disputes arising during the Games. When a dispute occurs, an application is submitted to the CAS and the arbitration panel is required to render a written decision within twenty-four hours. The ruling is final and binding, and may not be appealed or challenged (McLaren, 2002). The CAS procedure applies even if the athlete participates in a sport whose international federation has its own arbitration system for resolving disputes because the IOC's rules take precedence.

Generally, two types of disputes may be submitted to the CAS. The first focuses on contractual issues involving teams, players, and sponsors. Disciplinary cases represent the second group of disputes submitted to the CAS, of which a large number are doping related. In addition to doping cases, the CAS is called upon to rule on various disciplinary cases, such as in-game violence and abuse of officials (CAS Rules, 2010, Article 20).

No matter where the arbitrations are held, they are governed by the CAS rules, which state that arbitrators base their decisions on the Olympic charter and "general principles of law" (CAS Rules, 2010, Article 17).

## National Olympic Committees

Each nation competing in the Olympics must have an NOC. The NOCs "shall be the sole authorities responsible for the representation of their respective countries at the Olympic Games as well as at other events held under the patronage of the IOC" (Bitting, 1998). In the United States, the NOC is the United States Olympic Committee.

### The United States Olympic Committee

#### History

Created in 1896, the year of the first modern Olympic Games, the USOC is a nonprofit corporation which had a $560 million quadrennial budget for the years 2005–08. Unlike other national Olympic committees, which are government funded, the USOC obtains the majority of its funding from public donations and from corporate sponsorships.

Throughout most of its history, the USOC had surprisingly little power. Unlike many countries whose Olympic committees are government arms, the USOC is, at best, only quasi-governmental. As the "coordinating body" over all amateur athletic activity within the United States, it has exclusive jurisdiction over "all matters pertaining to the United States participation in the Olympic Games" and is the "ultimate authority with respect to United States representation in the Olympic Games" (Foschi v. United States Swimming, Inc., 1996). The USOC has the authority to recognize a national governing body for any amateur sport. Although this sounds like a powerful mandate, for many years the USOC was subordinate to powerful amateur athletic organizations. According to one commentator, the USOC was little more than a travel agency, which sent athletes to the Olympic sites every four years (De Varona, 2003).

While other countries were developing coordinated Olympic programs, the USOC was embroiled in jurisdictional problems throughout the 1950s and early 1960s. Three competing amateur sports organizations fought over athlete eligibility. First was the Amateur Athletic Union (AAU), which at the time was the national governing body for ten Olympic sports. Second was the school/college sports community. Finally, a number of independent national governing bodies, which conducted their programs apart from the AAU and did not have school/college participation in their sports, sought control. As a result, chaos resulted in the selection of the best athletes, and, to make matters worse, no dispute resolution mechanism existed to solve or address these problems.

In the mid-1970s, President Gerald Ford formed a commission to present recommendations for revising the organization of Olympic sports, resolving disputes, and improving ways to finance Olympic sports in

America. No disagreement surfaced on the central issue: The USOC had to be changed dramatically. Acting on the commission's recommendations, Congress passed the Amateur Sports Act of 1978 (now the Ted Stevens Olympic and Amateur Sports Act), which mandated the USOC as the one entity responsible for coordinating all Olympic athletic activity (Ted Stevens Olympic and Amateur Sports Act, 36 USC, sec. 220504).

### United States Olympic Committee Structure

A key goal of the 1978 Amateur Sports Act was to strengthen the USOC. Unfortunately, the result served as a case study in bad policy making because the law did not create a practical structure. A bloated policy board and executive committee with confusing reporting structures set the stage for frequent disputes. Two uncoordinated chains of command occurred, with some members reporting to the USOC president and others reporting to the chief executive officer (CEO).

The law "suggested" that the USOC president, a twenty-three-member executive committee, and a 125-member board set policies for the organization. Yet the CEO and his or her paid staff implemented the policies while also raising money. The president and CEO often fought over control and the use of that money. This created a revolving door of CEOs and presidents. From 1978 to 2003, the USOC had thirteen CEOs and eleven presidents (Scott, 2004).

The 125-person board of directors comprised past USOC presidents, IOC members, representatives of the national governing bodies, public-sector representatives, athletes who had competed in major international events within the past decade, and representatives from the thirty-nine Olympic sports. However, in an effort to accommodate other interested groups, the board also included members from such tangentially sports-related bodies as the Boy Scouts of America and the American Legion. It is no wonder that the organization was in such disarray.

A smaller executive committee, comprising twenty-two members that included the USOC president, vice-presidents, U.S.-based IOC members, and representatives of the national governing bodies, was the body that hired the CEO, and established policies and guidelines.

In 2003, responding to political pressures and bad publicity, the USOC agreed to eliminate twenty members of the executive committee and reduce the 125-member board to eleven. The board consists of four directors who have no USOC ties, two NGB representatives, and two athlete representatives (Michaelis, 2003). In addition, the board will include three U.S. IOC members with limited voting power. As we will see, this arrangement has not solved the personnel and governance problems of the USOC.

*Powers*

The Amateur Sports Act of 1978 mandated that the USOC was responsible for coordinating international sporting events for the U.S. NGBs (Ted Stevens Olympic and Amateur Sports Act, 36 USC sec. 220504). The USOC was allowed to recognize one NGB per sport, eliminating the earlier jurisdictional overlaps between different organizations claiming to represent the same sport. Once recognized, all the selected NGBs were required to report to the USOC. Although not a government agency, the USOC became a "quasi-governmental" organization, because the law mandated that it periodically report to Congress. However, Congress does not oversee the USOC on a day-to-day basis, leaving the USOC largely unchecked, but that could change if the USOC does not resolve its problems.

The recent difficulties surfaced after the failed bid by the city of Chicago to host the 2016 Summer Games (which ultimately went to Rio). Relations between the USOC and IOC became tense after the USOC intended to create an Olympic television network, without the approval of the IOC. Also, many IOC members felt that the USOC received too much money from global sponsorships and TV rights, an arrangement that will be renegotiated in 2013 (Thomas, 2009). A final criticism was that the leaders lacked expertise in the Olympic system, since they came from the corporate world.

Additionally, relations between the IOC and U.S. NGBs were equally strained. The following quote is an indication of the feelings by the then-USA Track & Field CEO Doug Logan, and for journalists it is illustrative of the problems (according to Logan) of a U.S.-centric approach to international athletics:

> As an institution, the United States Olympic movement in general, and the USOC specifically, does not have either the tools or the knowledge of what it takes to operate globally in today's day and age . . . The USOC is ensconced in the mountains of Colorado. Go check out the travel logs. They don't go anywhere. You go to them, they don't come to you . . . They don't go out there and mingle. They don't realize that the work of sports is out there. They're much more concerned with what's happening in that castle in the mountains. They're very inwardly focused rather than externally focused (Battaglia, 2009).

*Resolution of Disputes*

Because of court orders preventing the USOC from taking action against the figure skater Tonya Harding for her role in the planning of the assault against Nancy Kerrigan in January 1994, Congress amended the Amateur Sports Act in 1998 to strengthen the USOC's arbitration system. Under the amendments, a court may generally not impose any injunction against the USOC within twenty-one days of the beginning of a major competition. The amendments also established the office of an ombudsman, who, among other powers, may seek to mediate disputes (Ted Stevens Olympic and Amateur Sports Act, 36 USC, sec. 220509).

In 2004, the USOC adopted new bylaws covering the rights of athletes, coaches, trainers, managers, or other officials seeking participation in the conduct of international amateur athletic competitions (USOC Bylaws, sec. 9.7). Aggrieved parties may submit their claims to arbitration within six months of the alleged denial of rights (USOC Bylaws sec. 9.2).

*Sponsorships*

USOC partners receive marketing rights to the U.S. Olympic team and commercial access to the USA five-ring logo and Olympic themes, terminology, and imagery for use in sponsor marketing programs. This level of sponsorship is limited to the United States and is not a part of the IOC's international sponsorship program. Several levels of sponsorship exist. The top two are "Partner Level" and "Sponsor Level" companies, which have access to the above-mentioned items and the rights to list the year in which they first became Olympic sponsors or partners. In 2008, USOC Partners paid $20 million to $35 million over four years for a mix of licensing, hospitality, activation, and media rights. Sponsors paid $10 million to $15 million over four years and received a smaller mix of benefits, while the lowest level of rightsholders, known as suppliers, paid $3 million to $10 million over four years for rights to the image of the USA five-ring logo (Mickle, 2008a). "Partners" included Anheuser-Busch, Coca-Cola, General Electric, McDonald's, and Visa. "Sponsors" included Allstate Insurance, Nike, and United Airlines (USOC, 2008) However, the economic downturn of 2009 has cost the USOC some sponsors, such as General Motors and Home Depot.

## International Federations

International federations are the worldwide governing bodies of various sports, possessing the authority to regulate the sport, subject only to the limitations of the Olympic Charter. A federation's responsibilities include conducting international competitions, detailing eligibility rules, choosing judges and referees for competitions (including the Olympic Games), organizing world championships, and resolving technical issues in their sport. In contrast to the prior USOC model, which was inherently weak, by their nature the international federations have a more centralized decision-making structure. Often powerful (even autocratic) presidents or CEOs lead international federations.

In order to receive and maintain recognition from the IOC, international federations must agree to comply with the Olympic Charter, show compliance with IOC criteria, and receive approval by the IOC executive board. Like the IOC, for many decades, the international federations limited membership to amateur athletes. Most, if not all, now allow professionals to compete.

In recent years, the judging of events, particularly in the Olympics, has received criticism. At the 2004 Summer Olympic Games in Athens, questionable scoring in gymnastics, swimming, equestrian events, rowing, and fencing resulted in protests and appeals over medal results. Three gymnastics judges and a fencing referee were suspended for errors affecting the awarding of gold medals. Many remember the controversial judging at the 2002 Winter Olympics at Salt Lake City, where improprieties in the scoring of pair figure skating resulted in the awarding of joint gold medals. The relevant federations took a great deal of criticism regarding their selection of judges and the lack of damage control.

Athlete challenges to international federation rulings on disputes are heard by the CAS, which handles similar appeals involving Olympic athletes.

A list of the international federations for each international sport recognized by the IOC and their websites is given at the end of this chapter.

## National Governing Bodies

Each international federation has a corresponding NGB. An NGB is an organization in charge of running the sport in a given country. The particular international federation generally recognizes one domestic body as an NGB. The NGBs set eligibility standards for domestic participation in the sport, such as age limitations and professionalism. They also conduct competitions for selecting teams to participate in international competitions organized under the aegis of the international federation or the IOC. National governing bodies must abide by the rules of their corresponding international federation, as well as those of the IOC. Yet conflicts between the international federations and the NGBs have arisen in recent years regarding arbitration rules.

The USOC's bylaws outline the duties of NGBs in the United States. They include establishing written procedures to select athletes, coaches, and team leaders for the Olympic, Pan American, and Paralympic Games teams; selecting site(s) and date(s) to qualify for the Olympic, Pan American, and Paralympic Games teams; recommending a training plan for Olympic, Pan American, and Paralympic Games team members; establishing programs for the development of its sport; and preparing the requirements of its sport for submission to the USOC for apparel, supplies, equipment, training services, and transportation to service the Olympic, Pan American, and Paralympic teams (USOC Bylaws, sec. 8). The NGBs also must participate in the international federation activities of their sport and carry out those responsibilities required by the international federations.

In the United States, the Ted Stevens Olympic and Amateur Sports Act requires that NGBs "agree to submit to binding arbitration . . . the opportunity of any amateur athlete . . . to participate in amateur athletic competition, upon demand of the corporation or any aggrieved amateur athlete" (36 USC, 2003, sec. 220522(a)(4)(B)).

We next examine the structures of the international federations and national governing bodies representing track and field, figure skating, and swimming.

## Examples of International Federations and National Governing Bodies

### Track and Field

*International Federation—International Association of Athletics Federations (IAAF).* First established in 1912, the IAAF governs racing, walking, and other track and field events. In 1982, the sport moved away from its traditional "amateur" eligibility to the present rules allowing professionals to compete in its events. For example, the IAAF now offers prize money for its competitions based on a points system, as well as additional bonuses for outstanding performances such as breaking world records. The organization has procured increased financing from areas such as corporate sponsorship—a departure from merely collecting membership fees.

Headquartered in Monaco, the IAAF has 213 affiliated NGBs. The IAAF Council, the central body administering all IAAF affairs, includes the president, treasurer, four vice-presidents, six representatives, and fifteen individual members. Six committees and eight commissions assist the council. Council members are elected for four years, with the exception of the general secretary, who is appointed by the council (IAAF Constitution, 2007, Article 6).

*NGB—USA Track & Field (USATF).* The USATF is the IAAF member in the United States. It inherited that role from the old Amateur Athletic Union (AAU), which dated from 1878. The AAU governed track and field until 1979, when the Amateur Sports Act decreed that the AAU could no longer hold international franchises for more than one sport.

The officers and members of the USATF board, the chairs of all the committees, and twelve delegates from each association are permitted to vote at meetings. In addition, it requires that 20 percent of the delegates be athletes. Since the mid-1980s, USATF events have been open to professionals. The USATF has fifty-seven regional associations (USATF Bylaws, 2009, Article 7).

Disputes between athletes and the USATF are first submitted to an appellate tribunal. If one party wishes a further appeal, the CAS assumes jurisdiction. Its rulings are final.

During the last fifteen years, the USATF has suffered organizational and economic difficulties. Track and field lacks consistent popularity, which makes finding sponsors difficult. As a result, the organization has limited economic resources to stage competitions and otherwise promote the sport. Even worse, the USATF has been embroiled in controversy over its drug-testing rules. The IOC criticized the USATF for permitting the sprinter Jerome Young to run in the 2000 Sydney Olympics after having tested positive in the prior year for a banned steroid (Abrahamson, 2003).

Tense relations between USATF and the IAAF, the sport's international federation, over substance abuse have existed since the late 1990s, exemplified by an arbitration ruling in early 2003. The CAS concluded that USATF did not have to disclose the drug test results of thirteen athletes because of its, and the athletes', reliance on a confidentiality policy USATF had maintained, despite IAAF rules requiring such disclosure (Shipley, 2003). The IAAF claimed that its rules required all national track federations to disclose the results of the tests to the IAAF. Even if true, the USATF argued that such disclosure (from 1996 to 2000) was illegal under U.S. privacy laws. Despite the IAAF's disclosure requirements, the panel concluded that USATF's confidentiality policy took precedence, not necessarily because of the legal issues, but rather because of a procedural one (Shipley, 2003).

In a not-so-veiled criticism of USATF governance, in 2003 the USOC's board voted unanimously to mandate that USATF update its bylaws, improve its financial reporting, and improve its coordination with the United States Anti-Doping Agency (the agency now in charge of drug testing). Things did not improve, and in 2008 the USOC once again urged USATF to reform its organization structure and threatened to eliminate funding and even to decertify the body. Subsequently, Doug Logan, the former commissioner of Major League Soccer, was selected as the CEO and, at the end of that year, major governance changes were adopted reducing the board of directors from thirty-one to fifteen members and giving the CEO greater powers (Mickle, 2008b).

## Figure Skating

***International Federation—International Skating Union (ISU).*** The responsibilities of the ISU, the governing body over all national figure skating and speed skating associations, include jurisdiction over nonprofessional competitions, certification of national associations, and creating the rules for World Championship and Olympic figure skating championships. Founded in 1892, it espoused amateurism for many years but now allows professionals to compete, although under more limited circumstances than most other international federations.

Judging controversies have brought unfavorable publicity to the ISU, exemplified by problems in the 2002 Winter Olympics in Salt Lake City. In the pairs skating event, a gold medal was awarded to the Russian team of Yelena Berezhnaya and Anton Sikharulidze over a Canadian pair, Jamie Salé and David Pelletier. The result attracted considerable criticism, because, according to many, the Canadian pair skated a flawless program and the Russians did not. After a review, one of the judges, Marie Reine LaGougne (known in the media as "the French judge"), "confessed" that she was ordered by the head of the French skating governing body to vote for the Russian team as part of a deal with the head of Russia's governing body to vote for the French team in the ice dancing event. Ultimately, dual gold medals were awarded to the Russian and Canadian teams, a first in Olympic history (Weiler & Roberts, 2004, p. 1078).

The episode just described demonstrates the kind of sordid deal making of an organization that lacked adequate scrutiny. Why did the national skating federations select the judges for ISU events? In particular, why did countries participating in the World Championships or Olympics select the judges? Good reasons may exist, but it behooves journalists covering the governance of skating and other international sports to understand the basic functions of the international federations and NGBs and to ask those kinds of questions.

Fueled by the Salt Lake City scandal, the ISU altered its judging system. A computer randomly selects nine scores from fourteen judges, whose marks are kept anonymous even during the traditional postevent evaluation. The new arrangement apparently solves the problem of one or two judges affecting the outcome, but it creates other issues. Under the prior system, incompetent or biased judges could be identified and punished, but the new system makes it easier for corrupt judges to go undetected.

A more fundamental organizational change proposed is separating figure skating and speed skating into separate entities, much like the current structure in the United States. The ISU also governs speed skating, a much less popular sport in the United States than figure skating. Some have argued that the ISU is controlled by the speed skaters and is less attuned to the needs of competitive figure skating (Jones, 2003; Swift, 2003).

Unlike most other major international federations, the ISU contin-ues to cling to a modified form of "amateurism." If a skater wishes to remain eligible to compete at an ISU-sanctioned event, such as the World Championships, he or she is restricted from participating in certain pro-fessional tours (Crouse, 1998) but is eligible to participate in so-called "pro–am" events sanctioned by the ISU (ISU General Regulations, 2008).

*NGBs—United States Figure Skating and U.S. Speedskating.* As noted earlier, United States skating is governed by two separate NGBs, the United States Figure Skating Association and US Speed Skating. We focus on the United States Figure Skating (USFS), which was formed in 1921. USFS is the ISU's NGB in the United States for figure skating. It has several hundred member clubs throughout the United States that stage competi-tions, thus allowing athletes to move up the ladder to international com-petitions. Most recently, the USFS changed its scoring system, which is now modeled after the one used in international competition.

United States Figure Skating has a nine-member executive committee and a thirty-seven-member board of directors, of which twenty-nine are voting members (USFSA Bylaws, Articles IX and VIII). Athletes constitute 20 percent of the board. As noted earlier, the 1998 amendments to the Amateur Sports Act limit the power of U.S. courts to issue injunctions. US Speedskating, the NGB for the sport, is separate from United States Figure Skating, but a member of the ISU, just like its sister NGB.

## Swimming

*International Federation—Fédération Internationale de Natation Amateur (FINA).* Competitive swimming at the international level is governed by the Fédération Internationale de Natation Amateur (FINA). FINA is also in charge of other aquatic sports, including water polo, diving, and synchronized swimming. The national body governing swim-ming in any country is eligible for membership in FINA.

FINA's central governing group, known as "the bureau," consists of seventeen members: the president, honorary secretary, honorary trea-surer, five vice-presidents, and nine additional members. Its duties are to encourage development of swimming throughout the world, to ensure uniformity of rules, and to adopt rules for the control of competitions, as well as many other functions. The bureau is elected by the General Congress (FINA Constitution, Article 17).

As is typical in many international federations, FINA has an intricate organizational structure. The General Congress, the highest authority of FINA, has the power to decide upon all matters arising in FINA. The Technical Congress decides on all technical matters concerning the sports under FINA's jurisdiction. Both congresses meet once a year. The bureau's powers include interpreting and enforcing FINA rules, deciding on bylaws, and, not insignificantly, making decisions in case of "emergency" (FINA Constitution, Article 17).

FINA has its share of problems, most notably allegations of performance-enhancing drug use. This issue was at the forefront in the 1990s, when the Chinese swim team suddenly started dominating in a sport where it had previously made modest showings. Despite various protests, FINA claimed that doping was limited to individual Chinese athletes, but rejected the claim that it was part of a systematic pattern of abuse by the Chinese Swimming Federation. During the Asian Games in 1994, seven female Chinese swimmers tested positive for anabolic steroids and were suspended for two years by the Chinese Swimming Federation. These test results created widespread suspicion of team-wide doping, especially given the meteoric rise in the medal count. During the 1988 Seoul Summer Games, the female swimmers took home three silver medals and one bronze. In the 1992 Barcelona Olympics, they captured four golds, five silvers, and one bronze. In response to the growing concern over this problem, FINA joined the World Anti-Doping Association and adopted its drug-testing standards.

More recently, FINA adopted new regulations to ban the use of so-called "techno" or "super swimsuits," those made of "non-permeable materials," which helped break many world records in the 2008 Beijing Olympics. These swimsuits incorporated plastics and rubberized material, to enhance the ability of the athlete to be buoyant. Starting in 2010, the rules require swimsuits to be made of fabric (IBN Sports, 2009). An interesting question is whether the records set during the period of use of the "super swimsuits" will be acknowledged as official or not. At this time, FINA has not pronounced on this issue.

FINA embraced professionalism in the mid-1980s.

*NGB—USA Swimming, USA Diving, USA Synchro.* FINA has affiliations with several U.S. national organizations, including USA Swimming, Inc., USA Water Polo, USA Diving, USA Synchro, and U.S. Masters Swimming. Unlike areas of sports such as track and field, in which one organization governs all the various sports within its domain, aquatics have individual organizations for each particular sport.

## Information Check

When covering a international sports issue, a journalist should determine:

1 What are the applicable international federation and national governing body?
2 What powers do these bodies have that are applicable to the event in question?
3 Does the particular issue involve the Olympics? If so, when does the IOC or national Olympic committee have control of the matter?
4 Are copies of the organizations' constitutions and bylaws available? (If so, the journalist should read the appropriate sections and, if anything seems inconsistent or unclear, ask why.)
5 How have similar issues have been handled in the past?
6 Is there a right of appeal? If so, with whom and where?
7 How accessible are organization representatives for interviews?
8 How are the officials of the organization elected or appointed?
9 Is there any athlete representation in these organizations?
10 Does the organization have any age minimums or maximums for competition?

## Helpful Websites

International Archery Federation (FITA): www.archery.org

International Association of Athletics Federations (IAAF), the international federation for track and field: www.iaaf.org

International Basketball Federation (FIBA): www.fiba.com

International Bobsleigh & Tobogganing Federation (FIBT): www.bobsleigh.com

International Cycling Union (UCI): www.uci.ch

International Federation for Equestrian Sports (FEI): www.horsesport.org

International Federation of Rowing Associations (FISA): www.fisa.org

International Fencing Federation (FIE): www.fie.ch

International Gymnastics Federation (GIF): www.fig-gymnastics.com

International Ice Hockey Federation: www.iihf.com

International Judo Federation (IJF): www.ijf.org

International Olympic Committee: www.olympic.org

International Paralympic Committee: www.paralympic.org

International Skating Union (ISU): www.isu.org

International Swimming Federation (FINA): www.fina.org

International Tennis Federation (ITF): www.itftennis.com

International Volleyball Federation (FIVB): www.fivb.ch

International Weightlifting Federation: www.iwf.net

Royal and Ancient Golf Club of St. Andrews: www.randa.org

USA Archery: www.usarchery.org/

USA Track & Field: www.usatf.org

USA Basketball: www.usabasketball.com

United States Bobsled & Skeleton Federation, Inc.: www.usbsf.com

USA Cycling, Inc.: www.usacycling.org

US Equestrian Federation: www.usef.org

United States Rowing Association: www.usrowing.org

United States Fencing Association: www.usfencing.org

USA Gymnastics: www.usa-gymnastics.org

USA Hockey: www.usahockey.com

USA Judo: www.usjudo.org

United States Olympic Committee: www.teamusa.org

USA Paralympic Committee: www.usparalympics.org

The United States Figure Skating Association (USFSA): www.usfsa.org

US Speedskating: www.usspeedskating.org

USA Swimming: www.usaswimming.org

United States Tennis Association: www.usta.com

USA Volleyball: www.usavolleyball.org

USA Weightlifting Federation: www.usaweightlifting.org

United States Golf Association: www.usga.org

# References

*ABC News* (2008, October 20). Ex-China sports official tells of Olympic deals. Retrieved April 14, 2010, from http://abcnews.go.com/Sports/wireStory?id=8870799

Abrahamson, A. (2002, April 24). Salt Lake Winter Games turn a profit. *Los Angeles Times*. Retrieved April 10, 2010, from http://articles.latimes.com/2002/apr/24/sports/sp-usoc24

Abrahamson, A. (2003, December 2). Steroid secrecy upsets IOC; U.S. track officials haven't explained why gold medalist Young was cleared to run in 2000 Games despite a positive test, Olympic chief says. *Los Angeles Times*, p. D1.

Ansley, C. C. (1995). International athletic dispute resolution: Tarnishing the Olympic dream. *Arizona Journal of International Comparative Law, 12*, 277, 290.

Battaglia, J. (2009, November 2). On the record with Doug Logan. *Universal Sports*. Retrieved, April 14, 2010, from http://www.universalsports.com/news/article/newsid=365538.html

BBC News (2004). Green Olympic bill doubles. Retrieved January 5, 2005, from http://news.bbc.co.uk/2/hi/business/4007429.stm

Bitting, M. R. (1998). Mandatory binding arbitration for Olympic athletes: Is the process better or worse for "job security"? *Florida State University Law Review, 25*, 655.

*China Sports Review* (2009, March 7). Beijing Olympics made $16 million profit? Retrieved March 21, 2010, from http://www.chinasportsreview.com/2009/03/07/beijing-olympics-made-16-million-profit/

Court of Arbitration for Sport (2010). Arbitration rules. Retrieved April 14, 2010, from http://www.tas-cas.org/adhoc-rules

Crouse, K. (1998, February 6). Saving grace; Kwan puts sparkle back into women's figure skating. *Los Angeles Daily News*. Retrieved August 10, 2010, from http://www.thefreelibrary.com/SAVING+GRACE%3B+KWAN+PUTS+SPARKLE+BACK+INTO+WOMEN'S+FIGURE+SKATING-a083810163

De Varona, D. (2003, February 13). United States Olympic Committee Reform. Hearing before the Committee on Commerce, Science and Transportation, U.S. Senate. 108th Congress, 1st Session, p. 20. Retrieved May 11, 2010, from http://books.google.com/books?id=6Up7IrwLzpoC&pg=PA20&lpg=PA20&dq=USOC+was+little+more+than+a+travel+agent&source=bl&ots=rQNtiTzwWn&sig=EL1mmLogcGM4Rz2-zOy4aUQ1FT8&hl=en&ei=QBzsS6GkE4H58AaP5OyLBQ&sa=X&oi=book_result&ct=result&resnum=5&ved=0CB4Q6AEwBA#v=onepage&q&f=false

Executive Board, International Olympic Committee (n.d.). Retrieved April 10, 2010, from http://www.olympic.org/en/content/The-IOC/Commissions/Executive-Board/

Federation Internationale de Natation (FINA) Constitution (2009). Retrieved, October 24, 2009, from http://www.fina.org/project/index.php?option=com_content&task=view&id=42&Itemid=119#c17

Flatter, J. (2007). Thorpe preceded Dion, Bo. SportsCentury biography. ESPN Classic. Retrieved April 14, 2010, from http://espn.go.com/classic/biography/s/thorpe_jim.html

Foschi v. United States Swimming, Inc. 916 F. Supp. 232, 240 (E.D.N.Y. 1966).

Futterman, M., Moffett M., & Belkin B. (2009, October 5). Rio throws Chicago for a loop. *The Wall Street Journal*. Retrieved April 14, 2010, from http://online.wsj.com/article/SB125446379425258861.html

*IBN Sports* (2009, August 1). New swimsuit rules valid from January [2010]. Retrieved April 14, 2010, from http://ibnlive.in.com/news/new-swimsuit-rules-valid-from-january-fina/98337–5.html

International Association of Athletics Federation (IAAF) Constitution (2007). Retrieved April 14, 2010, from http://www.iaaf.org/mm/Document/imported/9585.pdf

International Skating Union, General Regulations (2008). Retrieved October 24, 2009, from http://www.isu.org/vsite/vfile/page/fileurl/0,11040,4844-192306-209529-141863-0-file,00.pdf

Jones, T. (2003, March 26). On thin ice; New figure skating body wants to bury the old guard. *Calgary Sun*, p. 63.

Lenskyj, H. (1998). "Inside sport" or "On the margins?" Australian women and the sport media. *International Review for the Sociology of Sport, 33*(1), 19–32.

Longman, J., & Thomas, J. (1999, February 9). Report details lavish spending in Salt Lake's bid to win Games. *New York Times*, p. A1.

Magnier, M. (2008, August 7). Many eyes will watch visitors. *Los Angeles Times*. Retrieved April 11, 2010, from http://articles.latimes.com/2008/aug/07/world/fg-snoop7

Masteralexis, L. P., Barr, C. A., & Hums, M. A. (1998). *Principles and practice of sport management*. Gaithersburg, MD: Aspen, p. 221.

McLaren, R. H. (2002). International sports law perspective: Introducing the Court of Arbitration for Sport: The ad hoc division at the Olympic games. *Marquis Sports Law Review, 12*, 515.

Merron, J. (2003, April 22). Montreal's house of horrors. Retrieved April 14, 2010, from http://a.espncdn.com/mlb/s/2003/0422/1542254.html

Michaelis, V. (2003, October 20). USOC hopes to take note of change. *USA Today*, p. 13C.

Mickle, T. (2008a, January 21). USOC sponsors slow to commit past 2008. *Sports Business Journal*, p. 11.

Mickle, T. (2008b, December 4). USATF approves bylaws; Size of BOD to be cut by more than half. *Sports Business Daily*. Retrieved October 22, 2009, from http://www.sportsbusinessdaily.com/article/126019

*Olympic.org* (2010). Olympic Sponsorships. Retrieved May 1, 2010, from http://www.olympic.org/en/content/The-IOC/Sponsoring/Sponsorship/?Tab=1

Rein, S. (2008, April 24). Beijing Olympic sponsorship's a waste. *Forbes*. Retrieved, September 22, 2009, from http://www.forbes.com/2008/04/23/china-olympics-sponsors-oped-cx_sre_0424olympics.html

Robinson, D. (2003, July 8). IOC thumbs its nose at the world. *Deseret News*. Retrieved, April 15, 2010, from http://findarticles.com/p/articles/mi_qn4188/is_20030708/ai_n11406924/pg_2/?tag=content;col1

Rose, J. (1999, September 22). Upton calls for Olympics cleanup congressional probe to look at committee's "culture of corruption." *South Bend Tribune*, p. A1.

Scott, M. S. (2004, January). Lloyd Ward: Victim or villain? *Black Enterprise*, Section BE Exclusive, p. 60.

Shipley, A. (1999, May 4). IOC retains right to conduct probes: Ethics panel declines to take over task. *Washington Post*, p. D01.

Shipley, A. (2003, January 11). Court rules in favor of U.S. Track; Refusal to identify athletes in drug testing case upheld. *Washington Post*, p. D01.

Swift, E. (2003, May 10). An insurrection among American figure skaters, fed up with the corruption of the international body that governs them has sent sparks flying this week at an annual convention in down Norfolk. *Virginian Pilot*, p. A1.

Ted Stevens Olympic and Amateur Sports Act, 36 U.S.C. (2010). Retrieved April 14, 2010, from http://videos.usoc.org/legal/TedStevens.pdf

Thomas, K. (2009, October 4). After Chicago's loss, critics assail U.S.O.C. *New York Times*, Sports p. 1.

United States Figure Skating Bylaws (date). Retrieved August 10, 2010, from http://www.usfigureskating.org/content/bylaws2.pdf

United States Olympic Committee (2008). *Annual Report*. Retrieved May 12, 2010, from http://assets.teamusa.org/assets/documents/attached_file/filename/14727/USOC_AR_for_PDF.pdf

United States Olympic Committee Bylaws (date). Retrieved August 1, 2010, from http://assets.teamusa.org/assets/documents/attached_file/filename/17354/Bylaws_7.01.08__executed_-_final_.pdf

USA Track & Field Bylaws (2010). Retrieved October 24, 2009, from http://www.usatf.org/about/governance/2009/09_Governance.pdf

Weiler, P., & Roberts, G. (2004). *Sports law: Text, cases and problems* (3rd ed.). St. Paul, MN: West Group, p. 1078.

# 5   Sports Contracts

Contracts are fundamental to professional sports. These documents determine the rights and obligations of the athletes, coaches, general managers, and the organizations that employ them. They also detail stadium leases, naming rights deals, and sponsorships.

Sports contracts have certain unique and important characteristics. First, an interplay between union agreements and individual service contracts exists. Therefore, player contracts are subject to the labor agreements negotiated between players' unions and their leagues (also a type of contract) and to the salary control mechanisms found in many of those labor–management agreements. Additionally, sports contracts contain particular duties and prohibitions not normally found in a standard business contract. Finally, as personal services contracts involving highly talented individuals, sports contracts enjoy particular remedies not available in most everyday contracts.

Although most sports contract issues receiving media coverage apply to professional athletes and their teams, contractual issues also apply to coaches and general managers, sponsorships, endorsements, and event participation. To understand the sports business, a journalist has to understand the very basics of contract law, the terms of such agreements, and the important negotiating points involved. This chapter focuses on these issues in considerable detail. We do not discuss purely amateur athletes, because NCAA rules prohibit them from earning compensation for their athletic involvement.

Often, professional athletes earn princely sums. In 2008, the average salary of a Major League Baseball player was $2.93 million (Bloom, 2008). For a National Football League (NFL) player, it was $1.1 million (Barra, 2009), for National Basketball Association (NBA) players, $5.85 million (Abrams, 2009), and for National Hockey League (NHL) players, $1.9 million (Shinzawa, 2009).

Even more telling are the total salaries paid to the few marquee athletes. *Sports Illustrated* annually lists the fifty highest-paid American athletes. The calculations take into account base salaries, winnings (for individual athletes), endorsements, and appearance fees. For 2009, Tiger

Woods (golf) led the list at over $99 million, of which $92 million comprised endorsements and appearance fees, followed by Phil Mickelson (golf) with $52 million, consisting of $6 million in winnings and $46 million endorsements, and the NBA star LeBron James earned $42 million ($14 million salary, $28 million endorsements). Alex Rodriguez (Major League Baseball), with a total of $39 million, Shaquille O'Neal (NBA) with $35 million, and Kevin Garnett (NBA), Kobe Bryant (NBA), Allen Iverson (NBA), Derek Jeter (Major League Baseball), and Peyton Manning (NFL) completed the top ten. NBA players made up nearly half the list, with twenty-two names (Freedman, 2009).

It has become routine for fans and journalists to question the contracts signed by professional athletes. Although these salaries are generous, even excessive according to many fans and writers, it must be emphasized that professional athletes constitute elite talent. The numbers tell the story. Hundreds of thousands of youngsters play basketball but there are only about 400 active players in the NBA. The same can be said of athletes in almost every other sport, including individual sports such as golf and tennis. The owners and general managers who negotiate contracts with the athlete or his or her agent base their offers on the skills of the athlete, as well as leadership ability, fan popularity, and, of course, the potential for that athlete to increase the club's success. True, many cases of bad deals exist. The Texas Rangers realized three years and three last-place finishes too late that they should not have signed Alex Rodriguez to a ten-year, $252 million contract. The contract left them little financial room to maneuver and improve the rest of their roster. But often the bad deals look bad in hindsight. At the time they are made, the contracts may seem perfectly sensible.

Contrary to popular belief, athletes rarely breach their contracts. The risks are too great from a legal, business, and public relations point of view. Legally, penalties in the form of damages and even injunctions issued by courts are possible (Central New York Basketball v. Barnett, 1961). From a business perspective, such an action weakens the credibility of the player and effectively limits his or her options to sign with another team in the particular league. It also creates ill will on the part of the team and its fans. Additionally, the move makes very little sense in this era of free agency, as an athlete attaining that status may simply pursue alternatives with other teams once his or her contract expires. Finally, a team inducing an athlete to breach will be dealt with harshly by the commissioner of the league under the "best interests of the sport" power in the league constitution, as discussed in chapter 1. Ironically, it's coaches—notably certain collegiate coaches—that have breached their obligations in recent years.

Knowledge of the basics of these agreements is crucial in understanding the parameters of the terms of an athlete's agreement. The mechanics of contract making are simple. Both parties make binding promises involving the exchange of a sum of money, services, or property. The terms of the agreement must be legal, and the parties must have the mental capacity to contract. This means attaining a certain age (usually eighteen years) and understanding the nature and consequences of the agreement they make. As a practical matter, the terms of a contract should be as definite and specific as possible. Otherwise, a court must interpret the contract for the parties.

It is best to view sports contracts as a variant of entertainment contracts. In both cases, talent performing personal services is the centerpiece of the contract. Unlike commercial contracts involving mass-produced goods, in an agreement involving talent (in this case, the sports-oriented talent) one party agrees to perform certain specified tasks at a level of expertise that may not be easily replaceable.

Before players unionized, general managers often imposed contracts on them because the players had little bargaining position. Professional athletes lacked free agency rights and lacked representation by agents. Additionally, such agreements were interpreted in unusual ways. Until the mid-1970s, most players signed one-year contracts, which contained a unique form of option clause, known as a "reserve clause," essentially binding the player to the team for his entire playing career. These onerous clauses were eliminated through collective bargaining, arbitration, or court rulings, as discussed in chapter 6.

## Contracts Involving Team Sports Athletes

Presently, each of the four major sports leagues (Major League Baseball, NFL, NBA, NHL) has unionized players and collective bargaining agreements (CBAs) between the union and the league. As noted earlier, the CBAs cover many of the items found in an individual player's contract. For example, grievance and salary arbitrations derive from the CBA. In some leagues, salaries and ranges of salaries, and minimums, especially for rookies but also for veterans, are regulated. The salary regulations found in the CBAs of Major League Baseball, the NBA, the NFL, and the NHL are discussed in more detail in chapter 6.

Bonus provisions sometimes serve as a key component. Examples include rewards for winning a championship or making it to a playoff round. Also, bonuses for certain individual achievements (1500 yards rushing, forty stolen bases, scoring fifty goals) are not uncommon, or, in the case of coaches, for winning a certain number of games and/or a conference championship.

Despite the fact that the parties—the team and the player—have concluded an agreement, the commissioner of the league retains the power to void the document if it is deemed contrary to the "best interests of the sport." Essentially, all contracts are conditional on the approval of the commissioner, even though in the four major leagues the athlete is employed by a particular team and signs a contract with the team, not the league. In a "single-entity" league, the athlete may be employed directly by the league.

## Contracts Involving Individual Sports Athletes

Contracts involving individual competitors offer different issues. Professional golfers, tennis players, and boxers, for example, are not employees. Rather, they are independent contractors: in essence, people competing for prizes in competition. Although a team athlete is paid a salary whether his or her team wins or loses, individual athletes sign a participation contract with stipulated winnings if they attain a certain level of success at that event. However, some athletes get paid "appearance fees" for simply participating in the event, often in an attempt to attract public interest (described in more detail in chapter 2).

There are other key differences between a team athlete and an individual competitor. In order to qualify to participate in an event, an individual athlete must demonstrate evidence of past success or a sports-wide ranking level based on a system like the Association of Tennis Professionals (ATP) in tennis. Also, athletes (or their sponsors) must pay expenses such as for transport, housing, and equipment, in contrast to team athletes, whose expenses, including transport, lodging, and meal allowances, are paid by their team.

## Key Clauses in a League–Player Contract

For those writing about sports, a working knowledge of a league's standard players' contract is beneficial. Such a contract (essentially a form) is found on various sites on the Internet, such as NBPA.com (the website of the NBA players' union). Similarities in the provisions among each of the four major league contracts outweigh the differences. A basic examination of the major provisions in a typical players' contract follows. A journalist should not focus simply on the salary provisions; other sections merit scrutiny as well.

*Salary.* A player receives a base salary, often coupled with performance bonuses. Often the bonuses will be contingent on surpassing a stipulated level in such statistics as field goal percentage, rebounds, or, in the case of an NBA contract, points per game. Additionally, bonuses for being picked for an All-Star team or winning awards such as the "most valuable player" title will be factored (Greenberg & Gray, 1998).

The use of "guaranteed" contracts varies from league to league. In Major League Baseball, as of 2005, 190 player contracts contained guaranteed salaries (often negating many of the standard grounds for termination;

Bodley, 2005). In the NFL, the practice is far less frequent. In addition, marquee players have also been able to negotiate guaranteed salary clauses or escape clauses allowing them to reopen the contract in the event that their salary does not place them within a specified number of top-paid players in that position. In other cases, teams, most frequently those in the NFL, have been able to persuade players to agree to deferred compensation, that is, delaying payment of portions of a salary or a signing bonus to a specified period after those payments would normally be due.

An escalator clause may appear in a player's contract. More than a simple bonus clause, this provision rewards a player's extraordinary performance by automatically raising the value of the player's contract to a level commensurate with, say, the NFL's elite performers at that player's position.

*Services.* This clause states what is required of the player. In the NBA agreement, the player is required to participate in training camp, team practices, exhibition games, regular season games, All-Star events, playoff games, and certain stipulated promotional activities (NBA Uniform Player Contract, 2010, sec. 2). A player cannot simply "feel like" not playing in the All-Star game. Likewise, unexplained absences from practices, games, and promotional events also violate this clause. Rarely does a team terminate a player based on individual violations, but the team can (and often does) impose fines on the player.

*Expenses.* With the kinds of salaries found in the major sports leagues, one does not think of incidental expenses. Yet this section mandates that a team must cover "proper and necessary" expenses, including lodging, food, and transportation. The precise meal expenses are set forth in the particular CBA.

*Conduct.* This provision is typically underestimated in any player contract. When examining this clause, note its broad language and the many types of potential misconduct that could be covered. An example is Paragraph 7(b)(1) of Major League Baseball's uniform players' contract, which states that a club may terminate a contract if the player should "fail, refuse or neglect to conform his personal conduct to the standards of good citizenship and good sportsmanship" (Major League Baseball Uniform Players' Contract, 2007–11, sec. 7(b)). To alleviate the potential harshness, punishment (usually fines and/or suspensions) may be challenged by the player in front of an independent arbitrator.

A player is required to give his or her "best services" as well as "loyalty" to the team. This is hard to define (an exception to what was said earlier about the precision of contracts) because it is extremely difficult to determine when a player does not give his or her "best" so as to constitute a violation. However, a more frequent violation involves a prohibition on taking any action "detrimental to the best interests of the team and the league." Examples of such actions include public criticism by a player of a team coach, owner, league, or referees. Such actions may result in fines or suspensions by either the team or the league. Even political statements and commentary may be deemed a violation. Journalists should understand the legal principle involved. Because the player works for a private organization, the U.S. Constitution's First Amendment protection against laws abridging freedom of speech does not apply and such a clause, although possibly unfair, is not illegal.

One interesting contract dispute centered on a "loyalty clause" inserted by Cincinnati Bengals management in the 2000 season. The clause, which appeared in many of its players' contracts, provided that "the Club, in its sole discretion," could withhold a signing bonus at any time if it felt the player made "any public comment to the media . . . that breaches Player's obligation of loyalty to Club and/or undermines the public's respect for the Club, Club coaches, or Club management" (Fielder, 2002). In other words, it was a gag order to prohibit criticism of the team's management. The idea originated after the Bengals' then wide receiver Carl Pickens publicly criticized the team and its management. Pickens was three months shy of receiving his $3.5 million signing bonus when he made the comments critical of the team's decision to re-sign coach Bruce Coslet. An arbitrator upheld the clause, concluding that it did not violate the terms of the CBA (Cyphers, 2001; Groeschen, 2001).

Most professional contracts include a clause prohibiting a player from betting or attempting to bet on any league contest. The NBA's standard contract, for example, specifically states that the commissioner has the sole authority to suspend the player or expel the player from the league (NBA Uniform Player Contract, 2010, sec. 5(e)). In contrast to the player's general right to challenge a determination of misconduct, a determination of gambling is unappealable. That distinction demonstrates the importance of a "no-tolerance" policy on gambling.

*Physical Condition.* All agreements mandate that players must be in "good physical condition" throughout the season. Often the failure to maintain such a level of playing condition, in the opinion of the team doctor, gives the team the right to suspend the player until he or she becomes so conditioned, again in the opinion of the physician. The player's salary will be reduced accordingly for the time suspended. If, however, the player is injured while playing, the player will retain his or her salary during that injury period.

*Prohibited Substances.* The professional sports leagues address the issue of substance abuse. The NBA has a detailed set of provisions regarding substance abuse by players, and a player's failure to adhere to those conditions will result in suspension and possible termination of the agreement. The issue of substance testing, particularly in regard to performance-enhancing drugs, and how it is handled differs among the leagues, individual sports, and Olympic sports, and is discussed in detail in chapter 10.

*Unique Skills.* All major league contracts contain a clause, such as that found in the NBA contracts, which state that all league players "have extraordinary and unique skills and abilities, such that a team can seek the remedy of injunction (as noted earlier) from a judge or arbitrator" (NBA Uniform Player Contract, 2010, sec. 9). This is an attempt to "force" a court or arbitrator to treat a breach of contract with an injunction. However, it does not necessarily mean that a court or arbitrator will impose this remedy. As mentioned earlier, this remedy is discretionary.

*Assignment (Player Trades).* In the overwhelming majority of cases, a player's contract permits assigning (the official term for trading) that player to another team. Note that the right to trade players is unique to the world of sports. In no other area of employment does it exist. Although some elite athletes have no-trade clauses or trade clauses limited to specific teams, teams do not like to have this right restricted.

*Validity, Filing, and Commissioner Disapproval.* Filing of league player contracts with the commissioner's office is usually required, and the commissioner retains the right to disapprove the contract, if authorized pursuant to a league's constitution, bylaws, or CBA with the union.

*Other Athletic Activities.* A team invests considerable money, benefits, and resources in its athletes, and it does not want its players engaging in conduct likely to cause injury or that may detract from his or her focus on the sport. This clause prohibits a player from engaging in "other sports [that] may impair or destroy his [or her] ability and skill as a player" (NBA Uniform Player Contract, 2010, sec. 9). Often written team consent is required for the player to engage in sports endangering his or her health or safety, notably boxing, wrestling, sky-diving, baseball, football, hockey, and off-season basketball. However, allowed sports often include amateur golf, tennis, handball, swimming, hiking, softball, and volleyball.

*Promotional Activities.* Although individuals have commercial rights in their names, voices, and likenesses, this clause allows the league or team to take photos and video of the player for use in promotional and publicity purposes. Often the player is restricted from participating in radio or television programs or sponsoring commercial products without the consent of the team. This section also requires the player to be available for media interviews.

*Group License.* Each of the leagues has a licensing division, and this clause states that a player consents to have his or her image used and shares in royalties generated from that image. The great majority of players in the major leagues consent to this, although there are some opt-out provisions. Chapter 12 details the licensing system.

*Termination.* Although rare, this provision gives a team the right to terminate a player's contract if the player fails to act with "good moral character," and good sportsmanship, to keep him- or herself in "first-class physical condition," and to obey the team's training rules. In the NBA's player contract, termination may occur if the player commits "a significant and inexcusable physical attack against any official or employee of the team or the NBA (other than another player), or any person in attendance at any NBA game or event" (NBA Uniform Player Contract, 2010, sec. 16(a)(ii)). The team must consider "the totality of the circumstances" in making its decision.

## Contract Negotiations

From a business point of view, any contract negotiation involves "give and take" between the parties. But the amount of compromise depends on the bargaining power of each party, an obvious but salient point for those involved in the contract process or those covering contract negotiations. A journeyman player often accepts whatever a team offers. On the other hand, a marquee player has the upper hand because the team needs that player more. The same can be said of a coach, general manager, or broadcaster.

The athlete's representative must have familiarity with the league constitution, the terms of the CBA, the salary cap rules (if applicable), the value of the player, and how that athlete compares with others. The prominent sports agent Leigh Steinberg noted the following:

> Once you understand the collective bargaining agreement and the trends, the second step is to try to understand the client's negotiation position. Aside from preparation, this is perhaps the most important step because it is not simply a function of what the name of your client is or what number he is picked. Rather, it is really a question of how much leverage you have. Leverage is the bottom line in my business (Falk, 1992).

Leverage encompasses several concepts, some obvious, others less so. The first is simply talent. A top draft pick has more leverage than lower picks. Then there is a record of performance. For veteran players, evidence of prior success (as compared with other players playing a similar position) is crucial. However, leverage also involves more intangible concepts, such as fan popularity. If the athlete has developed a public persona that attracts fans to games, that counts as an important advantage at the bargaining table, even if the athlete is not necessarily an All-Star. Finally, team leadership—the impact that the athlete has in the locker room with other members of the team—comes into play. Often this involves a veteran player whose statistics may not be first rate, but whose years of experience and presence motivate the rest of the team. Conversely, attitude problems weaken leverage. A talented but spoiled player causing dissension in the team is a negative. Additionally, players who do not perform well in "big" games suffer from a weakened bargaining position.

Many make the mistake of thinking that the only result of leverage is a high-salary contract. Of course high salary is very important, but a good negotiator looks at other key negotiating points. One is termination. A four-year, $5 million per year guaranteed contract, which limits or prohibits termination by the team, may be more valuable than a three-year, $10 million per year contract with a broader right to terminate.

In the NFL, the leverage focuses around the signing bonus. Many express surprise about high signing bonuses (much higher than in other sports), but, because NFL contracts are often not guaranteed and teams can "cut" players with relative ease, these bonus monies serve as the only "guaranteed" portion of the contract. Essentially a trade-off, the system fosters fewer guarantees for more bonuses. Another trade-off is current cash dollars versus deferred money. David Falk, another well-known agent, stated, "Deferred money is one of the most abused areas in professional sports contracts. That is why I like to call it 'funny money'" (Falk, 1992). He felt that the devaluation of money due to inflation makes the deferred amount worth considerably less than it would be if paid upfront. However, deferred income may be an area of compromise, as a team may be willing to pay more in deferred income than in upfront money. However, note that certain sports limit the amount of deferred compensation to be paid. In the NBA it is not more than 30 percent of the total salary (Falk, 1992).

Leigh Steinberg echoes the above strategy regarding incentive bonuses: "When you are negotiating a contract and you are apart in your positions, one area available to you to close the deal is incentive bonuses" (Falk, 1992). Although it is best to maximize guaranteed money, incentives can be used to close gaps. However, a contract loaded with incentives may put undue pressure on the athlete to succeed because so much of his income is based on surpassing the stipulated goals.

## Coaches' Contracts

### Collegiate Coaching

Although we have focused on athlete contracts, professional and college coaches often negotiate complex agreements covering many more subjects than simple compensation, as their jobs are far more involved than simply coaching a group of athletes. The college coach is required to be not only an instructor, but also a fund raiser, recruiter, academic coordinator, public figure, budget director, television and radio personality, and whatever else the university's athletic director or president may direct the coach to do in the best interest of the university's athletic program (Greenberg & Gray, 1998). Specifically, college coaches must address issues such as student graduation rates, prevention of criminal conduct, and National Collegiate Athletic Association (NCAA) rules enforcement. Even winning may not guarantee job security for a college coach. If attendance is down and the university's alumni simply do not like the coach's performance (even if he or she can demonstrate a winning record), tenure can be very short.

Contracts involving men's college basketball and football are increasingly lucrative because these sports generate large revenues in a number of institutions. In fact, the amounts paid in salary and other compensation for coaches have increased dramatically. In 2009, at least twenty-five college head football coaches drew annual compensation of at least $2 million. According to a study in *USAToday*, the average pay for a head coach in the NCAA's top-level, 120-school Football Bowl Subdivision (FBS) increased 28 percent from 2007 and an astounding 46 percent from 2006, to an average of $1.36 million. Many earn more than their college presidents (Wieberg, Upton, Perez, & Berkowitz, 2009).

Contracts for coaches of less popular sports and women's sports are more straightforward employment agreements. For journalists covering a particular contract controversy, coaches' contracts from public institutions are generally available under disclosure laws, and it is very important to read them.

Successful college coaches increasingly sign multiyear, seven-figure contracts laden with bonus provisions and income potential outside of coaching. In addition to base salary, a successful college coach can derive income from TV and radio shows, endorsement contracts with shoe companies, speaking engagements, and summer camps (Greenberg & Gray, 1998). College coaches must adhere to NCAA rules, and their failure to do so may result in suspension without pay or outright termination (NCAA Division I Bylaws, 2009, sec. 11.2.1). Among the prohibitions, coaches cannot give remuneration or compensation to student-athletes or pay assistant coaches extra money (NCAA Division I Bylaws, 2009, sec. 11.1.03).

The following are some key sections found in college coaches' contracts.

*Term.* Much like athletes' contracts, the term of a coach's contract is dictated by the past successes attained. A successful coach will often have a multiyear contract. Sometimes, a "rollover" provision will be included, which works as an extension of the contract if the university is "satisfied" with the coach's performance after a particular season. For example, coach X has a five-year contract and, after the first year, the university is satisfied with his performance; the contract term then increases to five more years, from four. Who benefits from this rollover clause? Of course, the coach does because his employment extends another year (or more, if the clause is activated more often). However, a persuasive argument can be made that the university benefits even more because (a) the school triggers the clause at its discretion and (b) the clause serves to "lock in" this coach for a longer period of time and prevents other schools from recruiting that person without inducing a breach of contract.

*Reassignment.* This clause, unique to a college coach's agreement, permits the university to remove the person as head coach, but not to terminate the contract. Instead, "reassignment" to another job commensurate with the person's skill and duties occurs. The disadvantage of a reassignment clause for a top-flight coach is obvious: It serves as a way to keep the talented person from going elsewhere. This form of "golden handcuffs" often stipulates that the failure of the coach to accept the alternative employment constitutes a breach of contract, possibly subjecting him or her to an injunction barring the coach from working elsewhere.

*Base Salary, Fringe Benefits, and Bonuses.* Every coach's contract will provide for some base salary. However, top-flight collegiate coaching agreements are filled with fringe benefits, such as free automobiles, free housing (or a down-payment toward a house), and moving expenses. The bonus provisions may turn out to be more lucrative than the base salary. They include a signing bonus, and bonuses for participation in postseason tournaments, attaining a certain win–loss record, victories in postseason tournaments, graduation rates for students, and increases in attendance (Greenberg & Gray, 1998).

*Termination.* As in the case of an athlete's contract, the termination clauses are especially important. There are basically two types of terminations: "just cause" and "without cause." "Just cause" means based on a proper, independent reason, usually a specific violation of law or regulation. For example, as part of the NCAA requirements, the coach can be terminated for "just cause" such as violating those rules. Usually the infraction is "major" (i.e., intentional), and can result from a subordinate's violation of the rules as well.

In 2003, two well-respected collegiate coaches lost their jobs as a result of off-field activities. Larry Eustachy, the former Iowa State men's basketball coach, was drinking with coeds and fraternizing with frat boys at a college party. Mike Price, who lasted just a few weeks as University of Alabama's football coach, allegedly visited a strip club and reportedly brought two strippers back to his hotel room for a night of sex (O'Donnell, 2003). Price sued *Sports Illustrated* for defamation and a settlement was negotiated in 2005. He became the head coach of the University of Texas–El Paso in 2003.

Neither action had any bearing on the individuals' ability as a coach. And neither coach committed a crime. But, whether or not each committed a crime, each suffered a public embarrassment that caused the university to reconsider the coach's continued employment. The schools thought that the bad publicity would limit each coach's effectiveness and would hurt the school's athletic program (Smith, 2003).

As an example of a college coach's contract, let us examine the agreement between the former men's basketball coach Bob Knight (who came to Texas Tech from Indiana University amid controversy over his coaching methods) and his then-employer, Texas Tech University. Because Texas Tech is a public institution, this contract is publicly available. Signed on March 23, 2001, the original agreement's five-year term was extended three years in 2004. Knight and the school structured the agreement to give Knight a base compensation of $250,000 per year (a low figure for someone of Knight's caliber).

Other details of this contract merit interest. Knight's term of employment was ten months per year, giving him two "free" months to earn extra income. Furthermore, the agreement permitted him to run private "summer camps" on school facilities. Following was a key section, entitled "Guarantee of Outside Athletics Related Income," stating that, if Knight's income outside of his base did not add up to $500,000 annually, the university guaranteed any of the shortfall. That outside income included endorsement agreements for clothing, shoes, TV and radio shows, sports camps, and some speaking engagements. Excluded were book contracts and TV advertisement contracts. This means the school could guarantee Knight three-quarters of a million dollars per season. Knight's contract also included a deferred compensation plan, deferring certain percentages of his income, and two free automobiles.

The contract specified that Knight risked termination if he violated any NCAA, Big 12 Conference, or university rules. Such a "morals clause" is a highly important provision in such contracts. For example, the University of Texas–El Paso negotiated such a clause in Mike Price's five-year contract, which required that Price "conduct himself with due regard to public convention and morals, shall not do any act that will tend to degrade him in society or bring him into public hatred, contempt, scorn or ridicule, or that will tend to shock or insult the community or offend public morals or decency." It was the first time the school ever included such a section in a coach's contract (Moore, 2004).

*Liquidated Damages.* More and more coaches' contracts contain a clause that specifies monetary damages in the event that the coach and/or the school breach the contract. Stating the damage amount is an effective way to impose a sanction because it avoids the difficulty of proving damages for the loss, a vexing problem in personal services contracts. For example, the former West Virginia football coach Rich Rodriguez had to pay $4 million in liquidated damages when he left that school to accept the head coaching position at the University of Michigan, the amount stipulated in his contract (although, as part of the settlement, Michigan paid $2.5 million of that amount) (RichRodriguezLaw Blog, 2008).

### Professional Coaching

Many of the issues just discussed also apply to professional coaches' contracts. As in the case of their collegiate counterparts, professional coach and manager contracts are personal services contracts with few legal requirements. Since coaches are not unionized, no labor law or collective bargaining requirements exist. Also, salary limitations due to "salary caps" do not apply. Lastly, professional coaches often lack job security. They can be dismissed at the will of the owner or general manager. In the case of an inexperienced or minor league coach, they will no longer be paid. Note that, because professional coaches work for private organizations, no legal requirement of public disclosure exists. An exception occurs if a coach or his or her team is in litigation, because court documents are public records.

Often a professional coach's contract will have a base salary, coupled with bonuses for on-the-field success. Team owners may further sweeten the deal by adding housing allowances, radio and television opportunities, and public speaking. In 1994, in his first year at the helm of the NHL's New York Rangers, Mike Keenan coached the team to its first Stanley Cup championship in 54 years. Keenan's contract consisted of the following provisions:

- Term: five years.
- Compensation: base salary of $750,000 (year 1), increasing to $850,000, $900,000, $950,000, and $1,000,000 annually for the ensuing four years.

- Signing bonus: $660,875.
- Loan to purchase residence: $400,000 (or 75 percent of the purchase price) at an interest rate of 5 percent per year.
- Incentive clauses: If the team attained these goals, Keenan would be paid the following:
  - Best overall regular season record in the NHL—$50,000.
  - Second best overall regular season record—$25,000.
  - First in the conference—$40,000.
  - First in the division—$25,000.
- Postseason bonuses: If the team participated in the NHL postseason playoffs the bonuses would be as follows: winning first round, $50,000; winning second round, $75,000; winning third round, $100,000; winning Stanley Cup, $200,000.
- Coach of the Year:
  - If Keenan received the "Coach of the Year" award—$25,000.
  - If he was second in the voting—$12,500.
  - If he was third—$7000.
- Miscellaneous: The club was willing to provide an annuity of $50,000 per year commencing when he reached the age of fifty-five years and continuing until his death (assuming he fulfilled the contract) (Conrad, 1995).

Keenan's contract specified that Keenan's bonus payments were to be sent within thirty days after the conclusion of the NHL season.

In return, Keenan was required to devote "substantially all of his time, attention, skills and energies to coaching the team, in consultation and subject to the prior approval of the General Manager of the club." He warranted "extraordinary and unique" skills and ability with regard to the sport of professional hockey. His services were therefore exclusive and irreplaceable to the club. Because of Keenan's stature, the contract specified that any loss or breach could not be adequately compensated with money damages, thereby granting the team injunctive relief to stop the questionable activities. The contract specifically forbade any services and duties for any other professional hockey team, or any business venture competing with the Rangers or the team's corporate parent at the time, Paramount Communications.

Because the team wanted Keenan's services, he negotiated some important protections. He could be discharged only for "cause"—meaning material (major) breach of obligations or unreasonable neglect. If such cause was involved, the contract gave him twenty days to cure the problem. If no cure occurred, the team's obligations would cease. The "morals clause" was quite limited, stating that Keenan's dismissal was justifiable only due to conviction of a felony or a plea of *nolo contendere* (no contest) with respect to a felony charge. Convictions for misdemeanors then would not be grounds for termination for cause. The agreement also provided that, if the team discharged Keenan "without cause," Keenan would receive a lump sum of 75 or 50 percent of his remaining base salary, depending on the date of notice.

One month after the team won the Stanley Cup, Keenan abruptly terminated his relationship with the Rangers, despite the fact that he had four years left on his contract. He claimed that the team breached the contract because his performance bonus check arrived one day later than prescribed in the contract. The Rangers sued Keenan in U.S. District Court in New York, but the case was settled through the intervention of the NHL commissioner's office (Swift, 1997).

## Insurance

Given the lucrative contracts that star athletes sign, player disability insurance policies have become a very important vehicle to protect the team from long-term injuries. These policies may be issued to athletes in all major sports, but the sport where insurance issues have been particularly important has been Major League Baseball, in which many player contracts are guaranteed. The following scenario provides the reason: Say that player X has a five-year guaranteed contract and gets a career-ending injury during a game or in practice after the first week of the first year. That player is entitled to the rest of his compensation—for the entire five years. With so much money at stake, it behooves the team to carry insurance.

Relatively little has been written about the costs of disability insurance contracts on overall team finances. One report put the total cost of insurance premiums paid by baseball teams in 2002 at $55 million (Chass, 2002).

Insurance contracts generally cover 60 to 80 percent of the value of the player's contract. At one time, these contracts covered up to five years of a player's contract. More recently, however, the term has been reduced to three years. In addition to the 9/11 effect, another reason cited is the case of Albert Belle. In 2002, Belle, an All-Star player who rarely missed games on account of injury, was diagnosed with a degenerative hip condition that forced his retirement. Belle was covered by an insurance policy that paid his team, the Baltimore Orioles, $27.3 million of his remaining $39 million salary. Belle was forced to retire after playing only two seasons of his five-year contract, valued at $65 million.

Brian D. Burns, the chairman and chief executive officer of Pro Financial Services, one of two companies that underwrite most professional sports contracts, said that Belle's injury "shook everybody." "He was the kind of guy you would always want to insure. [This injury] told insurance companies that the rates had to go up and they had to go up dramatically" (Quinn, 2001). Journalists should probe team officials to confirm the existence of such policies on a disabled player because it challenges the belief that a team had to "eat" the athlete's entire salary in the case of a permanent disability of a guaranteed salaried player.

## Endorsement Contracts

Athlete product endorsement agreements have become a very important source of income for the relatively few professional athletes who have the marketability and name recognition to be able to make such contracts. The greater exposure of sports and sports-related businesses over the last quarter-century has resulted in major increases in the compensation and scope of these agreements. At one time, endorsements were limited to local products. Dean Chance, a former Cy Young winner who pitched for the Minnesota Twins, signed an endorsement agreement with a local orange juice company. His compensation was $6000 per year and an unlimited amount of juice (Reed, 2003). Although agreements to endorse a local supermarket or auto dealership still exist, superstar athletes such as LeBron James and Tiger Woods have exemplified the modern trend of high-priced endorsement agreements. These contracts have bolstered the image of the company by branding the merchandise with the persona of that athlete and help turn the athlete into a cultural icon, with worldwide exposure. Two aspects make these deals different from past agreements: (a) The products endorsed are not niche products catering to a small class of enthusiasts, but products or brands that have general public appeal, such as Pepsi and Buick; and (b) even brands that are athletic in nature, such as Nike, are given a broader appeal because of the endorser. Such an agreement, although made with sports manufacturing companies, may include leisure clothing and eyewear. But this has to be put into perspective. Relatively few athletes achieve endorsement heaven. Many, if not most, athletes who are able to endorse products still do so on the local level or work for sports firms marketing to an audience of devotees. The few like James—who signed a $93 million seven-year deal in 2003 (which was extended in 2010)—hit the jackpot.

Any athlete (or coach) endorsing a product is bringing a level of public confidence and credibility to that product. Yet that can be destroyed quickly and easily by acts that are criminal, immoral, or offensive. Endorsement contracts contain a "morals clause" terminating the relationship in the event of such actions. In 1997, the Professional Golfers Association golfer Fuzzy Zoeller made racially charged comments about Tiger Woods. Woods was to host a champions' luncheon at the next year's Masters, to which Zoeller said, "Tell [Woods] not to serve fried chicken or collard greens or whatever the hell they serve." For his statement, which he considered a joke, Zoeller was dropped as a spokesman by Kmart. Certainly criminal acts would likely result in a loss of an endorsement contract despite a subsequent acquittal. O. J. Simpson's endorsement agreements were terminated, despite his acquittal of murder charges. More recently, in 2007, Nike terminated its endorsement deal with the then Atlanta Falcons quarterback Michael Vick, who was convicted and jailed for bankrolling a dog-fighting ring (Reuters, 2009). In 2009, the cereal maker Kellogg's decided not to renew its endorsement deal with the record-breaking gold medal swimmer Michael Phelps after pictures surfaced of him smoking marijuana (Lemke, 2009). Tiger Woods lost AT&T, Accenture, and Gatorade after it was revealed he had adulterous affairs with a number of women (NYPost.com, 2010).

## The Marketing Assessment

A firm seeking to engage an athlete to endorse its products must find a "marketable" athlete who projects a sellable image with a targeted group that the firm thinks is likely to buy its product. In the past, this meant a "positive" image, but more recently that is not necessarily the case. An executive vice-president of player marketing noted that bad behavior can sell a product, while a player of high character may not. Referring to the NBA player Tim Duncan, whom some consider "dull and boring," she noted that, if lawbreakers are considered better pitchmen, it legitimizes such bad behavior (Jacobson, 2003). For certain audiences, Allen Iverson's tougher, more rakish image has the pull for him to achieve financial success in the endorsement business and make millions in playing contracts and endorsement deals. In 2008, he reportedly made $7 million in endorsements (Freedman, 2009).

Of course, there is no magic formula to predict success. In an excellent primer to endorsement agreements, Pamela Lester noted:

> The athlete's desire for endorsements, willingness to make personal appearances in connection with those endorsements, his or her likes and dislikes, strengths and weaknesses should be considered. A successful advertising campaign promotes both the athlete and the endorsed product by matching the product to the athlete, and vice versa. [And] knowledge of all the athlete's past and present endorsements is critical (Lester, 2002, ch. 27, sec. 10).

In choosing an athlete, firms will consider public image, reputation, and personality. Just because an athlete is an All-Star does not make him or her a successful seller of the product. Conversely, just because someone did not win a championship does not preclude that person from consummating lucrative endorsement deals.

The former tennis pro Anna Kournikova serves as a telling example. Despite a career devoid of anything better than a quarter-final victory in a Grand Slam tournament and no more than a number 8 ATP ranking, she demonstrated the personality and sex appeal that resulted in agreements with firms such as Adidas (sportswear) and Lycos (search engines). In 1999, she earned an estimated $10–15 million in endorsements fees, making her second only to Venus Williams (who signed a $40 million deal with Reebok). Even in 2003, with her skills waning, she still earned more money in endorsements than Serena Williams. At the time, Kournikova had both a domestic U.S. following as well as an international one. Such popularity is increasingly important, as globalization has become a fixture in the business marketplace. But popularity in the U.S. market is still a crucial prerequisite for endorsement success. In 2008, thanks to her success and appeal, Maria Sharapova earned about $26–30 million (*Sports Business Daily*, 2009) She earned more money in endorsements than Serena Williams, who pocketed a reported $12–15 million annually on her endorsement deals (*Sports Business Daily*, 2008). In the case of Sharapova, her appeal has been so great that her representative hinted that she may drop some sponsors in favor of clothing deals that give her a fixed percentage of sales (Rossingh, 2010).

Team athletes have a more difficult time achieving international stature (especially for sports such as baseball and American football, which have less appeal abroad) than tennis players and golfers, who play in tournaments all over the world. Their names and faces may be as familiar to fans in Tokyo as in Tallahassee.

The economics of the particular firm or industry creates a certain "up-and-down" aspect to the endorsement market. Past economic prosperity expanded opportunities for endorsements, but more recent corporate downsizing has resulted in a diminution of opportunities. Changes in popular taste and social mores also have effects. Although "noncontroversial" white males were coveted in the past, that changed in the 1980s with the success of Michael Jordan and other African-American stars in the NBA. And, as noted earlier, the ability of "bad boys" such as John McEnroe and, later, Allen Iverson to secure endorsements demonstrates a change. Even Latrell Sprewell obtained an endorsement deal shortly after choking his coach.

## The Key Clauses

As noted earlier, some young journalists make the mistake of focusing solely on the compensation. One can argue that the most important sections are the "endorsed products" and termination sections.

*Endorsed Products.* Exactly what is to be endorsed must be specified in the agreement, not only so that the parties know exactly what they have to do, but also to avoid the problem of conflicting products. For example, let's say that golfer X has an endorsement agreement with a company that makes "golf equipment." Does that include shoes? If so, just shoes worn at golf tournaments? If the golfer wants to endorse sneakers for another company, does that conflict with the obligations under the first agreement? That point has to be addressed.

Some endorsement agreements—especially those with multinational firms that manufacture equipment, apparel, and shoes—may be "head-to-toe" deals, covering every product manufactured (e.g., hats, shirts, pants, athlete shoes). This is the goal of the companies, who want to "lock in" the athlete to everything they make as part of the compensation paid. On the other hand, an athlete (or coach) may seek individual deals for, say, golf clubs, leisurewear, and athletic shoes. If an athlete is relatively unknown at the time of the golf club agreement and becomes more successful and better known after that, that athlete's power to negotiate a more lucrative contract for the later deals remains intact.

*Termination.* In terms of negotiation, the athlete or coach wants more protection against termination and the company more power to terminate if certain stipulated events occur. If not taken seriously by both sides, the results can lead to acrimony and litigation.

Frequently, the company contracts the right to terminate if the athlete becomes disabled or retires from the sport. It may well be that certain compensation may be given, but a sports-oriented business may not find much use in a "former" athlete endorsing its tennis racquets.

Then there is the "morals" clause. We have already discussed the importance of the reputation of the endorser. This clause, in effect, makes the agreement dependent on continuation of that reputation. With so many news reports of athlete misconduct, the company does not want a "tarnished" endorser on its roster. Such an individual creates a public relations problem and does not inspire confidence in the company or its products by the public. And the company certainly does not want to continue paying the athlete after the athlete engages in particular transgressions.

Of course, the athlete wants this clause to be limited whereas the company wants broader enforcement. In any case, the scope of what is "immoral" is hard to define. A typical clause states that, if the athlete commits acts "tending to bring himself/herself into public disrepute, contempt, scandal, or ridicule, or tending to shock, insult, or offend the people of this nation or any class or group thereof, or reflecting unfavorably upon Company's reputation or products, then Company shall have the right, upon oral or written notice, to immediately terminate this agreement." This is far more than simple illegal conduct. And it should be. It includes noncriminal conduct such as obnoxious behavior, offensive public statements, or even controversial political actions. An athlete who decided to go to a country hostile to the United States and make public statements urging its leaders to attack the United States would not be endorsing the company's products (in the United States) for very long. A coach who made offensive statements directed at certain groups of people could very well suffer termination. Also, drug or alcohol abuse can serve to violate the morals clause. And, unlike some guaranteed coaches' or athletes' contracts, termination also means the end to compensation.

Alternatively, the athlete or coach may have termination rights as well, usually in the event that the firm becomes insolvent or fails to pay the required compensation. Possibly (but not frequently) the athlete may insist on a "morals clause" granting a right of termination in the event the company engages in improper or exploitative labor practices.

*Compensation.* The compensation is usually divided into two categories: base compensation and bonuses. Think of base compensation as a minimum wage. This payment is received no matter what the level of success. The bonuses are based on specific achievement. In the case of an individual athlete, bonus payments often apply to victories or high placements in given tournaments. In the case of a team athlete, criteria include selection to an All-Star team, team championships, or regular season division championship.

The breakdown between guaranteed money and bonus money depends on the nature of the negotiations and the strength of the parties. Especially for a younger athlete, focusing on larger base compensation is key, as no track record of achievement exists. The athlete need never win a match or have his/her team win a championship. For the company, limiting the base compensation (and the term) but basing the bulk of the potential monies on bonuses is a better strategy. It protects the firm from paying too much money in the event the athlete is a bust, either competitively or publicly.

A third method of compensation, known as a "royalty on products sold," is limited to what are known as "signature" products—products specifically carrying the athlete's name or likeness. An endorser may negotiate a provision creating such a "signature line," and a certain percentage of sales would be paid to the athlete. Usually, "signature-line" athletes are experienced, marquee performers.

*Term.* The time period of the agreement is always stated.

*Territory.* For an agreement with a national or multinational firm, the agreement is frequently worldwide in scope. It applies everywhere. If the deal is for a local firm, such as an auto dealership in Ames, it will cover Ames and its environs (as defined in the contract).

*Duties.* The agreement addresses the duties of the athlete or coach, which include personal appearances (the number and schedule to be specified or subsequently negotiated), and advertising in various media, notably print, broadcast, cable, and new media (Internet). Often the athlete or coach will have some right to approve advertising before a launch. As part of this duty, the company licenses the name and likeness of the athlete as part of its advertising and appearances. Also, the athlete must wear the clothing or use the equipment covered during tournaments and at other specified times.

*Other Provisions.* An endorsement contract should contain clauses dealing with options to renew or extend the term of the agreement, schedule of payments, and protections to the athlete in the event there is a lawsuit claiming liability for a defect in the manufacture and design of the equipment or the goods. These clauses, often called "right of refusal" or "right to exclusive negotiations" or "right to extend," are often drafted very carefully. A "choice of law" section, mandating what law applies in case of a dispute, is also a must.

## Sponsorship Agreements

For an event presenter, whether it be a local tennis match or the Olympic Games, paying sponsors are essential to the commercial success of the event. For the event organizer, the infusion of funds paid by one or more sponsors helps to defray the costs of planning and presenting the event. Sponsorships are also valuable because of the publicity the event gives the parties in terms of publicity, goodwill and advertising. Akin to the endorsement agreement, there are clauses of particular importance that can make the difference between a well-drafted agreement and one that leads to litigation.

Sponsorship agreements have been important for entities such as the National Association for Stock Car Racing (NASCAR) and the Olympics, as well as for tours, such as the Sony Ericsson Women's Tennis Association (WTA) and individual tournaments, such as a tennis or golf event. Various levels or categories of sponsorship include title or co-title sponsorship, team or vehicle sponsorship, associate or supporting sponsorship, broadcast sponsorship, or official supplier sponsorships. Beyond the fundamentals each provides, benefits can include on-site signage, on-court signage, or other on-field exposure. Moreover, benefits may include control over the sale of media rights (Yakovee, 2007).

The salient provisions of a sponsorship agreement are as follows.

*Product Categories.* There is nothing more important than exclusivity or sole sponsorship of the event in a particular "product category." Because the costs of sponsorship generally prohibit a single company from sponsoring the entire event, it is more frequent to award exclusive sponsorships for a certain type of product, such as "non-alcoholic beverage" or "automobile." Although simple enough, the problem is in the creation of the category. For example, does an "official credit card" include "charge cards" such as American Express? If it does, then the event cannot get sponsorship from American Express if it signs on MasterCard.

However, if "credit card" is defined as a credit instrument only, then it is possible to have both MasterCard and American Express as sponsors (with the latter being an official "charge card"). The latter benefits the event sponsor, while the former gives more power and marketing clout to MasterCard.

To avoid "product category creep" sponsors and sponsored organizations must create product terms that are precise. And they must think in marketing terms. For example, who are the competitors of the sponsor? For example, many sponsor deals use the term "financial services" to define a credit card since Visa and MasterCard function as lenders. Yet what if the event wishes to have an "official banking institution" as well as an "official financial services firm"? Problems may arise because both types of firm may perform some overlapping services.

The problem is exacerbated by the greater importance of digital technology. Creating product categories involving Internet service providers, Web-based search services, and voice over Internet protocol (VOIP) is terribly confusing and often involves considerable negotiations to craft the contours of these product categories.

*Renewals.* The process for renewing a sponsorship agreement poses some intricate issues. Is there an automatic right to renew? By which party? If not, what notice provisions are there to communicate the intention not to renew? Finally, what kinds of prerequisites must be fulfilled before a party decides to sign with a different sponsor?

The renewal provisions should be especially well drafted. If the agreement allows automatic renewal by one party based on certain conditions, then renewal is automatic if the conditions are fulfilled. For example, if a sponsorship agreement states that if ticket sales achieve a certain level then the sponsor must renew, extension of the contract occurs. More frequently, there are requirements of exclusive negotiations with the sponsor for a period of time before the athletic organization can negotiate with others. Or there can be a "right of first refusal" clause, which requires that any competing offers must be matched by the present sponsor.

This problem involving such renewals was evident in a recent dispute between FIFA, the international soccer federation, and MasterCard. MasterCard paid $100 million for the right to sponsor the World Cup tournament for sixteen years. The sponsorship included the right to put its name in stadium and broadcast ads around the world. The contract had a ninety-day "exclusive negotiating period" whereby FIFA could not enter negotiations with any other firm for those rights. It also had a "right of first refusal" if FIFA received an offer after that exclusive negotiating period concluded. It turned out that FIFA officials were actively negotiating with Visa at the same time. Ultimately MasterCard and FIFA settled the case, whereby MasterCard received $90 million to drop any claims to sponsorship rights for future World Cups. Visa is currently the official credit card sponsor (Lee, 2007).

## Information Check

When covering contract issues, a journalist should determine:

1 Does a signed contract exist?
2 Is obtaining a copy of the contract possible?
3 If so, what are the terms? Note the key clauses, including base pay, bonus, and termination.
4 Is a morals clause found and, if so, what conduct serves to terminate the contract?
5 Did the team take out an insurance policy on the player? On the coach?
6 How does the contract compare with others for similar players or coaches with similar experience?
7 Does the contract conform to the terms of the particular player's collective bargaining agreement?
8 What bonuses and guarantees are found?
9 Other than the morals clause, what grounds exist for termination?
10 What remedies are sought by either athlete or team or, in the case of an individual athlete, between athlete and presenter, in the event of a breach?

## References

Abrams, J. (2009, October 5). NBA players make their way back to college. *New York Times*. Retrieved October 22, 2009, from http://www.nytimes.com/2009/10/06/sports/basketball/06nba.html

Barra, A. (2009, September 10). Is the gridiron game the same? *Wall Street Journal*. Retrieved October 24, 2009, from http://online.wsj.com/article/SB100014240 5297020344010457440149318000078.html

Bloom, B. (2008, December 4). MLB salary increase lowest since '04. *mlb.com*. Retrieved October 24, 2009, from http://www.mlb.com/news/article.jsp?ymd=20081204&content_id=3702956&vkey=news_mlb&fext=.jsp&c_id=mlb

Bodley, H. (2005, March 24). $2.97 billion payroll debt faces MLB for years to come. *USA Today*, p. 1C.

Central New York Basketball v. Barnett, 181 N.E.2d 506 (Common Pleas Court, Cuyahoga City, OH, 1961).

Chass, M. (2002, December 1). Costs are dictating 3-year offers. *New York Times*, p. 5.

Conrad, M. (1995). Perspective: Mike Keenan's power play—A slap shot against the Rangers and a slap on the wrist by the NHL. *Seton Hall Journal of Sports Law, 5*, 637.

Cyphers, L. (2001, January 26). Free speech getting sacks in contracts, players getting hit with all-out blitz. *New York Daily News*, p. 91.

Falk, D. (1992). The art of contract negotiation. *Marquette Sports Law Journal, 3*, 1, 7, 13.

Fielder, T. (2002). Keep your mouth shut and listen: The NFL player's right of free expression. *University of Miami Business Law Review, 10*, 547, 553.

Freedman, J. (2009). The fortunate 50. *Sports Illustrated*. Retrieved October 20, 2009, from http://sportsillustrated.cnn.com/more/specials/fortunate50/2009/index.5.html

Greenberg, M., & Gray, J. (1998). *Sports law practice* (vol. I, 2nd ed., pp. 264, 266, 523, 534, 591). Charlottesville, VA: Lexis.

Groeschen, T. (2001, January 23). Bengals' loyalty clause is upheld; Will be included in "most" contracts. *Cincinnati Enquirer*, p. D01.

Jacobson, S. (2003, July 13). The only values are marketability. *Newsday* (New York), p. B23.

Lee, K. (2007, June 21) MasterCard settles suit with FIFA, gets $90 million settlement. *USA Today*. Retrieved April 22, 2010, from http://www.usatoday.com/sports/soccer/2007-06-21-1058545345_x.htm

Lemke, T. (2009, February 6). Kellogg's and Michael Phelps. *The Washington Times*. Retrieved November 4, 2009, from http://www.washingtontimes.com/weblogs/sportsbiz/2009/Feb/06/kelloggs-and-michael-phelps/

Lester, P. (2002). Marketing the athlete: Endorsement contracts. In *The law of professional and amateur sports* (ch. 27, sec. 10). St. Paul, MN: West Group.

Major League Baseball, Uniform Players' Contract (2009). Retrieved, October 22, 2009, from http://mlbplayers.mlb.com/pa/pdf/cba_english.pdf

Moore, J. (2004, May 31). Price's deal contains morals clause. *Seattle Post-Intelligencer*, p. D2.

NBA Uniform Player Contract (2010). NBA Collective Bargaining Agreement, Exhibit A. Retrieved April 16, 2010, from http://www.nbpa.org/cba/2005/exhibit-national-basketball-association-uniform-player-contract

NCAA Division I Bylaws (2009). Retrieved April 1, 2010, from http://www.ncaa-publications.com/productdownloads/D110.pdf

*NYPost.com* (2010, February 27). Tiger just can't hold his drink. Retrieved March 25, 2010, from http://www.nypost.com/p/news/national/tiger_just_can_hold_his_drink_TDojJjNyGFPq2VNA0N5KrI

O'Donnell, C. (2003, December 28). College coaches gone wild. *Bergen* (NJ) *Record*, p. S10.

Quinn, T. J. (2001, November 25). Paying for it. Injuries to stars increasing insurance costs for teams. *New York Daily News*, p. 80.

Reed, T. (2003, May 25). Show me the money; it's much more of late. *Akron Beacon Journal*, p. A18.

Reuters (2009, October 1). Nike denies endorsement deal with NFL player Michael Vick. Retrieved November 4, 2009, from http://www.reuters.com/article/sportsNews/idUSTRE5903SW20091001

RichRodriguezLaw Blog (2008, July 13). Final thoughts on West Virginia University v. Rodriguez. Retrieved March 23, 2010, from http://richrodriguezlaw.blogspot.com/2008/07/final-thoughts-on-west-virginia.html

Rossingh, D. (2009, September 2). Sharapova shifts sponsorship focus to equity deals, agent says. Bloomberg.com. Retrieved March 25, 2010, from http://www.bloomberg.com/apps/news?pid=20601079&sid=an0SCSNVAjiY

Shinzawa, F. (2009, June 22). NHLPA on salary drive. *The Boston Globe*. Retrieved October 24, 2009, from http://www.boston.com/sports/hockey/articles/2008/06/22/nhlpa_on_salary_drive/

Smith, M. (2003, May 8). Coach's contracts have clauses with some claws; Schools try to deal themselves out of embarrassments. *Louisville Courier-Journal*, p. 1E.

*Sports Business Daily* (2008, September 9). Serena Williams hopes to ride U.S. Open win to new endorsements. Retrieved November 5, 2009, from http://www.sportsbusinessdaily.com/article/123828

*Sports Business Daily* (2009, April 26). Pepsico, Maria Sharapova end partnership after deal expires. Retrieved November 5, 2009, from http://www.sportsbusinessdaily.com/article/129433

Swift, E. (1997, October 13). Odd man out: Mike Keenan, a proven big winner, is seen as prickly and power hungry. Those traits have kept him from getting another NHL coaching job. *SIVault*. Retrieved May 12, 2010, from http://sportsillustrated.cnn.com/vault/article/magazine/MAG1011117/index.htm

Wieberg, S., Upton, J., Perez, A.J., & Berkowitz, S. (2009, November 11). College football coaches see salaries rise in down economy. Retrieved, November 11, 2009, from http://www.usatoday.com/sports/college/football/2009-11-09-coaches-salary-analysis_N.htm

Yakovee, V. (2007, Summer). Legal aspects of big sports event management—Part II—Sponsorships. *Entertainment and Sports Lawyer, 25*(1), 1.

# 6   Labor Relations in Sports

Labor relations between sports leagues and athletes present some of the most contentious issues in professional sports. In the last three decades, the intricacies of union–management relations and the tensions arising from disputes involving salaries and other working conditions have been frequently discussed on the sports pages and increasingly on the business pages as well. Suffice it to say that a knowledgeable journalist must have a solid understanding of labor issues. This chapter reviews the history of labor relations in professional sports and discusses the current collective bargaining agreements in place (as of 2010) in the major professional leagues.

## The Labor Laws

For the last seventy-five years, the National Labor Relations Act (NLRA), a comprehensive law passed in 1935, structures labor relations in the United States. The NRLA grants workers the right to form unions and engage in collective bargaining. It also permits workers to strike (known in legal parlance as a "concerted activity") in order to achieve their goals of improved benefits and working conditions. In 1947, additions to the NLRA, known as the Taft–Hartley amendments, expanded employer rights during the collective bargaining process.

Not surprisingly, the bases of labor disputes are grievances over "wages, hours and working conditions" (NLRA, 29 USC, sec. 151). The ways to accomplish a new collective bargaining agreement (CBA) are steeped in leverage and tactics.

Generally, a union represents employees in negotiation with their employers, and, under the NLRA, employees cannot be fired for participating in union-related activities. Once a union is formed and recognized, the law permits the use of a strike as a method to attain the union's goal of an improved CBA in the event that contract negotiations fail. Conversely, the labor law gives employers the right to "lock out" employees after the expiration of a CBA as a preemptive measure to show their leverage in attaining an agreement more to their liking.

The NLRA lists a series of activities known as "unfair labor practices." Violations result in sanctions by the National Labor Relations Board (NLRB), an administrative agency created under the statute. The most important of the unfair labor practices is the refusal of the parties to "bargain in good faith" with regard to wages, hours, or working conditions—so-called "mandatory subjects of collective bargaining." Although seemingly straightforward at first glance, in reality, this requirement has been the subject of considerable discussion by courts and law professors.

One example of lack of "good faith" involves protracted delaying tactics by one or both sides. Another involves an employer who takes unilateral action regarding wages, hours, and working conditions without consultation with the union (Cozzillio & Levinstein, 1998). An important exception to that rule occurs during an "impasse"—a situation where, after honest and hard-fought negotiation, the parties cannot agree to a new CBA. In such a case, an employer does have the right to unilaterally impose changes in the mandatory subjects such as wages and working conditions. An employer can impose a new minimum salary or a new overtime policy after an impasse occurs and the employer's actions would not violate labor law. The standards for determining an impasse are not always clear and the issue has occurred in labor disputes in Major League Baseball and the National Football League (NFL).

Although the NRLA gives workers the power to strike, it permits an employer to hire replacement employees and even to fire the strikers (MacNeil & Lehrer, 1993). Although athletes have been spared the remedy of termination, replacement players were used in the 1987 NFL players' strike and for a short time during the 1994–95 baseball players' strike (Selig, 1995).

For the union, the strike—or the threat of one—is the chief weapon. For management, it is the lockout. Although the effect is the same—employees don't work and don't get paid—the strategic difference is great. Initiated by the union at any time after the expiration of the agreement, the union controls the timing of the strike. In 1992, the National Hockey League (NHL) Players Association (NHLPA) authorized a strike just before the Stanley Cup playoffs, even though the players worked most of the season without a CBA. Tactically, this strike gave the union members leverage because they had been paid most of their salaries for the season. For the league, it meant the possible elimination of the playoffs (the source of a great amount of team revenue). The 1994 Major League Baseball strike displayed a similar strategy. The players stopped working in August, six weeks before the beginning of the playoffs, after they worked for well over half the season.

On the other hand, the lockout serves as the league's and owners' gambit. The optimal time is the beginning of the season, before the players receive the bulk of their salaries. The owners can save money, put pressure on the union for settlement, and not pay out any salaries as the weeks go by. It could even deploy replacement players. The 1999 National Basketball Association (NBA) lockout cost the league half of the season, but, in what seems a league victory, the union agreed to a new CBA to salvage the season (and the paychecks). The 2004–05 NHL lockout cost the players and the league the entire season.

One last point: Traditionally, a union negotiated on behalf of employees for improvements in wages and working conditions, but more recently many unions seek maintenance of the status quo when management seeks changes. That scenario has been found in recent negotiations involving all of the major sports leagues.

## The Leagues

Presently, all of the major leagues and a number of second-tier leagues, such as Major League Soccer (MLS) and the Women's National Basketball Association (WNBA), are unionized. This means that each league's management must negotiate with the players' unions. Unions represent workers, in this case players, in discussions with the league for a CBA that outlines salaries, benefits, and working conditions.

In comparison with most labor organizations, sports athlete unions are small in numbers, consisting of elite, skilled practitioners. To become professional players, these athletes had to excel, either through a minor league system or through high school and college. The competition is fierce. Hundreds of thousands of young people play the sport, yet there are over 800 players on the opening-day roster in Major League Baseball, about 1200 in the NFL, 420 in the NBA, and 500 in the NHL. In the event of a strike or lockout, their elite status makes the management's use of "replacement workers" more difficult than in other industries. Replacing striking factory workers with others may not result in a significant decrease in the quality of the goods produced, but using substitute players (presumably ones who did not make it into the top pro leagues to begin with) has a tremendous effect on the quality of the game.

Professional athletes, unlike most of their unionized counterparts, negotiate their own contracts, although within the guidelines of the CBA, which focuses on broader issues such as free agency, salary constraints, luxury taxes, and minimum and maximum wage standards. Although the terms of the CBAs vary greatly among the various sports, in every case, players (often represented by their agents) have the right to make their own deals.

Despite the "elite" nature of professional athletes, considerable variation in the talent and salary of players exists even on a major league level.
The differences in pay of many unionized workers are often measured
in single dollars per hour. However, in professional sports, the differences are measured in hundreds of thousands, even millions, of dollars per
season. This adds tension to a union's cohesion. With some players being
paid the minimum salary and others commanding salaries many times that
amount, the goals and priorities differ. The minimum or near-minimum
wage player may be more inclined to go on strike, whereas a highly paid
free-agent All-Star may not.

Presently, sports labor relations involve rich owners and rich players,
but, at one time, neither sports franchise owners nor their teams exhibited great wealth. Salaries were artificially low and revenue streams were
limited. Today many owners are billionaires, sometimes a number of times
over. The list includes Microsoft's Paul Allen (NFL's Seattle Seahawks,
NBA's Portland Trail Blazers, and MLS's Seattle Sounders FC), and Philip
Anschutz (NBA's Los Angeles Lakers and NHL's Kings), both members of
the Forbes list of the 400 wealthiest individuals. Some owners are scions
of family fortunes, such as Robert Wood (Woody) Johnson (NFL's New
York Jets). Others are tycoons, such as Daniel Snyder (NFL's Washington
Redskins), who founded a successful marketing firm, and Mark Cuban
(NBA's Dallas Mavericks), who founded broadcast.com, a leading provider of multimedia and streaming on the Internet, and later sold it to
Yahoo!. The values of their franchises are in the hundreds of millions
of dollars. League revenues are in the billions and include revenue from
broadcasting, cablecasting, new media deals, sponsorships, and advertising, a far cry from the days of mere gate receipts (Quirk & Fort, 1997).

Over the years the values of franchises have generally increased, thanks
to more lucrative broadcasting and cable fees and the value of their stadiums or stadium leases. It should be pointed out, however, that profitability
can still be elusive, and owners often argue that their teams lose money.
A 2004 study commissioned by the NHL concluded that nineteen out of
thirty teams lost a total of over $270 million during the 2002–03 season
(Dupont, 2004). The unions often contest these conclusions, but it is difficult to determine which side is correct since the teams, as non-publicly
traded entities, are not subject to uniform accounting standards and federal securities disclosure requirements.

An excellent example of journalistic investigation of such claims came
in a report in the *Lawrence* (MA) *Eagle-Tribune*. It noted that the NHL
study was "not a true audit," as it relied on a disparate set of figures sup-
plied by the teams themselves and might have underestimated hockey revenue in some crucial areas, including the lucrative fees for luxury suites.
The newspaper interviewed NHL executives, players, union representatives, and others, and examined numerous internal documents and official

records over a period of several months for its study. Independent observers, including academics, were quoted to bolster the report's conclusion that this study did not constitute an independent audit, noting that figures were not independently derived and that not all the teams reported hockey revenue the same way (Strachan, 2005).

Players' associations began as "fraternal orders," not involved in negotiating on behalf of their players. Although the NLRA dates from the 1930s, it was only in the 1950s that the players of the major team sports unionized, and it was another two decades before their organizations developed negotiating clout. Their colleagues in blue-collar industries were decades ahead. Before CBAs limited its application, antitrust law was the weapon of choice of players' unions, most notably in the NFL.

The births of the unions representing the four major sports occurred at about the same time. The Major League Baseball Players' Association (MLBPA) and the National Basketball Players' Association (NBPA) were created in 1954. The National Football League Players' Association (NFLPA) and the NHLPA were founded in 1956 and 1957, respectively.

At first, these "unions" resembled trade associations of players, because the player sought not to use them as negotiating representatives. Because of this, the leagues quickly recognized and welcomed these unions. The first head of the MLBPA was the Cleveland Indians pitcher Bob Feller, who rejected the idea of negotiating with the owners. It was almost as if this organization assumed that a friendly roundtable discussion with management would redound to the collective benefit and assure contentment across the board (Dworkin, 1981).

## Salary Control

From a management point of view, salary control serves as the chief goal of every sports league. The need is obvious: Because the talent pool consists of many elite players, a "free market" results in a limitless range of compensation. Salary control is achieved by several different methods. Major League Baseball operates under a luxury tax in which owners are penalized for overspending, but the salaries of players, especially free-agent players, are not directly limited or capped. Although the luxury tax results in money flowing to poorer teams, it does not stop teams such as the New York Yankees from spending. The team's profitability ensures that the payment of the tax amounts to a cost of doing business, rather than a ceiling on spending.

The NFL's approach to controlling salaries from the early 1990s has been the utilization of a cap system. As explained later in this chapter, for most of those years, NFL teams have been unable to exceed a stipulated salary amount each season. The NBA also employs a salary cap system, with an important exception for players re-signed by their present teams.

In its recent collective bargaining agreement, the NHL also adopted a cap system.

Another method of salary control involves the power of termination. In baseball, player contracts are guaranteed, meaning a very limited right of termination. In the NFL, much greater discretion exists in terminating ("cutting") players, an important point for journalists.

Because the experience of each of the major sports differs, we examine the labor history of each separately. We also analyze the present collective bargaining agreements.

## Major League Baseball

Since 1972, Major League Baseball and its players' union have endured eight work stoppages. The sport's history of labor–management relations reveals an atmosphere rife with anger.

In 1876 William Hulbert, owner of the National League Chicago team and one of the league elders, declared, "It is ridiculous to pay ball players $2,000 a year when the $800 boys do just as well" (Fennell, 1994). In many respects, nothing has changed except the amounts of money quoted.

The close of the nineteenth century marked an era of confusion. Owners complained about escalating salaries and sought to control them. The players, angry over such attempts, engaged in strikes. Contract disputes ended up in court. Fans, angry and frustrated, talked about boycotting the sport. Attendance slipped in many cities, and some teams teetered on the brink of financial collapse.

In the 1890s, players' frustrations over salary and working conditions resulted in an unsuccessful attempt to unionize and start a "players' league." Until the middle of the twentieth century, the emergence of a rival league was the only way that players could secure better wages in a more open, competitive environment. With the emergence of the new American League in 1900, a number of baseball's best and brightest players left their National League teams because the American League promised "fairer contracts," including fringe benefits and no salary limitations, provisions unheard of in the National League. The American League President Byron Bancroft "Ban" Johnson also promised not to apply the dreaded "reserve clause" found in all National League player contracts for players who signed with teams in his league.

The "reserve clause," a standard contract option interpreted in an unusual way, arose from a secret agreement among the National League owners in 1879 as a means to control player salaries. The clause stated that if the player and the team could not agree to a new contract, "the [team] shall have the right to 'reserve' the [player] for the season next ensuing the term . . . provided that the [player] shall not be reserved at a salary of below [$]." Essentially, the player remained the "property" of the team for the following season. If the parties could not agree to a contract at the end of that option season, the "reservation" extended for the following year, year after year. This clause effectively barred players from negotiating with different teams to get the best deal. Additionally, in the 1890s, there was even a salary cap of $2500 (Dworkin, 1981).

The only way a player could move to another team would be through a trade. When the American League joined the National League, the reserve clause applied to American League players as well as those of the National League. A part of all baseball contracts until 1975, it served as the greatest salary restraint the owners had.

One can only guess the kinds of salaries the Babe Ruths, Joe DiMaggios, Ted Williamses, and Henry Aarons would have commanded in a free-market environment. Not surprisingly, many players resented the reserve clause, but the owners fought to keep it intact over the ensuing decades. Yet many in the press supported the system, concluding that it was needed to ensure economic stability of the sport. But even those in favor of the reserve clause acknowledged its draconian effect. In 1889, the St. Louis *Globe-Democrat* noted, "The reserve rule is, on paper, the most unfair and degrading measure . . . ever passed in a free country. Still . . . it is necessary for the safety and preservation of the national game." However, other journals criticized the clause as "tyrannical" and "un-American" (Seymour, 1960).

### The Antitrust Exemption

Before the players had an active union, they tried to challenge the reserve clause in the courts, as a violation of antitrust law. Unsuccessful attempts were made in the late 1940s, the early 1950s, and the early 1970s. In each case, the players argued that the reserve clause was unilaterally imposed on them by a group of employers (the baseball team owners) and that the concerted actions of the owners violated the Sherman Act of 1890 and the Clayton Act of 1914, the two most important antitrust laws.

Section One of the Sherman Act prohibits any person from making "a contract, combination or conspiracy to restrain trade" in interstate commerce. At first glance, it seems clear that the reserve clause violates this section of the Sherman Act. However, baseball owners got a lucky break from the Supreme Court. In 1922, the high court ruled the sport of baseball exempt from antitrust laws because baseball was not a "business in interstate commerce" (Federal Baseball Club v. National League of Professional Baseball Clubs, 1922). The Federal Baseball Club ruling is often misunderstood and misquoted. The mere three-page decision did *not* say (as some think) that baseball was not a business; rather it reasoned that the business was so localized that it did not rise to the level of systematic interstate commerce. In the words of Justice Holmes:

The business is giving exhibitions of baseball. . . . It is true that, in order . . . for these exhibitions [to attain] the great popularity that they have achieved, competitions must be arranged between clubs from different cities and States. But the fact that in order to give the exhibitions the Leagues must induce . . . persons to cross state lines and must arrange and pay for their doing so is not enough to change the character of the business. . . . [T]he transport is a mere incident, not the essential thing. That to which it is incident, the exhibition, although made for money would not be called trade or commerce in the commonly accepted use of these words. . . . Personal effort, not related to production, is not a subject of commerce (ibid.).

Despite changes in the business, the increase in revenue streams from the advent of radio, television, cable, and league-controlled merchandising, and a more expansive judicial interpretation of what activities constitute interstate commerce by the Supreme Court after 1935, the Federal Baseball precedent remained. Subsequent court rulings in 1953 and 1972 upheld the antitrust exemption.

The 1972 case of Flood v. Kuhn is well known. Curt Flood, an All-Star center fielder with the St. Louis Cardinals, refused a trade to the Philadelphia Phillies after an eleven-year All-Star career. His salary was $90,000 per year, one of the highest in the game in 1969. Flood challenged the reserve clause as an antitrust violation in the hopes of reversing the Federal Baseball ruling and thereby gaining him the right to play for whatever team he wished. On June 6, 1972, the Supreme Court in a 5–3 vote rejected his claim and concluded that, although the legal basis of the 1922 ruling was no longer sound and the exemption an "aberration" compared with other sports, the Federal Baseball ruling remained valid. The justices noted that Congress had ample opportunity to eliminate the exemption numerous times but chose not to. Curt Flood never became a free agent, and baseball kept its unique legal bonanza: near absolute protection in the realm of labor relations.

The Federal Baseball case distinguished baseball from other professional sports because the courts did not extend the antitrust exemption to football, basketball, or hockey. Yet just three and a half years later baseball became the first sport to introduce modern free agency, and the effect of antitrust exemption on labor relations was eliminated.

### Labor Agreements Make Headway

In 1966, the MLBPA became a negotiating representative for the players. The need for an effective union with a dynamic leader became evident, as the players did not achieve any improvements in their bargaining rights. For decades, the negotiation of players' contracts had often been reduced to annual take-it-or-leave-it offers, and long-term contracts were rare and unnecessary because of the continued enforcement of the reserve clause. To make matters worse, salaries were not released so players could not compare their salaries with those of their peers.

Yet many owners claimed, with some legitimacy, that their profits were small and they lacked deep pockets for long-term contracts. For the first half of the last century, revenues derived almost exclusively from gate attendance, and the balance sheet depended exclusively on bringing fans into the ballpark—something that poorly performing teams often could not do. Therefore, organized baseball argued the necessity of the reserve clause. However, in the 1960s the revenue streams changed significantly. Radio and television broadcasting agreements and income from licensing the teams' trademarks and players' names and likenesses brought greater amounts of money to the teams. And the players, hamstrung by the reserve clause, received little of it.

Marvin Miller, a labor economist and negotiator for the United Steelworkers Union, became the executive director of the MLBPA in 1966. To this day, many writers (and baseball owners) think of him as an uncompromising partisan with little appreciation for the traditions of the game. In reality, he was more nuanced. During his career with the Steelworkers, Miller also helped companies gain in productivity and profit. At the time of his ascension, Miller was not a leftist radical union-ist, but a tough labor negotiator respected by industry, government, and Steelworkers Union members alike.

He called the labor–management relations "as lawless, in [their] own way, as Dodge City in 1876" and classified baseball players as "the most exploited group I had ever seen" (Ryan, 1991). In a 1981 interview, he said, "It was comical. I discovered the three most important issues the players had brought before the owners in the previous negotiations were a faulty drinking fountain in St. Louis, a drain pipe in the outfield in Chicago and a splintered bench in the Fenway Park bullpen." He added, "I concluded that the owners were having a carnival at the players' expense." As an example, he noted that the players had not had an increase in their minimum salary since the 1940s (Down, 1981). Miller's transformation of the MLBPA from a struggling and ineffective organization to the most powerful union in sports is a testament to his leadership and vision.

Of course, the reserve clause remained Miller's major concern. However, Miller, aware he lacked the power to negotiate with the owners on an issue so dear to them, started with less controversial issues to build respect from the players. Given the ambivalence of many baseball players to an active union, that was not an easy task. In a 1991 interview, he said, "I would go as far to say that the players were brainwashed. They were led to believe they were the luckiest men on earth simply to be allowed to wear that uniform."

In 1966, the average salary of major league players was $19,000. In December of that year, Miller and then-commissioner William Eckert negotiated the first CBA in professional sports. The agreement raised the minimum salary for the first time in nearly two decades and covered pensions and insurance.

The 1966 agreement lasted two years. The next CBA (with Bowie Kuhn as commissioner, appointed after Eckert resigned) raised the minimum salary from $10,000 to $15,000. Moreover, Miller secured a clause requiring "grievance arbitration" of certain player disputes. This clause weakened the commissioner's power and gave the players a powerful new tool and, it turned out, a major concession by Kuhn.

Miller had delivered benefits for the players and by the early 1970s he had their confidence and backing. The MLBPA union became more assertive and sought the big prize—elimination or alteration of the reserve clause. In April 1972 the players walked out for two weeks, forcing the cancellation of eighty-six games. The elite players especially sought greater freedoms to negotiate their value. The players achieved some success as the owners agreed to arbitrate salary disputes for players with two years or more of service.

One year later, after a short lockout by the owners during spring training, a three-year CBA was reached. This agreement maintained the salary arbitration system, but tweaked it. Under this arrangement, any player with two years or more of service could bring a salary dispute to arbitration before a three-person board. The board was made up of one arbitrator appointed by management, one by the union, and a third "neutral" arbitrator. However, the board specifically lacked the power to consider the validity of the reserve clause.

Nevertheless, the reserve clause was doomed not by the courts (which, by crafting and upholding the antitrust exemption, over a fifty-year period, gave judicial approval of the provision), but rather by a labor arbitrator named Peter Seitz. In 1974, Seitz ruled that Oakland A's owner Charlie Finley had breached a contractual obligation to defer half of pitcher Jim "Catfish" Hunter's salary into an annuity. As a consequence, Seitz freed Hunter from his contract and made him a "free agent." At the time, Hunter was making $100,000 per season. One of the top pitchers of the game, he was free to sign with any team and he ultimately chose the New York Yankees, who offered him a five-year guaranteed contract for $750,000. It also included a then-unheard-of $1 million signing bonus, deferred compensation, and insurance benefits, making it worth $3.75 million. Hunter went from making $100,000 a year with the A's to earning over $3 million in his years with the Yankees. This unprecedented contract was the first indication of what a ball player could earn on the open market.

Other players now understood what Miller had been saying: They were grossly underpaid in a shackled environment. The Hunter case provided the impetus for baseball players to become free agents. Two pitchers, Andy Messersmith of the Dodgers and Dave McNally of the Expos, decided to "hold out" for the 1975 season, playing under the option period in the reserve clause. Then they planned to take their dispute to arbitrator Seitz in the hopes of making them free agents. The owners, fearful, offered them increasingly lucrative contracts, which both players refused.

Seitz, the "neutral" pick of the three-member arbitration board, cast the deciding vote in the Messersmith and McNally dispute. Although barred from ruling on the validity of the reserve clause because of the prohibition in the 1973 CBA, he could interpret its scope. The key question was: Was it a one-year option that concludes at the end of that one year or does it serve as a recurring set of options to be exercised by the team? Using basic contract interpretation rules, Seitz interpreted the reserve clause as having a one-year limit. He concluded that a plain meaning of the key term "for the period of one year" could only mean that, after the one-year "reserve" period, any player was free to contract with a team of his choice as he was released from his contractual obligations with the prior club. The modern age of free agency was born (National & American League Professional Baseball Clubs v. MLBPA, 1976).

After the award was unsuccessfully challenged in the courts (Kansas City Royal Baseball Corp. v. MLBPA, 1976), the baseball owners had to recognize a very different economic reality. When the 1973 CBA expired in 1976, the union had a much stronger hand to play in the negotiations for a new agreement. Owners, fearful of the effects of unfettered free agency and unprepared for its potential alteration of the baseball landscape, did not know what to do.

In one sense, Miller saved them. Miller did not favor complete free agency, but not because of concern about the owners. He thought it was not in the best interests of players, as younger and/or non-star players could be adversely affected. The owners had an incentive to negotiate short-term contracts, and to cast off mediocre players after bad seasons. What the union wanted (and received) was a system that allowed only veteran players free agency. The union hoped that free-agent veterans receiving market-level salaries would create a ripple effect benefiting younger players.

The 1976 CBA set the basic terms for all future agreements. During the first two years in the league, a player had to accept his club's contract offers, without right to arbitration or free agency. From years 3 to 6, salary disputes were referred to arbitration, where the independent third party determined the salary. After six years of service, players would become free agents. This new system produced a considerable increase in player salaries, as the average salary rose from $50,000 in 1976 to $370,000 in 1985 (Weiler & Roberts, 2004).

In 1981, a six-week midseason strike resulted in the cancellation of 712 games. The parties ultimately reached an agreement substantially identical to the 1976 CBA except that players could not demand arbitration until after three years of service (instead of two).

Salaries continued to increase and, in 1985, commissioner Peter Ueberroth encouraged owners to refrain from signing free agents from other teams. That "encouragement" occurred in a number of owners' meetings after the season. As a result, free-agent signings dropped dramatically. Only four of thirty-two free agents signed with other clubs. The other twenty-eight did not receive a single offer from another team. A similar pattern occurred in 1986. That class of free agents included stars such as Tigers pitcher Jack Morris and National League batting champion Tim Raines. Neither received offers from other teams. The lack of signings kept salary increases in check, but raised the union's suspicions of collusion by the owners.

If the owners in any other sports league tried the same tactic, a court would likely conclude an antitrust law violation. However, baseball's antitrust exemption protected the owners from that possibility. Therefore, the union relied on a clause shrewdly negotiated in the 1976 CBA that prohibited players and owners from negotiating contracts as a group. This had been proposed by the owners to avoid situations where players (such as Dodgers pitchers Sandy Koufax and Don Drysdale) tried to negotiate as one unit. The union agreed to the clause, but in return demanded a reciprocal prohibition on the part of the teams. An arbitration panel ruled that the owners' actions to shut out free agents violated this provision, and damages of $280 million were assessed (Matter of Arbitration Between MLBPA and the 26 Major League Clubs (1987), Grievance No. 86-2).

## The 1994 Strike

By 1994, both the NBA and NFL CBAs had provisions limiting the amount of money a team could spend on players' salaries. Many baseball owners wanted a "salary cap" system as well, especially those from smaller-market teams, who claimed economic hardship due to the rising costs of free agents and arbitration rulings using free-agent signings as a basis for their conclusions. Acting commissioner Bud Selig (who owned a small-market team, the Milwaukee Brewers) led the owners in a push for major changes in the way that baseball did business with its players. They sought a salary cap, and the elimination of arbitration. The union (led by Donald Fehr, who succeeded Marvin Miller) chafed at the proposals. The players decided that their best leverage was a strike in August, when the season is three-quarters complete. Despite efforts of members of Congress and President Clinton and the intervention of federal mediators, the strike continued and ultimately resulted in the cancellation of the World Series. Ultimately, the courts intervened and the strike ended in April 1995.

The players claimed that the owners engaged in an unfair labor practice in violation of the NLRA. As said earlier, management and the union must negotiate in good faith, and management can impose its proposed changes only when an impasse is reached and further negotiations would be fruitless. The owners claimed that point had been reached and unilaterally imposed their terms, which included a salary cap. The players claimed that there was no impasse and that the owners had engaged in an unfair labor practice.

The NLRB agreed with the players. The board's conclusions were upheld by a federal appeals court, which determined that the players could work under the rules of the expired CBA, noting that the issue of salary caps is a "mandatory subject of collective bargaining" and subject to the impasse rules noted above (Silverman v. MLBPRC, 1995). With this victory, the players ended the strike and returned to work in April 1995. However, it took almost two years to reach a new agreement. This 1997 CBA included some changes, including a "luxury tax," which effectively fined big-spending owners for having payrolls above a certain level, but no salary cap system.

As a result of the strike, fan attendance dropped, as did salaries, but that drop was temporary. Although average salaries dropped 10 percent in 1995, they grew 8.5 and 14.2 percent in the following two seasons (*Baseball Archive*, 1998). The result was an increasing gap between "small-market" and "big-market" teams. The luxury tax did not work to restrain salary growth.

### The Last Decade

In the summer of 2002, Major League Baseball and the MLBPA signed a collective bargaining agreement that ran through the end of 2006 and was then extended to 2011. The agreement combines salary control and payroll parity in an attempt to eliminate the disparity between "richer" and "poorer" teams. The ultimate compromise is more incremental than revolutionary. The 2007–11 CBA (known as the "Basic Agreement") includes the following.

*Revenue-Sharing.* The CBA provides that each team contributes 31 percent of its "net local revenue," after deductions for ballpark expenses, to a cash pool, a portion of which is redistributed equally to all thirty teams. This is known as the "Base Plan" (Major League Baseball CBA, Article XXIV). A second fund, the Central Fund Component, allocates another portion from that central fund from "richer" teams to "poorer" teams (Major League Baseball CBA, Article XXIV).

Note that a great deal of revenue is not included in this revenue-sharing system, including key sources such as revenues from national broadcast rights and merchandise sales (Major League Baseball CBA, Article XXIV).

*A Commissioner's Discretionary Fund.* A $10 million fund, with monies derived from equal contributions ($333,333), goes to the commissioner. The commissioner may make distributions from the fund to a club or clubs, in amounts and at times to be determined at the commissioner's discretion, as long as the amounts do not violate other terms of the CBA (Major League Baseball CBA, Article XXIV).

*A Luxury Tax on Excess Team Payrolls.* Officially known as the "Competitive Balance Tax," this is a central component of the agreement. Teams whose payrolls exceed set thresholds will be taxed on the portions above the thresholds. The bulk of that money is to be used to fund player benefits (Major League Baseball CBA, Article XXIII).

It works like this. There is a "tax threshold," the maximum payroll a team can have without triggering the tax. The threshold was $148 million in 2007, $155 million in 2008, $162 million in 2009, $170 million in 2010, and $178 million in the 2011 contract year. If a team's payroll reaches beyond the threshold, then the tax is computed based on two variables: (a) the year of the CBA and (b) the number of times the team has breached the threshold. First-time offenders pay a tax of 22.5 percent, second-time violators pay 30 percent, and third-timers pay 40 percent.

These rates may not be as onerous as they appear. Note that the tax kicks in only for payroll amounts above the threshold. Anything below the threshold is not a basis for the tax calculations. For example, if a team has a $200 million payroll in 2009 and is a first-time violator, the team pays $6.75 million in taxes. If the tax were based on the entire payroll amount, then the tax would be $45 million (Major League Baseball CBA, Article XXIII).

*Limits on the Debt a Team May Carry.* Also known as the "the Debt Service Rule," this states that a team's debt cannot exceed ten times EBITDA (earnings before interest, taxes, depreciation, and amortization, a commonly used financial formula determined by subtracting a company's operating expenses such as payroll, administrative costs, travel, and other items from gross revenues). For teams that moved into new facilities, the figure is extended to fifteen times EBITDA. The purpose is to ensure that a team's cash flow is sufficient to meet its present and future obligations. This rule, not widely discussed, came into effect in 2006, after a grace period of three years. It may have been one reason that the New York Yankees constructed its new stadium, which opened in 2009.

***Minimum Salaries.*** The annual minimum salary paid to players increased from $380,000 in 2007 to 390,000 in 2008 and $400,000 in 2009 and 2010 (Major League Baseball CBA, Article VI).

***Random Testing for Performance-Enhancing Substances.*** Discussion of these rules is found in chapter 10.

***Benefit Contributions.*** Major League Baseball will contribute $154.5 million for player benefits (Major League Baseball CBA, Article XXIII).

As of 2010, this CBA has had some success in controlling costs. Although news headlines trumpet the major free-agent contract signings, the average salary of Major League Baseball player on opening day rosters dropped 17 percent from the year before. More significantly, fourteen teams cut their payrolls (*Sporting News*, 2010; Boeck and Nightengale, 2010).

## National Football League

### History

Although the NFLPA was formed in 1956, the NFL players began collective bargaining negotiation with the league only in the late 1960s. As in baseball, the major issue centered on changes in wage restrictions based on a "reserve" system. However, unlike baseball, the NFL did not have immunity from antitrust laws, and until 1993 many of the labor controversies were decided by the courts.

Although NFL player contracts did not contain a "reserve clause" per se, the league commissioner, Pete Rozelle, imposed a requirement that had the same effect. The "Rozelle Rule" required a team signing a free agent to provide "fair and equitable" compensation to the team losing that player. The compensation could be in the form of active players and/or draft choices. The rule, unilaterally imposed in 1963, ultimately found its way into the first CBA made between the NFL and the NFLPA in 1968.

Over the next quarter-century, the NFLPA attempted to change the rule, but was not as successful as its baseball counterpart in creating a more open market for players. A 1974 strike failed after the union realized it lacked the leverage to ease the restriction. The union then turned to the courts, and in 1976 a federal appeals court concluded that the Rozelle Rule was an antitrust violation (Mackey v. NFL, 1976). Because the rule had been not negotiated, but imposed, it was held to be illegal.

After the court negated the Rozelle Rule, the union and NFL attempted to negotiate a new CBA. The league made proposals regarding free agency. One proposal (called "Plan B") provided free agency to a limited number of players on each team without a requirement of compensation to the old team. In return, certain players received diminished benefits. When negotiations failed, the NFL imposed Plan B unilaterally. Ironically, this system was even more restrictive than the Rozelle Rule, because it gave the prior team the right of first refusal for thirty-seven players on each team's roster, even if they were free agents. During the period from 1963 to 1974, 176 players became free agents, of whom thirty-four signed with other clubs. From 1977 to 1987, only one free agent player was signed by a new team.

In 1987, the NFLPA wanted to remove free agency restrictions and went on strike to force the owners to eliminate Plan B. The NFL employed replacement players, which was disastrous for the NFLPA. The use of replacements served two purposes for the owners. First, they were able to continue the season, although the quality of the games suffered. Second, the owners weakened the union's resolve. Ultimately, enough NFL players crossed the picket line to force the NFLPA to capitulate (Staudohar, 1988).

From the late 1980s to early 1990s, the union went back to court, unsuccessfully seeking antitrust protection. It lost, on account of a legal doctrine known as the "non-statutory labor exemption" to the antitrust laws, which states that the collective bargaining process supersedes antitrust law. A series of court rulings concluded that the players lost the protection of the antitrust laws when they negotiated free agency terms through the union (Powell v. NFL, 1989). In a final maneuver, the players voted to "decertify" the union, thereby revoking its authority to represent them in contract negotiations. By doing so, the players believed their antitrust claims would be resurrected, and a federal court agreed (McNeil v. NFL, 1992), finding that, once revocation of union authority occurred, antitrust law claims could be used as a basis of a lawsuit to eliminate the restrictive free-agent rules.

Ironically, the attempt to decertify brought the NFL and the NFLPA back to the bargaining table. The two sides, realizing the potential chaos that could result from decertification, negotiated a CBA in 1993, one so successful that it has been extended twice at the time of this writing. The result has been relative labor harmony for fifteen years.

### *The Present Collective Bargaining Agreement*

The CBA between the NFL and its players association is the longest running labor agreement among the four major sports. The present extension ends in 2011 and, as of early 2010, the possibility of a labor stoppage exists.

Aside from a salary cap, discussed in detail later in the chapter, the CBA contains the following.

*Non-free Agents.* Generally, free agency for players with less than three "accrued" seasons of NFL tenure does not exist. An accrued season means eligibility to play six or more regular-season games. The only exception occurs when a team fails to give one of its players a contract offer for at least one season by March 1 following the expiration of the prior season. In such a case, the player is free to negotiate a contract with any team (NFL CBA, Article XVIII, sec. 2).

*Restricted Free Agency.* A veteran with more than three and less than four accrued seasons in any capped year (or five in an uncapped year) shall, at the expiration of his last player contract during such period, become a restricted free agent. If, prior to the signing period set by the NFL and the NFLPA, such a player receives a contract proposal (known as an "offer sheet") from a new club, his old club may exercise a right of first refusal and match the offer and retain him. If the old club does not match the offer, the player may sign with the new team, but in many cases that team must "compensate" the former team by offering draft choices. The number and quality of the draft choices depend on the amount of the offer (NFL CBA, Article XIX, sec. 2). If the new team offers the player 110 percent of his previous year's salary, the current club has both "right of first refusal" and rights to a draft pick from the same round (or better) from the signing club (NFL CBA, Article XIX, sec. 2).

*Unrestricted Free Agency.* A veteran with four years or more of accrued service (six years in the uncapped final year of the CBA) may, once his contract expires, negotiate and sign a contract with any club, with no compensation awarded to the former team. Although players are eligible for unrestricted free agency sooner than their baseball counterparts (six years), one should keep in mind that the average playing time for an NFL player is about three and a half years (nflplayers.com, 2010) and only about 20 percent of all NFL players become unrestricted free agents (NFL CBA, Article XIX, sec. 1). However, with 2010 being an "uncapped" year, the free agency clock is six years, instead of four (NFL CBA, Article XIX, sec. 1).

*The Franchise Player.* In order to prevent a star player from leaving a team as a free agent, the CBA created a category known as a "franchise" player. Each team can designate one player, who would otherwise be an unrestricted free agent, as a franchise player per season. The player may negotiate only with his old club for that season, and the club must pay him based on one of two standards: either 120 percent of his prior year's salary or an average of the five highest league salaries for his position, whichever is greater (NFL CBA, Article XX, secs. 1 and 2(i)). A franchise player may sign a contract for more than one season, and, if so, the designation continues for the duration of the contract (NFL CBA, Article XX, sec. 10).

*Final Eight Plan.* This provision, which applies only in a non-salary-capped year, prevents, with limited exceptions, the top four teams in the league (those that participated in the National Football Conference (NFC) and American Football Conference (AFC) Championship games) from signing any unrestricted free agent except those from his own team. This section also restricts the signing of free agents by the next four teams which made the playoffs but were eliminated earlier (NFL CBA, Article XXI, secs. 2 and 3).

*Transition Players.* Each NFL club is permitted to designate one unrestricted free agent as a "transition player." Additionally, the club can designate a transition player in lieu of a franchise player, giving that team two transition players for the same season. Transition players are free to negotiate with any club during the designated time period, but the old club retains the right of first refusal over any offer with a new club. A transition player must receive the greater of either 120 percent of his prior year's salary or the average of the top ten players in his position (NFL CBA, Article XX, secs. 3, 4, and 11).

*Guarantees.* An NFL contract is generally not "guaranteed." Of all the major pro sports leagues, the NFL offers teams the most flexibility in releasing players, particularly given that most of an NFL player's contract is nonguaranteed income. Teams can cut players for performance reasons, business reasons, and also if a player misbehaves. Paragraph 11 of the standard player contract notes that a team may terminate a player's contract if the player has "engaged in personal conduct reasonably judged by Club to adversely affect or reflect on Club" (McCann, 2008).

In some cases, however, a contract may contain "skill" or "injury" guarantees. A skill guarantee obligates the club to continue paying under the contract even if the player has insufficient skill to make or remain with the club. An injury guarantee ensures full payment to the player in the event that he is unable to satisfy the team's physical exam requirements or becomes physically unable to perform as a result of on-field injuries suffered during the contract. The payment covers the present season and up to 50 percent of salary for the following year (NFL CBA, Article XII, secs. 1, 2, and 7).

From the union's standpoint, the weakest aspect of the CBA is the non-guaranteed salary. Despite the fact that the NFL has the richest television contract in sports and the league makes billions in revenue, NFL players do not enjoy the same security as many players in the other major league sports. In fact, by signing a nonguaranteed contract, an NFL player takes a considerable risk, as he can be terminated (or "cut") at any time. First, many agreements tend to be back-ended, meaning most of the base salary is located in the last two or three years of the contract. If he suffers a career-ending injury, his contract ends at the conclusion of the season and he risks termination by the team during the term of the contract.

Also, if the player becomes "too expensive" to the team owing to salary cap constraints (discussed shortly), the team can either force a renegotiation of the contract or terminate the player. Stanford University professor Roger Noll put it best when he said that "the absence of guaranteed contracts transfers the risk of injury or deterioration of skills from the team to the player" (Cunningham, 2004).

*A Fund to Supplement Salaries of Players Whose Playing Time Is Disproportionate to Their Compensation.* Implemented as part of the 2002 extension to the CBA, the "Performance Based Pool" established a fund (with the money coming from league revenues) that is used to supplement certain salaries. In 2006, the program paid $3 million per team, with 5 percent increases for each capped year. The figures for 2008 and 2009 were $3.3 million and $3.5 million, respectively (NFL CBA, Article XXXVIII-B, sec. 2).

Some may question why these restrictions exist. The answer centers around the fact that the NFL system is quite different in several respects from those of the other leagues, which may justify the lower salaries. Many professional baseball players and hockey players spend a great deal of time (or even their whole careers) in the minor leagues, where their compensation is dramatically lower than in the major league. With no feeder minor league in professional football, NFL players are drafted by a team, they sign with that team, and they play with that team right away. Another important point is that the NFL employs about twice as many players as baseball and hockey and more than three times as many as the NBA. Injury rates are also higher, creating a concern that owners would be stuck with paying out guaranteed contracts to many players, while seeking substitutes. And the benefits received by NFL players, which include long-term disability plans and pension eligibility after four seasons, are more favorable than those in the other leagues.

Yet average football salaries, as shown in the table at the conclusion of this chapter, lag behind those of other sports, in part because of the salary cap restrictions found in the CBA.

## The Salary Cap

In 1993, the NFL and its union agreed to implement a salary cap, making professional football the second major sport to do so (the first was basketball). The salary cap attempted to limit the potential for salary growth in a modified free agency system. Basically, player costs were limited to a specific percentage of league-wide revenues divided equally by the number of franchises existing in the league. The result, at least theoretically, limited the cumulative salary that a team can pay its athletes. Not only intended to control salary growth, the cap also promoted competitive balance amongst the teams in the league. With a cap, a "richer" team did not have an unfair advantage over a "poorer" team in signing marquee players.

In practice, the salary cap involved difficult dollars and cents budgeting. The tricky, accounting-oriented mechanics of the cap are often misunderstood (or not understood). The goal here is not to give readers an accountant's breakdown of every variable, but rather to provide a basic guide for journalists to the applicability of the salary cap standards in the NFL.

At the outset, the two most important considerations when discussing a salary cap have been (a) how the cap is calculated and (b) its exceptions. Many call the NFL salary cap system a "hard cap," compared with the "soft cap" system operated by the NBA. The inference is that the NFL system was stricter in operation than its NBA counterpart. However, the NFL system is filled with exceptions, just like the NBA's loopholes. The NFL cap was considered a "hard cap" in that it seems to establish a more definite predetermined limit on the amount a team may pay its players. Yet without those exceptions, the most important being the amortization of the signing bonus over the life of the contract, actual salary expenditures would have exceeded the salary cap in each season since 1993.

The NFL salary cap set a ceiling on the amount of money that any one team may spend on its players within a given season (known as "league year," starting from February 20 and lasting to February 19 of the following year) and effectively limited the number of teams with which a player may negotiate. For 2009, that ceiling was based on 57.5 percent of " 'projected total revenues,' less league-wide projected benefits (which include, among other things, player pension funding, group insurance, supplemental disability, workers' compensation, unemployment compensation, social security taxes, post season salary, practice squad salary and medical costs), divided by the number of Teams playing in the NFL during such year" (NFL CBA, Article XXIV, sec. 4). "Total revenues" included gate receipts, luxury box revenues, personal seat licenses, and broadcast rights tallied from the individual teams and the league's broadcasting and cable agreements (NFL CBA, Article XXIV, sec. 1(a)). In a change from the past, such revenues also include income from concessions, parking, program and novelty sales, local advertising and promotions, signage, and luxury boxes (NFL CBA, Article XXIV, sec. 1(a)). In 2009, the team cap came to $128 million. The salaries of the team's top fifty-three players count toward the cap.

To ensure that NFL owners did not pocket too much of their projected revenues, the CBA stated that, league-wide, the players were guaranteed to receive a *minimum* of 50 percent of total revenue in any capped season. If player costs for all NFL teams fell below 50 percent of total revenue in a capped season, owners must pay the difference directly to the players who played during that season by April 15 following that season. If such payment occurs, the funds would be distributed based on the reasonable instructions of the union (CBA, Article XXIV, secs. 3 and 4).This provision, overlooked by many, served as an important baseline to ensure that players are receiving some of the spoils of the revenues of the league. In addition to the league-wide salary cap, the current CBA mandates that individual teams pay their players a specified minimum percentage of the salary cap. In 2006, it was 84 percent of the salary cap. This minimum amount increases by 1.2 percent for each year so it was 86.4 percent for 2008 and 87.6 percent for 2009 but never exceeds 90 percent (NFL CBA, Article XXIV, sec. 5).

The calculation of the revenues was done before the season begins, and the amounts included estimates of expected growth, based on such factors as television contracts, new stadiums, and other revenue growth. Any differences were either added to the pool or subtracted from the pool for the next season. Hence, accounting skill was required to make accurate calculations. The number crunchers met with union representatives to inform them of the calculations and, if objections resulted, an arbitration proceeding occurred to resolve the dispute.

Even though the standard just described seemed strict, the cap rules have been applied in a clever fashion. Some amounts, such as a player's base salary and certain types of bonus payments, were to be calculated only for the particular season in which they are paid under the player's contract (*Sporting News*, 2004). But certain payments were prorated over the life of the player's contract in order to get "salary cap relief." This strategy can produce instant results by keeping high-quality players for an attempt at a Super Bowl championship. However, by using this accounting technique, teams mortgaged their future in favor of opening up salary room immediately.

Hypothetically, a highly touted first-round quarterback could receive a contract including (a) a signing bonus of $10 million; (b) a base salary of $5 million; (c) a roster bonus of $50,000; (d) a reporting bonus of $50,000; (e) $50,000 for playing in 80 percent of team games; (f) $100,000 for gaining 1200 yards in a season; (g) $200,000 for making the All-Pro team and being the most valuable player; and (h) $300,000 if the team goes to the Super Bowl. As described next, some of this money is prorated and some is not.

These rules were complex but important in calculating salary cap room. A summary follows.

*Signing Bonuses.* The signing bonus is the amount of money received by a player for merely agreeing to a contract with the team. The player and his agent attempted to maximize the signing bonus because it was *not* based on the player's performance and was typically the only guaranteed payment the player received. Thus, if a player had insufficient skill or was injured and not able to remain with his NFL team, the signing bonus was not forfeited or diminished in value. The rest of the contract, however, was usually terminated.

The signing bonus was the best-known and simplest method of circumventing the salary cap, because, at the time of this writing, it was prorated over the life of the contract or up to three years after the final capped year of the CBA (2009), whichever is sooner for salary cap purposes (NFL CBA, Article XXIV, sec. 7). In other words, the total bonus amount is divided by the number of years in the player's contract and, under the terms of the CBA, only the prorated amount is applied toward a given year's salary cap calculation. If player X signs a four-year contract with a $10 million signing bonus, $2.5 million will count toward the cap over those four seasons.

However, the use of prorated signing bonuses carried some risk. Releasing players with large signing bonuses early in their contracts penalized the team under the salary cap. So, if a player left the team before his contract expired, the remaining prorated portion of the bonus was counted immediately, in a lump sum, against the cap. Taking our last example, the team will take a "cap hit" of $5 million if the player with a four-year contract and $10 million bonus is released by June 1 before the upcoming season after playing two years.

Other types of bonuses existed, such as the guaranteed roster bonuses (a payment made in the preseason) and reporting bonuses (an extra payment for simply reporting to training camp). As described next, teams used other deferred compensation techniques to skirt the salary cap.

*Contract Renegotiation.* In order to save salary room and keep star players, owners have renegotiated player contracts. There are basically two ways to do this. The first is by reducing a player's salary and spreading it over a longer period of time. The reduction will create salary room in that given season. Also, money guaranteed in contract extensions and modifications is proratable (NFL CBA, Article XXIV, sec. 7(b)).

One way involves "reworking" a player's existing contract to get salary cap relief. This serves to diminish salary. Say a player under contract for $5 million per season accepts a modification to a lower amount, $3.5 million. The team then has an extra $1.5 million in salary cap room for the season. In some cases, the renegotiation may result in the player's salary being paid over a longer period of time. Let's take the following case.

An expensive veteran quarterback, under a four-year contract, making $9 million per season, coupled with a $15 million signing bonus, has two years left. The backup quarterback, making far less, played more games last season and achieved better production. The team does not want to continue paying such a high sum to a declining player. It could do several things:

(a) Force a salary reduction and use this quarterback as either a starter or a backup. The result would be a lower salary and a restructuring, and spreading the cap hit over future years (assuming a new signing bonus).
(b) Release the player and take about a $7.5 million hit against its salary cap for the remaining prorated portion of his past signing bonuses.
(c) Renegotiate the signing bonus.

Option (a) would save some salary cap room next year, but cost the team out-of-pocket cash (notably the signing bonus, which was paid upfront). However, option (b) would cost salary cap room because $7.5 million would have been charged to this coming year, but would not cost the team any cash, because it would not have to pay the player (Miller, 2003). Option (c) would involve renegotiating the signing bonus. Part of the player's base salary would be swapped into an added signing bonus. As a result, the player would receive more guaranteed cash, and the owner create more cap room, as well as retaining the player's services for a longer period of time if the contract term was extended. Also, this added bonus would not affect the proration of the original signing bonus.

If a club and a player renegotiated or extended a contract and increased the player's salary for the current season, the increase would be counted as salary for that league year if the negotiation was completed before the tenth week of the regular season. If the renegotiation occurred after the tenth week of the regular season, the increase in salary was treated as a signing bonus allocated over the remaining years of the contract (including the "current" year of that contract) (NFL CBA, Article XXIV, sec. 7(b)).

*Incentive Clauses.*  Incentive clauses are performance-based awards found in many NFL contracts. The number of incentive clauses and their values are a function of various factors, including the individual club's talent pool, the player's leverage, his expected and past contributions to his club, his salary, and the number of years the player has served. Typically, rookie and reserve players' contracts contain more incentive clauses because their base salaries are lower. Accordingly, as a player's salary increased, the number of incentive clauses usually diminished. The base salary theoretically reflects contributions that were covered by previous incentive packages.

"Playing-time incentives" rewarded a player for the amount of time on the field. Performance can be measured by games started or by a percentage of the team's total number of plays on offense, defense, and/or special teams. The playing-time incentive clauses were often used with players recovering from an injury.

"Statistical performance incentives" rewarded a player's on-field performance within various statistical categories based on terms and conditions set forth in the contract for a particular year. The scope of these clauses was limited only by the creativity and ingenuity of the negotiators. For example, a wide receiver can be rewarded if he leads the NFL in receptions, or a quarterback may receive extra money if he ends the season with the highest quarterback rating in the league.

"Honors incentives" rewarded a player for exceptional individual achievements. Such incentives are attractive to clubs because relatively few players, regardless of their ability, earn such incentives in any given season. Some of the awards include NFL Most Valuable Player, NFL Defensive Player of the Year, All-NFL First or Second Team, selection to the Pro-Bowl, and Rookie of the Year.

Additionally, players often received bonuses contingent on the performance and success of their team. Team performance incentives include bonuses based on the team's statistical performance or ranking. Examples of performance categories include the NFL's top-ranked offense or defense. Also, a team can reward each player with a progressively higher amount of money if the team advances into the playoffs or wins the division, conference championship, or Super Bowl.

As we can see, NFL contracts use incentive clauses with considerable frequency. But how the extra compensation fits into the salary cap during the many years of its use presents an important question. The NFL–NFLPA collective bargaining agreement created two different categories: (a) incentives "likely to be earned" based on whether the player's or the team's performance could have satisfied during the prior year and (b) incentives "not likely to be earned." If the incentive was likely to be earned, it counted toward the team salary in the current year's salary cap. If it was not likely to be earned, it was *not* to be counted against the cap even if the player met the incentive and got paid (NFL CBA, Article XXIV, sec. 7).

To interpret this very subjective standard, the CBA provided this example to help in determining whether an incentive clause is likely or not likely to be earned for salary cap purposes. Assume that player X receives an incentive bonus if he participates in 50 percent of the team's offensive plays this season. Assume further that last season the team had 1000 offensive plays. Therefore, as soon as player X plays in 500 plays in the current season (or 50 percent of last year's 1000 plays), the incentive will be considered "earned" for salary cap purposes. The same incentive is considered not earned if the same player in the current year participated in only one of the team's first 502 offensive plays. In this situation, it would be impossible for the player to achieve the 50 percent incentive based on last year's performance of 1000 plays.

Therefore, if the player receives money for attaining the "likely to be earned" incentive and that amount puts the team over the cap, the amount paid above the salary cap in performance bonuses will be subtracted from the team's salary cap in the next year (NFL CBA, Article XXIV, sec. 7(c)(ii)).

*Deferred Compensation.* The present CBA requires that base salary and bonuses that are deferred be counted in the year earned, not the year paid (CBA, Article XXIV, sec. 7). The use of deferred compensation had its risks. It could free salary room in the beginning but take up space in later years. In 2009, an example of this problem involved the difficulties of the Pittsburgh Steelers. Owing to salary cap limitations, Pittsburgh faced difficulties in extending the contracts of certain unrestricted free agents because of cap space taken by "dead money" of approximately $8.2 million. In past years, the Buffalo Bills suffered from this problem as well (Zasky, 2009).

*Retirement or Trading of Player.* If a player was traded or waived on or before June 1, the remaining signing bonus that had not been included in his salary "accelerated" and was included in that year's team salary for cap purposes. The team that waived or traded the player was responsible for the accelerated signing bonus. In most cases, if a player retired, the remaining signing bonus also "accelerated" and was included in that year's team salary. Thus, the team would take an immediate salary cap hit of the remaining signing bonus and the new team would not be responsible for any of the original signing bonus (NFL CBA, Article XXIV, sec. 7(b)).

Although the salary cap was eliminated in the 2010 season, it could be reinstated in the same or modified form in a future CBA. Therefore, journalists should be aware of the mechanics of the cap as it existed before that date.

## A Quick Summary

In summary, the NFL computed a player's cap number by adding the prorated signing bonus, base salary, and other bonuses, including roster, option, reporting, and workout bonuses, and likely to be earned (LTBE) incentives. When a player signed a five-year contract in 2009 that included a $5 million signing bonus, a $1 million roster bonus in the first year, a first-year base salary of $500,000, and $200,000 in LTBE bonuses in the first season, the player's salary cap number for that season was $2.7 million, or the total of $1 million (the signing bonus divided by the number of years of the contract), $1 million roster bonus, the $500,000 base salary, and the $200,000 LTBE (Seifert, 2004).

Before leaving the NFL collective bargaining agreement, this quotation merits inclusion: "Just remember the basics of this," Jay Zygmunt, the president of the St. Louis Rams Football Operations, said. "Every dollar you spend counts. The only thing you can control is when. But it's going to count. There's no way around it. No one's immune from the process" (Thomas, 2004).

## National Basketball Association

### History

The modern NBA arose from a merger of two rivals, the Basketball Association of America (BAA) and the National Basketball League (NBL), in 1949. Not surprisingly, NBA players worked under the same restricted salary arrangements as in other major sports leagues.

Like their football and baseball counterparts, NBA players slowly adapted to labor–management negotiation. Although formed in 1954, the National Basketball Players' Association (NBPA) and the NBA did not engage in collective bargaining negotiations for over a decade.

Similar to the other leagues, the NBA attempted to control salaries by a form of reserve system. And, like their NFLPA counterparts, the NBPA challenged the limitation based on antitrust theory. The lawsuit, known as the Oscar Robertson litigation (after the Hall of Fame player), was filed in 1970 and challenged the league's reserve clause that severely curtailed free agency and effectively limited salaries (Robertson v. NBA, 1970). The case was settled in 1976, and the reserve clause was eliminated and replaced with a compensation system whereby teams that lost free agents would be entitled to cash, players, or draft choices determined by the NBA commissioner from the signing team. Additionally, the player's former team would hold the right of first refusal on any free-agent signings.

At the time of the settlement, the NBA absorbed four teams from the defunct American Basketball Association (ABA) (1967–76), depriving players of a competitor league that attracted NBA players by offering more lucrative contracts. The terms of the settlement were memorialized in a CBA made in 1980.

In 1983, the NBA became the first professional sports league to establish a salary cap. At the time, many NBA teams experienced financial difficulties. Franchises in Cleveland, Denver, Indiana, Kansas City, San Diego, and Utah reported serious losses, and some fell behind on deferred payments to former players (Bradley, n.d.). In this atmosphere, the NBA and the NBPA decided to develop a novel salary structure. They created a salary cap on the amount teams pay most players, regardless of whether they are free agents or rookies. This agreement resulted in considerable success in stabilizing the finances of the league and its teams. The blueprint remains effective to the present day.

The players were to be paid an aggregate amount of at least 53 percent of the league's "guaranteed share of revenues," known as the "defined gross revenues," which included gate receipts, local and national television and radio revenue, and preseason and postseason revenues (Bradley, n.d.). However, free agency remained restricted.

During the term of the 1983 CBA, the NBA blossomed because of star players such as Magic Johnson, Larry Bird, and Michael Jordan. At the conclusion of this agreement, the players sought some form of unrestricted free agency and, like their NFLPA counterparts, went to the courts to challenge restrictions on free agency under the antitrust law. The NBA and NBPA settled the case, leading to the adoption of a six-year CBA in 1988, which for the first time granted unrestricted free agency. In a victory for the players, it eliminated the right of first refusal to a free agent's offer after a player completes his second contract (Bradley, n.d.).

The relatively harmonious relationship between the NBPA and the NBA ended in 1991 when the NBPA discovered that the NBA underreported revenues by excluding luxury box rentals, arena signage, and playoff ticket sales in the calculation of defined gross revenues. As arena economics began to shift in favor of suite and signage revenues, the union feared that the exclusion of such revenues would significantly hurt the players. The dispute was settled, as the parties agreed to a $2 million increase in the salary cap for the next two years (*New York Times*, 1992). At that time, the average salary for an NBA player was $1 million, up from $200,000 in 1976.

A period of strained labor relations followed. By 1994, the 1988 agreement ended and the players' union instituted another legal challenge to certain terms of the CBA, notably free agency, college draft, and the right of first refusal (which was limited, but not eliminated, under the old CBA). The courts ultimately ruled in favor of the owners and, once the litigation ended, contract talks continued (NBA v. Williams, 1995). The parties played the 1994–95 season without a contract, but after that season the NBA threatened a lockout if a new agreement was not concluded.

A new agreement was negotiated in the summer of 1995 and was supposed to last for six years. However, it faced criticism from a group of "dissident" players, mostly All-Stars, who objected to its provisions, notably a luxury tax on teams that exceeded the salary cap. This fissure showed divergent interests between highly paid marquee players, such as Michael Jordan, and the union leadership. The stars, opposed to such a tax, argued that it would depress their salaries because the teams had an economic incentive not to negotiate high salaries to avoid exceeding the cap. Like their counterparts in the NFL, these players and their agents sought termination or "decertification" of the NBPA as a bargaining representative. If that had happened, the unions would have lost the power to negotiate on the players' behalf. Also, these players claimed that, if the NBPA were decertified, the NBA clubs could not risk imposing team salary caps because of potential antitrust law challenges in the courts.

The decertification attempt failed, as the players voted to retain the NBPA as its bargaining representative. However, in a defeat for the union leadership, the players rejected the proposed CBA. The union, feeling the heat from the star players, took a tougher position with regard to a salary cap, and, after fruitless negotiations, the NBA decided to impose a lockout on July 1, 1995. This action was short-lived, as a new six-year CBA, without any "hard" salary cap or luxury tax, was concluded. Both sides bought labor peace. The NBA avoided the cancellation of games, whereas the union mollified the desires of the dissident players who sought decertification.

This CBA gave the players some tangible improvements, such as unrestricted free agency for all players following the conclusion of their contracts, and a guarantee of 48.04 percent of all basketball-related income (BRI) (an expanded version of the older "defined gross income"), characterized as the total of gate receipts, broadcast revenues, merchandise revenues, and concessions generated by all the teams in the league, which now included luxury suites, international television, and arena signage. The agreement also permitted unrestricted free agency after a player's third season.

For the owners, it provided for a reduction in the number of draft rounds to one and a rookie salary cap. It kept various exceptions to the salary cap rules (to be discussed later), including the so-called "Larry Bird Exception," which allowed teams to re-sign their own free agents at any price.

One consequence of this CBA was that it enhanced the bargaining power of star rookie players. To make sure they would not become free agents too quickly, some received lucrative contract extensions to "lock" them with the team for more than three years. Then Minnesota Timberwolves' Kevin Garnett received a six-year, $121 million extension.

The owners felt that the league gave in on the luxury tax issue. Fortunately for the NBA, the CBA had an "opt-out" provision. It provided that in three years, if total player salaries and *benefits* exceeded 51.8 percent of BRI, the NBA could "reopen" the CBA early and renegotiate the agreement. At the time of the agreement, team salaries constituted about 57 percent BRI level (Allen, 2002). By 1998, that amount was essentially the same. The average player salary approached $2 million. The minimum player salary was $225,000.

To no one's surprise, the league reopened the contract and many speculated that a work stoppage was likely. From the NBA's point of view, the salaries were so high that even the revenues from a lucrative, five-year, $2.4 billion television deal negotiated in 1997 did not alleviate the problem (In the Matter of National Basketball Players Association and National Basketball Association (Lockout Arbitration, Opinion and Award, 1998)). On July 1, 1998, the CBA officially terminated, and the NBA began what would become a six-month lockout, then the longest labor stoppage in sports history.

In such an event, the question becomes which side has more leverage. In most, if not all, of baseball's strikes and lockouts, it has been the union. However, in this case, it was the NBA and its owners. One important reason derived from an arbitrator's ruling that teams did not have to pay the players with "guaranteed" contract money (In the Matter . . . Association (Lockout Arbitration, Opinion and Award, 1998)). The October 19, 1998, decision threw the full balance of power in negotiations to the side of the NBA. As one commentator put it, "It simply became a waiting game until the union folded" (Michaelis, 1998).

Ultimately, after the loss of half of the season and the threat to shut down the league for the entire season, the parties came to their present labor agreement. Before the stoppage ended, 423 regular-season games and the NBA All-Star Game had been canceled.

### The 2005 Collective Bargaining Agreement

The CBA between the NBA and the NBPA, effective since the 2001–02 season, expired at the end of the 2004–05 season and was slightly modified by the current CBA, which began in July 2005 and expires in 2011 (or in 2012, if the NBA chooses to extend it).

Like its NFL counterpart, this CBA utilized a salary cap system, but, unlike the NFL's, it also specifically limited individual salaries, although with some significant exceptions. This CBA also set maximum salaries for players based on their years of service and regulated the salaries for rookie players' contracts. It also created an "escrow and tax" system if league-wide salaries exceed a certain percentage.

The NBA's salary structure offered, at least in theory, substantive control of salary growth. In return, the players received a minimum salary for veterans based on service, and methods to circumvent the cap, most notably by the continuation of the so-called "Larry Bird Exception."

The most important provisions of the current CBA are as follows.

*Player Salary Maximums.* This was an important concession by the union, because it put a drag on the salaries of the most elite players. The present CBA computes the maximums based on a flat amount, or a percentage of the salary cap, or a stipulated increase from the prior season's salary. For players with six or fewer years in the league, the annual maximum is the greatest of (a) 25 percent of the salary cap in effect at the time the contract is executed, (b) 105 percent of the salary for the final season of the player's prior contract, or (c) $9 million. For players in the league between seven and nine years, the maximum is the greatest of (a) 30 percent of the salary cap in effect at the time the contract is executed, (b) 105 percent of the salary for the final season of the player's prior contract, or (c) $11 million. For veterans with ten or more years in the NBA, the maximum is the greatest of (a) 35 percent of the salary cap in effect at the time the contract is executed, (b) 105 percent of the salary for the final season of the player's prior contract, or (c) $14 million (NBA CBA, Article II, sec. 7).

*Player Salary Minimums.* The parties agreed not only on salary ceilings but also to salary minimums for veteran players, as well as predetermined rookie salaries. According to this rookie salaries system, a player's salary was based not on his performance but rather on the position at which he was selected in the draft. Because a player's performance in college was not necessarily representative of his potential for success in the NBA, this system may have resulted in unfairness regarding a player's true market value. As of 2009–10, the breakdown was approximately as follows: rookies $457,588; one-year veterans, $736,420; two-year veterans, $825,497; three-year veterans, $855,189; four-year veterans, $884,881; five-year veterans, $959,111; six-year veterans, $1,033,342; seven-year veterans, $1,107,572; eight-year veterans, $1,181,803; nine-year veterans, $1,187,686; 10 years and up, $1,306,455 (NBA CBA, Exhibit C).

*The Salary Cap.* The NBA salary cap system has not changed appreciably since it was first introduced in 1983. A team's salary cap for each year was determined by a formula based on BRI. The cap amount was based on a figure of up to 51 percent of the projected BRI for the season subtracting player benefits, and dividing that amount by the number of teams in the league (30) (NBA CBA, Article VII, sec. 2(a)(1)).

Of crucial importance was how the BRI is computed. It includes aggregate operating revenues received by the NBA, such as gate receipts, broadcasting rights fees, proceeds from exhibition games and in-arena sales of concessions and novelties, parking, team sponsorships, 40 percent of fees from fixed arena signage, and 40 percent of proceeds from luxury boxes (NBA CBA, Article VII, secs. 1(a)(1)(vi), 1(a)(1)(vii), and 2(a)). The salary cap maximums have increased over the years as a consequence of the NBA's economic fortunes. For example, the 1983–84 season had a cap of $3.1 million per team. For the 2009–10 season, it was $57.7 million. During the same period of time, the average player salary rose from $250,000 to $5.356 million in the 2007–08 season. In the 2009–10 season, on account of economic circumstances, the cap decreased $1 million from the previous season's cap. However, the figure is deceptive because, if one took the cap exceptions into account, they pushed the average acceptable team payroll to almost $72 million (NBA.com, 2009; *USA Today*, n.d.).

When determining team salaries (e.g., to determine whether a team is over the salary cap), the following were included: salaries of all active players and players on injured reserve (including likely bonuses), salaries paid or payable to waived players, and any salary still being paid to retired players (Coon, n.d.; NBA CBA, Article VII, sec. 4(a)).

*Free Agency.* Restricted free agency, whereby the player's original team may match an offer by a prospective team, occurs after the fourth season for first-round picks, and after the third season for most veterans. For longer periods of tenure, unrestricted free agency applied in most situations (NBA CBA, Article XI, sec. 5).

*Escrow.* To protect teams against spiraling salaries, the CBA limits aggregate player salaries to 57 percent of the previously defined basketball related income (NBA CBA, Article VII, sec. 12). To enforce this limitation, an "escrow and tax" system was established. Under this system, an amount not to exceed 8 percent of players' salaries was placed in escrow for the years 2010 and 2011. If aggregate player salaries exceeded that percentage, the league would be reimbursed (with interest) the amount of the overage by the escrow fund (NBA CBA, Article VII, sec. 12(c)). Any money remaining in the escrow fund would be returned to the players with interest. In the 2008–09 season, about $205 million was returned to the owners because the player salaries exceeded the 57 percent BRI level.

*Luxury Tax.* In addition to the salary cap system, the NBA created another mechanism to control team spending. Known as the "tax" or "luxury tax," it is paid by teams whose payroll exceeds a predetermined tax level. The tax would be triggered when the league-wide salaries and benefits exceeded approximately 61 percent of BRI before the 2009–10 season.

If the tax was triggered, all teams over the luxury tax threshold had to pay, dollar for dollar, the amount by which their team salary exceeded the tax threshold (NBA CBA, Article. VII, sec. 12). The luxury tax threshold on 2009–10 salaries was approximately $69.9 million. Teams under the threshold would collect a percentage of this tax amount. By the end of the CBA, teams over the threshold generally did not collect any amount.

Note that the tax has not prevented teams from exceeding the salary cap but has presented strong monetary incentives to avoid doing so, similar to the luxury tax found in the present Major League Baseball CBA.

*Minimum Team Salary Threshold.* Under the CBA, a team could not have a team payroll lower than 75 percent of a team's salary cap. In the event this occurred, the league could force that team to pay the players the amount equal to the shortfall (NBA CBA, Article VII, sec. 2(b)). The minimum and maximum salary budgets could be spent by each team when signing new players, whether rookies or veterans. What constituted a "salary" was determined by rules regarding calculation of deferred compensation, signing bonuses, loans to players, incentive compensation, foreign player payments, one-year minimum contracts, and existing contracts entered into before the agreement was made (NBA CBA, Article VII, sec. 3).

*Maximum Contract Length.* The maximum length of a contract for most NBA players is five years. For "Larry Bird Exception" players, it is six years (NBA CBA, Article IX, sec. 1).

*Suspensions and Fines for Player Misconduct.* Players could be fined and/or suspended for noncompliance with the terms of their contracts. Fines range from $2500 for the first practice missed within a season, to $5000 for the second, $7500 for the third, and, finally, to "such amount as is reasonable" for the fourth or additional violations (NBA CBA, Article VI, sec. 2(a)). Also, the penalized player's cash compensation could be reduced by one 110th for each game that was missed (NBA CBA, Article VI, sec. 1). In addition, players could also be fined $20,000 for each promotional appearance and mandatory program that was missed (NBA CBA, Article VI, sec. 1). The NBA also had the authority to suspend a player for up to ten games when a player was convicted or pleaded guilty or no contest to a violence felony (NBA CBA, Article VI, secs. 3 and 4).

*Drug Testing.* The CBA permits two categories of drug testing: testing based on "reasonable cause" and "random testing." If either the NBA or the NBPA has information that gives "reasonable cause" to believe that a player is engaged in the use, possession, or distribution of a prohibited substance, an independent expert may order a drug test on the player (NBA CBA, Article XXXIII, sec. 5). The random testing regimen, on the other hand, requires all players to undergo testing for at any time, without prior notice to the player, no more than four times each season (NBA CBA, Article XXXIII, sec. 6). The list of "prohibited substances" includes marijuana and performance-enhancing drugs such as steroids (NBA CBA, Article XXIII, secs. 8 and 9).

A positive test for illegal substances, other than marijuana and steroids, results in dismissal and disqualification from any association with the NBA, although that player has the right to apply for reinstatement at a later date (NBA CBA, Article XXXIII, secs. 11 and 12). However, if a player tested positive for either steroids or marijuana he is required to enter a substance abuse treatment program, for a first-time violation. However, for the second, third, or additional violation, penalties of fines and suspensions occur, together with the requirement to enter the abuse treatment program (NBA CBA, Article XXXIII, secs. 8 and 9). More discussion on drug testing follows in chapter 10.

### Exceptions to the Salary Cap

The salary cap system has several important exceptions, most of which remain in effect in the present CBA. The following is a general description of each.

*"Larry Bird" Exception.* The most significant, known as the "Larry Bird Exception," allows a team to exceed the salary cap when it re-signs its own free agents. The exception covers up to the player's maximum salary. The player must have played at least three seasons without being waived or changing teams as a free agent (NBA CBA, Article VII, sec. 6(b)). The team can sign the player to a contract with annual raises of up to 10.5 percent. This exception thus permits the team's total payroll to exceed the salary cap in order to sign its own free agents. A new team signing such a player can also use the exception; however, it can only offer up to a 10.5 percent increase in the player's previous salary (NBA CBA Article VII, sec. 5(c)(2)). The exception is named after the Boston Celtics great Larry Bird, because he was the first player allowed to exceed the cap.

*"Early Bird" Exception.* This is a weaker form of the Larry Bird Exception. Players who qualify for this exception are called "early qualifying veteran free agents" in the CBA. A player qualifies for this exception after just two seasons without being waived or changing teams as a free agent. Using this exception, a team may re-sign its own free agent for 175 percent of his regular salary plus 175 percent of any bonuses for the final salary cap year or salary plus bonuses totaling 108 percent of the average player salary for the prior salary cap year, whichever is greater (NBA CBA, Article VII, sec. 6(b)(3)).

*"Non-Bird" Exception.* This applies to any free agent not in the first two categories. This exception allows a team to re-sign its own free agent to a salary starting at 120 percent of the player's salary in the previous season or 120 percent of the minimum salary, whichever is greater, even if they are over the cap. Raises are limited to 10.5 percent, and contracts are limited to six years when this exception is used (NBA CBA, Article VII, sec. 6(b)(2)).

*Mid-level Salary Exception.* This exception allows a team to offer any player a contract equal to 108 percent of the average NBA salary in a prior capped year, even if the team exceeds the salary cap. The exception amount for the mid-level salary exception is tied to the average player salary in the league. Thus, as the average salary in the league increases, the exception amount correspondingly grows. Contracts signed pursuant to the new exception may be up to five years. Finally, a team may utilize the mid-level salary exception every year instead of once every other year (NBA CBA, Article VII, sec. 6(e)). For 2009–10, it was about $5.85 million (Aldridge, 2009).

The CBA imposed severe penalties if teams and players attempt to circumvent these rules. A case in point involved a player named Joe Smith and the Minnesota Timberwolves. Smith signed with the Timberwolves for the amount of the mid-level exception, which at the time was $1.75 million. The parties made an under-the-table agreement that Smith would play under three consecutive one-year contracts at below market value, and the Timberwolves would reward him by using their Larry Bird Exception to sign him to a huge contract beginning with the 2001–02 season. The agreement was formalized in writing (not a wise thing to do under the circumstances), and the league eventually discovered the written agreement.

It had long been rumored that such under-the-table agreements existed, but this was the first time the league had hard evidence in the form of a signed contract. The league responded by fining the team the maximum $3.5 million, taking away its next five draft picks (two were later returned), and voiding Smith's $1.75 million contract and Smith's two previous, already completed contracts. This essentially stripped the Timberwolves of any Bird rights to Smith, preventing them from re-signing Smith for any salary above the minimum (they had already used their other exceptions) (Enlund, 2000).

## The National Hockey League

With only six teams (two in Canada and four in the United States) from the 1940s to 1967, ice hockey served as a niche sport, inaccessible to most areas in the United States. Since expansion started in 1967, its presence has grown considerably. So have its labor issues.

In the early 1990s, Robert Goodenow assumed the leadership of the NHLPA and sought a more aggressive stand against management than his more malleable predecessor, Alan Eagleson. As a result, relations between the NHLPA and the NHL have become more contentious. The problems began during the 1991–92 season, when the players and owners reached an impasse over free agency and the compensation system for restricted free agents. This led to a ten-day work stoppage between April 1 and April 11, 1992. However, the players and owners reached a new CBA and the season was completed.

Labor peace was short-lived. In the fall of 1994, after no agreement was made on account of issues of salary control and free agency, the owners locked out the players and the result was the cancellation of almost half the season, plus the All-Star game. On January 12, 1995, the parties came to an agreement, which became the governing CBA for the next nine years. That CBA expired after the 2004 season, which led to another lockout and the cancellation of the entire 2004–05 season.

The 1995 CBA permitted unrestricted free agency at age thirty-one for veterans with at least four years of NHL experience. A shared pool of draft choices compensated teams losing such free agents (Lapointe, 1995). It also contained a rookie salary cap and a restrictive free agency system (rarely used) for players who met either the specific age or experience requirements but did not attain unrestricted free-agent status. Restricted free agents were free to negotiate and sign a player contract with any club, although significant compensation in the form of draft picks by the signing club was required (NHL CBA, 1995, Article 10.2(a)(ii)). The prior CBA also had a unique salary arbitration system. If an owner disagreed with an arbitrator's salary determination, that owner could "walk away" from the obligation to pay. The teams can do this up to three times over two years, but no more than twice in any one year. Players who are affected will become free agents.

The 1995 CBA did not employ any general salary cap structure, except for the rookie cap. Since the league did not share revenues except for national broadcasting and cable contracts and merchandising, significant salary disparities occurred. A dramatic increase in player compensation resulted from signings by large-market teams in the United States. During the 1990–91 season, salaries averaged $271,000. Three years later the figure jumped to $572,161. In the 2000–01 season, the average salary was $1,434,884, which rose to $1.8 million in the 2003–04 season (Youngblood, 2004).

On first glance, largely as a result of expansion and licensing agreements, NHL revenue grew from $500 million to $1.93 billion from 1993 to 2004. But a very high percentage of that money has gone to the players, who have seen their compensation grow from $300 million to $1.46 billion during that same period (Heika, 2004).

## *The 2005 Collective Bargaining Agreement*

In 2004, the NHL locked out the players, resulting in the cancellation of the season. Only after 301 days of often acrimonious negotiations did the parties ultimately come to a new agreement. Reflecting the uncertain financial health of the league caused by a significant diminution of broadcast and cable revenues, as well as the financial difficulties of certain teams, the new agreement, concluded in July 2005, came about after the union agreed to the proposals sought by the NHL management.

The loss of their salaries during the season-long layoff obviously hurt the players economically, but it also hurt the league (at least temporarily), because the NHL had to win back alienated fans, sponsors, and advertisers. League officials argue that, although several teams are still struggling, NHL has recovered quite well and is in good health (Custance, 2009), using high attendance as evidence (Skolnick, 2008). However, the NHL pales in comparison with the other major sports leagues, which is reflected in its loss of its cable network contract with ESPN, less newspaper coverage, less prominent national endorsements, and fewer star names remembered by households (Skolnick, 2008).

However, almost half a decade after the lockout, league attendance has increased overall, with particularly high attendance at games in major markets. However, certain franchises have been hurting financially, notably the Phoenix Coyotes and the Nashville Predators. The Coyotes lost $30 million to $40 million in 2008–09 and has endured budget cuts, layoffs, resignations, loss of fans and a drawn-out bankruptcy court battle to keep the team in the Phoenix area (Allen, 2009). David Freeman, owner of the Predators, acknowledged that he had personal cash flow problems and sought to sell off assets to pay liens placed by the Internal Revenue Service in 2009 (*Sportsbusiness Daily*, 2009). Finally, television exposure is still a problem, particularly in the United States (Klein, 2009).

The present six-year collective bargaining agreement, which expires in 2011, provides for a league-wide salary cap, revenue sharing, a revised salary arbitration process, and greater restrictions on entry-level salaries. It consists of the following:

*Salary Cap.* The NHL becomes the third of the four major sports leagues to embrace a cap system. For the 2005–06 league year, salaries were capped at a level of about $39 million per team, with a likely minimum of $21.5 million. In the four years since it was introduced, the NHL salary cap has risen each year. For the 2009–10 league year, salaries were to be capped at $56.8 million, with a floor of $48.8 million (NHL CBA, 2007–11, Article 50, sec. 50.5(b); TSN.com, 2009).

*League Revenues.* For 2005–06, player compensation was based on 54 percent of hockey-related revenues (HRR). The formula for determining the percentage took months to establish and remains highly complex. The basis is 54 percent for a league year that has HRR of $2.1 billion. However, the players' share increases if revenues rise. They get 55 percent when NHL revenues hit $2.2 billion, 56 percent at $2.4 billion, and 57 percent at $2.7 billion (NHL CBA, 2007–11, Article 50, sec. 50.4(b)).

*Maximum Player Compensation.* No player may receive more than 20 percent of a team's revenue in a single season (NHL CBA, 2007–11, Article 50 Section 50.6(a)). This is a way to control spiraling salaries paid by richer teams for star players. As of the 2009–10 season, the highest paid player made $11.36 million.

*Revenue Sharing.* The top ten moneymaking clubs contribute to a fund shared by the bottom fifteen teams—ranging from $3 million to $8 million per club. Revenue sharing derives from league-generated revenues, player escrow, and playoff revenues and from the top ten teams, but teams receiving funds are subject to performance standards (NHL CBA, 2007–11, Article 49, sec. 49.5).

*Salary Arbitration.* Under the old CBA, teams had no control over which players could file for arbitration, and arbitrators looked to the compensation of other players of similar quality to make a determination, which could be any amount between the parties' requests. The present CBA states that players who sign their first NHL contracts are eligible for salary arbitration after four years of service. (It drops to three years if the player is twenty-one, two years if twenty-two or twenty-three, and one year if the player is twenty-four) (NHL CBA, 2007–11, Article 12, sec. 12.1(a)). It requires an arbitrator to choose between the club's offer and the player's request. Also, teams may seek arbitration for an unsigned player in an attempt to roll back the salary of a player whose production has slipped. As in the prior agreement, a team may "walk away" from an arbitration ruling, rendering the player a free agent. The ability to reduce the salary of a perceived underachieving player may be a real bonus for the owners (NHL CBA, 2007–11, Article 12, secs. 12.3(b) and 12.10(a)).

*Entry-Level Salaries.* Although the prior CBA imposed a cap on rookie salaries, bonuses paid to top rookies circumvented the limitations and, according to the owners, resulted in increases in salaries to veterans through salary arbitration. The new agreement capped salaries at $850,000 for 2005 (below the $1.075 million of the prior deal) and at $900,000 for 2009 and 2010, and ties bonus money to both team and individual success during a particular season. So, for example, bonuses could be awarded if the player's team plays in the Stanley Cup final round (NHL CBA, 2007–11, Article 9, sec. 9.3(a) and Article 50, sec. 50.2(b)).

*Free Agency.* Under the prior CBA, players over thirty-one or with ten years' experience qualified for unrestricted free agency. The new agreement reduces the age requirement to twenty-seven, phased in over the life of the new CBA. Specifically, in 2006, it dropped from thirty-one to twenty-nine, or younger if a player had eight years of NHL experience; for 2007, unrestricted free agency was age twenty-eight or seven years' experience; for 2008 and onwards it is age twenty-seven or seven years of experience (NHL CBA, 2007–11, Article 10, sec. 10.1(1)).

*Rollback of Salaries.* In one of the most unusual provisions in sports league CBAs, player salaries were decreased by 24 percent for the first season after the lockout. This marks the first time a players' union of a major sport agreed to an outright reduction in salary.

*Escrow Account.* Players are required to deposit a percentage of their salaries into an escrow account at the start of the season, where it remains until the league calculates revenues for that year. If league-wide salaries exceed a stated percentage of revenues, which ranges from 54 percent to 57 percent, the players will be obliged to return an undetermined portion of their incomes to the escrow account (NHL CBA, 2007–11, Article 50, sec. 50.4(b), (c), and (d)).

*Minimum Salary.* This was raised from $450,000 in 2005 to $500,000 in 2009, 2010, and 2011.

*Draft.* The CBA imposes a weighted NHL draft lottery in favor of poorer-performing teams: The club with the fewest regular-season points will have the greatest chance (25 percent) of winning the draft drawing. The only clubs with the opportunity to receive the first overall selection are the five with the lowest regular-season point totals.

*Limited Team Buyout Rights.* If a player is twenty-six or older, a team may buy a player out of his contract at two-thirds of its value at no cost toward the salary cap during a fifteen-day period between June 15 (or starting forty-eight hours after the conclusion of the season) and June 30. If the player is under twenty-six, that figure is one-third (NHL Standard Players' Contract, 2005, sec. 13(d)).

*Drug Testing.* The agreement requires a minimum of two drug tests a year with no advance warning. A player will earn a twenty-game suspension for a first-time offense, a sixty-game ban for a second, and a permanent suspension from the NHL after a third violation. Drug testing occurs between January 15 and the end of the regular season (NHL CBA, 2007–11, Article 47, sec. 47.6).

Finally, in a benefit to veterans, players with ten years of service and 600 games can request a single hotel room while on the road (NHL CBA, 2007–11, Article 16, sec. 16.9).

## The Women's National Basketball Association

Because of its recent vintage and smaller cash flow, the WNBA utilizes a salary cap structure more universally, but employs some novel methods to enhance player compensation.

In 2008, the WNBA and the WNBA Players' Association agreed to a new six-year collective bargaining agreement. Among key terms of the pact:

Veteran minimum salaries increased from $42,000 to $50,000. Rookie salaries also increased under the new deal, with the minimum in 2008 at $34,500, a rise from $32,400 in 2007.

The salary cap structure is unique: Cap systems encompass a hard salary cap and a "flex" cap, which is somewhat higher and can be utilized if the owners choose to do so. The "hard cap" increases result from a guaranteed 3 percent annual increase each year and the "flex cap" results give an additional 4 percent over the hard cap figure. For each club of the twelve-team league, the hard cap was set at $750,000 for the 2008 season, $772,000 for 2009, and $796,000 for 2010. For 2011 and 2012, the amounts are $810,000 and $844,000, respectively. For the flex cap, amounts during the term of the CBA are $772,000 for 2008, $803,000 for 2009, $827,000 for 2010, $852,000 for 2011 and $878,000 for 2012 (Dixon, 2008).

Players who enter their seventh year in the league became unrestricted free agents and restrictive free agency extends to those who have played more than five years (WNBA CBA, Article VI, secs. 9 and 5).

For the 2008 season two players per team could be designated "core players." For 2009–12, that designation is reduced to one player. Core players cannot be unrestricted free agents, but the team has to pay the maximum salary under the agreement, which in 2010 was $101,000 (WNBA CBA, Article VI, sec. 7).

If a restricted free agent receives an offer she wants to take from a new team, details of the contract proposal must be made to the player's old team, which has five days to match the offer (WNBA CBA, Article VI, sec. 7).

Marketing restrictions for players were lessened significantly. Under the previous CBA, players were prohibited from signing individual endorsement deals with companies competing against WNBA league and team sponsors in eighteen product categories. That has been limited to six product categories (WNBA CBA, Article XXVI, sec. 2).

## Major League Soccer

Unionization came relatively late to MLS players. After years of unsuccessful antitrust litigation, in which the courts ruled that MLS's attempts to impose salary caps and other cost controls were not illegal, the players commenced labor negotiations, which produced three CBAs. The most recent CBA between MLS and the MLS Players' Association concluded in March 2010. The five-year CBA provides:

- Guaranteed contracts for all players at least twenty-four years old with three years of MLS service. The majority of the players in the League will have guaranteed contracts each season.
- An increase in a team's salary budget from $2.315 million per club in 2009 to $2.55 million in 2010 (10.15 percent) and an increase of 5 percent per year thereafter.
- An increase in the minimum salary for senior roster players from $34,000 in 2009 to $40,000 in 2010 (17.64 percent) and an increase of 5 percent per year thereafter. For players whose annual compensation is less than $125,000, the minimum increase in base salary will be 10 percent for players who play in at least 66 percent of their club's games and 12.5 percent for players who play in at least 75 percent of their club's games.

Regarding player movement, no unrestricted free agency exists, but the League will establish a "re-entry draft" for players who are out of contract. Generally, this option is available for the players in the following categories:

A   A player who is at least twenty-three years old with three years of MLS service and whose option is not exercised is placed in a re-entry draft and made available to all clubs at his option salary.

B   A player who is at least twenty-two years old with one year of MLS service and who is asked to take a pay cut after contract termination is placed in a re-entry draft and made available to all clubs at his current salary.

C   A player who is at least thirty years old with eight years of MLS service and whose contract has expired is placed in a re-entry draft unless his team makes him a qualified offer that must be at least 105 percent of his last salary. If placed in the re-entry draft, the player will be made available to all clubs at a salary equal to 105 percent of his last salary.

D   A player who is at least twenty-five years of age with at least four years of MLS service whose contract has expired is placed in a re-entry draft unless his team offers him a base salary of at least as much as the base salary paid to him in the last year of his contract. If placed in the re-entry draft, the player will be made available to all clubs at a salary equal to the salary in the final year of his contract (Gooch, 2010).

## Miscellaneous Labor Issues

### Player Drafts—Age Restrictions

The NFL, Major League Baseball, the NHL, and the NBA take varying approaches regarding the minimum age of player eligibility for the leagues' entry drafts. Of the four major leagues, the NFL's policy is the most controversial.

Consisting of seven rounds, it requires a player to be three seasons removed from the graduation of his high school class. So if his class graduated in 2007, eligibility begins at the 2010 draft. (Note that the requirement does not mandate graduation from high school; NFL CBA, Article XVI, sec. 2.) In 2004, Maurice Clarett, a running back who played one year at Ohio State, challenged this restriction as a violation of antitrust laws. A lower federal court agreed and ordered him eligible for the NFL draft, concluding that, because the CBA between the NFL and the NFLPA did not specify the age restriction, it was not within the scope of the nonstatutory labor exemption to the antitrust laws. The U.S. Court of Appeals for the Second Circuit reversed that ruling, concluding that the age restriction was proper and within the scope of the antitrust law exemption, because it was agreed to by the union and the management, even though its specifics were not included in the current CBA (Clarett v. NFL, 2004).

This case, especially the trial judge's conclusions, received considerable press and public attention, much of it misdirected. The issue was not whether it was "fair" or "just" to ban Clarett, but rather whether it was legal under the meaning of the antitrust laws. Unfortunately, the appeals court's opinion—a more legally consistent ruling—received much less play (Hack, 2004; Zinser, 2004).

In Major League Baseball, the draft is held yearly in June. It consists of a multiple number of rounds, which can vary from year to year. Since the pool of potential players is large, the draft consists of many rounds. In 2007 and 2008, there were fifty rounds. Eligible players include those who have graduated from high school and have not yet attended college or junior college; college players, from four-year colleges, who either have completed their junior or senior years or are at least twenty-one years old; and junior college players, regardless of how many years of school they have completed. If the player doesn't sign with the team that drafted him and goes on to enroll in college, he cannot be drafted again until after his junior year. Generally, a player is eligible for selection if he is a resident of the United States or Canada and has never before signed a major league or minor league contract. This includes residents of Puerto Rico and other U.S. territories. Also eligible are residents who enroll in a high school or college in the United States, regardless of their place of citizenship (MLB. com, no date).

At this time, all thirty Major League Baseball clubs draft in the order of finish, worst to first. Any team can sign players from countries not covered by the draft. However, there is a one-year suspension for any player who fabricates his name, age, or nationality on documents such as U.S. entrance visas.

In the NBA, the draft is just two rounds. One notable difference in the NBA draft is that the National Collegiate Athletic Association allows college athletes to apply for early entry into the NBA draft by giving notice sixty days before the draft date without automatically forfeiting their remaining college eligibility. The rule permits athletes to declare for early entry, though they can opt out ten days after the NBA draft to return to collegiate competition (NBA CBA, Article X, sec. 8). The NBA rule permits players who choose not to attend college to be eligible, because the league now requires a prospective player to be at least one year removed from the graduation of a player's high school class or at least nineteen years old at the time of the draft (NBA CBA, Article X, sec. 1). Players from outside the United States must be twenty-two years of age during the calendar year of the draft to be eligible. The rule seeks to limit players opting for the NBA right out of high school, like LeBron James, Carmelo Anthony, and Amare Stoudamire, who either opted to go pro after high school or left college early to do so (Henderson, 2009).

In the NHL, to be selected in the June draft, players must turn eighteen by the following September 15.

### States' Nonresident Taxes on Athletes

It seems unusual to end this labor relations chapter with a subject as complex and arcane as taxes, but, given the substantial incomes of many professional athletes, cash-strapped states and localities have enacted laws to extract revenues from nonresident athletes. Such a scheme serves two purposes: first, to tap into a lucrative source of income, and, second, to do so without having to impose new taxes on their citizens.

In the early 1990s, Philadelphia was the first city to actively collect taxes on income earned by nonresident professional athletes within its city limits. Many other cities and states have since followed Philadelphia's lead by taxing nonresident professional athletes in both individual and team sports.

New York State takes an aggressive role in collecting taxes from nonresident athletes. Home to seven franchises in the four major sports leagues, this large number of professional teams means that a number of nonresident athletes compete in the state. This method of revenue raising serves New York well, especially given New York's high personal income tax rate (New York State Tax Law, sec. 631(c)).

## Summary of Key Information

### *Average Player Salaries (2009–2010)*

- MLB: $3.24 million
- NBA: $5.854 million
- NFL: $1.1 million
- NHL: $2 million

### *Salary Cap*

- MLB: No cap.
- NBA: A "soft cap" calculated annually based on an amount rising from 48 percent to 51 percent of "basketball-related league income" over the life of the agreement. Amount: $57.7 million per team (2009), and adding on exceptions, team average salary amount rises from $5.585 to $5.854 million. Also, individual player salary caps based on years of experience.
- NFL: A "hard cap" is set at 59.6 percent of "projected total revenues" or $128 million (2009). Teams can exceed the cap, but have to allocate a percentage of certain contracts to future years (in the form of signing bonuses or back-loaded contracts) to do it.
- NHL: A cap based on 54 percent of league revenues, or $56.8 million per team (2009).

### *Average Team Payroll (2009)*

- MLB: $88 million (twenty-five players)
- NBA: $72 million (fifteen players)
- NFL: $120 million (est.) (fifty-three players)
- NHL: $105 million (twenty-three players)

### *Player Share of Defined Gross Revenue (2009)*

- MLB: 51 percent
- NBA: 57 percent
- NFL: 59.6 percent
- NHL: 55 percent

## Contracts

- MLB: Guaranteed.
- NBA: Guaranteed.
- NFL: Not guaranteed. Teams can cut players at any time with no future obligations except signing bonuses, which for salary cap purposes are prorated over the life of the contract even if the amounts are paid upfront.
- NHL: Contracts are fully guaranteed and can be bought out at two-thirds of their value.

## Free Agency

- MLB: Players with six or more seasons are unrestricted free agents at the end of their contracts.
- NBA: Unrestricted free agency applies in most situations after three years, subject to a right to match option by the player's original team.
- NFL: Restricted free agency after three seasons and unrestricted after four in a capped year; in an uncapped year (2010), it is three to five years for restricted free agency and six years for unrestricted free agency. Teams designate transition players and franchise players, but must pay them from a stipulated standard.
- NHL: In 2009, players become unrestricted free agents at age twenty-seven. Players eligible after service of one to four years, depending on their first standard contract signing age.

## Arbitration

- Major League Baseball: Players with at least three seasons and fewer than six are eligible. Both parties must agree for arbitration to go ahead.
- NBA: None.
- NFL: None.
- NHL: Players eligible after service of one to four years, depending on their first standard contract signing age.

## Information Check

When covering labor issues, a journalist should determine:

1 Does a CBA exist? If so, most are available online.
2 If so, what are the relevant provisions at issue?
3 If the CBA has expired and labor negotiations occur, what are the main issues?
4 If either side tosses financial figures, try to get independent expert verification of the accuracy of those figures. Because professional leagues and teams are not public corporations, they are not subject to independent auditing.
5 Why was a strike or a lockout called at a particular point in time? (Note that players may continue to work after a contract expires.)
6 If an employer mandates an impasse, why did it make that decision? Ask experts to assess the likelihood of a labor law violation.
7 When a settlement occurs, ask several experts to assess its merits and ask each for a prediction as to whether the goals of the parties will be met.
8 What kind of salary cap system occurs? Obtain a basic knowledge of how it works.
9 What kind of arbitration system applies and what is its relative importance in the settlement?
10 If divisions occur within the ownership or union ranks, what are the reasons for those divisions and the possible ramifications?

## References

Aldridge, D. (2009, July 8). Worldwide recession affects NBA salary cap for 2009–10. Retrieved December 21, 2009, from http://www.nba.com/2009/news/features/david_aldridge/07/07/salarycap.feature/

Allen, B.-M. (2002). Embedded contract unionism in play—Examining the intersection of individual and collective contracting in the National Basketball Association. *Connecticut Law Review, 35*, 1.

Allen, K. (2009, December 15) Coyotes aiming to reconnect with fans after bankruptcy. Retrieved December 28, 2009, from http://www.usatoday.com/sports/hockey/nhl/coyotes/2009-12-14-reconnecting-with-fans_N.htm

*Baseball Archive* (1998). Minimum and average player salaries 1967–1997. Retrieved April 22, 2010, from http://www.baseball1.com/bb-data/bbd-mas.html

Boeck, S., & Nightengale, B. (2010, April 5). USA Today salary survey: 14 MLB teams cut payroll. *USA Today.* Retrieved April 10, 2010, from http://content.usatoday.com/communities/dailypitch/post/2010/04/sliding-mlb-average-salary-down-17-from-2009/1m

Bradley, R. (n.d.). Labor pains nothing new to NBA. *Association for Professional Basketball Research.* Retrieved April 22, 2010, from http://www.apbr.org/labor.html

Clarett v. NFL, 369 F.3d 124 (2d Cir. 2004).

Coon, L. (n.d.). NBA salary cap FAQ. Retrieved May 5, 2004, from http://members.cox.net/lmcoon/salarycap.htm

Cozzillio, M. J., & Levinstein, M. S. (1998). *Sports law: Cases and materials* (pp. 663, 776). Durham, NC: Carolina Academic Press.

Cunningham, M. (2004, February 29). Players pay price for booming NFL; Union members lag behind their pro counterparts. *Sun-Sentinel,* p. 1C.

Custance, C. (2009, May 12). Conversation: Gary Bettman. Retrieved, December 15, 2009, from http://www.sportingnews.com/nhl/article/2009-05-12/sporting-news-conversation-gary-bettman

Dixon, O. (2008, January 27) Players union and league agree on a new CBA. *USA Today.* Retrieved January 14, 2010, from http://www.usatoday.com/sports/basketball/wnba/2008-01-27-new-cba_N.htm

Down, F. (1981, May 30). Man in the news: Marvin Miller. *United Press International,* Sports Section.

Dupont, K. (2004, February 13). Report: NHL lost $273 million. *Boston Globe,* sports sec., p. 4.

Dworkin, J. (1981). *Owners versus players: Baseball and collective bargaining.* Boston: Auburn House.

Enlund, T. (2000, October 29). Timberwolves got caught by paper trail. *Milwaukee Journal-Sentinel,* p. 03C.

Federal Baseball Club v. National League of Professional Baseball Clubs, 259 US 200 (1922).

Fennell, T. (1994, October 3). Baseball's troubled history, edited by Tom Fennell. *Maclean's,* p. 8.

Flood v. Kuhn, 407 US 258 (1972).

Gooch, C. (2010, March 23). And now the MLS CBA details. *Kansas City Star.* Retrieved April 22, 2010, from http://www.kansascity.com/2010/03/23/1832173/and-now-the-mls-cba-details.html

Hack, D. (2004, February 6). Judge orders N.F.L. to permit young athletes to enter draft. *New York Times,* p. A1.

Heika, M. (2004, February 7). Stopped cold; High salaries, low scoring and dismal ratings have mucked it all up for the NHL. *Dallas Morning News,* p. 1C.

Henderson, L. (2009, April 15). History of players in the NBA draft. *Associated Content.* Retrieved April 22, 2010, from http://www.associatedcontent.com/article/1628384/history_of_high_school_players_in_the_pg3.html?cat=14

In the Matter of National Basketball Players Association and National Basketball Association (Lockout Arbitration, Opinion and Award) (1998). (Feerick, Arb.).

Kansas City Royal Baseball Corp. v. MLBPA, 532 F.2d 615 (8th Cir. 1976).

Klein, J. (2009, October 1). NHL preview: Matters of finance and safety unsettled as season begins. Retrieved December 30, 2009, from http://www.nytimes.com/2009/10/02/sports/hockey/02hits.html?_r=1

Lapointe, J. (1995, January 12). Pact reached for salvaging hockey season. *New York Times*, p. A1.

Mackey v. NFL, 543 F.2d 606 (8th Cir. 1976).

MacNeil, R., & Lehrer, J. (1993, September 6). *Strike, you're out? Weighing the benefits.* Broadcast/PBS.

Major League Baseball Collective Bargaining Agreement ("Basic Agreement"). Retrieved August 10, 2010, from http://mlb.mlb.com/pa/pdf/cba_english.pdf

Matter of Arbitration Between MLBPA and the 26 Major League Clubs, Grievance No. 86-2 (1987).

McCann, M. (2008, December 1). Answering the key questions in the Plaxico Burress case. Retrieved November 20, 2009, from http://sportsillustrated.cnn.com/2008/writers/michael_mccann/12/01/plaxico.burress/index.html#ixzz0Xpgn4BCj

McNeil v. NFL, 790 F. Supp. 871 (D. Minn. 1992).

Michaelis, V. (1998, October 20). Ruling shocks, disturbs; players admit owners now have the hammer. *Denver Post*, p. D05.

Miller, I. (2003, November 12). 49ers are in bind for 2004. *San Francisco Chronicle*, p. C1.

MLB.com (n.d.). First year player draft official rules. Retrieved January 15, 2010, from http://mlb.mlb.com/mlb/draftday/rules.jsp

National & American League Professional Baseball Clubs v. Major League Baseball Players Association, Labor Arbitration (1976), 66, 101.

National Labor Relations Act, 29 USC, sec. 151 *et seq.* (2010).

NBA CBA, various sections. Retrieved August 12, 2010, from http://www.nbpa.org/cba/2005

NBA v. Williams, 45 F. 3d 684 (2d Cir. 1995).

NBA.com (2009, July 7). NBA salary cap set for 2009–10 season. Retrieved, November 30, 2009, from http://www.nba.com/2009/news/07/07/salarycap.ap/index.html

*New York Times* (1992, February 10). Teams get higher salary cap, p. C4.

NFL CBA, various sections.

nflplayers.com (2010). NFL hopeful FAQs. Retrieved August 10, 2010, from http://www.nflplayers.com/about-us/FAQs/NFL-Hopeful-FAQs/

NHL, Collective Bargaining Agreement (1995). Article 10.2(a)(ii)). Retrieved August 10, 2010, from http://letsgopens.com/nhl_cba-old.php?id=10

NHL, Collective Bargaining Agreement (2007–11). Various sections.

NHL Standard Players Contract (2005). Exhibit 1, NHL Collective Bargaining Agreement. Retrieved August 10, 2010, from http://www.nhlpa.com/About-Us/CBA/

N.Y. tax. Law sec. 632 (McKinneys, 1988).

Powell v. NFL, 930 F.2d 1293, 1303 (8th Cir. 1989), cert. denied, 498 U.S. 1040 (1991).

Quirk, J., & Fort, R. D. (1997). *Pay dirt: The business of professional team sports.* Princeton, NJ: Princeton University Press.

Robertson v. NBA, 389 F. Supp. 867 (SDNY, 1970).

Ryan, B. (1991, June 23). Miller labored to make major leagues a better place to play. *Boston Globe*, p. 51.

Seifert, K. (2004, July 25). Vikings insider; Mad hatters; Vikings' innovative salary cap strategy has put them in great position for future. *Minneapolis Star-Tribune*, p. 1C.

Selig, B. (1995, April 9). Baseball hired temporary replacements. *New York Times*, sec. 4, p. 14 [letter to the editor].

Seymour, H. (1960). *Baseball: The early years* (pp. 111, 150, 232). New York: Oxford University Press.

Silverman v. Major League Baseball Player Relations Committee, 880 F. Supp. 246 (S.D.N.Y. 1995).

Skolnick, E. (2008, December 28). Outdoor game shows how NHL's trying to grow. Retrieved, December 24, 2009, from http://nbcsports.msnbc.com/id/28434036/ns/sports-nhl//

*Sporting News* (2004, March 22). Spending now will cost Snyder later, p. 56.

*Sporting News* (2010, April 5). MLB salaries are down 17 percent, according to report. Retrieved April 11, 2010, from http://www.sportingnews.com/mlb/article/2010–04–05/mlb-salaries-are-down-17-percent-according-report

*Sportsbusiness Daily* (2009, December 1). Predators owner Freeman having personal cash flow problem. Retrieved December 20, 2009, from http://www.sportsbusinessdaily.com/article/135233

Strachan, A. (2005, March 5). NHL isn't a clunker. *Toronto Sun*, p. 58.

Staudohar, P. (1988). The football strike of 1987; the question of free agency. Retrieved May 12, 2010, from http://www.bls.gov/opub/mlr/1988/08/rpt1full.pdf

Thomas, J. (2004, March 7). Higher cap brings spending to a head. *St. Louis Post-Dispatch*, p. D12.

TSN.com (2009, June 26). NHL, NHLPA, set cap at $56.8 million next year. Retrieved January 3, 2010, from http://www.tsn.ca/nhl/story/?id=282925

*USA Today* (n.d.). Salary databases, basketball. Retrieved December 15, 2009, from http://content.usatoday.com/sports/basketball/nba/salaries/totalpayroll.aspx?year=2008–09

Weiler, P. C., & Roberts, G. R. (2004). *Sports and the law* (3rd ed.). St. Paul, MN: West.

WNBA Collective Bargaining Agreement (2008). Various sections. Retrieved August 10, 2010, from http://www.womensbasketballonline.com/wnba/wnbacba08.pdf

Youngblood, K. (2004, January 20). Business of the NHL; Bucks beget blame; NHL salaries have risen fast, as the rate of finger-pointing about the cause. (Minneapolis) *Star Tribune*, p. 1C.

Zasky, J. (2009, August 4). Dead money on the Steelers' salary cap. Retrieved November 25, 2009, from http://www.nfltouchdown.com/dead-money-on-the-steelers%E2%80%99-salary-cap

Zinser, L. (2004, May 25). Federal appeals court denies Clarett's bid for the NFL. *New York Times*, p. D2.

# 7 Sports Agents

Agents are among the most misunderstood stakeholders in the sports business. The media often portray them as high-powered unethical deal makers who negotiate multimillion-dollar contracts for their clients and take large amounts of athletes' money to live a life almost as glamorous as those they represent. Good journalists should be wary of this simplistic characterization. Although unscrupulous agents exist, it is unfair and untrue to generalize all agents this way. Most agents are not wealthy, flamboyant, or criminally suspect individuals. In fact, many struggle and have to earn a living by combining agency with other work.

Agents have a number of important roles, depending on the particular athlete, the sport, and the nature of his or her representation. Some agents only negotiate player contracts; others specialize in endorsement deals; whereas still others manage the athlete's finances. Agents also serve as confidants, advisors, friends, and babysitters of their athletes. Often an agent, especially one representing a young and inexperienced athlete, serves as de facto guardian of the athlete's interests. Among their tasks: speaking to the press when their athlete's conduct results in criminal charges, finding legal representation for the athlete, counseling the athlete about his or her confidential personal issues.

The diverse roles of a sports agent make the position difficult to regulate, and the lack of uniform regulation and standards has resulted in a number of agents who lack the skills to do the job effectively and, even worse, a few who commit criminal acts against the athletes they represent. Even with haphazard regulation, many agents do their jobs well and are respected by athletes, their unions, and the team owners and general managers on the other side of the negotiating table.

## The Business

As noted earlier, most agents do not live a life of riches and glamour. Only a select few land the big athlete and the lucrative contract. Many more have to struggle to stay in business. Often their agency will be a side business of their law or accounting practices. The Baltimore-based agent Tony Agnone gives a word of advice for anyone interested in entering the sports agency business: "Don't." He adds:

> I try to explain to them it's not the best thing in the world. It's a very competitive business. I try to convince them there are other things to do besides being an agent. . . . It's a situation that's very competitive, very time consuming. It's got to be done very meticulously, and there is some involvement of luck. If the planets are all aligned, it works (Cohn, 2004).

Many enter the business with dreams of glory. But according to figures provided by the National Football League (NFL) Players' Association (NFLPA), which regulates anyone who represents an NFL player in contract negotiations with the league, of the approximately 1200 NFLPA-certified agents, almost 70 percent do not represent even one active player (Shropshire & Davis, 2003, p. 15). Ten percent of the agents represent 75 percent of the players (Cohn, 2004). According to Shropshire, in the National Basketball Association (NBA), there are 350 agents for about 400 active players. However, fewer than one-third of those agents represent players. In Major League Baseball there are about 325 agents representing 1200 players, and in the National Hockey League (NHL) there are about 150 representing 800 active players. As discussed later in the chapter, one must be certified with the appropriate players' association to represent active players (Shropshire & Davis, 2003, p. 125).

No matter what kind of sport is involved, one common thread permeates this business: difficulty in landing and keeping talent. Some agents expend considerable costs in travel and great amounts of time hoping to sign talent. With the growing internationalization of sports, many find basketball players playing in Europe or Canada.

Qualifications, or lack thereof, have created more headaches. Although some of the players' associations, such as the NFLPA, require agents to pass a qualifying exam, no uniform educational standards exist. Although many agents possess law or accountancy degrees, others do not. Even for those with professional licenses, a sports agency has particular rules and issues not found in a traditional law or accounting practice. The salary cap structure in the NFL and NBA and various arbitration rules among each of the major leagues are two important examples. Often the rules are technical (as shown in the preceding chapter), so even a competent and responsible person may forget or be unaware. In 2004, David Joseph, the agent for the then San Francisco 49ers' wide receiver Terrell Owens, admitted missing the NFL's deadline to file the necessary paperwork for free agency status. Although the player ultimately signed with the team of his choice, the Philadelphia Eagles, the result occurred through a player trade. Agents for two other elite NFL players made similar mistakes (Maske & Shapiro, 2004).

Ethical issues permeate the business. First, agents compete against other agents for clients. Although traditional legal rules forbid "tortious interference with contract"—one person attempting to get another to break a contract—in practice it is difficult to apply this prohibition. Athletes often sign with one agent and then change their mind and sign with another. If these terminations—whether by the athlete alone or with the encouragement of another agent—occur before the player signs a professional contract, there is little the first agent can do. If he or she sues the former client for breach of contract, two major problems exist: (a) The damages collected would be minimal or nonexistent because that aggrieved agent did not negotiate a contract for the player, and (b) the act would have serious business consequences. Other athletes could very well shy away from this agent, hurting the business. So in many cases, the former agent has to consider this a cost of doing business.

Rumors of agent payoffs to prospective clients abound, despite the prohibition of this practice under state and, more recently, federal law. Agents may do this using several techniques: outright payoffs, giving "loans" to athletes with repayment after a contract is signed, giving payouts to coaches to "deliver" clients, and the use of third parties—known as "runners"—to dispense money and gifts to players.

Examples of payoffs to athletes include a $6,000 shopping spree at a Foot Locker store in 1994 by a number of Florida State University football players and an alleged payment of $54,000 to a University of Iowa running back (Shropshire & Davis, 2003, pp. 2–3).

Despite attempts to regulate their conduct, cases of egregious behavior occur and make headlines. In the 1980s, the agents Norby Walters and Lloyd Bloom represented a number of NFL players. In 1988, a federal grand jury indicted the pair on racketeering charges, accusing them of using money, gifts, and threats of violence to obtain representation contracts with college athletes, which violated National Collegiate Athletic Association (NCAA) rules. One year earlier, a federal district court in New York took the unusual step of refusing to enforce a contract made by the agents and an Auburn University player, citing "overriding policy concerns" (Walters v. Fullwood, 1987). In a subsequent criminal prosecution, Walters and Bloom were convicted for mail fraud and racketeering. Walters received a jail term and had to pay restitution of almost $300,000. However, an appeals court overturned the conviction on the grounds that the trial judge failed to properly instruct the jury and other procedural grounds (U.S. v. Walters, 1993). In 2002, a Florida jury convicted William "Tank" Black of defrauding six NFL players out of $8.5 million (Pound, Pasternak, Madden, & Hook, 2002).

In November 2004, the former NBA star Scottie Pippen won an

$11.8 million judgment against a prominent Chicago financial adviser who was entrusted with $17.5 million of his money and proceeded to lose $7 million of it in questionable investments (Roeder, 2004). "It's a situation that goes on every day," Pippen was quoted as saying in the *Chicago Tribune*. "There's always a crook out there" (Isaacson, 2004). The article quoted Ron Shapiro, an agent and former securities commissioner for the state of Maryland, as saying "A significant number of professional athletes are de facto bankrupt [because of poor investments], meaning their debts outstrip their assets."

The former Los Angeles Laker star Kareem Abdul-Jabbar lost close to $5 million on failed hotel and restaurant ventures, as well as investments in Arabian horses, oil wells, and gold coins in the 1980s. He, like other athletes, gave their agents a power of attorney, meaning a legal right to invest the athlete's money in whatever manner the agent wanted. Presently, the NBA and NFL, in conjunction with their players' associations, include financial planning advice as part of their mandatory rookie orientation (Grossi, 2003).

## Mega-agencies

Although many agents either work alone or as part of a small group, the trend over the last twenty years has been the rise of large or "mega-agencies." If the agency has a strong stable of clients, the talent can be marketed into other areas of the sports business, such as event production and marketing, and licensing the intellectual property of their clients.

The first and most venerable mega-agency is IMG. Founded by the late Mark McCormack in the early 1960s, the firm grew from a small operation representing the interests of a few individual golfers to a behemoth. It has represented some of the top tennis and golf stars (IMGWorld.com, 2010). Just as important, IMG owns and operates professional tennis tournaments showcasing its talent pool. By owning these tournaments, IMG earns more money than just commissions from its athletes; it keeps the revenues from the tournament itself. More controversially, IMG operates "training academies" for young athletes. In 1987, it bought the Nick Bollettieri Tennis Academy (considered one of the premier training centers for talented professionals-to-be) and expanded it to include more sports and locations.

IMG is not the only mega-agency firm. Octagon also provides more services than contract negotiation, including marketing and endorsements, team relations, public relations, and financial planning services. Its website includes event management, TV rights sales, and new media planning (http://www.Octagon.com). SFX, in particular, grew from acquisitions of smaller agencies.

More recently, CAA Sports, founded in 2004, has become the dominant sports agency in the United States for representing athletes in the four major team sports. In 2010, CAA represents 130 NFL players, and the agent Tom Condon, a former president of the NFLPA, has personally represented six No. 1 overall draft picks since 1998. Condon negotiated the then-richest contract in NFL history for Indianapolis Colts quarterback Peyton Manning—a $98 million deal, including a record $34 million signing bonus—and has negotiated seven contracts with at least $20 million in guaranteed money (*SportsBusiness Daily*, 2008).

Large agencies have a mixed record of success. Individual agents, often used to working independently and having achieved notoriety by doing things their way, have not always fitted into a corporate culture. In 2005, Arn Tellem resigned and exercised an option to buy back SFX, which had merged with Octagon, and take his clients (*Los Angeles Times*, 2005). In 2010, Jeff Sperbeck, an NFL agent specializing in marketing and endorsements for, among others, John Elway, left Octagon and launched a new agency (Mullen, 2010).

## Duties of an Agent

Agency law governs the basic responsibilities of any sports agent (sometimes called an athlete agent). Simply put, an agent represents another person, known as a principal, and negotiates on behalf of that principal (in our case, an athlete or a coach) in order to secure a contract. Agents often possess considerable power (known as "authority") but remain a representative. An agent cannot overrule the wishes of the principal because the agent can only act within the authority given to him or her by the principal.

The nature and limitations of an agent's authority are illustrated by the circumstances surrounding the incentive-laden contract signed by the running back Ricky Williams after he was drafted by the New Orleans Saints in 1999 (Shropshire & Davis, 2003, p. 16). The New Orleans Saints traded to get a high draft pick so that they could pick Williams. That fact gave the player considerable leverage in the negotiations. But the ultimate contract seemed odd. Williams's contract included an $8.84 million signing bonus and base salaries that ranged from $175,000 to $400,000 over the course of the deal. Williams could earn another $500,000 each year if he reached at least ten of twenty-six goals worth $50,000 apiece (Mihoces, 2000).

Many criticized the deal, questioning agent Leland Hardy's judgment and competence, and pointed to his lack of experience in negotiating football contracts (Burwell, 1999). Ultimately, Williams fired Hardy and sought a trade to the Miami Dolphins because of his unhappiness in New Orleans. Upon arriving in Miami, his contract was reworked to a more traditional one, with fewer incentives and more upfront money.

What did not get proper attention was the fact that the idea for this incentive-laden agreement came not from Hardy, but from Williams. Williams reportedly told Hardy to reject a $25.6 million offer over seven years and to go with the incentivized contract. Williams later admitted: "I'm first and last when it comes to my decisions . . . I don't work for my agent. My agent works for me. This was my decision and my decision alone" (Shropshire & Davis, 2003, p. 16). Williams's statement perfectly summarizes the agent–principal relationship. The agent must follow the instructions of the principal, even if it may be against the agent's better judgment.

However, the agent has some important obligations to the principal, known as fiduciary duties. A fiduciary possesses a very high degree of loyalty to the principal and cannot engage in conduct considered a conflict of interest or act in bad faith. Based on this definition, an agent *cannot* do the following: (a) take payments from third parties to secure an agreement; (b) direct the principal to sign a contract with an entity owned or partly owned by the agent or a relative or close friend of that agent without disclosure of that fact; or (c) fail to reveal relevant information to the principal. The same fiduciary duties occur when an agent (or financial advisor) has the power to invest the athlete's money. The agent must invest it as a "reasonably prudent investor" would and must keep the athlete informed of the nature of the investments. Under no circumstance can the athlete's money be used for personal reasons. As discussed later, the NFLPA has drafted separate rules governing financial advisors.

A notorious example of a breach of fiduciary duty involved an agent named Jerry Argovitz, who represented Billy Sims, an All-Pro with the Detroit Lions. In 1983, Sims sought a new contract with the Lions and Argovitz tried to leverage more money because the Houston franchise of the new United States Football League (USFL) also sought Sims's services. Argovitz and the Lions were making progress in their negotiations. However, Argovitz gave the impression that the Lions were "dragging their feet" and brought Sims to Houston. The USFL team made an offer, which was accepted by Sims. However, Sims did not know that Argovitz owned 29 percent of the Houston team or that Argovitz never contacted the Lions with that offer so they could attempt to match it. He even asked Sims to sign a waiver stating that Sims could not sue Argovitz for breach of fiduciary duty (Detroit Lions & Sims v. Argovitz, 1984). Not surprisingly, the court ruled that Argovitz breached his fiduciary duty.

## The Rise of Agents

Although sports agents date from the 1920s, their numbers and use were at first limited. Most contract negotiations occurred directly between the athlete and the owner or general manager of a team. In the case of individual sports, the prohibition of professionals from the elite tournaments effectively negated the need for representation. A few highly regarded athletes negotiated endorsement agreements. A famous example occurred when the makers of the Baby Ruth chocolate bar signed the New York Yankees slugger Babe Ruth to an endorsement contract.

In the few cases where athletes sought agent representation, management was often contemptuous. An often recited story involves the late Green Bay Packers coach Vince Lombardi and a player named Jim Ringo. Lombardi, seeing a gentleman with Ringo, asked who he was. Ringo replied that the man was to help in the contract negotiations for the upcoming season. Lombardi then excused himself, stepped into an adjoining room, and made a telephone call. When he returned, Lombardi informed Ringo that he was negotiating with the wrong team because the Packers coach had just traded him to the Philadelphia Eagles (Shropshire & Davis, 2003, p. 10).

The then-existing salary structure presented a fundamental problem. Compressed salaries existed in all of the major league sports because of "reserve" clauses that prohibited outright or at best severely restricted free agency. In the 1960s and 1970s, the emergence of rival leagues such as the American Basketball Association (ABA), the World Hockey Association (WHA), and the American Football League (AFL) gave players more negotiating opportunities and increased their need for agent representation. To obtain credibility, these new leagues needed established stars and offered talented players more lucrative contracts than what they had. "Negotiations" in a true sense did occur, and agents represented these players. In time, the rival leagues either folded or merged with the more venerable league. Fortunately for the players, this coincided with the end of the reserve system and the rise of free agency either through arbitration or through collective bargaining. For the first time, bona fide arm's-length negotiations, often with several teams simultaneously, increased demand for agents. The creation of salary arbitration systems for non-free-agent athletes created yet another reason to obtain agent representation.

Off-field activities increased the demand for agents and increased the need for sophistication and expertise. The rise of endorsement opportunities required contract negotiations between agents representing individual professional athletes such as Arnold Palmer and nonsports entities. The greater incomes derived from player salaries and endorsements necessitated money management skills, something that many athletes lacked. Finally, the higher income brackets of more and more athletes necessitated the need for effective tax planning, and athletes used the services of agents or financial planners to limit the tax bite of federal and state tax laws. As a result, the higher salaries earned by players translated to more income for agents. Agents then (and now) normally take a percentage of the amount negotiated, so the higher the contract, the greater the reward for the agent's work.

## Agent Responsibilities

### Securing Talent and Contracting with Teams and Endorsers

The first (and possibly most difficult) task for the agent is to secure talent. A newly minted agent often must pound the pavement, speaking, cajoling, and charming a potential client. Unethical agents have offered money and goods to secure a representation contract for a talented athlete.

Often, the fiercest competition surrounds collegiate or even high school athletes entering the draft of the league. In too many cases (although not all), the athlete being solicited exhibits little experience in making a choice. His or her decision in choosing one particular agent over others may be based on many variables, such as personality and opinions of family members (who can have a major say). Without belittling the importance of these reasons, the major consideration in choosing an agent should be experience in contract negotiations and financial planning—in other words, a more hard-headed business decision. But, in many cases, a hotshot young athlete pampered since junior high school has developed a large ego and seeks a person who accedes to his or her every whim. Of course, more sophisticated and mature athletes (and their families) exist, especially among veteran players, who, by experience and perspective, have learned not to choose an agent just on personality and salesmanship.

A successful agent develops a reputation based on the satisfaction of clients. Negotiating a lucrative contract for a first-round draft pick in the NFL or a free agent in baseball may bring many more clients. But a lack of perceived success renders the opposite effect, as unhappy clients switch agents, often for subjective reasons, unfair reasons, or no reason at all. In May 2005, the NBA superstar LeBron James fired his agents, Aaron and Eric Goodwin, after they negotiated $135 million in endorsement agreements with Nike, Upper Deck, Sprite, and others, in addition to the $18.7 million he was guaranteed in his first four seasons under his player's contract. Instead, James decided to hire a former high school teammate to handle his affairs (Banks, 2005). To determine the "success" of an agent journalists should determine both how many new clients he or she signed, and how many he or she has retained. An agent who signed three NFL first-round draft picks but lost five established NFL players in a given year may arouse suspicion as to his success with veteran players. Reporters do not do enough of this kind of analysis.

After securing and retaining talent, the agent's goal remains signing the athlete to a contract. Without a player's contract, the agreement made between the agent and the athlete becomes practically meaningless. The athlete has no obligation to pay the agent because agent fees are based on a percentage of the contract consummated between the athlete and the team or endorsement company.

A highly drafted player or a top free agent generates a lucrative contract, with a good payday for the agent. If it is a long-term deal, the agent receives the percentage for as long as the athlete plays under the contract. However, an agent representing a journeyman player often incurs more legwork for less compensation. The agent may have to spend more out-of-pocket money to take the player to team tryouts or to shop him or her to teams in other countries. Ultimately, the time and effort may be for naught. The agent may spend thousands of dollars to no avail if the athlete is not picked and signed by a team.

Of course, the more money paid to the athlete, the more the agent receives in compensation. This is particularly important because most of the players' unions (except the Major League Baseball Players' Association) cap the fees agents may earn. In the NBA, the cap is 4 percent of the amount paid to the athlete. In the NFL, it is 3 percent. Because of these limits, the real money is made on endorsements and financial management. There is no limit on the percentages an agent may earn from endorsement deals (which usually is 15 percent, but can be as high as 20 percent of the contract amount).

### Understanding National Collegiate Athletic Association Rules

An agent who seeks student-athletes must understand the NCAA's restrictions. As described in chapter 3, the NCAA imposes a system of amateurism that prohibits compensation for student-athletes based on their athletic skills (NCAA Division I Bylaws, sec. 12.1.2). The rules also prohibit the student-athlete from signing any contract with an agent or receiving payments from an agent (NCAA Division I Bylaws, sec. 12.1.2(g)). However, securing advice from a lawyer concerning a proposed professional sports contract shall not be considered "contracting for representation by an agent" (NCAA Division I Bylaws, sec. 12.3.2). If an agent violates these rules, the student-athlete loses eligibility and scholarship support. However, before state and federal laws were enacted, the agent often went unpunished because the NCAA bylaws do not directly apply to agents.

---

#### Ethical Issue: Are these Rules Ethical Enough?

Like most NCAA rules, the above provisions are strictly enforced. The question involves the nature of the anti-agent rules. The following case illustrates the difficulties. In June 2006, after Andrew Oliver graduated from high school, the Minnesota Twins selected him during Major League Baseball's first-year player draft. During contract negotiations with the Twins, Oliver's agent (who was a licensed attorney) was present in the room. Oliver ultimately turned down the Twins' offer and instead enrolled at Oklahoma State University. He then fired his agent. The now-former agent informed the university of a violation under NCAA Division I bylaw section 12.3.2.1, which prohibits a lawyer from "being present during discussions of a contract offer with a professional organization or have any direct contact with a professional sports organization on behalf of the individual" (NCAA Division I Bylaw, 2009, sec. 12.3.2.1). In the spring of 2008, Oliver was declared ineligible for violating the NCAA's "no-agent" rule. Oliver challenged the no-agent rule in court, seeking damages and an injunction preventing its enforcement, arguing it was arbitrary under Ohio law because baseball players, unlike those in football and basketball, are draft eligible before they enter college, and the need for a "legal advisor" is imperative during negotiations. A trial judge ruled in Oliver's favor, ordering the NCAA to reinstate Oliver and prohibited the NCAA from enforcing its "no-agent" rule (so Oliver was eligible to pitch for the school's baseball team).

The NCAA and Oliver negotiated a $750,000 settlement. As part of the settlement, a prior court order forbidding the NCAA to enforce the two bylaws was vacated (Oliver v. NCAA, 2009).

A similar situation occurred in 2009 when James Paxton, a talented left-handed pitcher who attended the University of Kentucky, was drafted by the Toronto Blue Jays, but returned for his senior year after rejecting a $1 million signing bonus. He retained agent Scott Boras as an "advisor" but after it was reported that Blue Jays officials may have dealt "directly" with Boras, rather than Paxton and his family, the NCAA sought an interview with Paxton on the question of his amateur status.

Paxton refused the request on the basis of attorney–client confidentiality and was suspended by the NCAA. Paxton sued to enjoin the suspension and, after a Kentucky appeals court refused the request, Paxton left the school. His attorney said "They want him to answer questions no one else on earth would have to answer" (Mullen, 2010).

The two cases pose difficult questions about the enforcement of the agency rules. The question remains: What is the difference between an attorney acting as an "advisor" as opposed to an agent? Does the difference make sense or is it hair-splitting? Can the NCAA take the step of demanding that a client consent to an interview dealing with matters otherwise privileged between an attorney and a client?

## Understanding the Appropriate Sport's Collective Bargaining Agreement

Often agents specialize in only one sport for financial and practical reasons. Working in only one sport permits development of an expertise in the issues unique in that sport, which, in particular, include a detailed knowledge of the league's salary caps. An agent representing NFL, NBA, and NHL players must demonstrate knowledge of the salary cap system in the NFL, NBA, and NHL and have the challenge of negotiating in an atmosphere of "capped money" or "free money," a challenge not applying to their counterparts in Major League Baseball, which does not have a cap system.

## Engaging in Damage Control

One agent classified his job as "agent, manager, social worker, family counselor, and psychologist. All under one hat" (Shropshire & Davis, 2003, p. 28). Indeed, the agent's duties often transcend deal making. Often, the agent maintains a close relationship with the athlete and is the person the athlete turns to in the event of an arrest, family emergency, or general personal crisis. If the athlete is connected with an embarrassing event made public, the agent serves as the spokesman, hoping to deflect criticism and to polish the tarnished image.

### Study: Scott Boras

The baseball player agent Scott Boras has developed a reputation as one of the most dominant and aggressive agents in the game. His clientele included the prime free agents Carlos Beltran, Matt Holliday, Daisuke Matsuzaka, Adrian Beltre, Jason Varitek, Derek Lowe, Mark Teixeira, Barry Zito, and Magglio Ordoñez, as well as Alex Rodriguez, Bernie Williams, and Greg Maddux. This gives him considerable power not only to negotiate lucrative contracts, but also to time the negotiations in an attempt to control the market and increase the interest of teams battling to obtain one of those players (Klis, 2004; Cole, 2007).

Boras, like other top agents, limits his stable to only the top players, about sixty-five. Significantly, to avoid the problems of spoiled rookies (and, in baseball, of players whose lack of seniority limits their bargaining position), he said, "We're not for everybody. And not everybody's for us. We're looking obviously for the most skilled players. And we're looking for discipline and players who want to take information and want to improve themselves."

Boras often presents projections on the likelihood of success of his clients in the future, even ten years ahead. For example, if Carlos Beltran can maintain the averages he had during the 2001–04 seasons, he should have 436 home runs, 562 steals, and 2695 hits at age thirty-seven. At age forty, the numbers would be 523, 673, and 3208, which compares with the statistics of great players in the past. "When owners see these names, then it starts to click," Boras said. "They start to realize what kind of player we're dealing with. I tell them, 'Now do you understand why I'm placing a premium on this guy?' I say: 'This isn't what Scott Boras says. This is what the facts are'" (Klis, 2004).

Boras, like other agents, has received his share of criticism in the media. Some have questioned his calculations and his overselling of players to gullible owners, notably when in 2000 he negotiated the largest contract in sports history: Alex Rodriguez's $252 million, ten-year contract with the Texas Rangers (since renegotiated to $275 million for a new ten-year term as the now-Yankee exercised his option to open that contract three years before its expiration). But remember, that is an agent's job. He or she represents a client to the best of his or her ability within the guidelines of his or her fiduciary duties. And more than once, baseball club owners learned the hard way that Boras knew the collective bargaining agreement better than they did.

For example, Boras first attained success because he used the baseball amateur draft rules brilliantly. He told owners that a draft choice would go back to college or become a free agent if the team did not sign that player. The owners imposed a fifteen-day deadline to offer draft picks a contract—something they considered a formality. Boras did not think so and used the short time period as a sword to force contracts to talented but untested players. He stunned the industry by getting Brien Taylor a record $1.55 million bonus from the Yankees in 1991. Owing to a shoulder injury caused by a fight in a bar, Taylor never played one game for the team (Klis, 2004).

However, that does not mean that Boras is a fit for everyone. He has lost some prominent players in recent years, such as Alex Rodriguez and Kenny Rogers. Therefore, a key question for journalists is gauging how many athletes does the agent lose, as well as gain.

## Alternatives to Agents

### *Going Alone*

Before the advent of free agency, players generally represented themselves. Although most athletes now employ agents, a few still decide to negotiate on their own. One may question the wisdom of such a strategy, but if the athlete feels confident and sophisticated enough to represent himself or herself, there is no rule requiring procurement of an agent. Two notable baseball free agents—the slugger Gary Sheffield and the pitcher Curt Schilling—negotiated their own deals in 2003. Sheffield negotiated a three-year, $39 million deal with the Yankees, and Schilling a $25.5 million contract with the Boston Red Sox (Hohler, 2003).

In addition to confidence and sophistication, an athlete negotiating alone must display intestinal fortitude. Schilling admitted that his negotiations with the Red Sox were "intense and stressful" (Salisbury, 2003), but he negotiated a very favorable contract with the team. The three-year deal, beginning in the 2004 season, called for a $12 million salary for that season and increases for the following years. Presciently, he also negotiated a clause stating that, if the Red Sox won the World Series, his salary would rise by $2 million the following year, and a fourth year (originally an option) would become guaranteed. The team won the World Series in 2004 and Schilling received the additional compensation. What made Schilling's tactic all the more interesting was that the "World Series" clause violated baseball rules prohibiting contract bonuses based on team achievements. The Red Sox, which did not want to lose Schilling on a technicality, argued for the clause. The commissioner's office approved the deal, but later ruled that such a clause would be invalid in future cases (Chass, 2004).

Often, the player (or representative) discusses the "great abilities" possessed whereas the general manager points out the "weaknesses." If an athlete takes the negotiations personally and feels slighted by the team during the process, those bad feelings may linger, affecting the athlete's morale. Often it is best not to have the athlete in the negotiating room, but to delegate the sometimes ugly process to a representative.

Sometimes family members represent the athlete. A seeming middle ground between athletes negotiating their own contracts and employing an outside party, the family representative has advantages, but some particular pitfalls. A familial relationship between the athlete and the agent results in a strong bond of trust and respect, as opposed to a nonfamily agent who represents other similarly talented athletes and may not have the same bond. However, family members may also take management tactics personally, which will result in the same kind of hard feelings as if the athlete negotiates. Or the family member agent may interfere with the operations of the team. One reason for the deterioration in relations between the Philadelphia Flyers and its then-captain Eric Lindros in the late 1990s was the acrimony between Lindros's agent (his father) and the team's general manager, Bobby Clarke. The tension between Clarke and Lindros became particularly acute when Carl Lindros began advising Clarke on whom his son should play with and how long he should be allowed to recover from injuries (Gormley, 2001).

### Legal Representation

Although many agents are attorneys, their duties are different. An attorney retained to negotiate a contract has a more limited role, whereas the agent acts as a general representative and confidant for the athlete. A number of mature athletes—who do not need the wisdom and guidance of an agent, but require the expertise of a competent negotiator—may utilize legal help.

Lon Babby, formerly an attorney for the Washington, DC, law firm of Williams & Connolly, serves as an example of an attorney retained for the purpose of negotiating a contract. In return, the athlete paid an hourly rate for services, rather than giving a percentage of salary. When Babby negotiated Grant Hill's $45 million deal with the Detroit Pistons, Babby billed $100,000, based on his hourly rate. An agent charging the National Basketball Players' Association (NBPA) rate of 4 percent would receive $1.8 million. Babby's client list includes the basketball player Tim Duncan (Ludden, 2000). Currently, the agency firm of XTS Sports charges its players hourly for the amount of time spent negotiating a contract. The range is $1000–$2000 per hour. Its client list includes Alfonso Soriano.

## Standards and Regulations

### SPARTA

Unlike professions such as law or public accounting, agents are not licensed by a governmental body. However, after much debate over the last decade, Congress, in an attempt to impose uniform standards, passed the first federal law regulating agents: the Sports Agent Responsibility and Trust Act (SPARTA).

Enacted in September 2004, SPARTA makes it unlawful for sports agents to sign student-athletes into representational contracts with bribes or misleading information (Sports Agent Responsibility and Trust Act, 15 USC, 2004, sec. 7802). It permits prosecution of violators by the state where the misconduct occurred. Before SPARTA, thirteen states did not have any laws governing sports agents. Thus, sports agents could operate with relative impunity in those states.

Specifically, SPARTA makes it unlawful for a sports agent to (a) entice a student-athlete into entering an agency contract by giving false or misleading information or making false or misleading promises or representations; (b) provide anything of value to the student-athlete or anyone associated with the athlete; (c) fail to disclose in writing to the student that he or she may lose NCAA eligibility after signing an agency contract; or (d) predate or postdate contracts. In that sense, SPARTA mimics many state laws and NCAA rules. But SPARTA provides a uniform standard for prosecuting agents who choose to ignore NCAA rules and state law.

Under provisions of SPARTA, both the sports agent and the student-athlete are required to notify the school's athletic director within seventy-two hours of signing the contract or before the athlete's next sporting event (15 USC, 2004, sec. 7805). Additionally, SPARTA brings sports agents under the jurisdiction of the Federal Trade Commission (FTC), and considers sports agents who lure student-athletes with lies and gifts to enter into agency contracts in violation of the FTC's Unfair and Deceptive Businesses Act (15 USC, 2004, sec. 7803). It allows schools to seek civil remedies for any damages or expenses incurred through its violation.

Although already prohibited by the NCAA and many states, the behavior targeted by SPARTA had been difficult to prosecute because of jurisdictional issues. The passage of this federal law eliminates these issues by enacting nationwide standards. Before the passage of SPARTA, only non-agent-specific laws, such as the Racketeer Influenced and Corrupt Organizations Act (RICO) and federal mail fraud statutes, were used to criminally prosecute agents such as Norby Walters.

### State Statutes

SPARTA supplements and standardizes states' involvement with agents. In 2000, the Uniform Athlete Agents Act (UAAA) was proposed, and it was ultimately adopted in a number of states (in 2009 that number was forty). It requires agents to register in a given state, and requires specific contract language in agreements between an agent and an athlete, including the amount and method of calculating his/her fees, a description of the services to be provided, the duration of the contract, and, significantly, a notice that the student-athlete may lose eligibility to compete in the given sport and a requirement that the university's athletic director be notified within seventy-two hours. The UAAA contains a fourteen-day cancellation provision (UAAA, 2000, sec. 10c). Violators are subject to civil and criminal penalties. Its provisions served as the basis for the later federal statute.

There are a few states with different laws and, when writing on this topic, suffice it to say that it makes sense to access the appropriate laws, which can be found on databases such as findlaw.com or lexis.com.

## Players' Union Certification

The unions from the major sports certify the agents that represent their players, requiring that the agent abide by the union's rules and regulations in order to maintain their sports agent certification. In 1983, the NFLPA asserted its authority to regulate player agents. The NBPA did so in 1986, followed by the Major League Baseball Players Association and the National Hockey League Players Association.

## National Football League Players' Association

In order to represent an NFL player, the agent must be certified with the NFLPA. The NFLPA refers to these agents as "contract advisors," and its regulations require agents to pass a proficiency exam. Also, they limit how much compensation the agent receives from the player. The NFLPA regulations prohibit agents from providing inducements to college athletes and their family members and friends in order to sign a player; negotiating a contract in violation of the collective bargaining agreement; engaging in unlawful conduct; acts involving fraud or dishonesty; or violating the fee schedule. Penalties, including expulsion, exist for those who violate the rules. Unlike rules for agent counterparts in basketball and hockey, the NFLPA does permit an agent to represent both players and coaches (NFLPlayers.com, 2007).

In August 2003, over 300 more aspiring athlete agents sat the NFLPA's annual certification exam, and roughly 66 percent of those hopefuls passed, becoming contract advisors (Hall & Rothchild, 2004). More recently, this percentage has not changed.

The maximum an agent receives under the regulations is 3 percent of the amount paid to the player, except for players tagged as franchise or transition players. In those cases, the amount ranges from 1 to 2 percent. Because NFL player contracts are not guaranteed and are often incentivized, the rules prohibit the agent from receiving the 3 percent of the entire contract amount "upfront." Note that the compensation restrictions apply only to contracts negotiated with an NFL team. Other types of contracts, such as endorsements, have no fee restriction.

The NFLPA also regulates "financial advisors" based on a different set of standards. This program, the first of its kind, requires such advisors to have appropriate education and three years of experience as a broker-dealer, investment advisor, certified public accountant (CPA), or certified financial planner (NFLPlayers.com, 2007).

## National Hockey League Players' Association

The NHL Players' Association (NHLPA) regulates the conduct of agents who represent players in individual contract negotiations with clubs.

Anyone not designated by the NHLPA as being duly certified ("certified agent") cannot represent players.

Standards for applicants suffer in comparison with those in the NFLPA system. Although a criminal records check occurs, there is no requirement to pass an exam. A "certification guide" spells out the scope of the agent's services and business practices. Each prospective agent fills out a questionnaire about his or her qualifications and background, which goes to the NHLPA certification group. The NHLPA bases its decision on this questionnaire as well as on the background check. As is the case with the other players' associations, prospective agents do not have to be accountants or lawyers; agents need not possess a college degree. Although agents go through a background check, standards have been lax. In one case, the NHLPA certified an agent despite a conditional discharge after pleading guilty to assaulting a player (Weir, 2004).

### Major League Baseball Players' Association

The standards of the Major League Baseball Players' Association (MLBPA) for agent certification mirror those of the NHLPA, as they do not require a college degree or the passing of a test. Also, agent fees lack any limitation, so an agent can charge as much as he or she wishes (Shropshire & Davis, 2003, pp. 77–78). However, these regulations include a peculiar exception. No agent can charge a fee that drives the player's actual compensation below the minimum salary (MLBPA Regulations, 2003, sec. 4f).

According to officials from the MLBPA, in recent years, agents have become increasingly "bolder" and "often underhanded" in attempts to steal players from other agents. But stealing clients is not only unethical (and can result in an agent being decertified by the players' association), it is also illegal. Inducing someone to break a valid contract—called tortious interference—often results in civil liability. Generally speaking, players can change agents at their discretion so proving the "poaching" of a player must be difficult (McCann, 2009).

### National Basketball Players' Association

Athlete agents representing National Basketball Association (NBA) players must be certified with the NBPA. A person pursuing certification must have a degree from an accredited four-year college or university. Once a player agent is certified with the NBPA, that agent is subject to the NBA's "standard of conduct" regulations (NBA Regulations Governing Player Agents, 2004, sec. 3).

The regulations include several general requirements, mainly administrative provisions regarding fees (both to the NBPA and from the players), as well as several sections labeled "Prohibited Conduct Subject to

Discipline" (NBA Regulations, 2004, sec. 3). The prohibited acts mirror those prohibited by the other players' associations: providing inducements to college athletes, family, and friends in order to sign a player; negotiating contracts in violation of the collective bargaining agreement; committing fraud or deceitful acts; breaching the maximum fee schedule; and violating any provision of the standard player agent contract. The NBPA administers a comprehensive program involving mandatory instructional seminars and testing to ensure competence in contract matters. Presently, the maximum fee collected by the NBPA-certified agent is 4 percent of the contract amount.

## Information Check

When covering sports agent and financial advisor issues, a journalist should determine:

1 Does an agent represent the athlete?
2 If so, is the agent certified by the relevant players' association?
3 Did the agent negotiate a contract with a team or an endorsement agreement?
4 Did the agent engage in any conflict of interest or breach of fiduciary duty?
5 How many other athletes does the agent represent?
6 Is the agent's group of athletes increasing? Decreasing?
7 What is the background of the athlete's financial advisor? In the case of the NFL, did the players' association certify the financial advisor?
8 Has the athlete recently switched agents?
9 Did the athlete utilize someone other than an agent? Himself or herself? A family member? An attorney charging an hourly rate?
10 Does the agent work alone, in a small agency, or in a larger agency?

## References

Banks, L. (2005, May 20). James' switcheroo a youthful mistake; while there is nothing illegal about the move, there is much that is illogical and immature about it. *Chicago Sun-Times*, p. 155.

Burwell, B. (1999, October 11–17). Think Williams got bad deal? Don't try to tell him that. *Sports Business Journal*, p. 54.

Chass, M. (2004, November 7). Before helping Red Sox to a title, Schilling helped himself. *New York Times*, p. 5.

Cohn, B. (2004, May 4). Few Jerry Maguires; Aspiring sports agents find the clients scarce, the glamour nonexistent and the going tough. *Washington Post*, p. C01.

Cole, M. (2007). Who's in charge here? Scott Boros, for one. Retrieved January 22, 2010, from http://sports.espn.go.com/espnmag/story?id=3608950

Detroit Lions & Sims v. Argovitz, 580 F. Supp 542 (E.D. MI 1984).

Gormley, C. (2001, August 21). One question unanswered as Lindros leaves. *Cherry Hill* (NJ) *Courier-Post*, p. 3.

Grossi, T. (2003, July 13). Brown's health big factor in contract restructuring. *Cleveland Plain-Dealer*, p. C10.

Hall, T. J., & Rothchild, S. N. (2004, March 10). New York's Uniform Athlete Agents Act. *New York Law Journal*, 4.

Hohler, B. (2003, November 29). Red Sox hit jackpot, land Schilling; Boston signs Arizona ace to $25.5 million deal. *Boston Globe*, p. A1.

IMGWorld.com (2010). About IMG. Retrieved April 22, 2010, from http://www.imgworld.com/about/default.sps

Isaacson, M. (2004, December 19). Unscrupulous advisors, bad investments, lavish spending leave many athletes bankrupt. *Chicago Tribune*, p. 10.

Klis, M. (2004, December 20). Doing business Boras' way. *Denver Post*, p. C-01.

*Los Angeles Times* (2005, September 28). SFX sports chief to buy back L.A. business. Part C, p. 8.

Ludden, J. (2000, July 26). NBA law; Babby wins clients by acting like an attorney. *San Antonio Express-News*, p. 1C.

Maske, M., & Shapiro, L. (2004, May 2). Agent awareness in the NFL; Union considers screening process after costly mistakes. *Washington Post*, p. E01.

McCann, M. (2009, December 16). Did Aroldis Chapman switch agents because of tortious interference? Retrieved February 1, 2010, from http://sports-law.blogspot.com/2009/12/did-aroldis-chapman-switch-agents.html

Mihoces, G. (2000, November 14). Williams' loss doesn't deter Saints. *USA Today*, p. 1C.

MLBPA Regulations Governing Player Agents (2003). See 4F, found in Shropshire, K. D., & Davis, T. (2003). *The business of sports agents* (pp. 77–78). Philadelphia: University of Pennsylvania Press.

Mullen, L. (2010, January 8). Agent Jeff Sperbeck starts own agency after leaving Octagon. *Sports Business Daily*. Retrieved April 22, 2010, from http://www.sportsbusinessdaily.com/article/136036

NBPA Regulations Governing Player Agents (2004). Retrieved April 10, 2010, from http://www.nbpa.org/sites/nbpa.org/files/users/sean.brandveen/NBPA%20Agent%20Application.PDF

NCAA Division I Bylaws (2009). Retrieved August 10, 2010, from http://www.ncaapublications.com/productdownloads/D110.pdf

NFLPlayers.com (2007). NFLPA Regulations Governing Contract Advisors, Sample Representation Agreement, retrieved August 10, 2010, from http://images.nflplayers.com/mediaResources/files/PDFs/SCAA/NFLPA_Regulations_Contract_Advisors.pdf

Oliver v. NCAA, No. 2008-CV-0762, at 4 (E.C.C. Ohio Feb. 12, 2009).

Pound, E. T., Pasternak, D., Madden, M., & Hook, C. (2002, February 2). Money players. *U.S. News & World Report*, p. 30.

Roeder, D. (2004, December 1). Developer's dealings costly to ex-Bulls star. *Chicago Sun-Times*, p. 81.

Salisbury, J. (2003, December 26). Era of the sports agent is here to stay. *Duluth News Tribune*. Retrieved June 4, 2004, from http://www.duluthsuperior.com/mld/philly/sports/7572039.htm?template=contentModules/printstory.jsp.

Shropshire, K. L., & Davis, T. (2003). *The business of sports agents* (pp. 10, 14, 15, 16, 26, 28, 51–52, 78). Philadelphia: University of Pennsylvania Press.

Sports Agent Responsibility and Trust Act, 15 USC, secs. 7802, 7803, 7805 (2004).

*SportsBusiness Daily* (2008, August 20). CAA's Tom Condon named most influential sports agent. Retrieved May 12, 2010, from http://www.sportsbusinessdaily.com/article/123385

U.S. v. Norby Walters, 997 F.2d 1219 (2d Cir. 1993).

Uniform Athlete Agents Act (2000). Retrieved April 10, 2010, from http://www.law.upenn.edu/bll/archives/ulc/uaaa/aaa1130.pdf

Walters v. Fullwood, 675 F. Supp. 155 (SDNY, 1987).

Weir, T. (2004, May 7). Coach was "bad news." *USA Today*. Retrieved April 29, 2010, from http://www.usatoday.com/sports/hockey/nhl/2004-05-04-frost-cover_x.htm

# 8 Team Relocation and Facility Issues

Throughout the history of professional sports leagues, franchises have moved, sometimes two or three times. Within a twenty-year time frame, the Boston Braves moved to Milwaukee and then to Atlanta, while the Philadelphia Athletics moved to Kansas City and then to Oakland. Such moves sometimes result in acrimony and anger. The recent immigration and emigration of the NFL Raiders from Oakland to Los Angeles and back to Oakland has been one of the most controversial, drawing the ire of fans and resulting in considerable litigation.

Why does a team move? Lack of financial success in its present market is one reason. For example, in 2002, the National Basketball Association (NBA) franchise the Charlotte Hornets relocated to New Orleans, on account of lack of attendance, financial losses, and the refusal of voters to approve the financing of a new facility. Similarly, a year earlier, another NBA franchise, the Vancouver Grizzlies, relocated to Memphis.

The potential for greater opportunities in a larger and/or growing market serves as a second reason, the textbook example being the relocation of the Brooklyn Dodgers to Los Angeles in the late 1950s. However, in recent years, the availability of new markets has been limited by expansion, resulting in few locations to which teams can relocate. That leads to the third and most recent justification for team (or, more officially, franchise) relocation: the revenue stream from the facility.

As discussed later, the economics of having a first-class stadium or arena with opportunities to generate revenues by seat licenses, naming rights, signage, parking, concessions, luxury boxes, and premium seating has resulted in attempts by cities to woo teams to different locations or to keep teams. Often, part of the cost of building the stadiums or arenas is borne by taxpayers, directly through funding or indirectly from taxes and bond payments. Although the idea of public financing of facilities has caused controversy, the majority of stadiums and arenas have some public component to their funding. This chapter discusses these issues and also analyzes a typical stadium lease agreement. The subject of stadium economics deserves more media coverage, and young journalists must learn the basics of one of the most important issues in the business of sports.

## A Short History of Franchise Relocation

The first phase of the evolution of the major sports leagues demonstrates a gradual shift from smaller cities to larger ones as the league matures and becomes successful. Although all leagues commenced operations with some teams in larger cities, a surprising number of franchises hailed from the heartland. Teams from baseball's National League, the oldest continuous sports league of the four major sports, once hailed from Providence, Rhode Island, Syracuse, New York, and Worcester, Massachusetts. However, by 1899, the National League was ensconced in the eight largest U.S. cities. The rival American League started as a minor league but then decided to compete with the older league head-on by moving its teams from smaller cities to some of the larger cities where National League franchises were housed, such as from Milwaukee to St. Louis and from Baltimore to New York (Seymour, 1960). St. Louis had double the population of Milwaukee, and New York had over six times the numbers of Baltimore.

The history of the National Football League (NFL) also evidences this movement. The original franchises were in cities such as Canton, Ohio, Hammond, Indiana, and Green Bay, Wisconsin (with the last being the only surviving original NFL franchise in its city of birth). Professional football, initially given second-class status in favor of the far more popular college version, had its roots in these working-class Midwestern cities and towns. Most of the major urban teams such as the New York Giants, Detroit Lions, and Cleveland Browns were expansion teams.

The NBA, created after World War II, included teams from both large and smaller cities. In fact, teams from smaller cities such as Fort Wayne and Syracuse were more stable than their counterparts in larger cities, such as Detroit, Cleveland, Toronto, and Pittsburgh, which folded. Eventually, the Fort Wayne Pistons moved to Detroit and the Syracuse Nationals moved to Philadelphia (and became the 76ers).

For decades, the National Hockey League (NHL) contained only six teams, two in Canada and four in the United States. Each of the "original six" franchises—the Montreal Canadiens, Toronto Maple Leafs, Detroit Red Wings, Chicago Black Hawks, Boston Bruins, and New York Rangers—was financially stable and there was little reason to expand outside those cold-weather areas. A major expansion did not come until the mid-1960s. By the 1990s, team relocations, often from Canadian cities to the southern and western portions of the United States, occurred. The Quebec Nordiques moved to Denver and became the Colorado Avalanche in 1995. The Winnipeg Jets moved to Phoenix and became the Coyotes the following year.

## Waves of Relocation

It is best to look at franchise relocations episodically. Although the early relocations focused on playing in the largest markets (then in the Northeast and Midwest), a second wave of franchise movement—generally to the southern and western United States—began in the post–World War II era. These regions experienced major population growth and created fertile markets for sports franchises to flourish. By 1950, Los Angeles had become the third largest city in the United States, but it had no Major League Baseball franchises, whereas Chicago and Philadelphia, numbers two and four, respectively, had two teams each. Five years later, the Philadelphia Athletics of the American League moved to Kansas City. Then came the New York Giants' move to San Francisco and the Dodgers' departure to Los Angeles. Until that time, St. Louis was the westernmost location for a Major League Baseball franchise.

This era of franchise movement mirrored the movement of the nation as a whole. At the time, a Rustbelt–Sunbelt population migration began. Older stadiums and arenas, often found in decaying portions of cities, were not car-friendly. Fear of crime made fans less likely to come to night games. The facilities, often spartan and ancient, lacked modern amenities. New York's Polo Grounds dated from the nineteenth century and began as a facility for polo. Newer cities, such as Los Angeles, Phoenix, and Dallas, were more car-friendly, and spread over a larger area with swaths of empty space. Modern facilities could be built in undeveloped areas with little difficulty in the city's metropolitan area, rather than in the city proper. The Dallas Cowboys and the Texas Rangers, for example, play in stadiums located between Dallas and Fort Worth.

The popularization of air travel enticed leagues to set up franchises in the south and the west. With teams no longer dependent on railroad travel, a New York team playing a California team as part of a road trip would not cause undue schedule disruption.

With the advent of television, "nationalizing" a sport by opening every region to franchises became a greater priority. Teams in virgin territories could attract fans to a live game event and also to watching the sport on television. The television networks broadcast championship games nationwide, and the more interested the fans were in the sport, the higher the viewership.

The NFL and NBA were more amenable to setting up shop in the West. The San Francisco 49ers were born as an expansion franchise in 1949. In the NBA, the Minneapolis Lakers moved to Los Angeles in 1960 and the Philadelphia Warriors moved to San Francisco two years later. Although the movement of franchises south and west had exceptions (e.g., in 1970 the Major League Baseball Seattle Pilots moved to Milwaukee and became the Brewers), such movements were not the norm.

The first two phases of relocations—the pre–World War II exodus to the larger cities from the smaller ones and then the postwar moves from the Rustbelt to the Sunbelt—made economic sense in a time when gate attendance was the primary factor of financial success. Building a large and loyal fan base was crucial because, with the exception of the NFL, teams did not share local revenues.

Therefore, teams in growing markets with modern facilities could attract more fans and, later on, win more lucrative broadcasting rights for games. In 1953, the National League owners agreed to the first team relocation in Major League Baseball in fifty years when the Boston Braves moved to Milwaukee. The Braves agreed to play in County Stadium, a publicly owned facility, for a favorable lease agreement. Prior to that time, only one other team played in a publicly owned stadium. Every other facility was in private hands (Quirk & Fort, 1997).

## New Stadiums and Arenas

Teams in each of the major leagues keep all or most of the gate receipts, the money spent by fans to see a live contest. Additionally, teams keep revenues from stadium amenities such as concessions, parking, advertising, and luxury seating. These facilities may also include such attractions as angled seating (thus relieving postgame neck strains and giving excellent views of game action from all angles), walk-around open-air concourses that keep fans connected to the game, state-of-the-art video boards, breathtaking views, and retractable roofs. Therefore, the type of home stadium and the type of stadium lease agreement consummated between the franchise and the stadium owner become very important for a team's balance sheet.

New stadium construction boomed in the 1990s. Twenty-three of the thirty major league baseball teams have stadiums that were built after 1991. Twenty-three of the NFL's thirty-two teams built new or renovated facilities during that time period. And, in a departure from the past, all of the new facilities were constructed solely for the sports they were designed for. Another change was that many of these facilities were located "downtown" rather than in a suburban area.

The revenue-generating characteristics of the stadium or arena are a major, if not the main, reason why franchise relocation has occurred in the last fifteen years. This is not to say that stadiums or arenas were not important in past years, but the revenue potential of a state-of-the-art facility is a crucial component because franchises must find consistent revenue streams to earn income at a time of record-high player payrolls. A team may be enticed to a different locale based on a lucrative new stadium deal. Also, a new facility often serves to increase attendance, whether it is in a new city or an existing one.

In some cases, the stadium's ability to produce revenue trumps the size of the market. For example, the Los Angeles Rams moved to St. Louis, an open market, because its former team, the Cardinals, moved to Phoenix in 1987. The team went from residing in the second largest market to the twelfth largest. What enticed the Rams was the proposed stadium and its lease. The team receives 100 percent of concession revenues, 100 percent of revenues from luxury boxes and club seats, and 75 percent of stadium advertising sales revenues (Masteralexis, Barr, & Hums, 1998).

The 1990s and 2000s produced a spate of new stadiums and arenas on both the major league and minor league levels because the often functional but drab facilities built in the 1960s outlived their usefulness, and leases between the teams and the stadium owners (often governmental agencies) expired. Once the old stadium's lease agreement expired, teams often demanded a new facility. If this was not forthcoming, sometimes the teams threatened to move. The Chicago White Sox almost relocated from its venerable location to Florida until a stadium replacing old Comiskey Park was built. As of 2010, because of the construction boom, there are not many major league cities where new stadiums or arenas need to be built. The facility construction boom has also worked its way to the minor leagues, as state-of-the-art facilities are being built to cultivate the growing popularity of minor league baseball (Caldwell, 2005).

## Leagues' Control of Relocation

The rules codified in each of the major sports constitutions limit the right of a franchise to move without the approval of three-quarters of the other owners. In theory, this standard seems onerous, but in reality, few owners have blocked relocations. However, this process demonstrates the inherent conflicts in the relationship between a team and the league. On the one hand, the four major leagues have independently owned teams with their own staffs and their own independent revenue streams. On the other hand, they participate in a cooperative joint venture where certain rights are curtailed by provisions in the league's constitution and bylaws. This system has produced its share of operational difficulties (as explained in more detail in chapter 1) and legal controversies, especially in the area of antitrust law, but it remains the predominant form of team sports administration.

The main reason for prohibiting a relocation to a market where another league team already plays is that no owner will want a rival team moving into the same territory served by the existing team. Direct and potential destructive competition may result in the loss of fans and revenues.

Moreover, other owners and the league itself may not feel comfortable with a team's relocation—even one to a previously unserved market— because of the potentially bad publicity from fans of the departing market losing that team. That may hurt the reputation of the sport and cause resentment for years to come. Additionally, other owners and the league may fear that relocation may make that team either too valuable or not valuable enough. Although this seems counterintuitive, a logic behind this reasoning exists. An unsuccessful relocation may result in a drop in league-wide revenues, affecting the other owners' bottom lines, especially in a league such as the NFL, where virtually the entire broadcasting/cable revenue is shared (Cozzillio & Levinstein, 1997). Conversely, a success-ful relocation can hurt other teams as well, especially in a league such as Major League Baseball, where owners keep much more of their revenue. That in turn may drive salaries up, because the relocated team has more money to pay, increasing its market value. In a salary-capped labor struc-ture, the extra revenue may serve to increase the salary cap, costing the other owners more with little benefit in return.

Some have argued that most league attempts to block franchise reloca-tions were directed at specific owners of the teams that sought to move, such as Charlie Finley, Bill Veeck, and Al Davis, who were perceived as mavericks (Mitten & Burton, 1997). But these actions carry risks. An owner who blocks another's relocation attempt may expect retribution aimed at his own team's attempts in the future. So the result has been relocations without much challenge from the other owners.

From 1950 through 1982, seventy-eight franchise movements occurred in the four major league professional sports. Eleven of those relocations occurred in baseball, forty in basketball, fourteen in hockey, and thirteen in football. More recently, franchise relocations occurred when the NBA's Seattle SuperSonics moved to Oklahoma City and became the Thunder. The Montreal Expos relocated to Washington, DC, and became the Nationals.

In the 1980s, franchise relocation issues resulted in considerable legal and economic debate, which often resulted in litigation. No league wants a repeat of the Oakland Raiders case, in which a federal appeals court ruled that the NFL's relocation rules constituted an antitrust law viola-tion (Los Angeles Memorial Coliseum Commission v. National Football League, 1984). The federal appeals court did not conclude that all reloca-tion limitations are invalid, but it determined that even a league as central-ized as the NFL may not "improperly" block relocation. From a business as well as legal standpoint, that standard is vague and difficult to imple-ment. (Note that Major League Baseball was not affected by this ruling because its longstanding antitrust exemption.)

Given the steep penalties for antitrust violations (three times the jury's damage award), the NFL, NBA, and NHL did not block franchise relocations, thereby diminishing the risk of further litigation. Knowing that maverick owners such as Davis have not been bashful about using the courts to get their way, the leagues decided to pay it safe.

## Facility Attempts to Stop Relocation

Although we have focused on attempts by other owners to block a relocation, a related issue has been attempts by facility owners to stop a move. This issue does not affect a league or its other owners in the same way as relocation of a franchise from an older arena to a new arena in the same city. But a substantial immediate effect on the owner of the facility results because it loses its major paying client. Legally, a facility owner cannot stop a team from moving once its lease expires. However, an owner attempts to protect interests by drafting certain contract provisions in the lease agreement to make it more difficult for a team to terminate the lease before its expiration.

One common way to do this is to use a "liquidated damages" clause that spells out specific monies paid in the event the team breaches its contract and moves either to a facility in the same metropolitan area or to a different city. The amounts can be a flat amount or a per-game rate. For example, the lease agreement between the Minnesota Timberwolves and the Minneapolis Community Development Agency (the owner of the Target Center) stated that total damages for a breach would be $60 million, reduced by $3 million for each of the first ten years during the lease (Greenberg & Gray, 1998). In one NFL team lease, the damages are stated as $50,000 per game (Greenberg & Gray, 1998). The arena lease between the NHL's Phoenix Coyotes and the Jobing.com Arena had a complex liquidated damages clause that started at over $794 million (Dewey Ranch Hockey, LLC, 2009). When covering a possible breach of lease, a journalist should find out the terms of this clause, or whether it exists in the lease at all.

## Relocation and Cities

Much has been written about the effects of a franchise's relocation on the economy of the departed city and on the psyche of the team's fans. Probably the classic example was that of the Brooklyn Dodgers' relocation to Los Angeles in 1957. But the reasons for the move are probably more complex than the simple answer of "abandonment" of Brooklyn by the team. In reality, a generous offer of land for a new stadium, the economic opportunities of a growing market, and the failure of New York to condemn land for a facility in downtown Brooklyn served as the bases (Shapiro, 2004).

A more recent example of a similar public outcry came when the

Baltimore Colts moved to Indianapolis in 1984. To entice the team to relo-cate from its long-time home, the city guaranteed twelve years of annual ticket sales of more than 45,000, took out a ten-year, $12.5 million loan at an interest rate of 8 percent, and committed $4 million for a training facility (Leone, 1997). The Colts were negotiating with both Indianapolis and Baltimore, which wanted to keep the storied franchise. When word of the possibility of the team's move to Indianapolis was made public, the Maryland state legislature tried a novel approach: It considered a law authorizing Baltimore to condemn the team under the concept of "eminent domain," the seizure of private property by the federal or state government or governmental agency for a "public use."

After passage of the Maryland law, the Colts' owner, Robert Irsay, made his decision to move. Without consulting the NFL, Irsay accepted the Indianapolis offer and packed the Colts' property into moving vans in the middle of the night, one day before the Maryland law was to go into effect. Even though the city sued to enforce the law, the fact that the Colts' business, along with any property connected with it, were outside the state made the Maryland law ineffective.

Cities hoping to obtain franchises or keep them have often been gen-erous with funds and construction. To lure the Cleveland Browns to Baltimore, enticements included a $200 million rent-free stadium with 70,000 seats, 108 luxury boxes, and 7500 club seats and a $15 million training facility; 100 percent of revenues from ticket sales, luxury suites, club seats, concessions, stadium-naming rights, and parking; and half of all revenues from nonfootball events (Babington & Denlinger, 1995).

In 2009, the issue of league control over relocation came about in a dispute between the Phoenix Coyotes and the NHL over an attempt to sell the team and move it to Hamilton, Ontario. The Coyotes, losing millions of dollars through lack of fan support and a long-term lease commitment, wanted to sell the team to Jim Balsillie, reportedly one of Canada's rich-est individuals (he was a co-owner of the firm that makes BlackBerry) and move it to Hamilton. The league and the city of Glendale, Arizona (which built the facility for the team), protested the proposed sale and the move. The NHL did not want Balsillie despite making a bid for the Coyotes that was considerably higher than any other because of previous attempts to buy and move teams (which were rejected by the league's board of governors). Critical statements about the league's owners may have been a major reason for the board's rejection of his ownership application. However, he made a bid considerably higher than any other bidders.

In an attempt to circumvent the NHL's rules, the Coyotes' owner filed for bankruptcy, seeking a judicial sale of the team to Balsillie. However, the bankruptcy judge, in deferring to the NHL's franchise procedures, rejected that bid, emphasizing the primacy of the league's ownership approval rules. As of 2010, the team is under the control of the NHL and the issue of ownership and relocation is awaiting resolution (Dewey Ranch Hockey, 2009).

## Expansion

As in the case of relocation, each of the leagues requires that an expansion team application be approved by three-quarters of the owners.

Because of the league structure, a new team must go through an involved and often costly process before being selected as an expansion franchise. It has been argued that the limited number of teams entering a league stifles competition and may (except in the case of baseball) run afoul of the antitrust laws. Except for New York, Los Angeles, and Chicago, each city is limited to one team—if not by rule, then in practice. However, the leagues can offer legitimate business reasons for requiring franchise owners to have a certain level of financial security and to not hold ownership interests in other clubs in the same league.

Because a considerable capital investment is necessary to support a competitive professional sports team, a viable sports league must have financially secure franchise owners. Initially the franchise owner must pay expensive expansion fees and operating expenses, and must retain sufficient financial reserves to hire players and coaches, based on rules determined by the league. In all the major league constitutions, a clause limiting expansion and relocation in a "home territory" of an existing franchise exists. Usually that figure is between a fifty- and seventy-five-mile radius around a major metropolitan area (Kurlantzick, 1983). Although the very largest markets have more than one team, a new or relocating team often has to pay what is known as an "indemnity fee."

To obtain an expansion franchise, the applicant must not only be able to pay the expansion fee, but must go through a "due diligence" process to ensure the validity of the information that the potential expansion franchise owner releases. Essentially, this investigation process has not always received enough attention from journalists. Sometimes the leagues themselves have not done a proper investigation, which has led to embarrassing results. In 1997, the NHL approved the sale of the New York Islanders to a "businessman" named John Spano, who, despite practical insolvency, was able to obtain bank loans and to convince the league he had adequate financial resources. Spano ultimately pleaded guilty to fraud in connection with the attempted purchase (Valenti, 1997). More recently, in 2007, the NHL approved a purchase of a minority stake in the Nashville Predators by William "Boots" Del Biaggio, who secured loans to buy the team based on fraudulent financial statements. In so doing, he defrauded banks and investors of millions of dollars. Ultimately, Del Biaggio pleaded guilty to securities fraud and received an eight-year prison sentence (Mickle, 2009).

## Financing a Stadium

With contributions made by cities or states, or both ("public sector"), along with those made by the owner(s) of a franchise or private businesses ("private sector"), franchises have been able to finance and build new state-of-the-art stadiums that provide economic returns and enhancements not recognized in their old counterparts. Except for AT&T Park, the first privately financed ballpark in Major League Baseball since Dodger Stadium opened in 1962, most ballparks are financed with substantial public money (Keating, 2001).

Although most new state-of-the-art stadiums replace multipurpose facilities three to four decades old, new facilities can also replace more recent venues. In Memphis, Tennessee, an arena known as the "Pyramid" opened in 1991. Because the 19,000-seat facility was "antiquated," in that it did not attract restaurants and lacked other revenue generators, the public—through taxes to pay the debt from bond issuances—subsidized the construction of a $250 million arena that houses the NBA Grizzlies. The same occurred in Charlotte, North Carolina, where a new $265 million arena replaced the sixteen-year-old Coliseum housing the Bobcats.

The economic benefits to a franchise include revenue enhancements such as naming rights, advertising, luxury box leases, increased number of club seats, pouring rights (beverages), parking revenues, concessions, and favorable lease terms. This is in addition to the general increased attendance that results when the new facility opens.

## Funding Vehicles

In theory, the use of revenue enhancements mentioned in the preceding paragraph has provided a financial base that allows the franchise to secure funding for a new state-of-the-art stadium or arena. Today, most facilities are financed through a public–private partnership. At least thirty-eight major league sports venues were built or rebuilt using nearly $7 billion in tax-exempt financing from 1990 to 2003, according to a *Washington Post* review of more than forty professional baseball, football, hockey, and basketball projects (Whoriskey, 2003).

The public sector contributes equity (cash), pledges, and revenue from taxes, and/or issues debt through the issuance of bonds, often tax-exempt bonds. The private sector contributes private equity (cash contribution/guarantee from owner[s]), private debt (bank or institutional funds), and/or funds borrowed under a credit facility program run by a particular league (MLB or NFL in particular). Private debt is usually secured by guaranteed streams of revenue from naming rights, luxury suites, club seats, and advertising.

## Public Funding

The use of public funding for financing stadiums remains a controversial and important issue when writing about stadium financing. Public financing has drawn criticism from a number of economists, who argue that the money spent on the facilities does not result in increased revenues for cities, but provides considerable benefits to team owners. Studies by Zimbalist and Noll (1997) and Baade (1994) concluded that such arrangements were money losers (Krueger, 2002).

However, others have concluded otherwise. The essence of those arguments is that "the primary benefits provided by teams to the local communities are consumption benefits" such as the benefits provided by "parks, golf courses, swimming pools, zoos, concert halls" (Green, Klein, & Lebowitz, 1998). They argue that the mere presence of the team in the community confers additional benefits, including "identifying with the success of the team, following the team on television and radio, reading about the team in the newspapers, and talking with their friends about the team" (Dorocak, 1999).

Examining, analyzing, and writing about a proposed new facility requires a basic knowledge of financial lending techniques. It also involves asking pointed questions about the source of the money, the control of the facility once it opens, and the proposed lease terms. In financially troubled times, the monies spent on facility construction or even ancillary issues such as highway construction to and from the stadium or arena can siphon away funds from other governmental activities.

Although a municipality ("the public") owns many stadiums and arenas, the primary tenant team controls the majority of the revenue. Once the facility opens, the amount of money directly invested by NFL teams is quickly recouped, often within a few years—thanks to lucrative luxury boxes, club seats, and considerably higher ticket prices. Taxpayers, however, typically are committed to up to thirty years of debt payments.

Certain public interest or ad hoc groups representing public funding opponents have attempted to stop such funding by utilizing lawsuits, often on the grounds that the government lacked the power to seize land for a private stadium under its eminent domain power. However, such claims have been unsuccessful, particularly after the U.S. Supreme Court utilized an expansive view of "public use," allowing the state to seize private land for a private development as long as there is economic development (Kelo v. City of New London, 2005). Based on this ruling, the courts will not block seizure unless the scheme violates a specific law or regulation (environmental rules come to mind). Otherwise, the courts grant deference to governments to make such decisions (Goldstein v. New York State Economic Development Corp., 2009).

However, the question of the tax deductibility of bonds used to finance sports facilities is complex and has been the subject of controversy. In October 2008, the Internal Revenue Service limited the scope of the tax exemption, which could affect the financing of future stadiums (Internal Revenue Service, 2008, Treasury Reg § 1.141–4(e)(3)).

### Methods of Public Funding

*Bonds.* A bond is a loan, payable with interest, often issued by municipal governments. Purchased by individuals or organizations who serve as creditors, bonds are often secured (guaranteed) by a municipality or state's general taxing power.

Types of bonds include the following:

- *General obligation bonds:* These securities are to be repaid from general tax revenues of the particular government. Such bonds often require governmental approval and have become more and more difficult to use because of public opposition and the need for state and municipal governments to provide more basic projects in uncertain economic times.
- *Special tax bonds:* These securities are guaranteed from monies coming from a specific tax. The municipality, county, or state may levy an additional tax to be specifically used to pay these obligations.
- *Revenue bonds:* These securities are more complex, as they are secured by revenues coming from the facility and/or special taxes passed to pay for them. Often a hotel-use or other tourist-related tax (which is politically safe because tourists do not vote) or on tickets to events in the new stadium or arena, revenue bonds frequently serve as an effective funding vehicle.
- *Lease revenue bonds:* These securities are issued by a governmental authority distinct from the municipality, county, or state, not the government itself. These authorities, sometimes known as public corporations, often have the power to issue bonds and collect tolls or taxes. An example is a bridge or tunnel construction authority. Bonds will be issued as part of a lease agreement between the authority and the government, which leases the facility from the authority and then subleases it back to that very authority. Any revenues collected by the government (and the franchise[s] using it) may be used to pay the authority (Greenberg & Gray, 1996). A number of states have created such authorities, such as the Washington State Public Stadium Authority, which has a seven-member board appointed by the governor, and the Aloha Stadium Authority in Hawaii, whose boards consists of nine members.

Bonds are either taxable or tax-exempt. Tax-exempt securities, meaning those exempt from federal (but not necessarily state) taxation, are preferred, as more attractive to investors. Federal tax law permits the use of tax-exempt bonds to fund sports facilities (although with restrictions) if certain criteria are met. Basically, "private business interests" cannot "control" the facility's use (Greenberg & Gray, 1996).

*Taxes.* States, counties, and municipalities have the power to use tax revenues or levy new taxes to fund the construction of facilities. The type of taxes created is often dictated by the political popularity of the project as well as the creditworthiness of the proposal. Examples of additional taxes would be tax surcharges, sales taxes (or a portion thereof), special taxes on alcohol, tobacco products, restaurant- and hotel-use taxes, and car rental taxes. The laws creating the taxes may have a "sunset" provision that ends a tax at a certain date (i.e., completion of the facility, payment of the debt). The locality or the state may also enact a lottery to raise money either to pay for the facility or to guarantee payment of the bonds.

Governments may also issue certain tax abatements on the real estate taxes the facility would normally pay. And costs of additional road construction, such as special exits from a highway to the facility, are often borne by the local government (and, by extension, the taxpayers) as general expenditures.

### Private Financing

Most stadium and arena financing involves some private sources. Usually banks play a central role, as they lend money outright with some secured source of repayment, such as revenue from luxury suites or concessions. Additionally, private financing includes guarantees by the team owner backed by personal assets or by bonds backed by personal seat license fees. An additional method is the issuance of "stadium investment bonds," secured by the assets produced by the facility (Fraas, 1999). A final method is the use of personal seat licenses (PSLs), explained later in the chapter.

The economic benefits of granting generous stadium deals to lure or keep teams continue to be debated. An economic downturn, market saturation, and questionable economic benefits lead to increased public criticism. State and local governments, often forced to reduce public services or raise taxes, do not have the money to pay for new stadium or arena construction. Also, with expansion in all the major leagues, virgin markets are simply hard to find.

## The Stadium/Arena Lease

Often teams obtain stadium or arena leases on favorable terms, especially if a municipality or government agency owns the stadium or arena. In 1995, Slate Gordon, then a Washington Senator (a Republican who generally espoused the view of minimal intrusion of government in business), pulled together a deal to build a new stadium for the Seattle Mariners. Of the $414 million price tag, the team only paid $45 million. The rest was paid by state bonds. However, the team was given the naming rights, which, coincidentally or not, came to $45 million. In effect, the team did not put up one cent for the facility. Also, the Mariners got all the revenues—concessions, luxury boxes, parking. The only obligation the team had was paying the operating costs of the stadium (Quirk & Fort, 1999).

It is rare (but not impossible) that a team owns a stadium outright; more frequently, the team will lease to play its games in the facility. Given the public interest in sports franchises, the lease between the team and the stadium or arena it plays in is a document that should receive far more scrutiny and coverage than it often does receive, especially if the public and/or bondholders are paying for the facility's construction. The following sections break down the basic terms of such an agreement.

*Duration.* To recoup the cost of construction and upkeep, the stadium or arena lease often includes a long initial term—up to forty years—and some options to extend. The option clauses gives the team the opportunity to extend the lease, usually on similar terms. Some lease agreements require affirmative written communications if a team wishes to extend the lease under an option clause. Others do the opposite: They require that the team notify the facility owners or manager if they do not wish to extend.

*Termination.* All leases have termination clauses giving the team the right to terminate the lease before the expiration. A lease may permit termination if certain attendance minimums are not met. The Minnesota Twins were able to escape from their lease from their former home, the Metrodome, if the number of tickets sold for three consecutive baseball seasons was less than 80 percent of the American League average (Greenberg & Gray, 1996). A more common provision, known as a "force majeure" clause, allows termination after damage or destruction of the facility due to war, weather condition, or fire.

Additionally, some leases give the franchise the option to terminate at a specified period. The lease for the New Meadowlands Stadium, the home of the NFL's New York Giants and New York Jets, has a term of twenty-five years, but it contains options that, if fully utilized, extend it to reach ninety-seven years. It also contains an unusual termination clause, which allows either team to opt out of the lease every five years after the fifteenth year as long as that team gives the owner (a state agency) twelve months' notice. However, if one team exercises that option and leaves, the other team must stay for the remainder of the initial twenty-five-year lease term (Sports Facility Reports, 2009).

*Use.* The centerpiece of a stadium lease is the right for the team to use the facility and a corresponding right to limit use by others. Of course, a stadium or arena has many uses, such as concerts, rallies, and other sporting events. The way this section is negotiated evidences the scope of the control the franchise has.

A facility is very much like a commercial airline. It makes no money when it is not used. If an airplane sits in a hangar for one day, that one day of income is lost and never replicated. The airplane must fly with paying passengers taking up as many seats as possible.

Similarly, an unused facility does not generate revenues. So for the owner, frequent use is imperative. On the other hand, the principal tenant (team) may want to have "exclusivity" and limit other types of uses as much as reasonably possible. Too much use may result in wear and tear on the field and in seating, and requires the cumbersome job of putting away and taking out equipment.

Although rare, the lease may give the primary team absolute exclusivity, giving the franchise a veto right over any other events potentially held in the facility. Clearly that gives the tenant the right to dictate what events can and cannot be held. More frequently, the exclusivity right is more limited. For a baseball team, it may give the team exclusivity or a priority as to events during the season. For example, it can state that no other event may occur on the day of a baseball game, or that, if the team is involved in any postseason events, a conflicting event scheduled must be canceled to permit the playoff game to be held. Regarding the off-season, the lease may give the team "input" regarding the use of the facility, but not a veto power. If the event results in a likelihood of damage to the field, the team may have the power to reject the event. For example, a baseball team may have the right to bar an auto race on the grounds of the facility because of the likelihood of damage to the property. Finally, the lease often allows certain special events, such as a public memorial event, in the facility within the exclusivity period. In one case, a wedding was performed at Yankee Stadium after the groom received permission from the Yankees, the City of New York, and Major League Baseball to exchange vows with his fiancée on the same spot where Lou Gehrig made his famous farewell speech (Salamone, 2006).

Sometimes, a team will "reserve" event dates (meaning dates of potential home games). That may occur even before a final schedule of games is released by the league involved. Those dates are held exclusively for the team until the team specifically "releases" them (usually because of final schedule changes by the team or the league). Other leases may prohibit sporting events for a certain period of time before the team's games. As the principal tenant, the team does not want competition that may limit gate attendance. For example, the Orlando Magic had a clause in its lease with the City of Orlando (the owner of the arena) that prohibited the city from scheduling a non-Magic "basketball-related event" within the period three days before to three days after a Magic game (Greenberg & Gray, 1996).

Although most leases require the team to play all their home games at the facility, in some cases the lease may permit some games at a location within the home team's market. Before moving into the Staples Center, the Los Angeles Clippers played most of their games in the Los Angeles Memorial Sports Arena. However, their lease granted the team the right to play up to six home games at Arrowhead Pond in Anaheim (Greenberg & Gray, 1996).

Many stadium leases contain a provision permitting the team to have its offices in the facility, along with some training areas and places to store equipment. This is less common in arenas because of lack of space.

*Use by Other Teams.* Issues involving use of the facility by professional teams from other sports frequently occur, and, as noted earlier, the lease sets the priorities. However, two teams from the same sport rarely use the same facility as leases often prohibit this arrangement. However, exceptions occur. In the 1970s, the New York Yankees played in Shea Stadium, then the home of the rival Mets, during the reconstruction of Yankee Stadium and, more recently, the NFL's New York Giants and New York Jets agreed to share the cost of building their new football stadium, which opened in 2010 next door to the teams' former facility in New Jersey.

The New Meadowlands Stadium in New Jersey has a unique and complex bi-team arrangement. It marks the first time in NFL history that two rival teams have entered into a partnership for the purposes of building and subsequently sharing a sports facility. The two teams received a total of $1.3 billion for the stadium construction through separate private financing. The result was that each team completed separate $650 million financing deals. CitiCorp and the Royal Bank of Scotland financed the Jets' portion, while the investment banks Goldman Sachs and Lehman Brothers financed the Giants' deal. In addition, NFL owners approved $300 million in loans to help finance the stadium (Wolffe, 2007). The teams share the revenues generated at the new stadium.

## Stadium Naming Rights

The idea of naming a sports facility after a bank, brewery, or orange juice maker who pays for the privilege is relatively recent. Before the 1990s, facilities were named for their teams, present or past owners, historical figures, or in honor of war veterans. Yankee Stadium, Dodger Stadium, the Nassau Veterans' Memorial Coliseum (Long Island, New York), Veterans Stadium (Philadelphia), and Memorial Stadium (Baltimore) serve as examples. Older fans may remember the owners' names Shibe, Comiskey, Griffith, Crosley, Baker, and Ebbetts emblazoned on their teams' stadiums. In Pittsburgh, Forbes Field was named after a British general who helped found the city. In one interesting example, the Cincinnati Reds played at the "Palace of the Fans," probably the last time a team thought of the fans when naming a ballpark (Erardi, 1999). However, in the last decade and a half, naming rights have become an essential part of stadium and arena economics. As these facilities become more and more expensive, naming rights defray some of the costs of construction.

In 1973, Rich Stadium in Buffalo became the first stadium in any major league to utilize naming rights. The rights fee was $1.5 million for twenty-five years. By 1988, there had been only three naming-rights deals, with a total contract value of $25 million. In 2009, seventy-one "named" facilities existed, worth over $4 billion (ESPN.com, 2009). When the Los Angeles Forum was renamed the Great Western Forum in 1988, many callers hung up, thinking they had dialed a wrong number (Horovita, 1988). Since then, public acceptance of "named" stadiums has increased. In 2004, more than half the arenas and stadiums in professional baseball, football, basketball, and hockey bore corporate names. Some firms even have naming rights in multiple facilities. For example, American Airlines obtained naming rights for arenas in Dallas and Miami. The naming-rights trend has also extended to minor league and college stadiums and arenas. However, the economic recession of the late 2000s reduced the interest for expensive naming-rights deals. As of 2010, the New Meadowlands Stadium (home of the football Giants and Jets), Cowboys Stadium, and Nationals Park do not have naming rights, while Land Shark Stadium reverted back to Dolphin Stadium and was recently renamed "Sun Life Stadium." In contrast to prior deals, the time period and amount paid are modest: five years and a reported net fee of $4 million per year (Sandomir, 2010).

A long-term naming-rights deal provides an excellent funding device. Corporations wish to purchase naming rights for a number of reasons. The repeated use of the name countless times during broadcasts and in print article references constitutes a potentially cost-effective way to advertise. Often, broadcast contracts stipulate that team announcers use the corporate name in all references. Additionally, given that the naming rights are exclusive, competitor firms do not have many alternate facilities to obtain similar rights. The facility becomes attached to that corporation and that corporation only.

Naming rights help create a positive image and foster local goodwill toward a firm, especially if the teams using the facility are successful and popular. They make the business a part of the sports community in that city, especially in regions where the firm seeks to expand operations. A previously unknown financial institution can make a major impact in its new territory by buying naming rights. However, that notoriety has its risks. The Houston Astros' stadium was originally named Enron Field and kept that name for only two seasons. This proved embarrassing after Enron's downfall, with indictments of many of its top directors and officers. Because Enron filed for bankruptcy, the Astros were legally able to find another sponsor. The stadium was renamed Minute Maid Park in 2003, to the great relief of the team and stadium owner. Another issue is team performance. If a firm obtains naming rights for a team that is consistently unsuccessful, it may hinder rather than help the brand.

Naming rights facilitate cross-promotion and tie-ins. For example, Fleet Bank (since acquired by Bank of America) had the naming rights to the Fleet Center in Boston. As part of its rights, automatic teller machines from the bank were installed for patrons to withdraw cash. Chicago's United Center has an airline ticket booth. Also, the firm obtains a luxury box or other select seating, a marquee location for bringing prospective or potential clients. Finally, tax advantages exist. The costs incurred in the purchase of naming rights may be allowed as "advertising business expenses" under the Internal Revenue Code (Internal Revenue Code, sec. 162).

Naming-rights agreements generally last from ten to thirty years with options to renew. Annual payments are made by the firm to the team or to the local government or stadium authority in charge of building the stadium or arena. If a franchise decides to end its tenancy and move out of the stadium at any time during the term of the signage agreement, the firm usually has the right to terminate that agreement. If the stadium or arena is significantly damaged or destroyed by an unforeseen event, the firm may terminate the agreement. If the facility cannot be used for a relatively short time owing to an act of God (force majeure) event, the agreement may call for a suspension of payments for that period, but not a termination right.

Signage placement serves as a centerpiece of any naming-rights deal. A standard agreement involves placing signs on the side of the facility (able to be seen from a highway), on the roof (if it is enclosed), and on certain "exit" signs on the highway leading to the facility. In the interior, the agreement specifies the number of signs inside the facility and their locations (e.g., left field wall, back of home plate). Additionally, a sign is usually posted on or near the scoreboard. The agreement often specifies that the facility may contract with other advertisers, but the other advertisers cannot be competitors of the naming-rights firm. Or it may specify that the firm may have the right to veto the selection of any other advertiser inside the facility.

Houston's Toyota Center provides an example of a typical deal. The arena, which opened in September 2003, is home to the NBA Rockets and the American Hockey League Aeros. The sponsors are Toyota Motor Sales USA, regional distributor Gulf States Toyota, and the Houston

Power Team Dealers. The twenty-year, $100 million agreement includes the following:

- Signage at the five entrances to the facility, including a "large neon sign" at the main entrance.
- The name "Toyota Center" on the roof, along with the Toyota logo.
- Signage at four locations in the parking garage.
- A forty-one-foot-high by thirty-five-foot-wide graphic of the Toyota logo just inside the main entrance visible from outside the arena.
- The right for Toyota to name a courtside lounge adjacent to the luxury suites on floor level.
- Toyota's name or logo on video screens at each end of the building, in two places on the basketball court itself, and on the front of the courtside press table (Feigen, 2003).

## Concessions

Although many think of concessions as overcrowded stands selling over-priced hot dogs, pretzels, and sodas, the kinds of items sold and the agreements to sell them constitute important aspects of a stadium or arena deal. Successful concessions—based on variety and placement—can add significant revenues to both the stadium owner and the team.

For example, the Philadelphia Eagles, which moved into Lincoln Financial Field in 2003, have an official hot dog (Dietz & Watson), an official salty snack (Utz Quality Foods), and an official ice cream (Turkey Hill). The companies have their products sold exclusively at the new stadium, and their logos are displayed on signs throughout the concourses.

In addition, all three obtained the right to use the team logo and colors in Eagles-themed food products for sale to the general public and can do cross-promotions. Utz issued a limited-edition, one-pound Eagles commemorative bag of potato chips. Dietz & Watson sells "Eagles Beef Franks" in stores around Philadelphia, and Turkey Hill planned a new ice cream called "Eagles Touchdown Sundae."

Team players and other team personnel may also be involved. When the concession deals were announced, the then offensive tackle Jon Runyan, the Eagles cheerleaders, and Swoop, the team mascot, attended.

A particular segment of the concession deal, known as "pouring rights," applies to beverages. Pepsi and Miller Brewing secured pouring deals. Pepsi bought the rights to sell its soft drink and bottled water brands and to put its name on a gate and an open area to be known as the Pepsi Zone. Miller gets its Lite beer served and sponsors a party tent in the plaza outside the north end of the stadium (Brockinton, 2002).

In some facility agreements, the team gets 100 percent of the concession revenues, whereas in others the team may get 100 percent of concessions on game days (Greenberg & Gray, 1996). In yet other agreements (usually in older facilities), the owner gets 100 percent of the revenues. One other approach involves splitting the fees between owner and team based on total revenues or on products. For example, the owner may get 100 percent of revenues for food, whereas the team gets 100 percent for souvenirs and programs.

## Seat Licenses

For a team or governmental entity financing the costs of building a new stadium or arena, revenues derived from the sale of PSLs help defray the costs of construction of the new facility. These licenses consist of agreements by ticket holders to pay a fee for the *right* to purchase tickets at a specified location for a designated period. By purchasing a property right in their seats (which may or may not be transferred to others, depending on the particular PSL), the fans contribute to the success of the team in helping build the new facility.

The concept does have drawbacks. First, if fewer fans than expected pay for licenses, the construction financing may be in jeopardy. A municipality may have to guarantee the shortfall, which occurred when the City of Oakland agreed to refurbish the Oakland Coliseum (known as the McAfee Coliseum since 2004) (Miller, 2010). Also, the often considerable fees charged by licensors limit access to the stadium by fans of lesser means. And disputes have arisen over the "caliber" of the seating received by the license holder. In one case, a group of Pittsburgh Steelers season ticket holders who bought seating licenses for the team's new stadium sued because the seats they received were not comparable to what was promised (Yocca v. Pittsburgh Steelers Sports, 2004). Additionally, PSLs tend to reward wealth over loyalty (Hill, 2008).

## Seating Organization/Pricing

At one time, the typical seating plan in a stadium or arena had a graduated sectional approach. The facility consisted of four or five distinct sections (box seats, loge, reserved grandstand, and unreserved grandstand), with the best seats toward the front and the more affordable seating further back and higher up. The revenue generated from this arrangement was often unpredictable, unless many season tickets were bought.

Even for those facilities with a strong season-ticket commitment, teams and facility owners now create new levels of premium seating to increase revenue. Luxury suites are the best known and most successful form of seating-based revenue. Although many older stadiums had some "private boxes" (the first being eighteen private boxes furnished with drapes and armchairs in the stadium for the Chicago White Stockings in 1883), modern luxury suites have become far more ubiquitous in the newest facilities. The revenue derived often constitutes the second most important revenue stream for professional sports franchises, behind television revenues (Greenberg & Gray, 1996).

Often expensive, with prices in the hundreds of thousands of dollars per season, these suites frequently include a kitchen, waiter service, and comfortable seating in an enclosed, climate-controlled environment, somewhere toward the middle or top of the stadium or arena.

In considering the importance of such seating to the economics of a franchise, let's take the example of Citi Field, the present home of the New York Mets, which opened in April 2009. It contains fifty-four luxury suites of three levels (ten "Sterling Suites," thirty-nine "Empire Suites," and five "Party Suites"), available for prices ranging from $250,000 to $500,000 per season. This compares with only forty-five luxury suites located at one level in the team's prior venue, Shea Stadium, which cost only $4000 for a fifteen-person suite and $8000 for a thirty-person suite (mlb.com, n.d.; toptentopten.com, n.d.).

In some cases, the luxury suite prices will reach seven figures. As part of a renovation, Madison Square Garden plans twenty "bunker" (or event-level) suites to be priced at over $1 million. The best suites at the new Giants/Jets stadium range at $1.2 million per suite (Lombardo and Muret, 2010). Larger stadiums have more space to build premium seating. FedEx Field, the home of the Washington Redskins, includes 280 suites.

The revenues from luxury boxes may go to defray the costs of construction, to pay off debts, or to the stadium owner and the franchise according to some formula found in the lease. Often the franchise takes the lion's share of the money. The NHL's Anaheim Ducks get 45 percent of the first $1 million derived from luxury suite revenues, 50 percent of the next $10 million, and 55 percent of the next $10 million (Greenberg & Gray, 1996). In other cases, a flat percentage is used. The Arizona Diamondbacks pay 5 percent of the revenues to the owners of the Maricopa County Sports District, which owns Chase Field (Greenberg & Gray, 1996).

Club seats constitute a second class of premium seating. This idea came from the late Joe Robbie, the owner of the Miami Dolphins. The biggest difference between club seats and luxury suites is that club seating mixes with the general seating layout of the facility, although with more perks. Far less costly than luxury suites, club seats cost tens of thousands of dollars per season, rather than the six- or seven-figure amounts for suites. No uniform location exists for club seats, although they are often found at choice locations, such as center ice or the third-base dugout. Often club seat holders have waiter or waitress service and television monitors. Generally sold on an annual lease that can cover from one year to ten, the team usually keeps the bulk of the revenues from club seating, although facility agreements usually require that a small percentage go to the facility owner.

"Regular" seating generally follows the more traditional pricing model, although with higher prices than in the past. Some franchises, such as the San Francisco Giants and Phoenix Suns, have utilized alternative pricing techniques, whereby certain matches with more competitive or popular opponents will feature higher prices for all (or part of) the seats than for those with less attractive rivals. Others, such as the Dallas Stars, have become even more sophisticated, allowing real-time market conditions and consumer demand to set the "right" price for a single-game ticket. The application is designed to respond to changing conditions related to each individual game. Called "dynamic pricing," ticket prices can increase or decrease based on a variety of factors, including league standings, opposing team, star players, day of the week, and real-time supply and demand (Stepneski, 2009).

## Advertising

As anyone who has attended a sporting match can attest, advertising is a ubiquitous component of the viewing experience. Often placed in conspicuous locations in the stadium or arena, the size and frequency (in the case of rotating advertisements) of the material vary, depending on the agreement made. A key point is product exclusivity. Rarely will advertisements for two products of a similar type occur in one facility.

The heart of facility advertising is signage. The company with the naming rights will often have the pick of the best location(s) for signs, which often means the scoreboard display. However, the team and/or facility owner may contract with other advertisers for signage and or advertisements outside the location of play, such as near concession stands or near the entrances and exits. Ads even grace bathrooms. A firm called Stall Tactics places advertisements above urinals and in restroom stalls (Greenberg & Gray, 1996), claiming that patrons are likely to remember ads in unusual areas.

Advertisement procurement and revenues are controlled by the lease agreement with the facility owner and the team. In some cases, the lessor (facility owner) retains advertising selection and revenues, whereas in others it is the team that controls both. In some cases, revenues are split between the team and the owner.

## Parking

Fees from parking may be divided between the franchise and the stadium owner, or kept by one of the parties. Additionally, the fees may include nonevent parking.

## Other Revenue Generators

In addition to the options already described, a stadium or arena may include other devices designed to generate revenue. The facility may include one or more retail stores (with agreed-on amounts going to the team and/or the owners), sit-down restaurants open to the public on game and nongame days, paid public tours, and even museums. The lease agreements will often divide the revenues in some proportion between the team and the facility owner.

## Alteration of Existing Facilities

If an established team cannot construct a new facility or get the stadium/ arena owner or a locality to build one, expansion or alteration remains a viable option. Often done by adding more seats, or creating different seating tiers, it serves to modernize the facility and increase revenue potential. Fenway Park, the long-time home to the Boston Red Sox, added 274 seats above its left-field wall in 2003 and sold them at $50 per seat. In the following year, the team added more seats atop the roof of the structure and sold them for a minimum of $75 per ticket. The added seating was expected to bring in an additional $4–6 million for the team (Sandomir, 2004).

## A Final Word

Stadiums serve as major money machines for sports teams, and a state-of-the-art facility generates potentially more revenues than an older venue. Even in the NFL, with its equal sharing of important revenue streams, the changing economics driven by stadium deals has created significant revenue disparities between "stadium-rich" and "stadium-poor" teams. According to Forbes, the top team, the Redskins, earned about $345 million in revenues in 2008, while the least-producing team, the Detroit Lions, earned about $208 million, resulting in a disparity of about $137 million (Forbes.com, 2009).

Although the 1990s and 2000s were a boom period for new facilities, demands for new stadiums and arenas continue on the minor league and college levels. The questions of cost, governmental aid, and public support for new facilities costing hundreds of millions of dollars continue to be debated.

## Information Check

When covering stadium/arena construction and team relocation issues, a journalist should ask:

1  Why is a new/renovated facility needed?
2  What are the design plans?
3  Who owns the facility?
4  What is the proposed method of financing?
5  If government sources constitute all or part of the financing, how will be the money be raised? Taxes? Bonds?
6  If taxes serve as a revenue vehicle, what kinds will they be and whom will the taxes affect most?
7  If bonds serve as a revenue vehicle, who will issue them—the state or locality or a public corporation?
8  If private sources are involved, who are these sources and what are the amounts of contributions?
9  What are the details of the naming-rights deal, such as the term, placement, and costs, and who gets the revenue?
10  What are the details of any sponsorship deal, such as the term and coverage, and who gets the revenue?
11  What are the costs of luxury box and club seating?
12  Who gets revenues from nonsports events at the stadium?

## References

Baade, R. (1994). *Stadiums, professional sports and economic development: Assessing the reality.* Chicago: The Heartland Institute.

Babington C. and Denlinger, K. (1995, November 7). Modell announces Browns' move to Baltimore. *The Washington Post.* Retrieved May 14, 2010, from http://www.washingtonpost.com/wp-srv/sports/longterm/memories/1995/95nfl4.htm

Brockinton, L. (2002, September 9). Pepsi becomes Philly founder. *Street and Smith's Sports Business Journal,* p. 4.

Caldwell, D. (2005, May 1). Baseball's minor leagues more than just about baseball. *New York Times.* Retrieved April 21, 2010, from http://www.nytimes.com/2005/05/01/nyregion/01njCOVER.html?pagewanted=1&sq=Caldwell and minor league baseball parks and May 2005&st=cse&scp=2

Cozzillio, M., & Levinstein, M. (1997). *Sports law—Cases and materials* (pp. 568–569). Durham, NC: Carolina Academic Press.

Dewey Ranch Hockey, LLC. (2009) 414 B.R. 577.

Dorocak, J. (1999). Tax advantages of sports franchises: Part I—The stadium. *Law Review of Michigan State University—Detroit College of Law,* 579.

Erardi, J. (1999, April 5). A ballpark built for the fans. *Cincinnati Enquirer*, p. 8S.

ESPN.com (2009, September 29). Stadium naming rights. Retrieved May 15, 2010, from http://espn.go.com/sportsbusiness/s/stadiumnames.html

Feigen, J. (2003, July 25). Arena's sticker price for Toyota: $100 million. *Houston Chronicle*, p. A1.

Forbes.com (2009, September 20). NFL team valuations. Retrieved February 2, 2010, from http://www.forbes.com/lists/2009/30/football-values-09_NFL-Team-Valuations_Rank.html

Fraas, K. N. (1999). Notes & comments: "Bankers up!" Professional sports facility financing and other opportunities for bank involvement in lucrative professional sports. *North Carolina Banking Institute, 3*, 201, 210–223.

Green, K., Klein, B., & Lebowitz, B. (1998). Using tax–exempt bonds to finance professional sports stadiums. *Tax Notes, 78*, 1663.

Greenberg, M., & Gray, J. (1996). *The stadium game* (pp. 63, 71, 159, 161–162, 185, 339, 349). Milwaukee, WI: National Sports Law Institute, Marquette University Law School.

Greenberg, M., & Gray, J. (1998). *Sports law* (2nd ed., vol. 1, pp. 218, 225, 523). Gaithersburg, MD: Aspen.

Hill, J. (2008, August 4). Personal seat licenses, rising ticket prices spell doom. Retrieved February 8, 2010, from http://sports.espn.go.com/espn/page2/story?page=hill/080801&sportCat=nfl

Horovita, B. (1988, December 6). They are banking that it's a great advertising forum. *Los Angeles Times*, p. 2.

Internal Revenue Service, Treasury Reg, sec. 1.141–4(e)(3), 2008.

Keating, R. (2001). Baseline welfare cases: Stadiums, subsidies and the dole. Retrieved June 20, 2005, from www.newcolonist.com/stadium.html

Kelo v. City of New London, 545 U.S. 469 (2005).

Krueger, A. B. (2002, January 10). Take me out to the ballgame, but don't make taxpayers build the ballpark; The high cost and low benefit of sports subsidies. *New York Times*, sec. C, p. 2.

Kurlantzick, L. (1983). Thoughts on professional sports and the antitrust laws: *Los Angeles Memorial Coliseum Commission v. National Football League. Connecticut Law Review, 15*, 183, 203.

Leone, K. C. (1997). No team, no peace: Franchise free agency in the National Football League. *Columbia Law Review, 97*, 473.

Lombardo, J. and Muret, D. (2010, March 1). MSG prices bunker suites above $1M. *Sports Business Journal*, p. 1.

Los Angeles Memorial Coliseum Commission v. National Football League, 726 F. 2d 1381 (9th Cir. 1984).

Goldstein v. New York State Urban Development Corp., 13 NY3d 511 (2009).

Masteralexis, L. P., Barr, C., & Hums, M. (1998). *Principles and practice of sports management* (pp. 299–300). Gaithersburg, MD: Aspen.

Mickle, T. (2009, September 14). Del Biaggio gets 8-year sentence. *Sports Business Journal*, p. 6.

Miller, M. (2010, March 9). Owners v. fans: Owners win and it costs the fans, every time. *San Francisco Sports Business Examiner*. Retrieved May 14, 2010, from http://www.examiner.com/x-39410-SF-Sports-Business-Examiner~y2010m3d9-Owners-v-Fans—Owners-win-and-it-costs-the-fans-every-time

Mitten, M. J., & Burton, B. W. (1997). Professional sports franchise relocations from private and public law perspectives: Balancing marketplace competition, league autonomy, and the need for a level playing field. *Maryland Law Review, 56, 57,* 104.

mlb.com (n.d.). Citi Field vs. Shea Stadium. Retrieved February 12, 2010, from http://newyork.mets.mlb.com/nym/ballpark/comparison.jsp

Quirk, J., & Fort, R. (1997). *Pay dirt: The business of professional team sports* (pp. 131–132). Princeton, NJ: Princeton University Press.

Salamone, G. (2006, July 30). One of a kind weddings: tie the knot at some of N.Y.'s most famous landmarks. *New York Daily News.* Retrieved August 31, 2010, from http://www.nydailynews.com/archives/entertainment/2006/07/30/2006-07-30__one_of_a_kind_weddings__tie.html

Sandomir, R. (2004, April 16). To raise money, baseball tries new squeeze play. *New York Times,* p. A1.

Sandomir, R. (2010, January 19). Dolphins' home receives its 7th name since 1987. Retrieved January 20, 2010, from http://www.nytimes.com/2010/01/20/sports/football/20stadium.html

Seymour, H. (1960). *Baseball: The early years* (pp. 319–323). New York: Oxford University Press.

Shapiro, M. (2004). *The last good season: Brooklyn, the Dodgers and their final pennant race together.* New York: Doubleday.

Sports Facility Reports (2009). Vol. 10, sec. 3B. National Sports Law Institute, Marquette University. Retrieved February 1, 2010, from http://law.marquette.edu/cgi-bin/site.pl?2130&pageID=4239

Stepneski, A. (2009, September 9). More on the variable ticket pricing. Andrew's Dallas Stars Page. Retrieved April 29, 2010, from http://www.andrewsstarspage.com/index.php/ADSPblog/comments/more_on_the_variable_ticket_pricing/

toptentopten.com (n.d.). The top ten baseball's best skyboxes suites. Retrieved February 12, 2010, from http://www.toptentopten.com/topten/baseball_s+best+skyboxes+suites

Valenti, J. (1997, October 8). Spano cops plea; Admits he lied about wealth, could get 5 years in prison. *Newsday (New York),* p. A05.

Whoriskey, P. (2003, July 28). Stadiums are built on federal tax break. *Washington Post,* p. A01.

Wolffe, D. (2007, August 29). Giants, Jets land $1.3b stadium financing deal. *Real Estate Weekly.* Retrieved February 17, 2010, from http://www.allbusiness.com/construction/nonresidential-building-construction/5519082-1.html

Yocca v. Pittsburgh Steelers Sports, Inc., 854 A. 2d 425 (Pa. 2004).

Zimbalist, A., & Noll, R. (1997). *Sports, jobs and taxes: The economic impact of sports teams and stadiums.* Washington, DC: Brookings Institution Press.

# 9   Sports Injuries

Whether one is a professional athlete or a weekend warrior, almost every participant in sports incurs physical injury at one time or another. Sports such as football and ice hockey pose a risk of injury due to the frequent physical contact between players. Auto racing displays particular danger because of the limited space between drivers racing around an oval track at high speeds. Activities not associated with physical contact also have the risk of injury—recreational jogging and tennis come to mind. Even spectators at sporting events have suffered injuries.

In the majority of cases, sports injuries are minor, but serious, even fatal, accidents do take place. When a fatality results from a sports event, news coverage occurs. The death of Brittanie Cecil, a thirteen-year-old spectator at a National Hockey League (NHL) Columbus Blue Jackets hockey game in 2002, serves as a good example. After an errant puck hit her, she suffered fatal brain damage, prompting the league to utilize netting, in addition to Plexiglas boards, to protect fans sitting in back of the goals (Arace, 2003).

Frequently, the media cover an injury suffered by a professional or collegiate athlete that sidelines that athlete for a period of time and adversely affects the team's chances of success. Issues such as the causes and preventions of sports injuries have not always been examined, and the underlying business and legal issues surrounding the question of sports injuries are infrequently explored.

Another problem involves disclosure. Of the major professional sports, only the National Football League (NFL) makes its injury information public. Reporters covering other sports often have to speculate. In college sports, disclosure of injuries may be limited because the Health Insurance Portability and Accountability Act (HIPAA) and its accompanying privacy regulations restrict the dissemination of individuals' health information. However, the effect of the law is diminished because most college athletes sign a waiver, permitting such disclosure (Health Insurance Portability and Accountability Act, 29 USC, sec. 1191c).

The majority of the total number of injuries involve the millions of recreational athletes who participate simply for the fun and exercise. Yet such injuries and deaths receive little coverage since these athletes are largely unknown. That is unfortunate because, statistically, 40 percent of deaths and serious injuries related to athletics occur in swimming, diving, and boating, not team contact sports (Appenzeller, 2005, p. 40). Lack of training and lack of supervision are common threads that run through such cases—issues worth focusing on when reporting on the subject.

Despite the litigiousness of our society and the perception that plaintiffs have an easy time winning judgments from juries, difficult legal hurdles exist. Traditionally, the law often immunized liability of other participants, team owners, leagues, and schools. The responsibility rested almost solely on the person suffering the injury because he or she assumed the risk of harm or consented to participating in an activity with an inherent risk of harmful bodily contact. Successful lawsuits were rare.

Recent changes in law and society have made this issue less clear-cut. Although legal victory is far from guaranteed, stakeholders such as sponsors, municipalities, stadium/arena owners, and insurance companies may incur liability, with the possibility of considerable damages awarded against one or all of them by juries. The most difficult and increasingly important issues involve not the responsibility of one athlete for injuring another, but lack of adequate protection, such as safety standards provided by third parties to prevent injuries from occurring. This concept, known as risk management, merits discussion later in the chapter. Still, many of the rules outlining the inherent risks of sports activities and legal immunity remain in place.

This chapter discusses several topics: (a) the key legal standards governing sports injuries; (b) the consequences of dangerous athletic activities; (c) how sports organizations attempt to minimize the risk of injury to participants and spectators; and (d) facility safety in the post-9/11 environment. The goal is not to make journalists legal experts, but to convey general background so that journalists know what kinds of questions to ask when covering a sports injury story. What follows then is a general discussion. Therefore, a caveat: Specific standards do vary from state to state.

## Legal Theories

Sports injury cases combine two distinct areas of law: torts and contracts. A tort occurs when someone engages in conduct that violates a duty imposed by law resulting in financial responsibility. A tort involves certain levels of liability (never use the word *guilt* when writing about a tort case, because guilt is a criminal law concept). When a jury hears a tort case, it determines (a) the defendant's liability and (b) the amount of monetary compensation awarded to the victim.

It is important not to confuse torts with criminal law. In tort cases, the injured party, not the state, brings claims. A jury determines liability and a monetary amount for the damages, not a prison term. The standard for proving the tort is less onerous than for a criminal case. Liability is based on a "preponderance of the evidence," whereas a criminal case requires guilt "beyond reasonable doubt"—a high level of certainty.

### Who Can Be Liable?

Potentially, tort liability extends to many parties. And plaintiffs sue as many parties as practically possible, in an attempt to collect damages from the defendant with the most assets (known as "deep pockets"). The following list include potential defendants.

*Participants.* Participants are those who take part in the event. When one participant commits an intentional, reckless, or negligent act against another, liability accrues.

*Service Personnel.* These party include, but are not limited to, teachers, lifeguards, aerobics instructors, and trainers. Each has a duty of care to the students and may be liable for tortious acts. The liability of coaches and athletic personnel includes failure to provide competent personnel, adequate instruction, or proper equipment; failure to warn; failure to supervise; and improperly treating injured athletes. Liability also occurs for violations of association or conference rules, and injuries due to the improper design of a facility.

In January 2005, a jury awarded $135 million to the family of a seven-year-old girl paralyzed in a car accident caused by a drunken fan, holding the vendor liable for serving the patron (who is serving a jail term for vehicular assault). The stadium rule of buying no more than two beers at one time was violated when the patron gave the vendor $10 in exchange for buying six beers (Markos, 2005).

*Spectators.* Spectator injuries occur during sports events, and it is common to categorize fans as victims—one hit by a foul ball or a hockey puck—rather than producers of the injuries. However, cases where spectators instigate violence against other spectators, or even against athletes and officials, may result in liability against those aggressors. Nevertheless, as discussed later, owners, operators, and administrators are also liable for such transgressions, as they have responsibility for the safety of patrons, athletes, and officials.

*Administrative/Supervisory Personnel.* This category includes leagues, school principals, and the school districts, with liability based on their supervisory role, rather than participation in the act itself. If a plaintiff can prove that these defendants employed unfit personnel, failed to provide proper supervision, failed to have a supervisory plan, improperly directed an event or athletic program, failed to establish safety rules or comply with existing safety requirements, or failed to remedy dangerous conditions, liability (usually negligence) occurs.

*Employers.* A doctrine known as "vicarious liability" results in employers having responsibility for the acts of employees. Even if the employer shows no fault of his or her own, the employer's liability occurs through the negligent acts of the employees. For example, if an employee of an arena fails to attach the basketball court correctly and a spectator trips and breaks an ankle, that employer is vicariously liable. However, limitations exist. First and foremost, the employee causing the injury must have acted within the "scope of employment," meaning that the incident occurred during working hours and under the supervision and control of the employer. Courts have to determine how much control and supervision were present at the time of the injury.

### Liability

Torts are classified into four basic categories: intentional acts, recklessness, negligence, and strict liability. These require different standards of proof. The following describes the basic requirements to determine liability and defenses for the following torts.

*Intentional Torts.* Intentional torts require the plaintiff to prove that the defendant displayed a desire to injure. Most frequently, intentional torts in sports involve assault and battery cases among participants. Assault is defined as the intent of one person to put another in fear of imminent, unauthorized bodily contact. The battery is that unauthorized contact. Assault and battery tend to occur in body contact sports such as football, ice hockey, and soccer. However, considerable difficulties occur when applying these torts in an athletic context. A football tackle, for example, displays an intention to hit another player; the same applies to a body check in hockey.

Legal and practical reasons exist for the difficulty of proving assault and battery lawsuits in sports cases. Legally, an important defense known as "consent" applies in a great many situations. If the athletes voluntarily participate in a sport, have knowledge of the risks involved, and have an awareness of potential injuries that may occur, consent occurs (van der Smissen, 2003). A football player who steps onto the field consents to being tackled, and a hockey player on the ice consents to bodily contact. For youth and amateur participation, this standard is supplemented with a contract that the participant (or parent) signs, outlining the nature of these risks.

The consent defense covers activities within the reasonable contemplation of one who plays a particular sport. For example, an intentional high stick in a hockey game is not permitted and results in a penalty against the wrongdoer. But high sticking occurs in hockey, and the internal rules of the sport attempt to regulate this conduct. Therefore, an assault and battery lawsuit would likely be unsuccessful. When the act goes beyond those boundaries of reasonable activities—legal or illegal in the sport—then the consent defense fails.

Professional athletes are particularly reluctant to bring assault claims to court. Sports organizations, particularly professional leagues, frown on litigation and prefer to enforce penalties against transgressors by their own internal governance. Other players may ridicule the athlete for resorting to courts, rather than the league process (or, in some cases, for defending himself or herself on the field or in the rink). Then the reputation of the athlete and even of siblings entering the sport suffers. In one case, a hockey player for the NHL's Colorado Avalanche considered bringing a lawsuit against a Vancouver Canucks player whose improper body check rendered him unconscious, but decided not to because the victim's brother sought to play in the NHL (Berlet, 2004). Finally, the potential damage recovery may not be worth the effort. Those with guaranteed contracts will, in any event, be paid a salary for the rest of their contract terms.

Whether the event took place in an amateur or professional sports context, the keen journalist should ask whether the conduct was within the contemplation of the sport and subject to the consent defense.

*Recklessness.* Reckless conduct does not require intent to render a specific injury, but exists when a player "intends to commit the act but does not intend to harm an opponent." One commentator defined it as "highly unreasonable conduct where a high degree of danger is present" (Keeton, 1984).

The leading case defining this concept involved a professional football player who sued an opposing player and team for injuries suffered during an exhibition game in 1973. Dale Hackbart, a safety for the Denver Broncos, attempted to block Charles "Booby" Clark, a rookie running back for Cincinnati. Clark, "acting out of anger and frustration, but without a specific intent to injure," hit Hackbart on the back of the head and forearm. No penalty was called. After the game Hackbart was diagnosed as having a neck injury, ending his career. A federal appeals court concluded that Hackbart had a viable claim for recklessness, rejecting the view that the inherent danger of the sport precluded this action (Hackbart v. Cincinnati Bengals, 1979).

*Negligence.* Negligence, the most heavily utilized tort, is based not on intent, but rather on carelessness. Known as a "fault" standard, a plaintiff alleging negligence must prove that the defendant failed to act in a manner commensurate with a "reasonable person" in the same circumstances. To prove a case of negligence, the injured must show (a) that the defendant (the team, school, doctor) had a duty of care to the injured person; (b) that the duty of care was breached; (c) that the breach foreseeably caused the injury; and (d) that the injured person suffered damages. Although this standard seems easier than that of intent and recklessness, many claims involving sports injuries are precluded by dangers inherent in the given sport or by clauses in contracts prohibiting such claims.

As a prerequisite to a negligence claim, a duty of care must be present, meaning a legal responsibility of the defendant to the plaintiff. Although at first glance this may not seem difficult to establish, courts in sports injury cases often conclude that the facts fail to establish the duty, as in this example.

A member of a college rugby team broke his neck while participating in a tournament hosted by another college. The plaintiff sued both his school and the hosting school, claiming negligence. He claimed that the hosting school was responsible for the "negligent conduct" of its rugby team because the host school's team held a cocktail party the night before the tournament, even though two matches were scheduled on the next day. The court dismissed the lawsuit against the host school because no legal relationship was found between the parties (Fox v. Board of Supervisors of Louisiana State University, 1991).

Another issue involves a duty to warn of potential dangers. Many courts have noted that if the danger is so obvious there is no duty to warn. In 2004, a Massachusetts appeals court overturned a jury award of $486,909 in a lawsuit against the Red Sox filed by a spectator hit by a foul ball. The court concluded that "even someone with scant knowledge of baseball should realize that a central feature of the game is that batters will forcefully hit balls that may go astray from their intended direction. . . . [The Red Sox] had no duty to warn the plaintiff of the obvious danger of a foul ball" (Costa v. Boston Red Sox Baseball Club, 2004).

State law may limit the scope of the duty. A majority of courts in the United States have adopted a specialized negligence standard for spectators at sporting events known as the "no duty" or "baseball rule." The rule requires that:

> the proprietor of a ball park need only reasonably provide screening
> for the area of the field behind home plate where the danger of being
> struck is greatest, and that such screening must be of sufficient extent
> to provide adequate protection for as many spectators as reasonably

be expected to desire such seating in the course of an ordinary game (Atkins v. Glens Falls City Sch. Dist., 1981).

Some courts, however, have refused to adopt the baseball rule, preferring to determine the duty based on general negligence law requirements (Crespin v. Albuquerque Isotopes, 2009).

Once it is determined that a duty exists, the focus shifts to the second element—a lack of reasonable care in the defendant's actions. A core concept in the law of negligence, this means that a court compares the defendant's actions with those of a fictitious "reasonable person" under the same circumstances to determine whether a breach of that duty occurred. For example: Would a reasonable trainer permit a player complaining of severe headaches to continue playing? Or: Would a reasonable physical education teacher permit a student to stand directly behind another who was practicing a golf swing which might result in severe injury to that student?

The next issue concerns whether that breach of duty "caused" the injury. This is a complicated and abstract legal doctrine, and we do not have to engage in in-depth analysis here. For our purposes, causation means a direct connection between the act and the accompanying injury.

Let's take this example: D, a softball player, decides to take batting practice outside an area of the field designated for such practice. He disregards the signs posted in the locker room designating the area for batting practice. While taking practice swings, he hits P, another player, who was standing nearby. P suffers a concussion and a broken cheekbone. Analyzing this case based on the preceding standard, a legal duty existed between players D and P, and D acted below the standard of reasonable care by disregarding the sign and engaging in an activity involving a blunt instrument. Also, the injury to P was a direct result of D's improper activity. Even though D did not seek to hit P, the actions demonstrated negligence.

The preceding case is quite simple; however, negligence cases involving sports are often more complex and involve more than one defendant. A key issue surrounds the role of "supervisory" personnel, such as a coach, teacher, league, school district, or, in some cases, sponsor.

The focus of the liability on the supervisory personnel differs from that of the person who committed the act. Here, the liability results from a lack of an adequate safety plan, or proper training. For example, if a teacher acted negligently in failing to properly administer first aid to a student who suffered an injury, the principal, the school, or the superintendent of the school district can be held liable if that teacher did not possess the requisite first-aid certification mandated by the state's law, and that deficiency caused the injury.

The last element of a negligence case involves damages to the victim.

This monetary award, normally up to a jury, permits the panel to factor in pain and suffering, lost earnings and earning power, and costs of care (Owen, 2007). Punitive damages—a result intended to punish the wrongdoer for his or her actions—are also permitted.

### Defenses to Negligence Claims

Defenses to negligence exist. One is contributory negligence, which results if the plaintiff also acted in a negligent manner, contributing to the injury. Contributory negligence traditionally served as a complete defense and resulted in a dismissal of the lawsuit no matter how egregious the defendant's negligence. Even if the plaintiff was slightly negligent, the defendant won the case (Restatement of Torts 2d, 1965, sec. 463).

The harsh results of contributory negligence prompted most states to eliminate that defense and replace it with "comparative negligence." Comparative negligence rules vary from state to state, but basically this concept apportions the damages between the negligent plaintiff and one or more defendants. If both a defendant and plaintiff are deemed negligent, the jury's damage award is reduced to the extent to which the plaintiff contributed to his or her own harm. In some states, negligence plaintiffs can recover some percentage from liable defendants regardless of the extent of their own negligence, a concept known as "pure" comparative negligence (Li v. Yellow Cab Co., 1975). In other states, in a modified version, plaintiffs are allowed a partial recovery unless the plaintiff is either *more* negligent (greater than 50 percent at fault) than the defendant(s) or equally as negligent as the defendant(s) (McIntyre v. Balentine, 1992).

Taking the last example, under a pure comparative negligence system, if a jury determines that the plaintiff was 70 percent at fault and the defendant 30 percent, and the jury awards $100,000 in damages, the plaintiff receives only $70,000. However, under the modified system, the plaintiff cannot recover any award.

The final defense, assumption of risk, ranks as the most important used in sports injury cases. A participant in an athletic activity, who voluntarily and knowingly assumes a risk of harm arising in that activity, cannot recover damages for a negligent act occurring during that activity. Assumption of risk is a defense only in negligence and strict liability cases. Intentional tort claims, as mentioned earlier, employ the defense of consent.

For example, fans attending a baseball game know that a ball may be hit foul and into the stands. They assume the risk of that injury. An amateur hockey player hit by a puck causing injury to his eye also will likely lose any lawsuit on that basis. (Note that professional athletes are barred from most injury lawsuits based on workers' compensation laws, discussed later.) In most states, assumption of risk requires that the risk be "foreseeable." This issue of foreseeability is a key point to ask a lawyer representing any party in a negligence case.

Assumption of risk doctrine frequently involves contractual clauses in which participants agree before they can participate in an activity. Participants frequently contract to limit negligence liability arising from an injury in a sports event. Often explicit (known as an express assumption of risk) but sometimes implied from the general terms of the agreement, these limitations clauses are generally enforceable as to activity-related injuries.

## Limitation of Liability Clauses

Most organizations that sponsor sports competitions require participants to sign event participation agreements. These contracts contain provisions limiting the liability of sponsors, owners, schools, and other organizations in personal injury lawsuits. Known as "agreements to participate," they may include issues such as protective gear requirements, medical prerequisites, and the types of care available in case of an emergency.

An example of a simple agreement to participate follows:

> I know that participating in this event is a potentially hazardous activity. I agree not to enter and participate unless I am medically able and properly trained. I agree to abide by any decision of an event official relative to my ability to safely complete the event. I am voluntarily entering and assume all risks associated with participating in the event, including, but not limited to, falls, contact with other participants, spectators or others, the effect of the weather, including heat and/or humidity, traffic and the conditions of the course, all such risks being known and appreciated by me. Having read this Waiver and knowing these facts, and in consideration of your acceptance of this application, I, for myself and anyone entitled to act on my behalf, waive and release [organization, parent organization, national governing body, city and state], all sponsors, and their representatives and successors, from present and future claims and liabilities of any kind, known or unknown, arising out of my participation in this event or related activities, even though such claim or liability may arise out of negligence or fault on the part of any of the foregoing persons or entities (New York Road Runners, 2010).

When writing about a negligence lawsuit and an assumption of risk defense, a journalist should examine the agreement containing the particular assumption of risk provision. For those participants under the age of eighteen years, a parent or guardian must sign; otherwise, the waiver may not be enforceable because the minor lacked the legal right to consummate the contract. Note that the agreement serves as evidence of notification of the risks involved.

Courts tend to scrutinize these agreements to ensure that they are not manifestly one-sided. If so determined, a court can strike them down as "unconscionable" and the injured person may sue based on traditional tort concepts. Most states do not enforce a clause that "limits all liability to the presenting organization, league, school, coach and other participants," even if signed with free will. Instead, the courts usually enforce a clause limiting liability for negligence, but not for intentional torts such as assault and battery (Connell & Savage, 2003). Keep this point in mind when interviewing an attorney representing a defendant in such a case.

The language in such agreements must be clear and concise. If not, courts may refuse to enforce them on the basis of public policy. Consider the following example.

The plaintiffs, an auto racer and his wife, sued for damages after the racer suffered injuries. Before the race, the racer signed a "Release and Waiver of Liability/Indemnity Agreement" as a precondition of participating in the race. During a race, his vehicle crashed and burned. He suffered burns and incurred substantial medical costs. He sued based on negligence alleging the lack of care in fighting the fire by the racetrack.

The agreement barred legal actions for, among other things, injuries compounded by "negligent rescue operations." That term was undefined and the racer argued that it made the limitation of liability "vague and unenforceable." The court ruled otherwise, noting that, even though it did not specifically state that the waiver applied to "negligent firefighting" claims, the waiver did include the term "negligent rescue operations" when it stated that injuries received might be compounded by negligent rescue operations (Groves v. Firebird Raceway, 1995).

## Strict Product Liability

In the last half-century, the concept of strict product liability for acts that lack intent or fault on the part of the defendant has become an accepted standard for certain "unreasonably dangerous" items. Product liability cases focus on defects in design, manufacture, or warnings making the product "unreasonably dangerous," rather than the actions of individual players, coaches, or supervisory personnel. The reason or cause of the defect is not important. Liability extends to both manufacturers and retailers, as long as a third party does not alter the product.

Note that the "no-fault" standard of product liability does not guarantee liability. Many of these lawsuits fail to make it to court because of the difficulties in determining "defect," "unreasonable dangerousness," and "cause." Also, the defenses of assumption of risk may be applicable.

As a result of product liability litigation, manufacturers attempt to limit their liability by posting warnings on both the product and in the instructions. They should carefully craft the language in the advertising, marketing, and promotion of the product. Clear and unambiguous warnings should mark the packaging as well. Product liability lawsuits center on athletic equipment. Frequent claims allege design defects in football helmets. Some plaintiffs have suffered tragic consequences, such as quadriplegia or head injury (Arnold v. Riddell Sports, 1994; Rodriguez v. Riddell Sports, 1999).

## State Law Immunity

States and localities are favored defendants in personal injury lawsuits because of their "deep pockets"—considerable resources to pay legal judgments. A bar to unfettered lawsuits against these defendants is the use of "sovereign immunity," a traditional doctrine aimed to protect the state from lawsuits for its actions. Many jurisdictions retain laws limiting lawsuits; others have granted permission for parties to sue them. If a plaintiff sues a town for an injury sustained in a town park, claiming negligence due to inadequate supervision, the existence of an immunity law may prohibit the lawsuit. Even when lawsuits are allowed, states and localities can require "notice of claims" filed in an expedited manner (ninety days in New York) or mandate that the trial be held before a special judge, not a jury (New York General Municipal Law, sec. 50e; New York Court of Claims Act, 2009, sec. 12). When writing about a lawsuit against a municipality or state, it is important to know whether an immunity law exists and how it affects the claim.

## Medical Malpractice

The issue of the conduct of medical personnel in servicing athletes (and sometimes spectators) has two distinct components: the malpractice of the physician or emergency medical technician and the responsibility of the team or organization for that conduct. Often, the distinction between the two is blurred.

First, consider the malpractice of physicians, trainers, and emergency medical technicians. Similar to negligence, medical professionals have a duty to the patient to exercise the level of care that a reasonable medical expert of their level of training would provide, given the circumstances. If the care falls below that standard and causes or exacerbates the injuries, liability accrues—for example, when a doctor performs duties below a general, competent standard, or when a trainer fails to promptly refer an injured athlete to a physician for evaluation and treatment (Mitten, 1999).

Over the last three decades, the rise of sports medicine as a distinct specialty and the increase in the quality of medical care in general have increased the standards of "reasonable care." Professional teams often employ sports physicians as consultants and, even if that is not the case, most franchises are located in cities with major medical centers. On the collegiate and high school level, presenters of sports events commonly have some emergency medical assistance on hand or nearby. The failure to do so may result in negligence.

Courts appear to be most receptive to suits by athletes alleging that a physician or athletic trainer has improperly treated their injury, thereby causing "enhanced harm" to the athlete. In addition, courts have found that an athlete has a valid claim against a physician for improperly providing medical clearance to resume or continue playing a sport, or failing to fully inform the athlete of the material risks of athletic participation with his or her medical condition (Mitten, 1999).

However, courts have dismissed negligence suits by athletes against team physicians and athletic trainers employed by public educational institutions based on state immunity laws. On the professional side, many lawsuits against teams and team physicians have been dismissed under state workers' compensation laws prohibiting employees from suing employers or other employees for negligence. These laws provide back wages and compensation for medical costs to victims of work-related injuries. They do not require fault, but, in return, injured employees give up the right to sue their employers for damages. For one who is injured by falling on a loading dock and experiences a temporary backache, this system works reasonably well. But for athletes whose careers end prematurely or who experience permanent injury, workers' compensation is a difficult barrier. If the team doctor is an "employee" of the team, many states bar or limit suits against the employer and the doctor under workers' compensation (Brinkman v. Buffalo Bills Football Club, 1977).

Often the relationship between the team physician and the athlete differs from the typical doctor–patient relationship. In a typical scenario, the doctor serves the patient, not the employer. Communications are confidential, protected by the doctor–patient relationship. In the case of team doctors, the physician receives payment from the team and works for the team. The duty of reasonable care in skill and treatment remains, but questions of confidentiality, conflict of interest, and loyalty surface, especially when the medical advice or treatment results in an incomplete recovery or, worse, in a permanent injury (DiCello, 2001).

Athletes who allege that they were "forced" to play despite their injuries include the former National Basketball Association (NBA) star Bill Walton. In order to play, Walton claimed he "reluctantly accepted" injections of cortisone and novocaine and ingested other medications for several years. Walton eventually settled a lawsuit filed against his former team, the Portland Trail Blazers (Habib, 2002).

The former NFL players Charles Krueger and Dick Butkus also sued their respective teams, alleging that the teams and team physicians failed to disclose the nature and extent of their injuries, and failed to inform them of the risks associated with painkilling treatments. The Krueger case involved not claims of malpractice but rather the failure of team personnel to discuss relevant medical information, which constituted fraud (Krueger v. San Francisco Forty-Niners, 1987).

In 2002, a New Jersey jury awarded the former Philadelphia Flyers defenseman Dave Babych $1.37 million for his claim against the Flyers' team doctor. Babych alleged that the doctor "deviated from standard medical practice" and "failed to inform Babych of the ramifications of playing with the injury" (Roberts & Conrad, 2002).

The traditional arrangements between a team and its medical professionals have been changing. Owing to the increasingly competitive health-care market, hospitals and medical practices have sought to pay professional teams for the right to treat their players. In addition to the revenue, sports franchises get the services of the provider's physicians either free of charge or at substantially discounted rates. In return, the medical groups and the hospitals obtain the exclusive right to market themselves as the team's official hospital, health maintenance organization, or orthopedic group, a point worth noting when writing about malpractice claims.

Criticism of this practice occurs. "These groups should have to put out a disclaimer: 'We paid for the ability to treat these top athletes,'" said Dr. Robert Huizenga, a former team doctor for the Oakland Raiders and past president of the NFL Team Physicians Society. "What's it say about our profession when the most high-profile jobs are awarded not by merit, but by auction?" (Pennington, 2004).

Note that an imperfect result does not automatically make the doctor or the team liable. Athletes share responsibility. Often, the athlete pressures the physician for certification to play. Professional athletes realize their tenure is limited and do not want to end their careers prematurely because of being sidelined by an injury.

### Ethical Issue: Who Is Responsible for Player Concussions?

The condition of a number of former NFL players who have been incapacitated by head injuries deriving from their playing experience has been well reported in recent years (Crossman, 2007). The long-term effects of the concussions received from on-field hits and the lack of treatment for the cumulative effects of these injuries have resulted in dementia, early-onset Alzheimer's disease, and depression. Not only serious, concussions are frequent. The NFL reports approximately one concussion every two games. Given that the NFL stages about 320 games per year, that translates to about 160 reported concussions per season (Benjamin, 2009).

Because many retired players did not receive adequate compensation or, more importantly, adequate pensions (because of their low salaries and because the NFL Players' Association (NFLPA) was in its infancy or not created as the time they played), their illness resulted in the depletion of their financial resources. The plight of these former players, what they feel is poor treatment by the NFL and its players' association, has resulted in considerable adverse publicity for those organizations.

Before 2009, the NFL's "Concussion Committee" flatly rejected a connection with on-field concussion and later brain injury (Kain, 2009). The NFLPA also rebuffed attempts to increase compensation for disabled former players by using pension money for current players. Then NFLPA Executive Director Gene Upshaw bristled at criticism of his perceived failure to help. "It's just like water off a duck's back. It had no effect before and it will have no effect [now]" (Sando, 2008).

The issue of present player and league responsibility for the injuries of former players raises difficult questions. Certainly, a compelling case exists for a rich league and a players' association of wealthy players to help out players who have been debilitated by injury. Since these stories became public, both the NFL and NFLPA are making efforts to help. However, at the time of this writing, friction between the union and the former players continues (Kaplan, 2009).

The problem is not limited to NFL players. High school football players alone suffer 43,000 to 67,000 concussions per year, though the true incidence is likely to be much higher, as more than 50 percent of concussed athletes are suspected of failing to report their symptoms (Gregory, 2010). For the players, the dangers are real, but, unlike professional players, interscholastic football involves young people who are, for the most part, minors. Should rules be changed to provide extra protection? Legally, should courts expand liability rules by limiting the effect of releases and waivers? Should the state scholastic associations mandate insurance and a no-fault payment system to avoid costly and time-consuming litigation?

## Information Check

When covering issues involving personal injuries, a journalist should determine:

1 The circumstances and facts surrounding the injury.
2 The accurate diagnosis and comments from experts about the effect of such injury.
3 The parties sued and, if a verdict occurred, those responsible and their levels of responsibility.
4 The legal theories behind the lawsuit.
5 The claims of the defendants.
6 Whether waivers of liability were signed.
7 Whether the medical care was adequate.
8 The kind of relationship that the team doctor has with the team.
9 Whether the doctor is an "employee" or "independent contractor."
10 How long the treatment in question was.
11 Whether the athlete has a history of similar injuries.
12 Whether the athlete has a history of prior medical conditions possibly complicating the treatment.
13 Whether the athlete sought alternative medical opinions.

## Risk Management

The bulk of the preceding text focused on remedies following a personal injury. This portion details attempts by leagues, teams, and facility operators to *reduce* the risk of injury. This concept, known as *risk management*, involves the planning and logistics of a sports event, whether it is the Super Bowl or a local high school soccer game. The failure to adequately cover potential risk results in injuries, bad publicity, the diminution of the reputation of the organization or team (or even sponsor), and, of course, litigation. The goal of risk management is first to minimize the amount of injury overall and second to insure that, when injury does occur, someone else pays. For journalists, knowledge of these issues results in better reporting and more in-depth questions.

In a sports setting, risk management involves many stakeholders: players, coaches, managers, teams, facility owners, the equipment manufacturers, vendors, spectators, and, yes, the media. A well-organized and safe event is the goal. The potential for mishaps is high, and it behooves the organizations sponsoring or running the event to attempt to limit the injuries that occur on their watch. Think of the possibilities: a riot in or outside the facility, people falling over slippery surfaces, inebriated fans, a natural disaster, or a terrorist attack.

Risk management procedures include planning to provide a prompt response to incidents. Organizers of an event should establish a response team and develop a well-defined strategy so that each member of that team knows what to do (Appenzeller, 2005, p. 44).

As noted earlier in the chapter, all sports club participants should be required to sign a waiver or release form prior to participating. But this only scratches the surface of risk management. Presenters, including sports clubs, leagues, and stadium or arena owners or sponsors, should develop a disaster handbook, obtain insurance, provide equipment and facilities fit for that particular use (which they should inspect regularly), and develop an emergency medical plan (Appenzeller, 2005, pp. 42–44). Often, they consult with independent firms specializing in this kind of work. A good risk assessor sizes up the potential risk of the event or events. Journalists covering an incident should inquire about the level of risk prevention planning involved.

### Common Risk Management Issues

*Athlete Protection.* The stabbing of women's tennis star Monica Seles in 1993 by a deranged fan and the assault on figure skater Nancy Kerrigan in 1994 resulted from security breakdowns. In the latter case, the only transportation provided by the organizing committee hosting the U.S. National Figure Skating Championship was a hotel shuttle van with no security protection (Graham, Neirotti, & Goldblatt, 2001). Event promoters, teams, and leagues must have plans to protect the talent. First comes the identification of potential harms. Who had access to the dressing room areas? Did he or she enter from restricted entrances? What kind of security detail existed? What steps were taken to prevent fans from going on to the playing area? Were the athletes made aware of the security protections available to them? In the case of a team, did the coaches and general managers know the extent of the protection?

*Financial Protection.* During many sporting events, significant amounts of cash change hands. Purchases of food, beverages, souvenirs, and payment of game-day tickets result in the need to store the money to prevent theft. Where was the money kept? And, in the case of credit card information, were the records secured in password-protected computers? Other questions include: How was the theft or loss discovered? What access did employees have to the information?

*Crime Protection.* No organization guarantees spectator safety from criminal acts, such as thefts of wallets and pocketbooks. Frequently, the victims carelessly left these items in open pockets or simply hanging on a seat. But what if the facility gave access to non-ticket holders through an unguarded passage? In one example, at R.F.K. Stadium in Washington, DC, it was discovered that kids would sneak under the end of zone bleacher seats and steal bags and purses. To prevent this, fences with gates had to be constructed to close off the ends of the bleachers and ushers placed at every gate (Graham, Neirotti, & Goldblatt, 2001). After a number of fans, upset over a controversial boxing decision, threw chairs into the ring in Madison Square Garden, resulting in a number of injuries and arrests, it was reported that only seventy security guards and fifty ushers serviced the entire arena (Schultz, 1996).

*Storage of Personal Belongings.* Since 9/11, a number of sports facilities have limited what items can be brought into the facility, and many have implemented inspection checkpoints (Yankees.com, 2010). These measures, designed to prevent terrorist acts in marquee sports events, have increased facilities' operating costs, and burdened fans by delaying their entrance. Yet, if event planners did not take such action and a terrorist act occurred, questions would surely arise as to the adequacy of the precautions.

*Credentialing.* For the press, access to nonpublic areas of the facility requires credentials. Often, the sports organization or presenter issues the credentials, and a person without the proper credentials lacks the access needed to adequately cover the event. In the case of a team playing a number of games at "their" stadium or arena, the credential procedures are well known to editors and reporters. But for an individual event, such as a national competition, the organizers must specifically state the requirements and procedures for seeking credentials. It also helps to give the credential holder proper directions and rights. Often, the presenters will not "advertise" these areas, to prevent the general public from seeking access.

---

### Ethical Issue: Bloggers and Credentials

In most cases, bloggers lack credentials to access private areas. That raises the issue of how a "traditional" journalist differs from a blogger and whether some bloggers are entitled to traverse the same areas as print and broadcast reporters. The problem even applies to full-time journalists who blog. In 2008, Mark Cuban, the owner of the National Basketball Association (NBA) team Dallas Mavericks, sought to ban bloggers from the Mavericks' locker room, but the NBA intervened, ruling that bloggers from credentialed news organizations must be admitted. Cuban then decided to let in any blogger—"someone on Blogspot who has been posting for a couple weeks, kids blogging for their middle school Web site or those that work for big companies" (Arango, 2008). The issue of blogging is discussed in chapter 13.

*Staffing.* For major events, private firms, working with local police, handle security matters. Hiring those employees involves a "reasonable" job search. In many cases, these firms do not advertise, but hire based on referrals. If a staff member embezzles money from an event, the question becomes whether the security firm failed to adequately check that employee's background. Or, if the security staff members carry weapons, what is the nature of their training? Note that laws regulating such training vary, so no uniform standard exists.

*Ingress and Egress.* How quick and easy is it to enter and exit the facility? Are the exits well marked and easy to find? In older or smaller venues, the issue deserves particular attention when a crowd control problem or riot occurs. Questions to ask include: How many exits exist? Are the exits well marked? How do disabled spectators exit in an emergency?

*Pyrotechnics.* As part of the entertainment, many sports events feature half-time, pregame, or postgame shows involving special effects, such as smoke and fireworks. If problems occur, questions should be asked about whether the producers of the show and the sports event complied with local fire code requirements.

*Use of the Public Address System.* What kinds of announcements are made on the facility's public address system? Often, announcements notifying fans of risk of injury from foul balls or hockey pucks are broadcast during sports events. But what announcements occur in the event of an emergency? Are they audible? Presenters should script such announcements in advance to ensure that announcers do not "ad lib" any statements.

*Outside Climate and Indoor Climate Control.* What is done in the event of inclement weather? If the weather forecast calls for snow or ice, this mandates the existence of procedures alerting the staff to clear passageways and stairways. Bad weather *before* an event requires greater steps. The clearance of snow and ice prevents injuries and ugly occurrences, such as the throwing of snowballs onto the field. Snowball incidents at a few NFL games caused injury to those on the field and raised questions about the organizational planning of the event (Freeman, 1995). For indoor events, the facility engineers should frequently test the climate control system.

*Medical Emergencies.* It has become standard to have some medical personnel on premises in the event of an unanticipated need. Particular challenges occur in events that take place over a large area, such as a marathon, where water stations, medical technicians, and transportation are spaced through the entire course. Questions should focus around the training, accessibility, and amount of the equipment and personnel. Even if one operates a park or gym used by the general public, questions regarding the first-aid training and other qualifications of personnel may exist. One study reported that only 10 percent of the respondents indicated that an on-site automatic external defibrillator was available in their recreation areas (Miller & Veltri, 2003).

## Alcohol and Public Safety

Public safety remains a primary concern of anyone involved in presenting a sports event. In a time of heightened sensitivity to mishaps, injuries, and intentionally violent acts, the sports industry must spend adequate time and resources on presenting a safe event. If not, the responsible parties are questioned by the press.

In November 2004, during a match between the Indiana Pacers and the Detroit Pistons, three Pacers players were suspended by the NBA for a total of 128 games, and five Pacers players and seven fans were charged with misdemeanor assault and battery related to the brawl between players and the fans that created national headlines. This type of stadium or arena violence has recurred over the last two decades, resulting in questions of adequate security during games. At times, fans have hurled bottles, batteries, snowballs, and racial slurs at players, who have sometimes responded with verbal and physical actions. In 2002, a Kansas City Royals first-base coach was attacked while standing in the coaches' box by a father and his son at Chicago's Comiskey Park (Brown, 2004). In 1974 the Cleveland Indians hosted the Texas Rangers in a game at which over 25,000 fans consumed more than 65,000 cups of beer that night—thanks to the 10-cents-a-cup promotion. Not surprisingly, the crowd became unruly, and some fans ran onto the field and attacked players, who feared for their lives. The Indians were forced to forfeit the game (Johnson, 2008). In an article published shortly after the melée between fans and players at the Pacers–Pistons game, George Hacker, the Alcohol Policies Project Director at the Center for Science in the Public Interest, a non-profit health advocacy group, summed up the source of the problem. "It's the beer talking," Hacker said. "Most people don't do that kind of stuff when they're sober. Who in their right mind wants to attack a big athlete? You've got to be nuts to do that" (McAllister, 2004).

As a result of the violence, the NBA created a "Fan Code of Conduct," which sets forth expected standards for all attendees of NBA games. It also restricts the size of drinks to twenty-four ounces and limits purchase to two drinks at a time. The guidelines prevent alcohol sales after the fourth quarter begins.

Other leagues do not have a uniform policy, but many teams stop beer sales after a certain point in the event. However, prevention of dangerous incidents may involve greater measures. Hacker proposed the following:

- Selling beer with lower alcohol content (3.2 percent alcohol).
- Selling beer in smaller quantities—for example, reducing the common sixteen-ounce cups to ten-ounce cups.
- Raising the price of beer.
- Not only cutting off beer sales before the game ends, but limiting the amount of time before the game when beer is sold.
- Increasing vendor vigilance in terms of heavy drinkers by requiring every adult fan to wear a wristband to indicate how many drinks the fan has bought. With stated limits on the number of drinks sold in a game, this method helps enforce the numerical limit.

A complete ban on alcohol sales is highly unlikely, given the adverse fan reaction and the importance of the beer advertising in sports (spending more than $540 million on sports TV advertising in 2003).

## Defamation

Knowledge about the rules of written and spoken defamation by journalists helps avoid lawsuits. Presumably, many students and reporters have already learned the basics in other classes or through their publication's editors or attorneys. We do not intend to rehash them here, but we will point to particular issues involving reporting sports.

Defamation, a tort that involves false statements causing injury to reputation, is based on traditional English law. Two types of defamation exist: libel (written defamation) and slander (spoken defamation). As it was a "strict liability" tort, winning a defamation case meant that the plaintiff had to prove that the information was false and caused injury. It did not matter whether the statement was an honest mistake or an intentionally malicious comment (Kimmerle v. *New York Evening Journal*, 1933; Chalpin v. Amordian Press, 1987).

Because of the potential for chilling free speech, the Supreme Court altered the rules in its famous *New York Times* v. Sullivan (1964) ruling. Today, if the plaintiff is a "public figure," he or she must prove that the statement was false, and done with "malice" or "reckless disregard of its truth." The complex definitional elements of this standard have received a great deal of debate and discussion, but it remains good law.

Defenses to defamation include truth and opinion. If the statement in question is factual and truthful, no grounds for defamation exist. Opinion is less clear and merits greater discussion. A fine line exists between fact and opinion, and the courts often have difficulty in making that designation.

And sports commentary—whether in print or in broadcast—is ripe for this kind of lawsuit.

A sports column accusing a coach of being a liar could be libelous, according to a 1990 opinion by the U.S. Supreme Court. Even though the claim came from a "column," rather than a straight news story, the Supreme Court concluded that the opinion defense does not automatically excuse the journal and the journalist from liability as long as the column was "sufficiently factual to be susceptible of being proved true or false" (Milkovich v. *Lorain Journal*, 1990). It also serves as a lesson to sports writers and broadcasters to exhibit care in their writing, even in an "opinion" piece.

The issue of defamation has taken on greater urgency with the advent of sports talk radio. Given the often brash personalities of the announcers of these stations, their viewpoints sometimes constitute wicked criticism, some of it plainly unfair or nasty. Saying that a player "stinks" or is "over the hill" does not lead to successful defamation suits. But claiming that a player missed a game because he was drunk could be another matter.

In 1997, an announcer on radio station WIP-AM in Philadelphia stated that the then Philadelphia Flyer Eric Lindros missed a game because of a hangover caused by drinking the night before. The report claimed four undisclosed sources, one of which was inside the team's organization. The team's owner sued the station for defamation. Earlier that year, another announcer on the same station claimed that Lindros was friendly with a local mobster. "I've had enough," owner Ed Snider was quoted as saying. "The WIP hosts constantly misrepresent the facts." Ultimately the radio station settled, issuing a public apology and contributing an undisclosed amount of money to a charity (Manley, 1997).

---

### Ethical Issue: Privacy and Athletes

"There is no privacy," said Michael Levine, a prominent Hollywood publicist who has represented athletes and actors (Brown, 2010). If true, does it mean that no aspects of an athlete or coach's personal life are out of bounds in the age of Internet, blogs, and Twitter all tied to a 24/7 news cycle? Should there be any legal or ethical limits in reporting one's private life?

Rooted in both law and social mores, a right of privacy has been recognized in varying degrees over the last century. "The right to be left alone" has been a well-worn quote that remains as valid today as it was in 1890 when first penned by the future Supreme Court Justice Louis Brandeis and his partner Samuel Warren (Warren & Brandeis, 1890). Involving matters as diverse as the rules against intrusion on private property to confidentiality of information on social websites, privacy regulations are a patchwork of state and federal laws and regulations.

Yet a conflict exists, especially regarding those who qualify as "public figures." Professional and amateur athletes, and, to a lesser extent, team owners and sports executives, fit into this category, and, consequently, their privacy rights are limited. Because of the public interest generated about their achievements, information about the lives of these individuals is subject to greater dissemination. The question is how far journalists should and can go.

Answering the second portion first, the answer is—very far. Most courts have concluded that public figures (including well-known athletes and coaches) have limited privacy rights. The standard many courts consider is whether the publication of truthful information concerning the private life of a person would be both highly offensive to a reasonable person and not of legitimate public concern (Restatement of Torts 2d, 1977). Inherent subjectivity permeates the test. Are Tiger Woods's extramarital affairs a subject of legitimate public concern or are they nobody's business? Are allegations made during a divorce proceeding a matter of public concern? The sexual orientation of a coach who never made the matter public? Recreational drug use during the off-season? Criminal activity by members of an owner's family? On the one hand, if these personal aspects of an athlete's life have no effect on his or her performance, should they be reported? On the other, does the oft-used cliché "the public's right to know" justify the dissemination of such information?

Ethical questions surround the issue whether the journalist should report such information. Although media companies do have ethics guidelines regarding issues such as conflicts of interest and impartiality (New York Times Company, 2005), issues of newsworthiness are not always addressed. The Code of Ethics of the Society for Professional Journalists (SPJ) tends to focus on general points, such as "fairness, conflicts of interests and plagiarism" (SPJ, 1996). Finally, complicating the issue of what is newsworthy is the rise of nontraditional sources of information, such as blogs and websites, which often aggressively expose—through photos, rumors, and innuendo—certain conduct and activities by athletes. Many of these bloggers or websites do not follow traditional journalistic standards,. Should reporters quote such websites, thereby further exposing the rumors and innuendo? Is it justified even if the website exposes a particularly private act that turns out to be true?

## Criminal Law and Sports

As stated in the introductory chapter, this text does not cover criminal law issues in sports in great detail, despite the seeming frequency of the connection between crimes and athletes. Highly publicized athlete-defendant trials such as those of O. J. Simpson, Kobe Bryant, and Michael Vick receive considerable media coverage. But the issues involving most criminal charges against athletes are not related to their sport or sports in general. And the laws and procedures utilized are the same as those against any defendant.

Note that criminal laws differ from state to state. Definitions of crimes can and do vary. An offense in one state may not be prosecutable in another, especially in the realm of sexually oriented activities. That means, when writing about or discussing an arrest, indictment, or trial, it is important to read the charges to avoid generalizations. Often, copies of criminal indictments can be found on the web for easy access.

The notoriety of elite athletes cuts two ways. On the positive side, the athlete may create a positive reputation in the minds of his or her fans, if not the public at large, by demonstrating success on the field. Competent, even stellar, legal counsel and crisis management experts are available, given the financial resources. On the negative side, the scrutiny of the athlete's conduct by ambitious prosecutors may give rise to "overcharging" in an attempt to obtain publicity.

Athletes, especially star athletes, enjoy a great deal of press coverage, a fact well known to prosecutors, who ultimately have the discretion to bring charges (victims of crimes do not make the decision). The prosecutor's discretion, often based on strategic as well as legal reasons, is rarely second-guessed by courts. For prosecutors, conviction is the goal—and the favorable publicity resulting from the conviction of a high-profile athlete can lead to public acclaim for that prosecutor.

The Kobe Bryant sexual assault case in 2003 demonstrates a powerful interplay between a famous athlete with high-powered legal representation and an aggressive local district attorney. Ultimately, it turned out to be a fiasco for the district attorney, who was forced to drop the sexual assault charges because the victim chose not to proceed with the trial. Some of the mistakes included staff members of the trial judge inadvertently releasing *in camera* (closed hearing) transcripts with the name of the victim (a violation of Colorado's rape shield law) and then the judge demanding a "gag order" barring publication of those transcripts. The Colorado Supreme Court, in a 4–3 ruling, permitted their publication (People v. Kobe Bryant, 2004). Had a trial occurred, it is likely that the superior quality of Bryant's attorneys would have outshone those of a rural district attorney's office, especially in a case where the alleged victim's sexual activities could be an issue.

Yet high-quality lawyers do not necessarily win in the court of public opinion. Although the tactics they utilize may work in a courtroom, the athlete may suffer a loss of reputation even if an acquittal results. Therefore, wealthy athletes often hire public relations experts to deal with the public fallout.

Criminal charges against athletes are not a rare occurrence. This raises the question of whether there is more such activity today than in the past. Some have argued that professional athletes are held to a higher standard (Robinson, 1998), whereas others see the opposite (*Harvard Law Review*, 1996). Certain commentators have suggested that there is a greater incidence of off-the-field criminal activity, drug-related gambling, and domestic violence by athletes for three reasons: (a) Athletes are conditioned to believe that the rules do not apply to them; (b) the subculture of sports perpetuates violence and drug use; and (c) the subculture of sports glorifies violence and denigrates women (Cart, 1995; Nack & Munson, 1995). It is up to journalists to form their own conclusions.

### Examples of On-field Criminal Activity

Although violent activity occurs at football fields, hockey rinks, and basketball courts almost every day, participants rarely are charged with criminal conduct. District attorneys are reluctant to get involved in matters traditionally handled under the enforcement powers of a professional or amateur sports organization. What may constitute a criminal assault outside of sports could be within the rules of the game. However, egregious acts do occur, and in such cases players have been criminally charged.

In 2000, the chief prosecutor in Vancouver, British Columbia, charged the then Boston Bruins player Marty McSorley with assault after he hit the Vancouver Canuck Donald Brashear from behind with his stick. A quick two-handed swing of his stick clubbed Brashear on the side of his face. Brashear suffered a severe concussion and was hospitalized. McSorley was handed a one-year suspension from the NHL and was found guilty of assault with a weapon by a provincial court in British Columbia. The trial judge rejected McSorley's defense that the act occurred during the "heat of the game" (Regina v. McSorley, 2000).

A different result occurred in a 1969 NHL exhibition game. Ontario prosecutors charged Edward "Ted" Green and Wayne Maki with assault for a harrowing on-ice incident. It began when Green hit Maki in the face with his gloved hand and in the shoulder with his stick. A fight then erupted in which Maki ultimately fractured Green's skull. Both players were acquitted, however, based on their "consent" to play a violent sport (Regina v. Green, 1970; Regina v. Maki, 1970).

In 2004 another NHL player, Todd Bertuzzi, was charged with assault causing bodily harm over an on-ice incident in which he gave a behind-the-head punch to an opponent. Steve Moore, the injured player, was carried off the ice unconscious. He suffered two fractured vertebrae, and his hockey future remains unclear. The charge carries a maximum penalty of ten years in jail. The NHL suspended Bertuzzi indefinitely, causing him to miss the remaining thirteen games of the regular season and the playoffs with a corresponding loss of $500,000 in salary. However, in a plea bargain, the British Columbia court sentenced Bertuzzi to a conditional discharge that also included a $500 fine and eighty hours of community service (Joyce, 2004). Both this incident and the McSorley case a few years earlier received heavy media attention. Because the actions were recorded, millions viewed the injury.

Many other examples of potentially criminal conduct occur that have not been prosecuted, such as the infamous choking of the then Golden State Warriors coach P. J. Carlessimo by the player Latrell Sprewell during a practice in 1997. Another instance was the 1977 mauling of the NBA player Rudy Tomjanovich (of the Houston Rockets) by Kermit Washington of the Los Angeles Lakers. Tomjanovich suffered several bone fractures, a brain concussion, and leakage of spinal fluid from the brain cavity; the blow ended Tomjanovich's career as a professional basketball player (Howard, 2003; *Newsweek*, 1977).

Criminal prosecution and civil injuries arising from injuries and deaths caused in the ring are nonexistent because the nature of the sport sanctions assault. In the history of boxing, deaths in the ring, though rare, have occurred. In 1930, Frankie Campbell died after a knockout by Max Baer. Four decades later, Emil Griffith knocked out Benny "Kid" Parente and the brain damage was so severe that he died. On April 2, 2005, Becky Zerlentes became the first female boxer to die as a result of a punch, received during a Colorado Golden Gloves match. She died the next day from "blunt force trauma" to her head (Bianculli, 2005).

## Ethical Issue: The Duke Lacrosse Case

The allegations that three members of the Duke University lacrosse team raped a hired stripper in 2006 received extensive coverage and caused debate nationwide. What made this case fascinating and troubling was the media's reliance on the statements of a rogue district attorney, claims that played into assumptions and even stereotypes about the individuals involved. District attorney Mike Nifong's egregious conduct—at times bending the rules of the criminal justice system and engaging in political grandstanding during his re-election campaign—suckered many in the media, who should have known better. Portraying the players as privileged white kids who flouted rules and acting in a delinquent variation of "boys will be boys," he alleged that they abused an African-American woman whom they hired as a stripper to entertain them. If the boys were not outright racists, they were implicitly bigoted by their backgrounds and their actions (Ghiglione, 2008). However, bad behaviour should not be confused with criminal conduct. Even if some members of the team were not choirboys and had a rowdy reputation, one should not impose guilt on them as rapists before they were tried and convicted. Simple point, but one overlooked.

Many in the media—including New *York Times*—accepted the district attorney's claims without investigating inconsistencies and without hard evidence. Criminal defendants are innocent until proven guilty, but implications of guilt were often present in the coverage (Taylor & Johnson, 2007). A detailed review of the case and the resulting media coverage is found in Stuart Taylor and K. C. Johnson's *Until Proven Innocent—Political Correctness and the Shameful Injustices of the Duke Lacrosse Rape Case* (2007), which should be required reading.

Inaccuracies in reporting included "really, really strong evidence" of rape when no evidence existed; the refusal of all forty-six white lacrosse players to cooperate with police (no player refused); and the players' denial of "participation or knowing anything" (the players interviewed had described in detail what had taken place) (Taylor & Johnson, 2007; Ghiglione, 2008). Dan Okrent, New *York Times*'s public editor until 2005, said that the case "had everything that would excite the right-thinking New York journalist: It was white over black, it was male over female, it was jocks over a nonstudent, it was rich over poor." Reporters who visited the Duke campus often interviewed bombastic professors who perpetuated the image of the university as an elitist, racist institution. Especially on television, the author Dan Yaeger argued, calm, intelligent voices were less likely to be heard than hysterical, hyperventilating ideologues. Yaeger and his co-author Mike Pressler quoted Stephen Miller, a columnist for *The Chronicle*, Duke's student newspaper, about an advertisement from a faculty group titled "We're Listening": "The people turned it from an issue about a specific charge about a specific situation into all-out class and race and gender warfare" (Yaeger & Pressler, 2007).

The ramifications of this case reverberate beyond sports or the business of sport, and should serve as a lesson to reporters covering high-profile cases. Do not trust authority figures. Rather, verify, verify, verify.

**Information Check**

When writing about risk management issues, a journalist should ask:

1 Are written procedures covering security, injury prevention, and emergency evacuation in place?
2 Were those procedures followed?
3 How recently were those procedures enacted?
4 Were drills or practices utilized?
5 How well or poorly are security personnel trained?
6 Was intoxication an issue in the event?
7 How did the facility prepare for the potential of or realization of unrest or terrorist activity?

**Information Check**

When writing about criminal issues and sports, a journalist should ask:

1 What is the nature of the event? Do not rely solely on the district attorney's press conference, but speak also to defense lawyers for the athlete.
2 Who are the defense lawyers? Are they well known?
3 How much experience do the prosecutors have in prosecuting a high-profile case?
4 What is the precise definition of the crime (as state laws vary in this regard)?
5 Does the defense of consent occur if the act is committed during a sports contest?
6 Is the district attorney elected? If so, is he or she running for re-election soon?
7 Do you have any independent legal experts to call for analysis or advice in writing the story?

## References

Appenzeller, H. (ed.). (2005). *Risk management in sport: Issues and strategies*. Durham, NC: Carolina Academic Press.

Arace, M. (2003, September 24). Blue Jackets put up new protective nets at Nationwide. *Columbus Dispatch*, p. 01F.

Arango, T. (2008, April 21). Tension over sports blogging. *New York Times.* Retrieved February 13, 2010, from http://www.nytimes.com/2008/04/21/ business/media/21bloggers.html?adxnnl=1&emc=eta1&adxn nlx=1266088040-EQScpNZ1cc8RIP8I11eJzw

Arnold v. Riddell Sports, Inc., 853 F. Supp. 1488, 1489 (D. Kan. 1994).

Atkins v. Glens Falls City School District, 53 NY2d 325 (1981).

Benjamin, J. (2009, June 22). League, union must redouble efforts to protect players' health. *Street and Smith's Sportsbusiness Journal,* p. 21.

Berlet, B. (2004, March 11). Pack's Moore focuses on job. *Hartford Courant,* p. C2.

Bianculli, D. (2005, April 19). A welter of emotions: Documentary looks back at fatal '62 fight. *New York Daily News,* p. 74.

Brinkman v. Buffalo Bills Football Club, 433 F. Supp 699 (W.D.N.Y. 1977).

Brown, M. (2010, March 28). Privacy evaporates for athletes, particularly the superstars. *Pittsburgh Tribune-Review.* Retrieved September 2, 2010, from http://www.pittsburghlive.com/x/pittsburghtrib/sports/steelers/s_673736.html

Brown, T. (2004, November 19). Things don't sit well in the stands; Fans respect the games but not a lot of athletes, and answers to violence are not always obvious. *Los Angeles Times,* p. D1.

Cart, J. (1995, December 27). Crime & sports '95: Sex & violence. *Los Angeles Times,* p. C4.

Chalpin v. Amordian Press, 128 A.D.2d 81; 515 N.Y.S.2d 434 (1st Dept. 1987).

Connell, M. A. and Savage, F. G. (2003). Releases: Is there still a place for their use by colleges and universities? 29 J.C. & U.L. S79.

Costa v. Boston Red Sox Baseball Club, 61 Mass. App. Ct. 299 (2004).

Crespin v. Albuquerque Isotopes, 216 P.3d 827 (NM Ct. App., 2009).

Crossman, M. (2007, June 19). Concussions create living hell for former NFL players. *The Sporting News.* Retrieved April 10, 2010, from http://www.sportingnews.com/yourturn/viewtopic.php?t=224682

DiCello, N. (2001). No pain, no gain, no compensation: Exploiting professional athletes through substandard medical care administered by team physicians. *Cleveland State Law Review, 49,* 507.

Fox v. Board of Supervisors of Louisiana State University, 76 So. Wd, 978 (La. 1991).

Freedman, M. (1995, December 28). Pro football: Giants express regret over snowball throwers. *New York Times.* Retrieved May 16, 2010, from http:// www.nytimes.com/1995/12/28/sports/pro-football-giants-express-regrets-over-snowball-throwers.html

Ghiglione, L. (2008) The court of public opinion: the practice and ethics of trying cases in the media: back to the future—questions for the news media from the past. *Law & Contemp. Prob., 71,* 1.

Graham, G., Neirotti, L. D., & Goldblatt, J. J. (2001). *Guide to sports marketing* (p. 119). New York: McGraw-Hill.

Gregory, S. (2010, January 28). The problem with football: How to make it safer. *Time.* Retrieved April 29, 2010, from http://www.time.com/time/nation/ article/0,8599,1957046,00.html

Groves v. Firebird Raceway, 1995 U.S. App. Lexis 28191 (9th Circuit).

Habib, H. (2002, June 16). When injuries rob athletes, who's to blame? *Palm Beach Post*, p. 1C.

Hackbart v. Cincinnati Bengals, 601 F.2d 516 (10th Cir. 1979).

*Harvard Law Review* (1996). Out of bounds: Professional sports leagues and domestic violence. *109*, 1048.

Health Insurance Portability and Accountability Act, 29 USC 1191c (2000).

Howard, J. (2003, December 24). Spree delivers words, deeds. *Newsday* (New York), p. A69.

Johnson, P. (2008, June 4). The night beer and violence bubbled over in Cleveland. ESPN.com. Retrieved February 22, 2010, from http://sports.espn.go.com/espn/page2/story?page=beernight/080604

Joyce, G. (2004, December 23). Bertuzzi on probation one year; plea bargain to conditional discharge carries chance of no criminal record. *Toronto Star*, p. A10.

Kain, D. (2009). "It's just a concussion." The National Football League's denial of a causal link between multiple concussions and later-life cognitive decline. *Rutgers Law Journal, 40*, 697.

Kaplan, D. (2009, October 19). Friction between NFL alumni and union continues. *Street and Smith's Sportsbusiness Journal*, p. 26.

Keeton, W. P. (1984). *Prosser and Keeton on the law of torts* (5th ed., p. 215). St. Paul, MN: West.

Kimmerle v. *New York Evening Journal*, 292 NY 99 (1933).

Krueger v. San Francisco Forty-Niners, 234 Cal. Rptr. 579 (Cal. App. 1st Dist. 1987).

Li v. Yellow Cab Co., 532 P.2d 1226 (Cal. 1975).

Manley, H. (1997, June 8). Throwing a check at talk radio. *Boston Globe*, p. C7.

Markos, K. (2005, March 5). $135 million DWI award in crash upheld. *Bergen Record* (New Jersey), p. A07.

McAllister, M. (2004, November 24). Beer muscles; Fans take leave of senses when alcohol involved. Retrieved May 6, 2010, from http://sportsillustrated.cnn.com/2004/basketball/nba/11/23/alcohol/index.html

McIntyre v. Balentine, 833 S.W.2d 52 (Tenn. 1992).

Milkovich v. *Lorain Journal*, 497 U.S. 1 (1990).

Miller, J., & Veltri, F. (2003). Symposium: General aspects of recreation law: Security issues in public recreation centers. *Journal of Legal Aspects of Sports, 13*, 265.

Mitten, M. J. (1999). Medical malpractice liability of sports medicine care providers for injury to, or death of, athlete. *American Law Review, 33*, 619.

Nack, W., & Munson, L. (1995, July 31). Sports' dirty secret. *Sports Illustrated*, p. 62.

*Newsweek* (1977, December 26)., In brief: Basketbrawl. p. 79.

New York Court of Claims Act, sec. 12 (2009).

New York General Municipal Law, sec. 50e (2009).

New York Road Runners, Inc. (2010). Waiver of liability. Retrieved May 5, 2010, from https://www.nyrrc.org/cgi-bin/htmlos.cgi/1467.3.082666709165301005

*New York Times* v. Sullivan, 376 U.S. 254 (1964).

New York Times Company (2005). Policy on ethics in journalism. Retrieved March 29, 2010, from http://www.nytco.com/press/ethics.html#A1

Owen D. (2007). The five elements of negligence. *Hofstra Law Review, 35*, 1671.

Pennington, B. (2004, May 18). Sports turnaround: The team doctors now pay the team. *New York Times*, p. A3.

People v. Kobe Bryant, 2004, 94 P.3d 624 (Colo. 2004).

Regina v. Green, 2 C.C.C.2d 442 (Ont. Provincial Ct. Sept. 3, 1970).

Regina v. Maki, 1 C.C.C.2d 333 (Ont. Provincial Ct. Mar. 4, 1970).

Regina v. McSorley, B.C.P.C. 0117 P 21 (2000).

Restatement of the Law of Torts, 2d (1977). The American Law Institute. Retrieved May 6, 2010, from. http://cyber.law.harvard.edu/privacy/Privacy_R2d_Torts_Sections.htm

Roberts, G., & Conrad, M. (2002, November). Jury awards $1.3 million to former Flyers player against team doctor. *Sports Lawyers Association Newsletter.* Retrieved September 25, 2005, from www.sportslawyers.org

Robinson, L. N. (1998). Professional athletes—Held to a higher standard and above the law. *Indiana Law Journal, 73*, 1313, 1322–1323.

Rodriguez v. Riddell Sports, Inc., No. B-CV-96-177 (S.D. Tex. Mar. 16, 1999).

Sando, M. (2008, January 31). Upshaw: NFLPA won't take from current pensions to help ex-players. ESPN.com. Retrieved April 11, 2010, from http://sports.espn.go.com/nfl/news/story?id=3225087

Schultz, J. (1996, July 13). Brawl another low blow for boxing; Officials point finger at "reckless individuals." *Atlanta Journal and Constitution*, p. 01G.

van der Smissen, B. (2003). Symposium: General aspects of recreation law: Legal concepts related to youth responsibility. *Journal of Legal Aspects of Sport, 13*, 323.

Society of Professional Journalists (1996). Code of ethics. Retrieved March 31, 2010, from http://www.spj.org/ethicscode.asp

Taylor, S. & Johnson, K. (2007). *Until proven innocent: Political correctness and the shameful injustices of the Duke lacrosse rape case* (pp. 63–65, 122, 125). New York: Thomas Dunn.

Warren, S., & Brandeis, L. (1890). The right to privacy. *Harv. L. Rev., 4*, 193.

Yaeger, D., & Pressler, M. (2007) *It's not about the truth: The untold story of the Duke lacrosse case and the lives it shattered* (pp. 147–49). New York: Simon & Schuster.

Yankees.com (2010). Stadium A to Z guide. Retrieved May 15, 2010, from http://newyork.yankees.mlb.com/nyy/ballpark/guide.jsp#Entry Guidelines

# 10  Performance-Enhancing Drugs in Sports

One of the most complex issues in sports involves drug use by professional and amateur athletes. The use of performance-enhancing drugs, testing standards, and punishments involving competitive athletes has generated debate among fans, players, sports executives, and politicians. And the almost weekly nature of this coverage makes it an evolving news story. With all this in mind, a basic primer of the drug-testing standards in various sports organizations serves readers best. As of the end of 2009, implementation of the enforcement standards varied among the professional leagues, which contrasts with the almost uniform enforcement standards for international sports organizations and their national governing bodies.

Drug use in sports has changed over the last thirty years. At one time, drug use—at least in the United States—constituted *illegal* "recreational" drugs, such as smoking marijuana, popping amphetamines, or snorting cocaine. In the 1980s, Major League Baseball, stunned by the convictions of four Kansas City Royals players on cocaine possession charges, suspended them for one year.

Note the word *illegal*. For the leagues and other sports organizations, little difficulty occurs in drafting a policy against illegal drug use. Such activities violate criminal laws, and those involved are subject to prosecution by the state. Both the unions and leagues recognized the problem and drafted sections in their collective bargaining agreements (CBAs) to address illegal drug use.

Athletes used legal substances (particularly alcohol) for years with little consequence and little publicity from the media. Often occurring after a game, alcohol use was within accepted standards of conduct at the time, and sports writers, not wanting to reveal the dark side of star athletes, refrained from such coverage (Sprattling, 2010).

More recently, a different type of drug abuse has evolved: of substances, some legal, many not, that boost performance, giving the athlete a competitive edge. Leagues and sports organizations have grasped for ways to control these drugs, often "designer" compounds created specifically to boost athlete performance. Although athletic federations have banned "stimulating substances," the lack of a comprehensive testing program makes these rules almost useless. Early drug tests were first introduced in the 1960s. Nevertheless, the use of the first-generation class of drugs, known as *anabolic steroids*, continued.

Anabolic steroids enhance muscle development, and allow athletes to train harder and recover more quickly from strenuous workouts. In the 1970s, athletes from East Germany were given these drugs in a government-ordered quest for athletic glory. The policy worked. In a short time, that nation's athletes won a striking number of medals at the Olympics. At the 1976 Olympics at Montreal, East German women won eleven of the thirteen swimming events, an astounding achievement in a nation of only 16 million people (steroid-abuse.org, n.d.)

In non-Communist countries, some individual athletes started using these drugs. Yet, despite occasional mention, the issue did not generate much attention until two events propelled this issue into the public eye: the suspension of the Canadian sprinter Ben Johnson after testing positive for anabolic steroids, and the revelations of state-sponsored doping after the fall of Communism. Johnson won the gold medal in the 100-meter sprint at the Seoul Olympics in 1988, but afterward tested positive for the steroid stanozol. Subjected to a torrent of negative publicity along with the ire of millions, he was forced to forfeit his medal. Shortly thereafter, the demise of East Germany revealed a state-run pattern of performance-enhancing drug abuse among its athletes. Some 10,000 East German athletes took steroids to boost their performance. The revelations resulted in criminal convictions and jail sentences for doctors and trainers (Ungerleider & Wadler, 2004).

Performance-enhancing drugs pose different pharmacological issues from traditional illicit drugs, which serve as addicting agents. Unlike those drugs (or alcohol), which may adversely affect an athlete's performance, performance-enhancing drugs aid in performance and are taken solely for that purpose. And, as said earlier, many of them were *not* illegal, although in 1990 Congress passed the Anabolic Steroids Control Act, which categorized certain anabolic steroids (although not all) as *controlled substances* (Anabolic Steroids Control Act of 1990, 2003, 21 USC, sec. 802). The 1990 act was tightened by enactment of the Anabolic Steroids Act of 2004, which prohibits over-the-counter sales of "steroid precursors" such as androstenedione, which act like steroids once ingested (Iwata, 2004). Further, in 2006 President Bush signed into law the Office of National Drug Control Policy Reauthorization Act, which prohibits the use of gene doping, and bans from athletic competition anyone who uses genetic modification for performance enhancement. The law came three years after the World Anti-Doping Agency (WADA) banned gene doping for Olympic athletes (21 USC, secs. 2001 and 2007).

Still-legal performance-enhancing substances, classified as either prescription drugs or nutritional supplements (which escape the rigorous regulation of the Food and Drug Administration), are available for purchase at drug stores or laboratories. As of early 2010, Congress was considering greater oversight of the dietary supplement industry, but no action has yet been taken (steroidlaw.com, 2010). But, even with more regulation, detection is often difficult as athletes may take other substances, known as "masking agents," to hide the presence of those substances in the athlete's system, thus avoiding a positive urine sample test (the preferred method of drug testing).

Finally, privacy issues mix into the debate. U.S. law and society value a right of privacy, and many argue that random drug testing, especially during nonwork time, is intrusive and a violation of individual rights (Ludd, 1991). Unless specific cause exists, testing should be limited in time and scope. In professional sports, certain players' unions have used this argument to forestall strict drug testing (Barker, 2004).

Only in recent years have professional leagues and international and domestic athletic organizations tightened standards. But, as noted earlier, variations exist between the professional sports leagues, and between the international athletic organizations (whose participants are not unionized) and professional league athletes, whose unions negotiate collective bargaining agreements detailing the drug-testing regimen and the rights of players who test positive.

When indictments of several individuals associated with an alleged steroid distribution ring occurred in 2004, the issue exploded onto the sports and news pages. Congressional hearings were held in 2005 and 2008, and many politicians and commentators demanded strict drug testing and punishment by professional sports and even proposed a nationwide standard. The critique of "lax" standards may be justified (Dvorchak, 2005). However, a counterargument also merits attention. If an athlete uses legal or even illegal drugs during the off-season, is it his or her employer's business? And, if so, how invasive should the tests be? The drug-testing procedures governed by international and amateur athletic organizations are far more invasive than those in the pro leagues. They raise greater privacy concerns and the system exists that many people find burdensome and intrusive.

Given that the rules and standards are changing rapidly, the rest of the chapter consists of a short summary of the drug-testing standards implemented in various organizations as of 2010.

## National Collegiate Athletic Association

The National Collegiate Athletic Association (NCAA) executive committee has created a list of banned substances, updated yearly, for which they test athletes for use by urinary analysis. The listing is found at the NCAA's website (ncaa.org). The classes of drugs banned include stimulants, and so-called "anabolic agents" (NCAA.org, 2009).

Each student-athlete must sign a drug-testing consent form annually, in which the student-athlete agrees to be tested for prohibited drug use. Failure to complete and sign the consent form results in the student-athlete's ineligibility to participate in all intercollegiate athletics. Since 1999, NCAA drug-testing programs have been administered by the National Center for Drug Free Sport.

Essentially two plans exist, one for the season and another for post-season events. As far as the seasonal tests are concerned, the program, implemented by the NCAA in 1990, applies to about 10,000 student-athletes each year, and its focus was to deter the use of anabolic steroids (Espn.com, 2007). During the regular season, the center randomly selects football and track and field programs for short-notice testing (less than forty-eight hours of notice to the schools). The center also randomly selects the individual athletes for testing based on the institutional squad lists. Every Division I and II football program conducts tests at least once each academic year. Selection is based on such criteria as player position, competitive ranking, athletics financial-aid status, playing time, an NCAA-approved random selection, or any combination thereof. A student-athlete who tests positive cannot participate in at least one season of competition, which includes any postseason play.

The National Center for Drug Free Sport selects NCAA postseason events for testing and submits the confidential testing schedule to the NCAA president for approval on behalf of the NCAA executive committee. Each NCAA championship competition is tested at least once every five years. Approximately 1500 athletes are tested at those events each year, and any who test positive lose their collegiate eligibility for at least one year.

The NCAA list of banned drug classes is composed of substances that are generally considered to be performance enhancing and/or potentially harmful to the health and safety of the student-athlete. The NCAA recognizes that some banned substances are used for legitimate medical purposes. Accordingly, exceptions can be made for those student-athletes with a documented medical history demonstrating the need for regular use of such a drug. Exceptions may be granted for substances included in the following classes of banned drugs: stimulants, beta blockers, diuretics, and peptide hormones (NCAA Division I Bylaw 31.2.3.5, 2009).

The NCAA drug-testing program grants an appeals procedure by the institution for a student-athlete who tests positive for a banned drug or who violates an NCAA drug-testing protocol. At least three members of the drug-education and drug-testing subcommittee of the NCAA Committee on Competitive Safeguards and Medical Aspects of Sports hear appeals (NCAA Division I Bylaw 31.2.3.3, 2009).

## The Olympic Movement

### *United States Anti-Doping Agency*

Although the International Olympic Committee (IOC) has the ultimate drug-testing authority for Olympic sports, it assigns this duty to the individual national bodies such as the U.S. Olympic Committee (USOC). The USOC in turn created an independent organization to manage a comprehensive, independent drug-testing program. That organization is the United States Anti-Doping Agency (USADA). The USADA began operating on October 1, 2000, with full authority for testing, education, research, and adjudication for U.S. Olympic, Pan-American, and Paralympic athletes.

The USADA drafts principles, standards, policies, and methods of enforcement in antidoping policy. In addition, the USADA is responsible for educating athletes about the rules governing the use of performance-enhancing substances and the harmful health effects of the use of such substances. As a requisite of recognition by the USOC, any national governing body or Paralympic sports organization must comply with the USADA procedures.

The USADA has authority to test any athlete who is a member of a national governing body, such as USA Track & Field, who participates in a USOC-sanctioned competition, or who has given his or her consent to testing by the USADA. Generally, the prohibited substances fall in the following categories: anabolic agents, diuretics, masking agents and peptide hormones, stimulants, and narcotics. Alcohol also may be tested in certain circumstances.

What makes this system comprehensive (or an egregious violation of privacy rights, depending on one's point of view) is the testing of individual athletes in an out-of-competition setting with little or no notice. Once athletes are identified by the national governing body and/or the USADA for inclusion in the program, the USADA will select athletes to test based on an automated draw that considers a number of factors, including ranking, risk of doping within each sport, and test history (USADA Protocol for Olympic Movement Testing, 2009). A "doping control" officer may come to the athlete's home, school, or training facility. The athlete's failure to cooperate may result in suspension.

An athlete submits urine samples to the USADA. After the USADA receives notification from the laboratory that a sample is positive, it notifies the athlete, the USOC, and the particular national governing body. The test results are turned over to the USADA's Anti-Doping Review Board (a group of experts independent of USADA) for review and the review board then presents its recommendation to the USADA. The USADA is then responsible for proceeding to an adjudication of the matter or closing the matter based on the review board's recommendation. The USADA will forward the review board's recommendation to the athlete, the national governing body, the USOC, the relevant international federation, and the WADA (USADA Protocol for Olympic Movement Testing, 2009).

The athlete has the right to a hearing if USADA proceeds with adjudication as a result of a positive or elevated test. He or she may choose between two separate hearing procedures:

1  The athlete may elect to proceed to a hearing before the American Arbitration Association.
2  The athlete may elect to proceed directly to a final and binding hearing before the Court of Arbitration for Sport (CAS) held in the United States.

The second option may be more practical because it saves time.

In many cases, a proposed sanction is provided by the arbitrator or, if accepted by the athlete without a hearing, forwarded to the national governing body to impose. In some cases, the sanction may be determined by the national governing body or the USADA.

The USADA replaced programs by the USOC and national governing bodies that were perceived as hiding drug cheaters. There have been doping allegations, most notably those involving the members of USA Track & Field, in which the names of athletes who reportedly tested positive for performance-enhancing drugs were not released, causing discord between USA Track & Field and its international federation, the International Association of Athletics Federations (Conrad, 2001). For example, Jerome Young tested positive for a steroid called nandrolone the year before going to the Sydney Olympics in 2000 to compete in the $4 \times 400$ m relay race; nonetheless, it remained secret and he was cleared to participate in the race. On June 29, 2004, the CAS ruled that Young be stripped of his gold medal. Alvin Harrison, who was also on the same team as Young and took home a silver medal in Sydney, is currently facing a lifetime ban due to a doping charge, as he is accused of using steroids. His brother Calvin Harrison was suspended and declared ineligible for the Athens Olympics after testing positive for modafinil (Gloster, 2004).

Enhancing the credibility of U.S. testing efforts "by eliminating the negative perceptions inherent" in prior programs was a key reason for the USADA's creation.

### World Anti-Doping Agency

The creation of WADA, an international version of the USADA, resulted from a doping scandal at the 1998 Tour de France bicycle race. In a police raid during the race, a large number of prohibited medical substances were discovered. The amount seized and the accompanying bad publicity and embarrassment suffered encouraged a coordinated effort to stop doping in all sports. Before the establishment of the WADA, the IOC and other international federations suffered the same problems as their domestic counterparts: These governing bodies adopted their own standards and procedures, resulting in confusion and inconsistency.

In 1999, the WADA was established, headquartered in Montreal. The WADA proposed a World Anti-Doping Code, which has since been adopted by an impressive array of national Olympic committees, international federations, national governing bodies, and national antidoping organizations (such as the USADA). As of this writing, most of the international sports bodies have adopted the code and its procedures. Notably, the major professional sports leagues in the United States have not, despite political pressures to do so.

The Code imposes a strict liability standard involving the use of banned performance-enhancing substances. Whether one takes the drug intentionally or accidentally does not matter. It states:

> It is each *Athlete's* personal duty to ensure that no *Prohibited Substance* enters his or her body. Athletes are responsible for any Prohibited Substance . . . found to be present in their bodily specimens. Accordingly, it is not necessary that intent, fault, negligence or knowing Use on the *Athlete's* part be demonstrated in order to establish an *anti-doping violation* (World Anti-Doping Code, Article 2.1.1, 2009).

The code calls for a two-year ban for a first offense and a lifetime ban for a second, barring mitigating circumstances. However, it allows for the use of certain prohibited substances for "therapeutic" purposes on a case-by-case basis (World Anti-Doping Code, 2009, Article 4.4).

## Professional Sports

Before we examine the drug-testing policies of the individual professional sports league, some major differences between the NCAA, the Olympic movement, and professional leagues deserve mention. As noted earlier, unlike the first two, pro sports involves a core relationship between employers and employees. Since the players in each of the major leagues are represented by unions, labor law principles must apply. Drug-testing standards—a mandatory subject of collective bargaining—must be negotiated between those parties and memorialized in the CBA between the union and management. Therefore, unlike collegiate or international sports, implementing or changing a drug-testing regime must be done by agreement. It cannot be mandated by one party, despite what certain critics hope to do. With this in mind, we will examine the policies of the major sports leagues.

## National Football League

Of the major sports leagues, the strictest drug policies come from the National Football League (NFL). The illegal use of drugs and the abuse of prescription drugs, over-the-counter drugs, and alcohol are prohibited for NFL players. Moreover, the use of alcohol may be prohibited for individual players in certain situations, such as following a charge for driving under the influence. The NFL and the NFL Players' Association (NFLPA) have maintained policies and programs regarding substance abuse. They can be found in Article XLIV, section 6(a) of the NFL CBA (NFL CBA, 2006, Article XLIV, sec. 6).

The NFL has separate drug-testing policies for "substances of abuse" and steroids. The so-called Intervention Program serves as the cornerstone of the substance abuse policy. Under the Intervention Program, players are tested, evaluated, treated, and monitored for substance abuse. The NFL tests for illegal use of drugs and the abuse of prescription drugs and alcohol every year on a specified date, with notice given to players far in advance. If a player fails the first test, he gets a second test before any disciplinary action (suspension) is taken.

The philosophy rests on the belief that recreational drug use is a medical issue. Players who fail a drug test are placed in the Intervention Program, with the goal of treatment and rehabilitation. Only players who do not comply with the requirements of the Intervention Program are subject to discipline. If a player has been suspended indefinitely under the substance abuse program, he is eligible to apply for reinstatement after a given period of time. The commissioner then determines whether or not to accept the reinstatement (National Football League, Policy and Program for Substances of Abuse, 2003).

The NFL also, and more strictly, tests for steroids and performance-enhancing drugs, giving random tests for steroids to players. A computer randomly selects six players on each team each week to be tested. On the first positive test result for a performance-enhancing drug, a player is suspended for four games without pay. A six-game suspension follows a second positive, and a third positive results in at least a one-year suspension. The league also tests for masking agents. If a player tries to pass a test by using masking agents, suspensions occur, even if a steroid is not detected (Collinsworth, 2004).

All disciplinary action provided under the policy is imposed through the authority of the commissioner of the NFL. The commissioner maintains the ability to impose other sanctions as he deems necessary, and, significantly, no appeals process exists.

## National Basketball Association

The National Basketball Association (NBA) policy on drug testing and drug use was considered a bellwether when first adopted in 1983. The players and the owners agreed to a drug detecting system administered by an independent expert. However, it did not provide for mandatory testing, but only required testing based on "reasonable cause." For non-performance-enhancing drugs, the regimen remains essentially the same today. Actual drug testing does not occur unless confidential evidence brought to that expert demonstrates a drug abuse problem. Only then can "authorization for testing" occur. The policy also encourages players to come forward and admit their problems. If they do, then treatment is available without the threat of disciplinary sanction.

In the 2006 CBA, the illegal addictive drugs and performance-enhancing drugs are covered, including amphetamines, cocaine, LSD, opiates (heroin, codeine, and morphine), PCP, marijuana, and steroids (NBA CBA, 2005, Article XXXIII, sec. 4(c)).

Notably, the league, the team, and the union are prohibited from publicly disclosing information regarding the testing or treatment of any NBA player in the program, except as required by the suspension or dismissal of a player in the program. This differs from the approach of the WADA and USADA.

A player may come forward voluntarily regarding his use of a prohibited substance and seek treatment in the program. There is no penalty the first time a player comes forward voluntarily. A player may not come forward voluntarily when he is subject to an authorization for reasonable cause testing or when he is subject to in-patient or aftercare treatment in the program (NBA CBA, 2005, Article XXXIII, sec. 7).

A player tests "positive" for a prohibited substance at the concentration levels set forth in the CBA. The player is also deemed to have tested positive if he fails or refuses to submit to a drug test, or if the player attempts to mask, substitute, dilute, or adulterate his urine sample. A player notified of a positive result has two business days to request a retest from the NBA and National Basketball Players' Association (NBPA). The retest will be performed at a laboratory different from the laboratory used for the first test (NBA CBA, 2005, Article XXXIII, sec. 4(c)).

If the NBA or NBPA receives information that provides "reasonable cause" of a player's use, possession, or distribution of a prohibited substance, the NBA or NBPA will request a hearing with the other party and the independent expert within twenty-four hours of the receipt of that information. If the independent expert decides that "reasonable cause" exists, an authorization for testing is granted and the NBA arranges for testing of the player four times during the next six weeks (NBA CBA, 2005, Article XXXIII, sec. 5).

If, after the test, the NBA or NBPA believes that there is sufficient evidence to show use, possession, or distribution of a prohibited substance, the matter may be taken directly to the league's grievance arbitrator. If the grievance arbitrator determines that the player has used or possessed amphetamine or one of its analogs, cocaine, LSD, opiates, or PCP, or has distributed any prohibited substance, the player will be dismissed and disqualified from the NBA. (NBA CBA, 2005, Article XXIII, sec. 5).

Presently, all rookies are subject to unlimited drug testing and veteran players are subject to four random tests per year. All random tests are at the discretion of the NBA and without prior notice to the player. As noted above, when a player tests positive for illegal substances, other than marijuana and steroids, he is dismissed and disqualified from any association with the NBA, and can apply for reinstatement at a later date. However, if a player tests positive for either steroids or marijuana, he is required to enter a substance abuse program.

If a player tests positive for amphetamines or one of their analogs, cocaine, LSD, opiates, or PCP during reasonable cause testing, first-year testing, or veteran testing, he will be dismissed and disqualified from the NBA. However, veterans can seek reinstatement after two years and rookies after one. Reinstatement occurs only with the approval of both the NBA and the NBPA, and such approval may be conditional on random testing and other terms (NBA CBA, 2005, Article XXXIII, sec. 12(a)).

A player will also be dismissed and disqualified from the NBA if he is convicted of a crime involving the use or possession of amphetamines and its analogs, cocaine, LSD, opiates, or PCP (NBA CBA, 2005, Article XXXIII, sec. 5(d)).

The above rules do not apply to performance-enhancing drugs, or to marijuana possession. Both merit more lenient treatment. For a first offense, a player will be suspended for five games and will be required to enter the antidrug program. A second positive test for steroids will result in a ten-game suspension and the player's reentry into the program. A third (or any subsequent) positive test for steroids will result in a twenty-five-game suspension and the player's reentry into the program. A player will be dismissed and disqualified from the NBA if he is convicted of a crime involving the use or possession of steroids (NBA CBA, 2005, Article XXXIII, sec. 10(c)).

If a player tests positive for marijuana for the first time during reasonable cause testing, first-year testing, or veteran testing, or he is convicted of the use or possession of marijuana in violation of the law, he will be required to enter the antidrug program. A second such violation will result in a fine and the player's reentry into the program. A third (or any subsequent) such violation will result in a five-game suspension and the player's reentry into the program (NBA CBA, 2005, Article XXXIII, sec. 9(c)).

## Major League Baseball

In the wake of allegations of use of performance-enhancing drugs by star players such as Barry Bonds and Jason Giambi, and resulting pressure from politicians, commentators, and the public, Major League Baseball and the Major League Baseball Players' Association twice amended their CBA to tighten their drug-testing procedures in 2005.

The first change, agreed on in January 2005, increased the penalties for violators and expanded the list of illegal performance-enhancing drugs (Fisher, 2005). It provided that every player will undergo at least one random test during the playing season, and included random testing during the off-season, irrespective of a player's country of residence. It also provided for additional tests for an unspecified number of randomly selected players. In addition, testing would occur during the off-season for the first time.

The agreement also revised disciplinary penalties for positive test results, with first-time offenders suspended for ten days. Second-time offenders would be suspended for thirty days. Third-time offenders would be suspended for sixty days. Fourth-time offenders would be suspended for one year. All suspensions would be without pay. Significantly, offending players would be publicly identified, a departure from the prior policy of keeping the names of first-time offenders secret (Bodley, 2005).

The new policy expanded the list of banned substances to include diuretics, masking agents, human growth hormone, and steroid precursors. The penalties fell far short of those stated in WADA's code, which calls for a two-year ban for first-time offenders unless there are mitigating circumstances.

The January 2005 changes did not mollify critics and, after months of continuing criticism and Congressional pressure, Major League Baseball players and owners agreed to significantly tighten the policy in November 2005. The new policy, effective from the 2006 season, sharply increased penalties for steroid use to a fifty-game suspension for a first offense, 100 games for a second offense, and a lifetime ban for a third. It also established mandatory random testing for amphetamines, a first for any of the major professional leagues. First-time amphetamine offenders will be subject to mandatory follow-up testing. Second-time offenders will be suspended for twenty-five games and third-time offenders for eighty games. Players could be banned for life for a fourth offense. Any player banned for life has a right to seek reinstatement after two years (Hohler, 2005).

Regarding illegal drugs, Major League Baseball players who possess, sell, or use such controlled substances risk disciplinary action by their individual clubs or by the commissioner. This prohibition also applies to agreed-upon steroids or prescription drugs. The Health Policy Advisory Committee, a group composed of doctors and lawyers representing the league, the players, and the office of the commissioner, is responsible for administering and overseeing the anti-drug program.

Once a player tests positive, he enters a treatment program under a "clinical track." The medical representatives will help tailor a treatment and counseling program for the player. However, if the player fails to comply, by continuing to use or sell banned drugs, the player is put on an "administrative track" and is subject to immediate discipline.

In the summer of 2004, Major League Baseball and the players' association banned the use of androstenedione, the substance used by Mark McGwire when he hit seventy home runs six years earlier. However, this was done after the Food and Drug Administration banned its sale. Other leagues and organizations had banned "andro" years earlier.

In 2007, former U.S. Senator George Mitchell was asked to report on the use of performance-enhancing drugs among present and former Major League Baseball players. The report identified eighty-five players who used one or more of such substances, including Barry Bonds and Roger Clemens. Because Mitchell could not force individuals to speak to him (as he lacked subpoena power), the report was general and not as comprehensive as it would have been had he had such powers (Mitten, Davis, Smith, & Berry, 2009).

### National Hockey League

Before the present CBA, the National Hockey League (NHL) did not randomly test for steroids, stimulants, or any other performance-enhancing drugs; instead, it offered education and counseling (Wilstein, 2004). The present agreement requires that every player is subject to up to three "no-notice" tests from the start of training camp through the end of the regular season. It breaks down as follows: Ten teams are subject to one no-notice test, ten teams subject to two no-notice tests, and ten teams subject to three no-notice tests.

If a player tests positive for a banned performance-enhancing substance, he is subject to a twenty-game suspension without pay and mandatory referral to the NHL Players' Association (NHLPA)/NHL Substance Abuse & Behavioral Health Program for evaluation, education, and possible treatment. A second positive test results in a sixty-game suspension without pay and a third positive test results in permanent suspension (although he is eligible to apply for reinstatement after two years). The NHL utilizes the WADA list of prohibited substances (NHLPA.com, 2010).

### The Bay Area Laboratory Co-operative Case

Athletes have sometimes gone to impressive lengths to circumvent drug screening, notably in the case of certain track and field athletes. An edge, even a slight edge, can make a difference between winning an Olympic gold medal or finishing out of medal contention. In the summer of 2003, the Bay Area Laboratory Co-Operative (BALCO) created at least one undetectable steroid.

Tetrahydrogestrinone, or THG, was that undetected steroid. Unknown until an unidentified track and field coach sent a syringe containing the substance to the USADA in June 2003, THG was administered in drops placed under the tongue. Detection was difficult, because its half-life was short and no traces existed by the time a routine drug screening occurred. After the creation of a test procedure for THG, four American track athletes tested positive for the steroid. One track and field star, Kelli White, the world sprint champion at 100 and 200 meters, admitted that she used undetectable steroids provided by BALCO (Patrick, 2004). Other athletes, notably in baseball, were also implicated, such as the Yankees' Jason Giambi and the San Francisco Giants' Barry Bonds (NBC Sports.com, 2007). These allegation cast a pall over their achievements.

Dr. Don H. Catlin, of the University of California (UCLA) lab that first discovered THG, said:

> It's not one little athlete reading something in a book or magazine and writing away for something. There are a lot of people involved. It shows you the stakes are high and getting higher. These are not just last-stringers trying to make the team. These are name athletes, champions. It's terribly disturbing. The drugs work, and high-level athletes take them. That's the highest form of crime in a sense for an athlete (Longman, 2004).

But the methods used in the BALCO investigation present issues of privacy, due process, and basic civil rights. Under the U.S. legal system, an accuser must prove guilt (in a criminal case) or liability (in a civil case). The USADA, with federal prosecutors, has attempted to use what one commentator called "sloppy-nasty" tactics, to make "cheaters now look like victims, and the innocent like potential martyrs" (Jenkins, 2004). Leaks of athletes' grand jury testimony to the press by prosecutors violate the confidentiality of such testimony. Press conferences and statements by USADA officials strongly implying guilt under the ongoing criminal investigations are similarly debatable. Journalists should probe accusers and ask why information was leaked.

When writing about this issue, note the level of proof required. For example, the USADA changed its definition of proof from "beyond a reasonable doubt" (the standard for criminal prosecutions) to a standard of "comfortable satisfaction." Why did the agency do this? Did it think the older standard too difficult? One answer is that the change clearly makes the USADA's job much easier in attempting to prove guilt (Jenkins, 2004).

Other recent performance-enhancing controversies involved Floyd Landis, the winner of the 2006 Tour de France. After performance-enhancing drugs were found by the French police in the car of the team trainer, Landis was tested and found to have elevated levels of testosterone. He sought arbitration under WADA rules. The first arbitration panel ruled against him in a 2–1 margin, despite the fact that the initial screening test was not done in accord with WADA rules. Stripped of his title and barred from the sport for two years, Landis appealed to the CAS, which denied his appeal (Weiler & Roberts, 2008).

Also in 2007, Marion Jones, the star of the 2000 Summer Olympics, admitted having used performance-enhancing drugs. Jones, who had won three gold and two bronze medals at Sydney, told a federal judge that she had been taking the banned substance named "the clear" produced by BALCO after its founder Victor Conte had earlier named her as one of its recipients. In January 2008 Jones received a six-month federal jail sentence for having made false statements to the federal investigation of BALCO. Jones also returned the medals she won in Sydney and accepted a ban from going to the 2008 Summer Olympics in Beijing, China (Weiler & Roberts, 2008).

The issues of drugs and drug testing will continue as a major concern in the sports landscape. See Table 10.1 for a summary of sanctions in the four major team sports and the Olympics.

*Table 10.1* A Comparison of Penalties for Performance-Enhancing Drug Test Violations among Sports Organizations

| Organization | First Violation | Second Violation | Third Violation | Fourth Violation | Fifth Violation |
|---|---|---|---|---|---|
| NFL | Four games (min.) | Six games | One year | One year | One year |
| NBA | Five games | Ten games | Twenty-five games | Twenty-five games | Twenty-five games |
| NHL | Twenty games | Sixty games | Lifetime ban | n/a | n/a |
| MLB | Fifty games | One hundred games | Lifetime ban | n/a | n/a |
| Olympics | Two years | Lifetime ban | n/a | n/a | n/a |

## Information Check

When covering substance abuse issues, knowledge of the standards discussed here is required. After that, the journalist should determine:

1 What substance(s) was discovered?
2 What does the athlete or his or her representative say about the circumstances leading to the alleged discovery?
3 Was there a "medical" reason to take the substance?
4 Is it an illegal drug in the United States?
5 Does the athlete plan to appeal and, if so, what are his or her main claims?

## References

Anabolic Steroids Control Act of 1990, 21 USC, sec. 802 (1999).

Barker, J. (2004, December 9). White House pushes MLB to crack down on steroids; North Dakota senator says players union must put end to "stonewalling." *Baltimore Sun*, p. 3C.

Bodley, D. (2005, January 12). Baseball officials announce tougher steroids policy. *USA Today*. Retrieved September 2, 2010, from http://www.usatoday.com/sports/baseball/2005-01-12-steroid-policy_x.htm

Collinsworth, C. (2004). The best policy: NFL's drug testing. Retrieved July 6, 2004, from www.nfl.com/new/story6744864

Conrad, M. (2001, July 13). USA Track criticized for "lax" enforcement of anti-doping rules. Retrieved June 1, 2005, from www.sportslawnews.com/archive/Articles%202001/USATrackDoing.htm

Dvorchak, R. (2005, May 19). Congress remains skeptical; grills, prods sports czars on steroids. *Pittsburgh Post-Gazette*, p. C-1.

Espn.com (2007, June 27). NCAA committee rejects proposal to test for street drugs. Retrieved May 10, 2010, from http://sports.espn.go.com/ncaa/news/story?id=2918911

Fisher, E. (2005, January 13). Baseball beefs up steroid penalties. *Washington Times*, p. C01.

Gloster, R. (2004, August 3) Harrison hit with 2-year drug suspension. *Ventura County Star*, p. 4.

Hohler, B. (2005, November 16) Baseball gets tough about doping. *Boston Globe*, p. A1.

Iwata, E. (2004, December 21). Andro users, sellers push to beat ban. *USA Today*, p. 1A

Jenkins, S. (2004, June 26). Due process? Not for track stars. *Washington Post*, p. D1.

Longman, J. (2004, June 11). Edge is all to athletes, BALCO case reveals. *New York Times*, sec. D, p. 1.

Ludd, S. O. (1991). Athletics, drug testing and the right to privacy: A question of balance. *Howard Law Journal, 34*, 599.

Mitten, M., Davis, T., Smith, R., & Berry, R. (2009). *Sports law and regulation* (p. 602). New York: Wolters Kluwer.

National Football League (2003). Policy and program for substances of abuse. Retrieved September 27, 2005, from www.nflpa.org/Members/Main.asp?

NBA CBA, Article XXXIII, sec. 4(c) et al.(2005). Retrieved August 31, 2010, from http://www.nbpa.org/cba/2005

NBCSports.com (2007, October 5). Key figures in BALCO steroid scandal. Retrieved May 15, 2010, from http://nbcsports.msnbc.com/id/21154643/ns/sports-other_sports/

NCAA Division I Manual (2009). Bylaws, secs. 31.2.3.3 and 31.2.3.5. Retrieved August 31, 2010, from http://www.ncaapublications.com/productdownloads/D110.pdf

NCAA.org (2009). *NCAA Drug-Testing Program Handbook* (chapter 1). Retrieved May 10, 2010, from http://www.ncaapublications.com/productdownloads/DT10.pdf

NFL CBA, Article XLIV, sec. 6 (2006). Retrieved August 20, 2010, from http://images.nflplayers.com/mediaResources/files/PDFs/General/NFL%20COLLECTIVE%20BARGAINING%20AGREEMENT%202006%20-%202012.pdf

NHLPA.com (2005). NHL drug testing program. Retrieved January 7, 2010, from http://www.nhlpa.com/About-Us/Drug-Testing-Program-Summary/

Patrick, D. (2004, December 2). Sprinter reveals career demise. *USA Today*. Retrieved May 15, 2010, from http://www.usatoday.com/sports/olympics/2004-12-02-white-demise_x.htm

Sprattling, S. (2010). Tiger's transgressions: a look at how sports coverage has changed. USCAnnenberg.org. Retrieved May 15, 2010, from http://blogs.uscannenberg.org/neontommy/2010/01/tigers-transgressions-werent-a.html

Steroid-abuse.org (n.d.). Women and steroids—The wonder girls. Retrieved May 6, 2010, from http://www.steroid-abuse.org/the-wonder-girls-women.htm

steroidlaw.com (2010, Feb. 3). Senator McCain to introduce legislation regarding FDA's Current Regulations on Dietary Supplements. Retrieved March 1, 2010, from http://www.steroidlaw.com/page.php?pageID=40

Ungerleider, S., & Wadler, G. I. (2004, June 20). A new world order in elite sports. *New York Times*, sec. 8, p. 12.

USADA Protocol for Olympic Movement Testing (2009). Sections 4, 9, 11. Retrieved March 10, 2010, from http://www.usada.org/files/active/policies_procedures/USADA%20Protocol-%202009-%20FINAL.pdf

Weiler, P., and Roberts, G. (2008). *Supplement to Sports and the Law* (3rd ed., p. 9). St. Paul, MN: West.

Wilstein, S. (2004). NHL can't afford to be aloof about drug testing. Retrieved July 16, 2004, from http://msnbc.msn.com/id/4569409

World Anti-Doping Code (2009). Retrieved April 21, 2010, from http://www.wada-ama.org/rtecontent/document/code_v2009_En.pdf

# 11 Discrimination in Sports

A good journalist tackles a discrimination story with caution. With the possible exception of labor–management issues, allegations of race, gender, ethnic or sexual orientation discrimination may be the most difficult subject to cover, in part from the nature of the claim and the resulting charges and countercharges from those involved. Because of the broad and controversial legal and social issues, understanding the basis of a discrimination claim and obtaining information from as many parties as reasonably possible is a must. This chapter provides a general background on the various kinds of discrimination that exist and the appropriate standards used to determine the validity of a discrimination claim.

Note the distinction between *illegal* discrimination and policies that, although not illegal, result in the lack of representation of certain groups of people. Witness the case of the Augusta National Golf Club, the home of the prestigious Masters' competition. Protests against the all-male club were launched during the 2003 tournament, which received notable coverage, especially in *New York Times*. William "Hootie" Johnson, the chair of the club, said, "There never will be a female member, six months after the Masters, a year, 10 years, or ever" (Bisher, 2003). Although controversial and possibly unethical, the action of the club and the statement is not illegal. The club has the right to exclude women, because a private facility has the discretion to select the members it wishes, no matter what sex (or race) they are.

Discrimination laws often apply in the employment relationship, and these laws—state and federal—prohibit discrimination based on race, ethnicity, religion, age, and in some cases sexual orientation. Employment discrimination issues can exist in sports (Kahn, 1991).

In addition to employment, discrimination laws apply to actions by government entities and private organizations that receive governmental funding. In particular, gender-based discrimination has received a great deal of coverage and discussion, owing to the considerable litigation resulting from the interpretation of Title IX of the Education Amendments of 1972, the statute governing equity in federally funded institutions. The standards have produced intense debate about the nature of the enforcement of the law and the resulting claims by certain male athletes of "reverse discrimination." Discrimination against those with disabilities has also resulted in discussion and lawsuits, notably in high school and collegiate sports.

In 1964, the passage of Title VII of the Civil Rights Act barred discrimination in employment based on race, color, religion, sex, or national origin. Since then, outright, intentional discrimination has been illegal. Essentially, Title VII prohibits intentional discrimination in hiring, promotions, and termination. A basic question arises of how to prove such acts. It is safe to say that most employers and their managerial and supervisory employees (even in the sports industry) refrain from making openly racist statements regarding employment standards. Therefore, limiting discrimination laws to purely intentional statements would result in few successful cases. Instead, a system based on "disparate impact" or statistical underrepresentation has been devised by the courts. Simply put, if such a statistical imbalance can be shown between the number, rank, or termination of employees as compared with a general population, a basic presumption of employment discrimination occurs. For example, if only two of the NFL's thirty-two head coaches are black, as compared with the percentage of players or even the percentage of African Americans in the United States (which is far higher), it can merit a disparate impact claim by those eligible black candidates denied head coaching positions. However, the employer has a defense of "business necessity," and, if the team or the league proves that the disparity is based on success (meaning victories) and that a full and fair job search yields candidates who are qualified, then the employer wins (Griggs v. Duke Power, 1971).

With this in mind, let us tackle some of the major issues.

## Race Discrimination

If one thinks of an example of an egregious discriminatory policy in sports, the lack of African Americans in professional baseball ranks at the top. From the late nineteenth century to 1947, Major League Baseball enforced a ban on "Negro" ball players. The policy was never formalized, but the effect was pernicious. During the reign of commissioner Kenesaw Mountain Landis, not one Black person played in the major leagues. While baseball denied it had a race problem, it had existed under the veneer of impartiality. As reportedly noted by Landis's successor, Albert "Happy" Chandler, "so long as Landis remained commissioner, . . . there wasn't going to be any black boys in the league" (Rogosin, 1995).

Certainly, talent existed. Marvelous players from Negro Leagues toured the country and even competed against White major leaguers in exhibitions (Weiler & Roberts, 2004). The foolishness and outrageousness of this policy resulted in a great talent pool of players being excluded from the major leagues. The segregation policy also violated good business sense. A greater number of players for owners to pick from would exist and owners' leverage over their players in a pre–free agency era would increase, keeping salaries low, possibly even lower than was the case.

After Landis died in 1944, the color barrier broke down with the entry of Jackie Robinson (Brooklyn Dodgers) and Larry Doby (Cleveland Indians). It took another decade to integrate all major league teams. But changing attitudes about minority players, unfortunately, took years longer.

In 1987, the issue of race in sports became national news when Al Campanis, a vice-president for the Los Angeles Dodgers, made inopportune remarks on an ABC News *Nightline* broadcast when asked about the lack of Black managers and front-office personnel in the sport. He said, "I don't think it is prejudice. I truly believe that they may not have some of the necessities to be, let's say, a field manager or perhaps a general manager" (Johnson, 2007). Campanis was fired after that broadcast, and Major League Baseball instituted an affirmative action program to expand opportunities for minorities on the coaching and managerial level. A few years before that, the National Football League (NFL) and National Basketball Association (NBA) instituted such programs. In 1985, the league worked with Benjamin Hooks, the National Association for the Advancement of Colored People (NAACP) executive director to hire Blacks in the front office. The NFL hired its first Black head coach in the modern era, Art Shell of the Los Angeles Raiders, in 1989.

Another example of offensive comments occurred a few years later. In the early 1990s, the principal owner of the Cincinnati Reds, Marge Schott, made anti-Semitic and racist comments that received wide publicity. Ultimately, she accepted a one-year suspension from day-to-day control of the team's operations and a fine. Although her opinions constitute protected free speech under the First Amendment, that immunity does not apply to a private organization such as Major League Baseball, which was well within its rights to enact sanctions against her for those comments. More recently, in 2003, the conservative radio talk show host Rush Limbaugh stated that the Philadelphia Eagles quarterback Donovan McNabb was overrated by the media and the NFL because of their interest in seeing Black quarterbacks and coaches do well. The resulting criticism forced Limbaugh's resignation from his role on ESPN's *Sunday NFL Countdown* (Siemaszko, 2003).

Players have joined in this chorus of ill-timed statements. The Atlanta Braves relief pitcher John Rocker made insulting comments about various minority groups and gays in an interview in *Sports Illustrated* in 1999. In it, he ranted against the kinds of people who took the subway to Shea Stadium (then the home of the New York Mets) and then stated: "The biggest thing I don't like about New York are the foreigners . . . Asians and

Koreans and Vietnamese and Indians and Russians and Spanish people and everything there. How did they get into this country?" (Pearlman, 2000). Commissioner Bud Selig suspended Rocker for the spring training and the first twenty-eight days of the 2000 regular season. Unlike the situation with Schott, Rocker, a unionized employee subject to the collective bargaining agreement, pursued arbitration. The arbitrator reduced the fine to $500 and the suspension to fourteen days during the season (Standora, 2001).

The Rocker case presents an important question when dealing with insensitive racial, ethnic, or religious comments. Rocker made them during the off-season, in a nonbaseball setting. Should his employer sanction him for his opinions, as odious as they are? If Rocker got along with his teammates and did not engage in any racial or ethnic insults while engaged in his job, should the league mete out punishment?

Another issue involves double standards. The rap group led by the then-Philadelphia 76ers' Allen Iverson made a CD replete with comments about those with "faggot tendencies," and "fucking bitches." NBA commissioner David Stern criticized the lyrics as "repugnant" but did not take any disciplinary action (Smith, 2000). Given Rocker's statements and punishment, do these comments deserve equal sanction?

## Underrepresentation of Minorities

Although underrepresentation of African Americans exists on the management level, with the exception of ice hockey the problem is not found among players. In 2008, 10.2 percent of baseball players, 67 percent of NFL players, and 77 percent of NBA players were African-American. What has become striking, however, is the increase in percentage of other minorities in professional sports. Today, 27 percent of baseball players are Hispanic, up from 14 percent in 1990, and 2 percent are Asian, an increase from 0 percent in 1992 (Lapchick, 2009a,b,c). The selection, cultivation, and compensation of these athletes are commensurate with their abilities and the likelihood of illegal discrimination is scant, since professional athletics is the ultimate meritocracy, as only the very best make it to the major league level.

For sports league and team management, the survey found that baseball had eight general managers who are people of color—the fewest among the big three leagues. One person of color and no women had minority shareholdings of Major League Baseball teams, 34 percent of Major League Baseball's central office employees were people of color, second only to the NBA's 35 percent, while 18 percent of central office employees at the senior executive level were people of color. Women occupied 18 percent of the senior level positions (Lapchick, 2009a).

The same report gave the NBA the best racial and gender diversity.

The NBA led all men's pro leagues for people of color among players (82 percent), league office vice-presidents (14 percent), league office professional staff (35 percent), head coaches (40 percent), chief executive officers/presidents (15 percent), general managers (10 percent), and team professional administration (29 percent). The NBA was best for women in men's pro leagues in league office vice-presidents (18 percent), league office professional staff (43 percent), and owners (7 percent) (Lapchick, 2009b).

Although frustration exists regarding the slow pace of recruitment of African Americans, Hispanics, and women to head coaching, general manager, and other executive positions, litigation is rare in the professional leagues. The time, cost, uncertainty of success, and, possibly most importantly, limited prospect of employment after bringing such a lawsuit serve as disincentives to undertake such a strategy.

## Title IX

Title IX of the Education Amendments of 1972 has become the signature law banning gender discrimination in interscholastic and college sports. Title IX merits recognition by many in the general public, something few laws achieve. However, public recognition is not always synonymous with accuracy, and some of the reporting and commentary about Title IX lacks substantive knowledge about the language, history, and enforcement of this important statute. The law's controversy lies in the enforcement issues created by regulatory bodies and the courts, rather than the actual text.

Although the main interpretation issues have been settled for at least fifteen years, the social ramifications of Title IX continue, resulting in much debate and, at times, rancor. Explaining, rather than advocating, is the goal in this chapter. Journalists must exercise caution and prudence when tackling this tricky subject and ask the right questions.

Let us dispel several myths: (a) Title IX applies only to gender equity in sports; (b) the law constitutes a government-mandated affirmative action program; and (c) the law applies only to women. None of these assertions is true. Title IX, enacted by Congress with the signature of President Richard Nixon, is an educational rights law, pertaining to *all* educational programs receiving federal assistance. It states: "No person in the United States shall, on the basis of sex, be excluded from participation in, be denied the benefits of, or be subjected to discrimination under any educational program or activity receiving federal financial assistance" (Civil Rights Restoration Act of 1987, 2000, 20 USC 1681(a)). That means that, if university X has a biology program that limits participation to men and receives a federal grant of $1 million, the institution is in violation of Title IX. Note that the law applies to both public and private institutions. Federal funding is the key, and many private institutions receive such funding.

Affirmative action involves a voluntary or court-ordered remedy for past discrimination. Title IX, however, is a statute barring discrimination, not a judicial remedy to ameliorate the effects of past discrimination. Also, Title IX deals with opportunities for a historically "underrepresented sex." Although the great majority of cases involve females, it is at least theoretically possible for males to sue, if they meet the statute's threshold requirements.

Yet the enforcement questions belie the outward simplicity of the law. The seemingly broad language of the statute led to years of interpretation questions. Although Congress passed the law, it empowered the Office of Civil Rights (OCR), a federal administrative agency, to craft the particular regulations needed to implement and interpret the law. As was the case with the Americans with Disabilities Act (discussed later in this chapter), the regulations caused the most controversy and required judicial intervention to ensure a uniform interpretation.

It took three years of input and drafting for the issuance of the first set of regulations by the Department of Health, Education, and Welfare in 1975. When the regulations were criticized as vague, the OCR (the successor agency in charge of implementing Title IX) reconsidered and came up with more specific recommendations in 1979. Although the 1975 regulations addressed broad terms such as admissions and employment of students, the 1979 rules, for the first time, specifically applied the statute to issues of gender equity in intercollegiate sports. These standards, despite criticism from certain quarters, remain in effect.

At the same time, a debate developed concerning the scope of Title IX's application. Is it institution-wide or merely applicable to the particular program funded by federal monies? If it is the latter, virtually no athletic programs fall within its ambit, because few if any athletic departments receive federal funding. Institution-wide application, however, results in school-wide enforcement. So, if the college or university accepts $100,000 for its biology lab or its cyclotron, athletics must comply with Title IX and its regulations. The Supreme Court concluded that the more limited standard applied in Grove City College v. Bell (1984). Four years later, Congress overturned Grove City when it passed the Civil Rights Restoration Act (1988), which explicitly extended Title IX coverage to all programs of an institution that receive federal money.

By the late 1980s and early 1990s, Title IX litigation regarding athletic programs began in earnest. In addition to the federal government, the courts allowed individual lawsuits for money damages for violations of Title IX. Most cases have arisen from private litigants, and the plaintiffs emerged victorious in the great majority of these cases (Weiler & Roberts, 2004).

Unequal treatment in the participation, funding, and scholarship opportunities in athletic programs served as the basis of these lawsuits.

Because of these disparities, the argument went, colleges and universities lacked compliance with Title IX. The courts had to determine whether a violation of Title IX existed, and, in answering that question, they looked to the 1979 OCR guidelines. These important—and controversial—rules serve as the basis for Title IX interpretation.

To ensure compliance in *participation* of athletic programs, the college or university must prove one of three alternatives (or "prongs"):

1 Demonstrating that intercollegiate athletic participation is "substantially proportionate" to the respective enrollments of each sex in the particular institution; or if not
2 Demonstrating that the institution has a history of and continuing practice of expanding participation opportunities for the underrepresented sex; or if not
3 Demonstrating that the institution fully and effectively accommodates the abilities and the interests of the underrepresented sex in the current program (Title IX, Policy Interpretation, 44 Fed. Reg. 71, 418, 1979).

Revenue-producing sports such as men's football must be included in the calculation, despite the lack of women's football teams.

The rules cover not just participation, but also scholarships. Many schools grant athletic scholarships based on National Collegiate Athletic Association (NCAA) rules. The OCR guidelines require that male and female student-athletes receive such scholarships proportionally to their participation. The OCR policy outlines "nondiscriminatory factors" such as equipment and supplies, scheduling of goods and practice times, travel and daily allowances, access to tutoring, coaching, locker rooms and competitive facilities, and other support services. Violation of the rules may result in monetary damages and judicial remedies to rectify the situation.

It is best for an institution to show prong 1, the "proportionality" ratio. Basically, if an institution shows "substantial proportionality" in the numbers of male and female athletes, compliance occurs. Let's take an example: College X has 5000 students, 53 percent female and 47 percent male. Two hundred and fifty students participate in intercollegiate athletics. Of those 250, 100 are female and 150 are male (including a number of men's football players) or a breakdown of 40 percent female and 60 percent male. Because these numbers do not fit the proportionality of the student body, noncompliance occurs (unless one of the two other prongs is fulfilled). However, the regulations did not specify the parameters of "substantial proportionality." What if the student body is 53 percent female and athletic participation is 49 percent? Does that result in compliance? That question is left up to the courts. One court concluded that an 11 percent discrepancy is not substantial proportionality (Cohen

v. Brown University, 1993). Presently, many college and university athletic programs lack substantial proportionality (Department of Education, 2002).

The second prong, a demonstration of the institution's current and historical practice of program expansion, means that, although a disparity remains between the ratio of male to female students and the proportion of those engaged in intercollegiate athletics, the institution has a history of expanding opportunities for the underrepresented sex and a plan for continuing that practice. Applicable in the case of an institution seeking to remedy past practices, this prong requires greater resources to expand the numbers of athletes of the underrepresented sex.

The standard involves considerable factual data. A court must examine the past practice of the institution. How many years has the college or university attempted to correct the disparity by adding programs for the underrepresented sex? Have new teams been created? Have club teams "graduated" to varsity teams? Have those teams been created or expanded to meet the interests of that gender? Simply creating new teams does not ensure compliance if little demand exists for them. Louisiana State University learned that lesson when a court concluded that its decision to add women's softball and soccer did not constitute an adequate response to student interest (Pederson v. LSU, 1996).

Once the history of program expansion is adequately demonstrated, the institution must then demonstrate a continuation of that practice. The regulations do not specify a particular timeline but do require the demonstration of consistency. An example of the difficulty of fulfilling prong 2 occurred in a lawsuit against Colgate University. Colgate added eleven women's varsity sports in the 1970s and 1980s, but did not add any women's sports from 1989 to 1993, when the lawsuit was filed. Afterward the court refused to rule in favor of the university and did not dismiss the case. Basically, the court determined that factual questions still existed as to whether the second prong's requirements were met (Bryan v. Colgate University, 1996). The parties settled the case shortly afterward.

The second prong benefits wealthier schools, those possessing the resources to invest in larger athletic activities. Many less affluent institutions lack this ability. The question becomes: What can these schools do to eliminate the disparity? That is the role of the third (and by far the most difficult) prong.

This last alternative allows an institution that maintains a disparity between men's and women's programs to determine that, despite the disparity, the interests and abilities of student athletes are "fully accommodated." In making this determination, the OCR regulations consider these factors: "(a) whether there is unmet interest in a particular sport, (b) sufficient ability to sustain a team in the sport, and (c) a reasonable expectation of competition for the team."

To show that the underrepresented sex's interest is met, the regulations require proof by such methodologies as surveys of students in the institution and potential students in the community. In addition, personal interviews may be utilized. If the institution so proves, then compliance occurs. If not, then a court considers the "ability to sustain an intercollegiate team," a particularly subjective and questionable consideration. The institution must show, through the opinions of coaches, administrators, and athletes, whether it possesses the ability to field a particular team. What makes this ludicrous is that "a school may ask the women's softball, basketball and swimming coaches whether the school has the potential to sustain a varsity bowling team" (Bentley, 2004). If, somehow, the institution can show a lack of ability to sustain new teams, then compliance occurs.

In March 2005, the federal Department of Education (which has since assumed enforcement power over Title IX) issued a "clarification" of the third prong of the OCR standard. The burden of proof was on students and government investigators to show that a college was not doing enough to accommodate women's (or, in some rare cases, men's) athletic interests and abilities and allowed student surveys to gauge student interest and demand for participation in a particular sport. The failure to respond could indicate lack of interest. The regulation noted that, even where an interest exists, schools were not obligated to add a women's team unless the interested students have ability and there are opponents in a school's competitive region (The Secretary of Education's Commission on Opportunity in Athletics, 2002). The "student survey" rule was never widely implemented because it was opposed by the NCAA, which advised its members to ignore it. In 2010, the Obama administration repealed the 2005 clarification (Thomas, 2010).

Before the passage of Title IX, women constituted only 15 percent of the total number of athletic participants in college. By 2009, the figure had increased to 42.6 percent (1981–82 – 2007–08 NCAA Sports Sponsorship and Participation Rates Report, 2009).

Although many Title IX controversies centered on collegiate athletes, the law also applies to primary and high schools, and more litigation has occurred in athletic programs affecting interscholastic sports programs, with the number of complaints involving sex discrimination in high school and even middle school athletics outpacing those involving colleges by five to one since 2001 (Pennington, 2004). The increased level of interest constitutes a reason why. In 1972, when Title IX was enacted, there were 295,000 girls participating in high school sports, or roughly one in twenty-seven. In 2008, there were more than 3,114,000 girls and 4,422,000 boys participating in high school sports, or roughly four out of ten (National Federation of High School Athletic Associations, 2009).

Title IX does not only involve numbers, but also requires equality in playing conditions. The statute also applies to gender discrimination due to poorer playing fields, equipment, and locker rooms (Women's Sports Foundation, 2008).

The federal government is not the only enforcer of Title IX. State athletic authorities have become more aggressive in reviewing member schools' compliance. In Kentucky, the state athletic association's decision to annually review all 284 member school districts for Title IX compliance (a process that often leads to fines and penalties for the noncompliant) has brought about the construction of more than seventy softball fields (Pennington, 2004). After the filing of a lawsuit, two Westchester, New York, high schools were ordered to move girls' soccer from the spring to the fall, so the girls' teams would have the same opportunity as the boys' teams to compete in regional and state soccer championships (Paskin, 2003).

In researching a Title IX issue, considerably more information is available regarding collegiate athletic programs than those of primary and secondary schools. Under the Equity in Athletics Disclosure Act, a federal law enacted in 1994, colleges and universities must disclose all pertinent data on the financial support and numbers of male and female athletes (Equity in Athletics Disclosure Act, 20 USC, sec. 1092, 1999). In primary and secondary public schools, no such federal requirement exists, and much of the enforcement is sectionalized among local school districts.

## Criticisms of Title IX

Title IX greatly helped create the boom in women's athletics in the United States. However, Title IX enforcement comes at a cost, and some have criticized the method by which it is enforced. In June 2002, the Secretary of Education created a fifteen-member commission to study Title IX and possibly recommend changes in its enforcement. Its conclusions, published eight months later, showed that, although the panel agreed on many issues, sharp differences existed on others, prompting a dissenting report. The majority reaffirmed the ideal of Title IX but called for modification and "clarification" of the three-prong test. For example, it called for elimination of the category of "non-traditional" students (meaning older students) from the calculation of proportionality and permitting the Department of Education to allow for a "reasonable variance" from equality if proportionality is retained as a way of complying with Title IX (The Secretary of Education's Commission on Opportunity in Athletics, 2002).

Although the commission's recommendations did not translate into legislation, they demonstrated a discomfort with the proportionality standard (prong 1 of the three-part test) and the adverse consequences of Title IX for male teams. In certain situations, male athletics suffered in the quest for proportionality. The argument that men's teams had to "suffer" unfairly to ensure compliance with Title IX resonates strongly in sports such as men's wrestling that have seen reductions and eliminations in a number of schools.

The impetus for the establishment of the commission was a lawsuit filed by the National Wrestling Coaches Association claiming "reverse discrimination." The organization alleged that Title IX discriminated against male athletes with respect to participation opportunities because sports programs had been eliminated at many schools as a result of the regulations. Neither the lower federal court nor the federal appeals court decided the merits of the case. The federal appeals court, in a 2–1 ruling, dismissed it on procedural grounds (Nat'l Wrestling Coaches Ass'n v. U.S. Dept. of Education, 2004). However, one judge did note that the claims of the plaintiffs were "speculative" because individual schools had discretion to utilize various methods to comply with Title IX, and even a favorable ruling would not result in the likelihood that the men's programs would be protected (ibid.). The following year, the Supreme Court rejected an appeal of the ruling (Nat'l Wrestling Coaches Ass'n v. U.S. Dept. of Education, 2005).

However, some men's programs have been eliminated or reduced to satisfy compliance (McEldowney, 2009). The question journalists should research or ask is the possibility of alternatives—most notably, changes in the numbers and scholarships in the football program, which is generally all male and quite large in many institutions. Because women generally do not have football teams and men's teams contain high numbers of players (with high numbers of scholarships in some cases), this creates difficulties for other men's programs. Men's wrestling or swimming lacks the constituency and alumni interest that football has, so diminution or elimination of football, especially in an institution with a "football tradition," is less likely.

Another argument criticizing Title IX focuses on primary and secondary schools. It concludes that such enforcement provides a disincentive to engage in any improvements because of the costs of compliance. If new training facilities are built, the argument posits, then they have to accommodate women's as well as men's teams. In other words, why commit to new men's facilities unless one can ensure that they are used by women as well?

These costs have become more acute in the face of the belt-tightening by many states and localities. With many school districts forced to cut funding, is it always practical to construct or upgrade facilities? Or should there be a demonstrated commitment to participate in the sport before a school district takes such an action? Consider this example. Let's say that twenty girls wish to compete in interscholastic swimming, but their high school lacks a swimming pool and cannot afford to build one. Therefore, the girls are denied an opportunity to compete and, after parents' complaints, the OCR investigates. Ideally, the OCR would require the school to build a competition-sized pool (which would benefit boys as well), but the prohibitive costs prevent this. The school settles (as opposed to being drawn into time-consuming litigation with the government) and the settlement provides that the school rent the only competition-sized pool in the area (located fifteen miles from the school) and provide transportation to and from that pool for the girls after school for practice sessions for the next two years at a cost of tens of thousands of dollars.

If the settlement spurs momentum for girls' swimming, then the settlement helps ensure the goal of increased participation. However, if fewer girls—and more boys than expected—decide to participate, then the settlement raises difficult questions about priorities and economics. The result is that the school district committed resources that helped only a few students at a considerable cost.

This example raises unpleasant questions, but ones that must be addressed in such a circumstance. Like any law designed to remedy past social inequities, the results may not always be ideal.

Finally, Title IX poses a conflict of race and class. Many of the beneficiaries of Title IX have been women of middle- or upper-middle-class means. Does the proportionality test benefit such women over minority men from underprivileged backgrounds? A sensitive point rarely argued publicly, it was summarized in a 1997 speech given by the Rev. Jesse Jackson in Sacramento, California. In it, Jackson stated:

> There are those who say affirmative action is hurting whites. Let's look at that reasoning. The primary beneficiaries are the white family. The majority of beneficiaries under Title IX are white women who with education, as they join the work force, and get contracts, help stabilize the white family and expand the economy (Jackson, 1997).

Like the prior example, this argument, if true, raises a difficult moral and ethical dilemma. For example, say that a university must spend a proportionate amount of money on athletic scholarships between men and women but, in doing so, disproportionately affects poorer or minority male students. In many cases, an athletic scholarship is the only opportunity for many of these male students to attend college.

## Disability

Disabled people have attained legal protections through legislation passed in 1973 and 1990. Some of the protections mirror those for other groups with a history of discrimination. However, unlike race or sex discrimination, the disabled have unique obstacles in terms of athletic participation.

First, the central focus of disabled athletics rests in the secondary schools and colleges, rather than the professional sports. Given that professional athletes must rank at the pinnacle of those playing the sport, it is difficult, not to say unlikely, for someone without an arm or leg to perform competitively with others. And, in the rare event that someone with a life-altering disability makes it to the pros, that person should understand the risks involved in participation.

Discrimination laws protecting the disabled in public education have been in effect for over thirty-five years, and a body of jurisprudence has developed from the many lawsuits that have been filed against school districts. The first of the two major disability protection laws, section 504 of the Rehabilitation Act of 1973, prohibits the exclusion of participation from any program or activity receiving federal financial assistance (29 USC, sec. 794, 2010). The second, the Americans with Disabilities Act of 1990 (ADA) (42 USC, sec. 12101 et seq., 2002), expanded this mandate. Enacted to protect disabled people from discrimination in the workplace, by private entities offering public accommodations and services, and by the government, it ensures that disabled Americans are offered the same opportunities as all others in society. The ADA incorporated section 504 of the 1973 act and has been utilized by student-athletes when faced with exclusion from participation in a sport.

In order for an athlete (or just about anyone else) to bring an ADA claim, the person must demonstrate a "disability," and, despite that disability, the person must be "otherwise qualified" to obtain the benefit sought. The ADA defines disability as "a physical or mental impairment that substantially limits one or more of the major life activities of such individual" (42 USC, sec. 12132, 2002). An athlete has a claim when he or she proves that, if not for his disability, the person qualifies to engage in the activity. Once shown, the burden shifts to the defendant to show that the eligibility requirements are essential and neutral, and that the proposed accommodations for the disabled athlete fundamentally alter the nature of the athletic program.

Under Title II of the ADA, which applies only to state or local governments or agencies, the individual must show that the defendant is a public entity, that he or she is a qualified individual with a disability, and that this person has been excluded from participation or denied benefits offered by the entity because of the disability. Public educational institutions or state public school athletic associations fit into this definition. Typical disability claims under this title involve denials of student requests for waivers of certain eligibility requirements. More specifically, in the sports context, maximum age requirements, the eight-semester rule (which prohibits a student from participating in interscholastic sports if he or she has spent more than eight semesters completing grades 9–12), and physical requirements are frequently litigated. The following examples illustrate the point: A nineteen-year-old in a special education program seeks the right to try out for the football team but is barred because of an eighteen-year-old maximum age ceiling; a student in his ninth semester because of a neurological condition seeks the tryout for the track team; or a student blind in one eye seeks a spot on the school's hockey team.

Cases against private entities offering public accommodations or services are brought under Title III of the ADA. The accompanying regulations define a place of public accommodation as "a facility operated by a private entity whose operations affect commerce and come within at least one of twelve enumerated categories." Under a Title III action, a plaintiff must show a disability, that the claim is against a private-entity defendant operating a "place of public accommodation," that the athlete was denied the opportunity to participate or benefit from services or accommodations on the basis of his disability, and that reasonable accommodations could have been made without fundamentally altering the nature of the entity.

The intricacies of disability laws in the sports contexts under Title III were found in the Supreme Court decision in PGA Tour, Inc. v. Casey Martin (2001). Martin, a professional golfer, suffered from a circulatory disorder that causes severe pain and that had already atrophied his right leg, making it virtually impossible for him to walk an eighteen-hole golf game. Despite this condition, Martin, an accomplished golfer, progressed to the point where he sought qualification to the PGA Tour, the top professional level for men's golf. Unlike the PGA's other levels of competition, the PGA Tour rules stated that no participant may use a golf cart. Martin applied for a waiver from that rule but was denied. The PGA claimed that the use of the cart gives one participant an advantage over other players who have to walk a course.

Leaving aside the issue of poor public relations caused by the PGA's act, Martin's case brought forth a slew of comments, many of them off point. The key issues were (a) whether a private golf course (where most PGA tournaments are staged) becomes a "place of public accommodation" under the ADA because it hosts a golf tournament and, if so, (b) whether Martin fitted the definition of someone disabled. The majority opinion of the U.S. Supreme Court concluded that a golf course was indeed a place of public accommodation, for the players as well as the audience, thus bringing the dispute within the jurisdiction of the ADA. This key point received far too little coverage. Then the court had to determine whether Martin fitted the definition of "disabled," which he did because his impairment substantially limited one or more major life activities.

Some mistakenly compared Martin's case to that of Ken Venturi, who suffered through heat stroke while competing in a golf tournament in the 1960s, to show the importance of this "walking only" rule. But that also missed the point. Venturi was not disabled, because it was the weather conditions that caused his serious heat stroke, not a life-limiting physical condition. In rejecting the views of many golfers, the court noted that access to a cart would not fundamentally alter the competition, because other levels of PGA competition permitted a cart. Therefore, a denial to accommodate Martin's disability was a violation of the ADA. The court reasoned that walking between holes was not an "essential attribute of the game itself." Even if it were to alter the game, Martin endures much more fatigue even with the use of the cart than his able-bodied competitors.

## Information Check

When covering discrimination issues, a journalist must proceed with caution. This issue, sensitive at the least and incendiary at worst, must be covered carefully, with an understanding of the allegations made and the appropriate legal standards. Ask the following questions:

1 What is the basis of the claim? If it is racial, what laws are allegedly violated? If it is sexual, is it Title IX and/or another law? If it is based on disability, does it come under the ADA and/or section 504 of the Rehabilitation Act?
2 How many individuals are making this claim?
3 Was the conduct intentional? For example, were discriminatory words or conduct alleged?
4 Was the discrimination more institutional, based on disparate numbers of student-athletes versus the percentage of those students in the institution?
5 If Title IX is alleged, what defenses does the institution have? Have any of the three prongs of the 1979 OCR guidelines been satisfied?
6 If the first prong is violated, how does the institution demonstrate compliance with the second or third prong?
7 What remedies do the plaintiffs seek?
8 If the institution decides to reduce men's teams, in numbers of teams, numbers of players, or numbers of available scholarships, has the institution considered cuts in its men's football program and, if applicable, the number of scholarships?
9 When covering professional sports issues, does a particular organization have a plan to increase participation by traditionally disadvantaged groups, notably in coaching and the degree of success of the program?
10 If the sport has a players' association, what procedures are in place, if any, in the collective bargaining agreement to combat discrimination?

# References

1981–82 – 2007–08 NCAA Sports Sponsorship and Participation Rates Report (2009, April). Retrieved March 12, 2010, from https://www.ncaapublications. com//productdownloads/ParticipationRates2009c2f40573-60aa-4a08-874d-1aff4192c5e4.pdf

Americans with Disabilities Act, 42 USC, sec. 12101 et seq. (2002).

Bentley, E. (2004). Title IX: How Title IX should be interpreted to afford women the opportunities they deserve in intercollegiate athletics. *Sports Lawyers Journal, 11*, 89.

Bisher, F. (2003, April 16). Johnson: Club will never have female member. *Atlanta Journal-Constitution*, p. C1.

Bryan v. Colgate University, 1996 WL 328446 (N.D.N.Y. 1996).

Civil Rights Restoration Act of 1987 (20 USC, sec. 1681, 2000).

Cohen v. Brown University, 991 F. 2d 888 (1st Cir. 1993).

Department of Education (2002). Equal opportunity in intercollegiate athletics: Requirements under Title IX of the Education Amendments of 1972. Retrieved August 25, 2010, from http://www2.ed.gov/about/offices/list/ocr/docs/inter-ath.html

Equity in Athletics Disclosure Act (20 USC, sec. 1092, 1999).

Griggs v. Duke Power Co., 401 U.S. 424 (1971).

Grove City College v. Bell 465 U.S. 555 (1984).

Jackson, J. L., Sr. (1997, October 27). Save the dream: March on the Capital, speech delivered October 27, 1997, Sacramento, CA. Retrieved January 17, 2005, from http://www.inmotionmagazine.com/jjsave.html

Johnson, E. (2007, April 12). 'Nightline' Classic: Al Campanis. ABCNews. com. Retrieved August 25, 2010, from http://abcnews.go.com/Nightline/ESPNSports/story?id=3034914

Kahn, L. (1991). Discrimination in professional sports: A survey of the literature. *Industrial & Labor Relations Review, 44*, 395. Retrieved May 15, 2010, from http://www.questia.com/googleScholar.qst?docId=98939559

Lapchick, R. (2009a, September 24). Racial and gender report card: National Football League (Appendix I). Retrieved April 1, 2010, from http://www.tide-sport.org/RGRC/2009/2009_NFL_RGRC.pdf

Lapchick, R. (2009b, April 15). Racial and gender report card: Major League Baseball (Appendix I). Retrieved April 1, 2010, from http://www.tidesport.org/RGRC/2009/2009_MLB_RGRC_PR_Final_rev.pdf

Lapchick, R. (2009c, June 10). Racial and gender report card: National Basketball Association (Appendix I). Retrieved April 1, 2010, from http://www.tidesport. org/RGRC/2009/2009_NBA_RGRC_PR_UPDATED.pdf

McEldowney, H. (2009, August 9). As colleges cut athletics, Title IX creates an injustice to men. *The Washington Post*. Retrieved May 10, 2010, from http://www. washingtonpost.com/wp-dyn/content/article/2009/08/05/AR2009080503089. html

National Federation of High School Athletic Associations (2009). 2008–09 high school athletics participation survey. Retrieved March 10, 2010, from http:// www.nfhs.org/content.aspx?id=3282&linkidentifier=id&itemid=3282

Nat'l Wrestling Coaches Ass'n v. U.S. Dept. of Education, 366 F.3d 930 (D.C. Cir. 2004), aff'g, Nat'l Wrestling Coaches Ass'n v. U.S. Dep't. of Education, 263 F.Supp.2d 82 (D.D.C. 2003).

Nat'l Wrestling Coaches Ass'n v. U.S. Dep't of Education, 126 S. Ct. 12 (2005).

Paskin, J. (2003, July 16). Spring soccer for girls found unfair. *Journal News.* Available at http://www.nynews.com/newsroom/071603/a0116titleix.html

Pearlman, J. (2000). At full blast. *Sports Illustrated, 91*(25), 60.

Pederson v. LSU, 912 F. Supp. 892 (La. 1996).

Pennington, B. (2004, June 29). Title IX trickles down to girls of generation Z. *New York Times*, p. C1.

PGA Tour, Inc. v. Casey Martin, 532 U.S. 661 (2001).

Rehabilitation Act of 1973, Nondiscrimination under federal grants and programs, 29 USC sec 794 (2010).

Rogosin, D. (1995). *Invisible men: Life in baseball's minor leagues* (p. 192). Lincoln: University of Nebraska Press.

The Secretary of Education's Commission on Opportunity in Athletics (2002). *Open to All: Title IX at 30.* Retrieved June 10, 2005, from http://www.gpoaccess.gov/eric/200405/ed480939.pdf

Siemaszko, C. (2003, October 2). He quits ESPN gig over race remark. *New York Daily News*, p. 4.

Smith, S. (2000, October 13). Iverson's rap? NBA will take the rap. *Chicago Tribune*, p. 9.

Standora, L. (2001, June 23). Now, Rocker is headed to the Bronx, instead of Queens. *New York Daily News*, p. 4.

Title IX, Policy Interpretation (1979) 44. Fed. Reg. 71, 418.

Thomas, K. (2010, April 20). Policy change takes aim at loophole in Title IX. *New York Times*, p. B11.

Weiler, P., & Roberts, G. (2004). *Sports and the law—Text and cases* (3rd ed., p. 85). St. Paul, MN: West.

Women's Sports Foundation (2008). Understanding Title IX and Athletics 101. Retrieved May 15, 2010, from http://www.womenssportsfoundation.org/Content/Articles/Issues/Title-IX/U/Understanding-Title-IX-and-Athletics-101. aspx

# 12 Intellectual Property and Sports

Unlike a business that produces machinery or apparel, a league, team owner, college, or individual athlete does not need an engineering plant, heavy equipment, or a fleet of trucks to manufacture or transport its product. Instead, the leagues, teams, athletes, colleges, conferences, and independent tournaments possess rights to "intangible" property—the trademarked names, logo designs, and general rights to license and reproduce those items for merchandising purposes. Over the last quarter-century, the marketing and sale of the team names, designs, uniforms, and player images have constituted a lucrative revenue base.

The licensing and merchandising of sports properties has been transformed from a relatively small and fragmented sideline into a highly profitable $19 billion global industry. Retail sales of sports licensed goods account for 15 percent of worldwide retail sales of licensed merchandise (Brochstein, 2008). Owners of the intellectual property enter into licensing agreements that account for the bulk of the revenue. In 2006, the National Football League (NFL) led the major leagues, earning $3.25 billion, followed by Major League Baseball ($2.2 billion) and college basketball ($3 billion) (Freedman, n.d.). It has been reported that in 2007 the National Basketball Association (NBA) received $2.5 billion, the National Association for Stock Car Auto Racing (NASCAR) $2.1 billion, and the National Hockey League (NHL) about $1 billion (Lindeman, 2008).

What is licensed? Merchandise carrying the names, logos, and designs associated with a particular sport, league, team, college, athletic conference, or other governing body. The licensee, often a firm manufacturing clothing, shoes, or sports equipment, contracts with the intellectual property owner or licensing firm for the use of its names, logos, and designs on items sold to the public. The licensor often receives a stated percentage of the sales, and, even more importantly, has control over the production, design, and overall quality of the product. The major aspects of these agreements are discussed later in this chapter.

## Trademarks

Intellectual property contains a broad category of rights; the most important for sports purposes is trademark protection and licensing. All too often, writers and broadcasters confuse trademarks with copyrights. They are quite different. Defined as "any word, name, symbol or device used to identify and distinguish goods from those manufactured or sold by others" (Trademarks, 2010), a trademark is a brand name, design, symbol, shape, color scheme, slogan, or even smell for use in commerce. For example, the brand name Coca-Cola identifies a particular soft drink. The name *Coca-Cola* is trademarked—a rival cannot use that name without permission. If the rival does, it faces severe penalties, including civil fines, injunctions, even criminal prosecution (Trademarks, 2010). The law requires that a trademark owner use the mark. An unused mark loses protection after a certain period of time, opening it up for use by another entity.

Most U.S.-based trademarks are registered with the U.S. Patent and Trademark Office in Alexandria, Virginia. In order to obtain trademark protection, the mark has to be "distinctive." Examples of distinctiveness involving sports-related marks include "arbitrary" titles—common words applied in an unfamiliar way. The *Detroit Tigers* and the *Carolina Panthers* come to mind. In the context of their sport, these words connect a fan's mind to the particular team. There are also "suggestive" marks—those requiring imagination, thought, and perception, such as the *New York Yankees*. Another basis for distinctiveness comes from "fanciful" marks—made-up names with no dictionary meaning. "Super Bowl" is a trademark of the NFL (although it did not coin the term and was hesitant to use it at first).

A generic term cannot be trademarked, as it lacks distinctiveness. The terms *football* and *baseball* themselves have no protection, so, if anyone wanted to design a sweatshirt with those terms, no trademark infringement would result. The NFL and Major League Baseball cannot own those terms.

Once a trademark is registered, the owner uses a circled R (®) as evidence of the existence of the mark. A protected trademark cannot be used for a *commercial purpose* without the owner's permission. Trademark infringement occurs when one improperly uses another's protected trademarks or uses a mark "likely to cause confusion about the source of a product or service." The focus of trademark infringement analysis is on the confusion of actual or potential customers. Accordingly, an infringer's products or services need only be sufficiently related to the trademark owner's products or services so that it is likely that both are promoted to and/or used by common customers (inta.org, 2010). This rule protects consumers from being misled by the use of infringing marks and also protects producers from unfair practices by an imitating competitor.

Infringement involves one of two situations. The first involves creation of a design similar or substantially similar to an existing trademark, creating a "likelihood of confusion." Courts consider the following factors to determine whether confusion exists: the degree of similarity between the plaintiff's and defendant's mark, the proximity of the products or services, and the existence of actual confusion (Trademarks, 2010). No one factor is necessarily controlling, and in general infringement is evaluated on a case-by-case basis, based on the totality of the circumstances.

It is incumbent on a sports organization to consider the trademark ramifications of a name or logo seriously. That requires *due diligence*, a legal term meaning a comprehensive search to see if the name or design is used by someone else or is sufficiently similar to the other mark. The failure to do so may not only lead to infringement claims. After the NFL's Colts left Baltimore for Indianapolis, that city was awarded a Canadian Football League (CFL) franchise, under the name "Baltimore Colts." The NFL and the Indianapolis Colts sued and a federal appeals court enjoined the CFL team from using the "Colts" name (Indianapolis Colts v. Metropolitan Baltimore Football Club, 1994).

In another example, the Atlanta Thrashers of the NHL received their name in an expeditious but risky manner. After the NHL awarded the franchise to Ted Turner, Turner, asked about the name of the team by a reporter, blurted out "Thrashers . . . I like the name Thrashers." (The brown thrasher is the state bird of Georgia.) A California team owned the mark, and Turner paid a settlement to avoid a lawsuit (Unger, 1998).

The second basis for infringement is clear-cut counterfeiting of goods, known as "knock-offs." Known as "unfair competition," such acts are prohibited by the Lanham Act (Trademarks, 2010), which is the most important law protecting trademarks. The act provides the courts with the right to enjoin the manufacture of knock-off merchandise, coupled with monetary penalties. Fake goods costs sports organizations sizable amounts of money, and, because these counterfeit goods are often made cheaply, such items hurt the image of the trademark holder. Seizure of the fake goods by the FBI and local police occurs, but, despite that power, it is often difficult to catch infringers because it is easy for them to make knock-offs and they are able to work quickly and sell their fake goods in locations such as street fairs and small shops. Larger and more reputable stores usually won't carry them.

More recently, a third method of trademark infringement, known as dilution, was created. Although dilution does not involve a likelihood of confusion, it applies when a similar, though not identical, mark "blurs" or "tarnishes" that trademark. The necessary elements to a claim of dilution by blurring require: that (a) the first mark must be distinctive and (b) the second user attempts to capitalize on the first mark's status. Dilution by tarnishing occurs when a new trademark's similarity to a famous mark causes consumers mistakenly to associate the famous mark with the second user's inferior or offensive product (Kimpflen, 2004). A hypothetical example of blurring exists when a minor league lacrosse team calls itself the New York Yanquis; in the case of tarnishing, it would be a strip club called the New York Spankees.

Whereas every nation has its own trademark laws, an international treaty known as the Madrid Protocol enables a person or entity from a member state to simultaneously register a trademark with all member states at the time of original filing in the home country. Adoption of this treaty means that trademark applicants do not have to file separately in every member country, making it easier and more cost-efficient to obtain international trademark protection. Since the adoption of the treaty by the United States in 2003, domestic sports organizations have expanded their trademark applications to countries all over the world (http://madridprotocol.info).

## Copyright

As noted earlier, the concepts of trademarks and copyrights are frequently confused. Although trademark law protects names, designs, and logos, copyright protects "original words of authorship in any tangible medium of expression" (Copyright Act, 2010). Examples include books, music, recordings, broadcasts, films, theatrical presentations, and choreography. Recent changes in the copyright law have expanded protection to the life of the author plus seventy years, whether the work is performed or not.

The right to broadcast and rebroadcast sporting events has been a central topic involving copyrights. In copyright law, infringement can be direct (done by volition of the infringer), contributory (occurring when one, with knowledge of the infringing activity, induces, causes, or materially contributes to the infringing conduct of another), or vicarious (when one has the right and ability to control the infringer's conduct, and receives a direct financial benefit from the infringement) (Fonovisa v. Cherry Auction, 1996). New media such as YouTube have been accused of copyright infringement due to the posting of portions of copyrighted sports events. The claim centered on whether YouTube engaged in copyright infringement for individual uploads of copyrighted materials, and, if so, what kind of infringement occurs. The case was dismissed by a federal trial court in 2010 because of statutory protection for Internet providers as long as the providers take down the infringing materials after they receive notice that the materials have been uploaded (Viacom v. YouTube, 2010).

## Athletes' Right of Publicity

In addition to trademark protection, which concerns designs and logos used in commerce to identify products, there is an additional intellectual property right in one's name, likeness, and voice. Known as the right of publicity, this concept allows an individual to protect and control the use of his or her identity for commercial purposes. Laws recognized by most states cover the unauthorized use of all recognizable aspects of a person, including image, name or nickname, biographical data, and a distinctive feature such as voice or walk, all of which are often referred to as a celebrity's *persona* (ETW Corporation v. Jireh Publishing, Inc., 2003). Unlike copyright or trademark law, which are based on federal statutes, the right of publicity is a creature of state law, and states vary on the amount and length of protection for this right (Cal. Civ. Code, 2009, sec. 3344; NY Civ. Rights Law, 2009, secs. 50 and 51).

In addition, tension exists between the scope of publicity rights and the constitutional protection of free speech under the First Amendment, which has vexed courts and commentators and resulted in inconsistent rulings. Two cases demonstrate this problem. The first involved a painting entitled "Masters of Augusta," which commemorated Tiger Woods's victory at the 1997 Masters' tournament. The painting shows Woods in three different poses. Also featured are the Augusta National Clubhouse and likenesses of Arnold Palmer, Sam Snead, Ben Hogan, Walter Hagen, Bobby Jones, and Jack Nicklaus looking down at Woods.

The artist, Rich Rush, sold "limited-edition prints" of the work. When Woods discovered this, he (or to be more precise, his corporation, ETW, Inc.) brought suit, claiming a violation of his right of publicity. A divided federal appeal court concluded that Woods's right of publicity was outweighed by the First Amendment. Noting that the painting constitutes a "creative" work of art, not simply an illustration or photograph of Woods, it was protected expression and not an infringement of Woods's rights. The majority of the court noted that Rush's work consisted of a "collage of images" that in combination described a historic sports event and conveyed the significance of Woods's achievement in that event (ETW Corporation v. Jireh Publishing, Inc., 2003).

Other courts, however, have ruled in favor of the athlete. Tony Twist, a former NHL player known as an "enforcer," filed suit claiming that a comic book producer misappropriated his likeness. After learning of the existence of a comic book that contained a villainous character named "Tony Twistelli," Twist sued the creators, publishers, and marketers of the comic book. Twistelli engaged in activities such as multiple murders, abduction of children, and sex with prostitutes. The fictional Twistelli and the real Twist bore no physical resemblance and, aside from the common nickname, were similar only in the sense that each had an "enforcer" or tough-guy persona, according to the court. Unlike the ruling in the Woods case, the Supreme Court of Missouri concluded that the comic-book creators and publishers intended to gain commercial advantage by using Twist's name to attract consumer attention to the comic books and that they marketed the comics and the character to hockey fans who knew Twist and his reputation. This, according to the court, outweighed First Amendment protections (Doe v. TCI Cablevision, 2003).

More recently, the issue of the rights of players in fantasy sports games has resulted in an important federal court ruling. The controversy involved a former licensee of Major League Baseball fantasy games which continued to market a baseball fantasy game utilizing only the players' names and statistics, but not any photographs or uniform numbers. A federal appeals court concluded that First Amendment free speech considerations override any property rights in the use of purely statistical information (CBC Distribution v. MLBAM, 2007). Since then, similar disputes have been considered by the courts, but there is no general rule as of 2010 (CBS Interactive v. NFLPA, 2008). In the wake of these cases, leagues have attempted to create a more varied array of fantasy products (Fisher, 2010).

Like holders of trademarks, athletes protect their image for economic and personal reasons. The more celebrity status an athlete has, the more leverage he or she has to enter into endorsement and marketing deals. Using that athlete's name or likeness without permission undercuts control of his or her reputation and results in damages for lost business opportunity. For example, if someone uses an athlete's name in connection with a tawdry business, the athlete will stop this use (usually by a court order) to protect the athlete's image. The failure to take action could create public perception that the athlete assents to the representation.

The public's interest in particular athletes based on their success and personality has resulted in the achievement of celebrity or near-celebrity status. Athletes such as Babe Ruth, Michael Jordan, Wayne Gretzsky, George Forman, Venus and Serena Williams, and Derek Jeter have a protected property right in their personas. They can license their names or likenesses in posters, apparel, toys, and video games, generating fees often based on a percentage of each item sold.

## Licensing Agreements

Merchandising encompasses the practice of companies selling products with the trademark of a league, conference, team, college, or other organization on those products. The theory behind sports merchandising is that the market power of that organization as a brand attracts fans of the sport to buy the merchandise and therefore enhances the value of the product sold. Although licensing agreements can involve individual names and likenesses, for our purposes we will focus on trademark licensing, as agreements are more frequent and standardized.

A licensor (usually a league) and licensee sign a "trademark license agreement" granting permission from the licensor trademark owner for the licensee to use a trademark for a defined purpose. An agreement using the name of an athlete often results in a similar agreement (even if the name was not trademarked). The agreement specifies the scope of the license. In addition to identifying the parties to the agreement and the specific trademarks licensed, the agreement states what rights are licensed and, particularly in the case of goods manufactured bearing the trademark, the standards, and quality control mechanisms.

The major segments of a license agreement involve the following.

*Quality Control.* In almost every license agreement, the licensor exercises quality control over a licensee's goods and services. The importance of this power cannot be overstated. Because a trademark represents the trademark owner's brand name and reputation, the owner wants to ensure that the goods and services possess a high level of quality, as consumers tend to rely on this reputation in making purchasing decisions. A licensed product of inferior quality hurts the reputation of the licensor.

For example, say that the Winnetka Wombats licensed their trademark to X Clothiers, Inc., to make apparel bearing the team's logo. If X Clothiers makes poor-quality goods, customers are apt to complain and, although the team did not make the goods, the image and brand of the team will be damaged by adverse reaction from buyers. That could translate to lower sales in the future and even to a diminishing interest in the team.

*Specific Use of the Trademark.* The licensor often specifies the manner in which a trademark will be used on or in connection with the goods and services of the licensee and on advertising and promotional materials. Often, the agreement requires that the licensee obtain the licensor's permission before using any new presentation of the trademark.

*Term.* The trademark license usually states a fixed term for the license and the conditions under which the license may be renewed for an additional period of time. For example, in August 2003, Major League Baseball announced a five-year deal whereby the league and its thirty teams were guaranteed at least $500 million from 2005 to 2009, owing to the signing of new contracts with its licensing partners (Walker, 2003). By 2009, it had exclusive licenses with MasterCard, Pepsi, New Era (for caps), and Topps (trading cards).

*Exclusivity.* An agreement almost always gives the licensee an exclusive right to use that trademark in connection with the manufacture of a certain line of products. If a shoe company obtains a license, it should have the exclusive right to use the name and logo owned by the licensor. If the licensor could negotiate with another shoe company, this would severely compromise the branding of the first shoe company.

*Royalties.* The royalty payments—usually a percentage of sales—are stated and defined to ensure that both parties understand the calculation.

In recent years, the four major professional sports leagues have reduced the number of licensees, seeking long-term exclusive agreements. Examples are deals with Reebok by the NFL and NBA to produce various NFL- and NBA-branded merchandise. In December 2000, the NFL signed an exclusive ten-year contract with Reebok to provide all on-field and sideline apparel for all thirty-two teams (Sandomir, 2003). The deal remains in effect even though Adidas acquired Reebok in 2006. A year later, in August 2001, Reebok signed a ten-year agreement to provide apparel and footwear for the NBA and Women's National Basketball Associtaion (WNBA) (McCarthy, 2001), which was extended for eleven years in 2006 after the Adidas acquisition.

An exclusive deal makes sense. A few major licensing agreements with marquee firms outweigh a multiplicity of deals, which cheapens the brand and generates public confusion. However, such deals are not without the threat of litigation, as was the case when the apparel manufacturer American Needle brought an antitrust action against the NFL (discussed in chapter 1) claiming that the exclusivity violated its rights (American Needle v. NFL, 2010).

## Professional Leagues and Group Licensing

Each of the four major sports leagues has created separate corporations in charge of licensing the uses of the names, logos, symbols, emblems, signs, uniforms, and identification of the league and its member clubs. Note that the individual teams no longer control such licenses (with a few exceptions), but the leagues brought this power "in-house." Specifically, NBA Properties, NFL Properties, NHL Enterprises, and MLB Properties hold the exclusive trademark and licensing rights for each of the leagues and oversee the marketing and protection of individual trademarks and products. Revenues from these agreements are shared by all the teams in the respective league.

The advantages of the league-wide licensing approach are uniformity of licensees, standardized quality control, and equality in revenue distributions. But league-wide licensing has problems. Marquee teams, such as the New York Yankees or Dallas Cowboys, must share royalties with teams that sell less merchandise. That did not sit well with Jerry Jones, who purchased the Cowboys in 1989. Jones, who paid $150 million for the team (a large sum at the time), sought to increase revenues for his investment. He made private deals with firms in competition with firms that had league-wide licensing deals. For example, he licensed "official card" rights to American Express, although Visa had such rights league-wide. After a series of lawsuits, Jones and the NFL settled, allowing him to license specific promotions only within Texas Stadium, the home of the team (Foldesy, 2004).

The unions representing major league players often act as agents for the licensing of athletes' names and likenesses and have, in some cases, made separate agreements with licensees from those of the league. These licenses focus around the athletes, not the team-owned property. Such agreements contain a royalty formula for the sharing of licensing revenues.

Both the leagues' and players' associations' licensing systems are group-wide and do not apply to deals negotiated by athletes individually (Ferber, 2005). For the NFL players, it is any program involving six or more players. For Major League Baseball players, the minimum is three.

The vast majority of league athletes participate in these arrangements by signing annual contracts with their union, allowing the leagues to market various items bearing their likeness (Players Choice Group Licensing Program, n.d.). The licensed items—T-shirts, trading cards, and video games—are often controlled by the licensing division of the league. Revenues derived from the licensing are distributed among the athletes. Licensing agreements are made by a firm with both the league and union to ensure uniformity.

Players may opt out of the group licensing agreements, and on occasion some do, in the hope of negotiating more lucrative marketing deals. One of the first players—and probably the most famous—to opt out of a group licensing agreement was Michael Jordan. He withdrew the use of his name and likeness for licensed NBA products. Jordan's superstar status and economic impact to the league afforded him the opportunity to go solo. However, most players remain a part of the agreement because they lack that kind of economic and marketing leverage.

A summary of the licensing systems in each of the four major sports leagues follows.

### National Basketball Association

NBA Properties, Inc. (NBAP), the marketing and licensing arm of the NBA, owns and exclusively licenses all trademarks, service marks, trade names, and logos of the NBA and its member teams. NBA Properties has complete control over all the league's trademarks and logos outside of each team's own arena. In addition, NBA Properties possesses the right to market the trademarks and logos internationally. All income that is generated from such intellectual property is split evenly amongst all the teams.

NBAP acts as the exclusive licensor for NBA teams and controls all merchandising contracts. Regarding players' rights, the NBA and the players' union, the National Basketball Players' Association (NBPA), negotiated a group license agreement in their collective bargaining agreement (CBA). That agreement allows the league to retain the right to license a player's name, number, and likeness for uniforms, trading cards, posters, video games, and other products. It granted a license to Reebok (as current apparel licensee) to manufacture player jerseys, and revenues from sales of these jerseys are split between the league and the team. Retired NBA players also share in this agreement, whereby revenue from sales is split among the league, the National Basketball Retired Player's Association (NBRPA), and in some cases the retired player (NBA CBA, Article XXXVII, sec. 1, 2005–2011).

In 2007, sales of NBA-licensed merchandise came to $2.5 billion, with the league capturing about $94 million (Brochstein, 2008) In addition, the NBAP has signed non-exclusive, multiyear videogame licensing renewals with EA Sports, Take-Two, Sony, Midway Games, and Atari. The agreements began in October 2005 and their value was reported to be $400 million for five to six years (Consumer Electronics Daily, 2005).

Unlike the other major sports leagues' unions, the NBPA does not distribute licensing revenue or enter into group licensing agreements on behalf of the players. NBAP has the sole authority to enter into such licensing agreements (NBA Uniform Players Contract, 2005).

## National Football League

The NFL teams created NFL Properties (NFLP) in 1981 to act as the exclusive agent for negotiating and entering into merchandise licensing and sponsorship agreements. The NFLP is equally owned by the franchises of the NFL, and its role consists primarily of holding the team and league trademarks and the receipt and distribution of any income derived from the licensing efforts of NFLP.

The income derived from these licensing deals passes to the NFL Trust, which controls these revenues before passing it to the teams on an equal share basis, regardless of the amount earned by any particular team's "club marks," which include a team's name, helmet design, uniform design, and identifying slogans (NFLP v. Dallas Cowboys, 1996). In March 2004, team owners voted in favor of a fifteen-year extension of the NFL Trust. However, dissents and abstentions from certain owners prompted the league to appoint a commission to consider ways to rectify certain disparities that had occurred (Bell, 2004).

The NFL's licensees sold $3.25 billion worth of goods in 2007 and the league captured $148 million in royalty income (Brochstein, 2008). That year, the NFL and Anheuser-Busch InBev entered into a six-year

deal, including rights fees, marketing, media, and team spending com-
mitments—more than double the prior agreement with Coors beer
(now MillerCoors). The rights fees for the beer category increased from
$30 million a year now to an average of $50 million over the life of the
deal (Lefton, 2010).

Unlike the other leagues, the NFL Players' Association (NFLPA) has its
own marketing and licensing subsidiary, known as PLAYERS, INC., which
represents 1800 active and 2700 retired players. Although a player may
opt out of the arrangement, PLAYERS, INC. represents the overwhelming
majority of NFL players.

PLAYERS, INC. negotiates the licensing of player names and images in
trading cards and collectibles (such as bobble heads, figurines, and pen-
nants), video games, fantasy football, apparel and novelties, and other
retail licensed products. PLAYERS, INC. grants licensees the rights to use
players' names, numbers, likenesses, and images. It handles group licensing agreements involving six or more players. PLAYERS, INC. receives
a royalty percentage for the licensing, which after administrative costs is
distributed among the players. Licensing and sponsorship revenue totaled
$135 million in fiscal year 2008. The biggest licensee was Electronic Arts,
which paid the NFLPA $35.1 million in the fiscal year ending February
29, 2008. Sports trading card sales also constituted a significant revenue
source, totaling $29.4 million in fiscal year 2008 among the big three
companies in the category: Upper Deck, Topps, and Donruss. During that
year, Reebok's Onfield Apparel Group paid the NFLPA $17.8 million
(Belter & Hanna, 2009).

Although retired players are now a part of the royalty pool, controversy remains as to the amounts they received. In 2008, a jury awarded
over $28 million in favor of a group of retired players in a class action law-
suit claiming that the union failed to actively pursue marketing deals on
their behalf with video games, trading cards, and other sports products.
As proof, the retirees pointed to a 2001 letter from an NFLPA executive
telling Electronic Arts Inc. executives to scramble the images of retired
players in the company's popular "Madden NFL" video game, otherwise
the company would have to pay them (Feldman, 2008).

## Major League Baseball

Major League Baseball Properties (MLBP), established in 1966, controls
the marketing and licensing of all league-wide and team trademarks.
Individual teams retain some exclusive control of their trademarks within
a specified radius of their home stadiums (New York Yankees & Adidas
v. MLBP, 1997) All domestic promotional and retail licensing income is
shared among the teams in equal amounts, regardless of the actual income
generated from a single team. MLBP obtains a percentage of fees based
on their gross income.

The royalty revenue derived from licensed merchandise is placed in a general fund, but the individual teams can increase their revenue by selling game souvenirs, such as bats and baseballs used during games. In 1997, team owners granted the Major League Baseball commissioner authority to distribute the shared sources of revenue unevenly, so that "poorer" teams receive a larger share to make up for their losses or disproportionately low amount of local revenue. The commissioner also has discretion in giving these poorer teams a larger share to develop new players and to build new parks. In 2009, about $400 million went from big-market to small-market teams (Brown, 2009). MLBP licensed merchandise amounted to $3.3 billion in sales and $150 million in royalties in 2007 (Brochstein, 2008).

For the past forty years, Major League Baseball players have signed annual contracts with the Major League Baseball Players' Association (MLBPA) to market their names and likenesses on merchandise. Any firm seeking to use the names or likenesses of more than two Major League Baseball players in connection with a commercial product, product line, or promotion must sign a licensing agreement with the MLBPA. The most recent agreement includes interactive rights, including group rights to player likenesses. The license grants the use of the players' names and/ or likenesses only, not the use of any Major League Baseball team logos or marks. Examples of products licensed by the MLBPA include trading cards, video games, T-shirts, and uniforms. Players receive a pro rata share of licensing revenue, regardless of popularity or stature. Each player's share is determined by his actual days of Major League Baseball service in a given season (Peters, 2004). Players can opt out of the agreement, but that rarely occurs. In 2003, Barry Bonds opted not to re-sign the annual licensing agreement (Raine, 2003).

In 2010, Major League Baseball Properties settled a trademark dispute against the trading card maker Upper Deck, which continued to issue baseball cards after the expiration of its license with Major League Baseball. The company lost its license to use team logos and uniforms on its cards three months before issuing the cards. Upper Deck issued the cards, removing team trademarks from packages and card designs, but failed to delete the team logos on hats and uniforms from players pictured on the cards. The settlement terms were intricate. Upper Deck agreed to pay over $2 million in back license fees for the cards and not to produce "any new sets of cards using MLB logos, uniforms or color combinations" (Freeman, 2010).

## National Association for Stock Car Auto Racing

In the past, NASCAR teams managed their licensing rights in-house— each team operated as an independent contractor, separate from the sanctioning body. That model was considered cumbersome and confusing for licensees because they had to negotiate five different contracts to get the licensing rights to five different drivers.

As of early 2010, NASCAR planned to create NASCAR Properties, a trust that will serve as a centralized licensing agency. Under this system, NASCAR Properties will control the licensing for drivers, teams, and NASCAR marks. Revenue will be distributed to the race teams based on sales rather than by a equal revenue-share agreement. Participation in the program would be voluntary. Under the new trust, those team, driver, and NASCAR marks will be available under the umbrella of the licensing arm, creating a "one-stop shopping" business model (Smith, 2010).

### Olympics

The International Olympic Committee (IOC) owns the name and controls the trademarks to the Olympic Games, including the Olympic symbol (the five rings), the Olympic flag, the Olympic motto (Citius, Altius, Fortius), the Olympic flame, and the Olympic torch (Olympic Charter, 2010, Chapter 1, rule 7-2). The IOC obtains legal protection both domestically and internationally, to protect against trademark infringement of the above trademarks. In cases where the national law or a trademark registration grants to a national Olympic committee (NOC) the protection of the Olympic symbol, the NOC may use the ensuing rights only in accordance with instructions received from the IOC executive board (Olympic Charter, 2010, Chapter 1, bylaw to rule 7-14).

Each NOC shall take the necessary steps to prohibit any unauthorized use of the Olympic trademarks. In the United States, Olympic trademarks are given automatic protection under the Amateur Sports Act and its amendments, meaning that the United States Olympic Committee (USOC) does not even have to show "likelihood of confusion" to successfully prosecute an infringement case (US Olympic Committee, 2002, 36 USC, sec. 220506(a)). The USOC successfully sued an organization not affiliated with the USOC to stop it using the term *Gay Olympics*. After lengthy litigation, the Supreme Court upheld the USOC's rights (San Francisco Arts & Athletics, Inc. v. USOC, 1987).

Corporations wishing to use any Olympic trademarks must first pay the IOC a rights fee and sign a general sponsorship agreement. For example, IBM provided the IOC with $40 million worth of computers and cash in return for use of the interlocking rings in its advertising efforts in 1996. For the 2008 Beijing Olympics, a dozen multinationals such as Coca-Cola, Lenovo, McDonald's, and Samsung paid as much as $100 million each to be global sponsors of the Summer Games. An additional eleven firms—including Volkswagen, Adidas, and Air China—paid as much as $50 million each for the right to link ads within China to the Games (Balfour, 2008). For the 2010 Vancouver Winter Games, Bell Canada paid $200 million, Royal Bank of Canada $110 million, and Hudson's Bay Co.

$100 million for the rights to these Games and the next three Olympics (Fong, 2010).

There have also been sponsorship disputes between athletes and NOCs concerning apparel sponsors. In the 1992 Barcelona Games, Michael Jordan and other players under contract to Nike draped a U.S. flag over the Reebok logo of their basketball warmup suits. More recently, Kim Clijsters, then the number 2-ranked player in women's tennis, withdrew from the 2004 Athens Olympics because she could not wear apparel from her own sponsor. The Belgian Olympic Committee prohibited its athletes from wearing apparel not made by the team sponsor, Adidas (which has sponsored the Belgian team since 1976), whereas Clijsters had a deal with Fila, which stipulated she could play only wearing the company's clothing (*Guelph Mercury*, 2003). The speed skaters Chad Hedrick, Shani Davis, Derek Parra, and Chris Witty split from U.S. Speed Skating and signed their own sponsors, paid their own expenses, and worked with their own coaches and trainers before competition in the 2006 Turin Winter Olympics. In addition, six snowboarders set up their own team to avoid the sponsorship rules of their national governing body, U.S. Ski and Snowboard Association (Clark, 2006).

For all licensing agreements, the conditions set forth under the Olympic charter state that NOCs will receive half of all net income from "exploitations derived from use of the Olympic symbol and Olympic emblems, after the deduction of all taxes and out-of-pocket costs relating thereto" (Olympic Charter, 2010, bylaw to rule 7-14).

Sponsorship conflicts may also exist between a particular sport's governing bodies and its athletes. The U.S. Olympic gold medalist Gary Hall, Jr., said that swimmers "need a unionlike association to protect themselves from organizers and sponsors," after USA Swimming threatened to sanction swimmers for failing to display a bib with the FINA (the International Swimming Organization) sponsor Argent. Hall was fined $5000 by USA Swimming for not wearing designated Speedo gear in Athens and said: "What seems like a step forward for marketing people was actually 20 steps back. What happens if Speedo takes over a meet? What happens if, say, Nike is trying to get involved? Would the Nike swoosh have to be covered up by Speedo?" (Frauenheim, 2004).

## National Collegiate Athletic Association

The bylaws of the National Collegiate Athletic Association (NCAA) provide that institutions may give third parties permission to use a student-athlete's name, photo, and so on, as long as all money is paid to the member institution and not to the student (NCAA Division I Manual, 2009, sec. 12.5.1.1). Student-athletes are also prohibited from accepting compensation from any non-NCAA institution as an award for their athletic performance. But no restriction exists on the colleges themselves profiting from using the player's likeness for promotional purposes.

Many universities are now getting into the trading card business, a practice deemed by the NCAA as a permissible promotional activity. Because NCAA players consent to the use of their likeness, they give up any right to sue for compensation. Additionally, players are not entitled to compensation when their coach or university contracts with a company to endorse their product, such as having the players wear Nike sneakers or other apparel (NCAA Division I Manual, 2009, sec. 12.5.2.1). The Collegiate Licensing Company (CLC), a for-profit firm licensed by the NCAA and about 200 schools, is the organization's official licensing representative. In 2009, collegiate-licensed merchandise generated about $4 billion (Reitmulder, 2010).

As noted in chapter 4, the class action antitrust case involving the former UCLA basketball player Ed O'Bannon may change the present licensing system and may result in student-athletes having rights to their names and likeness for merchandising purposes. A federal judge has refused to dismiss the lawsuit by O'Bannon and other former players (no current players are a part of claim) (O'Bannon v. NCAA, 2010). As one commentator stated:

> The stakes of O'Bannon v. NCAA are enormous. If O'Bannon and former student-athletes prevail or receive a favorable settlement, the NCAA, along with its member conferences and schools, could be required to pay tens of millions, if not hundreds of millions, of dollars in damages . . . The marketplace for goods may change as well, with potentially more competition over the identities and likenesses of former college stars (McCann, 2009).

## Information Check

When covering intellectual property issues, a journalist should ask:

1  Has the item in question been licensed by the owner of the trademark (usually one of the major league's property divisions)?
2  What products are covered by that licensing agreement?
3  Has an athlete consented to his or her name and likeness being used, under either the CBA or another agreement?
4  Has the athlete's name/likeness been misappropriated without permission?
5  What rules exist between an organization with a licensing agreement with one firm and an athlete who signed a contract with a rival firm wearing apparel with its logo at a competition?

# References

American Needle v. NFL, 130 S. Ct. 2201 (2010).

Balfour, F. (2008, March 11). Ambush in Beijing. *Business Week*. Retrieved April 5, 2010, from http://www.businessweek.com/magazine/content/08_12/b4076054803579.htm?chan=search

Bell, J. (2004, July 6). NFL tug-of-war over revenue. *USA Today*, p. 1C.

Belter, C., & Hanna, J. (2009, October). The business of sports product licensing. *DRI Newsletter*. Retrieved March 31, 2010, from http://www.dri.org/(S(bziiss45tipaog452rxxmpjf))/articles/CommercialLitigation/FTD-0910-BelterHanna.pdf

Brochstein, M. (2008). Introduction. *The Licensing Letter's Sports Licensing Report*, pp. 5–6.

Brown, M. (2009, November 24). MLB can't have their cake and eat it too (revenue-sharing). Bizofbaseball.com. Retrieved March 20, 2010, from http://www.bizofbaseball.com/index.php?option=com_content&view=article&id=3765:mlb-cant-have-their-cake-and-eat-it-too-revenue-sharing&catid=26:editorials&Itemid=39

California Civil Code (2009). Sec. 3344.

CBC Distribution v. Major League Baseball Advanced Media (MLBAM), 505 F.3d 818 (8th Cir. 2007).

CBS Interactive v. NFLPA (2008). No. 08-cv-5097 (D. Minn.).

Clark, H. (2006, February 8). National teams get the cold shoulder. Forbes.com. Retrieved April 25, 2010, from http://www.forbes.com/2006/02/08/olympic-athlete-endorsements_cx_hc_0208endorsements.html

*Consumer Electronics Daily* (2005, March 23). Videogames. p. 1.

Copyright Act of 1976, 17 USC, sec. 102 (2010).

Doe v. TCI Cablevision, 110 S.W.3d 363 (Mo. 2003).

ETW Corporation v. Jireh Publishing Inc., 332 F.3d 915 (6th Cir., 2003).

Feldman, G. (2008, November 10). Retired NFL players win suit against NFLPA. *Sports Law Blog*. Retrieved, March 31, 2010, from http://sports-law.blogspot.com/search?q=Retired+Players+Win+Suit+Against+NFLPA

Ferber, T. (2005). Symposium: Trademark and publicity rights of athletes. *Fordham Intellectual Property, Media & Entertainment Law Journal, 15*, 449, 488.

Fisher, E. (2010, March 8). MLBAM, Yahoo! build official fantasy game. *Street and Smith's Sportsbusiness Journal*, p. 04.

Foldesy, J. (2004, June 17). NFL owners fear death of golden goose; Revenue sharing divides teams into two camps. *Washington Times*, p. C01.

Fong, P. (2010, January 22). Official sponsors take on Olympic marketing wannabes. *The Toronto Star*. Retrieved April 5, 2010, from http://olympics.thestar.com/2010/article/754290--luluemon

Fonovisa v. Cherry Auction, 76 F.3d 259 (9th Cir. 1996).

Frauenheim, N. (2004, November 20). Hall says swimmers should form union. *Arizona Republic*, p. 19C.

Freedman, M. (n.d.). NFL still king in sports licensing, fans. *Pressbox*. Retrieved March 15, 2010, from http://www.pressboxonline.com/story.cfm?id=2247

Freeman, M. (2010, March 4). Upper Deck settles MLB trademark suit. *San Diego Union-Tribune.* Retrieved May 6, 2010, from http://www.sportsbusinessdaily. com/article/137499

*Guelph Mercury* (2003, December 2). Clijsters to skip Olympic Games, p. B7.

Indianapolis Colts v. Metropolitan Baltimore Football Club, 34 F.3d 410 (7th Cir. 1994).

inta.org (2010). Trademark infringements and statutory redress (U.S.)—What is trademark infringement? Retrieved March 17, 2010, from http://www.inta. org/index.php?option=com_content&task=view&id=181&Itemid=59&ge tcontent=1

Kimpflen, J. (2004). Trademarks and tradenames. In *American jurisprudence* (2nd ed., sec. 116). St. Paul, MN: West.

Lefton, T. (2010, May 10). Strong brew. *Street and Smith's Sportsbusiness Journal,* p. 01.

Lindeman, T. (2008, May 18). Hedging their bets: Stanley Cup playoffs force retailers to gamble on winners. *Pittsburgh Post-Gazette.* Retrieved March 15, 2010, from http://www.post-gazette.com/pg/08139/882571-28.stm

McCann, M. (2009, July 21). NCAA faces unspecified damages, changes in latest anti-trust case. SI.com. Retrieved April 16, 2010, from http://sportsillustrated. cnn.com/2009/writers/michael_mccann/07/21/ncaa/index.html

McCarthy, M. (2001, August 2). Reebok to be exclusive apparel provider of NBA. *USA Today.* Retrieved May 2, 2010, from http://www.usatoday.com/sports/ nba/stories/2001-08-01-reebok.htm

National Basketball Association, Uniform Players Contract, paragraph 14 (2006). Retrieved March 20, 2010, from http://www.nbpa.org/cba/2005

National Football League Properties, Inc. v. Dallas Cowboys, 922 F. Supp. 849, 851 (S.D.N.Y. 1996).

NBA CBA (2005–2011). Group Licensing Rights. Retrieved August 20, 2010, from http://www.nbpa.org/sites/default/files/ARTICLE%20XXXVII.pdf

NCAA Division I Manual (2009). Retrieved August 25, 2010, from http://www. ncaapublications.com/productdownloads/D110.pdf

New York Civil Rights Law (2009). Secs. 50 and 51.

New York Yankees & Adidas v. Major League Baseball Properties (1997) No. 97-1153-civ-T-25B (Complaint for injunction and jury trial). Retrieved May 11, 2010, from http://www.ncbusinesscourt.net/FAQ/plaintiff/COMPLAINT. htm

O'Bannon v. NCAA, 2010 U.S. Dist. LEXIS 19170 (N.D.CA).

Olympic Charter (2010, February). Retrieved April 5, 2010, from http://www. olympic.org/Documents/Olympic%20Charter/Charter_en_2010.pdf

Peters, S. (2004, May 15). Phone conversation regarding MLBPA licensing, May 15.

The Players Choice Group Licensing Program (n.d.). MLBPA.com. Retrieved August 25, 2010, from http://mlb.mlb.com/pa/info/licensing.jsp

Raine, G. (2003, November 21). Giant's slugger to negotiate his own merchandise deals. *San Francisco Chronicle,* p. B1.

Reitmulder, M. (2010, February 25). Lawsuit threatens big business of collegiate licensing. *University of Minnesota Daily.* Retrieved April 16, 2010, from http://www. mndaily.com/2010/02/25/lawsuit-threatens-big-business-collegiate-licensing

Sandomir, R. (2003, August 20). Reebok strikes exclusive deal with NFL. *New York Times*, p. D3.

San Francisco Arts & Athletics, Inc. v. United States Olympic Comm., 483 U.S. 522 (1987).

Smith, M. (2010, March 8). 'Much healthier' licensing model for NASCAR near. *Street & Smith's Sportsbusiness Journal*, p. 1.

Trademarks (Lanham Act of 1946), 15 USC, sec. 1114 (2010).

Unger, H. (1998, January 7). Thrashers' name at heart of federal lawsuit. *Atlanta Journal & Constitution*, p. C.01.

US Olympic Committee: Exclusive right to name, seals, emblems and badges, 36 USC, sec. 220506 (2002).

Viacom v. YouTube, 2010 U.S. Dist. LEXIS 62829 (SDNY, 2010).

Walker, D. (2003, August 5). MLB announces licensing deals. *Milwaukee Journal-Sentinel*, p. 2C.

# 13 Traditional and New Media in Sports

Dissemination of sporting events through any one of various media outlets constitutes the single most important source of revenue for professional and amateur sports organizations. For sports leagues and individual events, fees earned from media rights bring in billions of dollars per year. The media also have benefited, since sports events constitute an important source of programming. Marquee sports events such as the Super Bowl draw large numbers of viewers or listeners, resulting in premium fees charged to advertisers.

This chapter examines the basics of the business of sports broadcasting, both involving the "traditional" media (defined for our purposes as radio, broadcast television, cable television, and satellite) and new technologies (Internet, broadband, social media, and mobile telephone communications). It outlines the history, the nature, and variety of sports broadcast deals, and concludes with some thoughts on the future of sports and media.

## The Property Right

Think of a sports broadcast as a form of property. Some entity (usually a league or a team) owns the rights not only to the game itself, but to how it disseminates to the public. At one time, that only meant a performance in front of paying fans, but since the advent of radio and television, it means reproducing the event to audiences far away from the site of the event.

That property right to distribute the game, or, more precisely, to license that right to broadcast the event to others, is central. Usually, this right involves licensing to a particular broadcaster, who receives the permission to disseminate the event through a particular communications platform (television, radio, cable, Internet) but *not* the right to own the product. When the National Football League (NFL) licenses broadcast rights, it permits the broadcasters, under prescribed conditions, to broadcast games. The radio, television, and cable licensees are, in essence, delivery tools. They produce the event and pay a sum to the owner (the league) to produce it.

This system has resulted in a number of legal issues. A patron paying a fee to see a match has the right to see it with his or her eyes at the stadium or arena; or a fan can remain home and watch it on free or cable television. But if that person recorded the event and charged a fee to anyone who wanted to see it, that would violate the rights of the property owners (the team, and/or the league) and the broadcast licensee.

Initially, with the exception of boxing, organized sports were skeptical at the licensing of broadcasting rights. In particular, many in baseball felt that broadcasting games on the radio would siphon off fans coming to the ballpark. Boxing, however, took to licensing early on. As a dominant sport in the early decades of the twentieth century, boxing matches were filmed and distributed to theaters (Ward, 2004).

In a day when most broadcasts are recorded, sports events remain one of the last bastions of live programming. For broadcasters and cablecasters, this has advantages and poses challenges. Live broadcasts offer excitement and unpredictability that few other programs match. However, the economic value of the event diminishes sharply once the event concludes. Whereas broadcasters and cable network owners rerun successful entertainment programs—often for years—sports broadcasts do not command high audiences—or value—when rebroadcast, since the result is already known.

In part to add value to the event, broadcasters have added news programs, features, documentaries, and sports talk shows to their package. Pregame and postgame analyses of the games, including press conferences, expert opinion, and highlights—add to the fan's interest.

## The Key Audience

Radio and over-the-air television earn their revenues through advertising. Advertisers choose particular types of programs to target certain audiences, based on demographics such as gender, age, race, ethnicity, and income. Sports broadcasts have traditionally appealed to a male demographic. For all four major sports leagues, approximately two-thirds of the viewers are male (Mullin, Hardy, & Sutton, 2007). Producers of items of interest to males found such events to be an excellent way to reach that audience. Hence, broadcasters paid fees to broadcast such events to earn money from advertisers. The more popular the event, the more the outlet charges for ads. Cablecasting differs in some respects. It earns money from advertising, but in addition it has another revenue stream—subscriber fees from local cable operators. For carrying a particular cable network, the operators pay a negotiated fee.

At one time, audiences were primarily White. However, because of the increased buying power of African Americans, Asians, and Hispanics, and the fact that these groups are increasingly making up the fan base in baseball, marketers are eager to reach them. More Blacks and Hispanics are tuning in to television and radio to listen to baseball games. From 1996 to 1999, the number of Hispanics who said they watched a baseball game in the past year grew 12.2 percent; among African Americans, there was a 6 percent increase. A marketing director for the New York Mets noted that much larger companies, such as Toyota, have begun advertising on Hispanic radio stations, whereas in the past it was mostly small-scale companies that advertised there (Gardyn, 2000).

## Radio

Once Major League Baseball teams discovered that radio (and eventually television) created new revenue streams by rights fees and by publicizing their teams and attracting more fans, they became more amenable to allowing game broadcasts. Generally, local radio broadcasts remain an important part of baseball coverage. Presently, ESPN Radio has exclusive national radio broadcast rights with Major League Baseball (through 2010 for $55 million). Included in the Major League Baseball package is a full schedule of Saturday afternoon and Sunday night baseball games each season, opening-day and holiday doubleheaders, select pennant race games, and all postseason games including the World Series and the All-Star game. Also, Major League Baseball has a long-term contract with XM Satellite Radio, which will pay the league $650 million over eleven years. Major League Baseball splits the proceeds equally among all the teams.

The National Basketball Association (NBA) also has a national radio deal (through 2015–16, as part of the total $7.4 billion broadcasting package). ESPN is entitled to broadcast regular weekend afternoon games, select playoff games and doubleheaders, all conference and NBA final games, and the All-Star game, as well as weekend events and the NBA draft until 2016 (NBA.com, 2007). In 2004, the National Football League (NFL) signed a seven-year deal with Sirius Satellite Radio to broadcast all professional games. The NFL received $188 million in cash and $32 million in Sirius stock (Mullen, 2004). Although network radio broadcasts produce significant revenue, the amount is secondary to television.

Locally, just about every team in the four major leagues license broadcasts with individual radio stations serving their markets. These teams—in all the professional leagues—keep the revenue earned.

## Broadcast Television

Even in an age of newer technologies, television remains the primary economic and technical engine for sports broadcasting. Although introduced at the 1939 New York World's Fair, television broadcasting as we know it developed after World War II. As part of its programming, sports events—especially those in confined areas such as boxing—were standard fare.

Sports television—which at the time included the World Series, boxing matches, and college football games—received increased interest and, by 1950, 10.5 million receivers rested in U.S. homes (Kumar, 2008).

Although it is hard to fathom, early sports broadcasts did not help the bottom line for many teams. Home attendance dropped precipitously in many instances. For example, after the Boston Red Sox started televising home games in 1950, attendance dropped from 1.45 million in 1948 to fewer than 300,000 in 1952. The Los Angeles Rams' gate receipts dropped 50 percent in the first year of home broadcasts. Ultimately most teams adopted some kind of "blackout" policy for their home games. By the end of the decade, teams and leagues became more sophisticated in parceling out broadcast rights, making adept use of the blackout rules to focus on road games, which would result in fan interest without any diminution of attendance (MacCambridge, 2004).

In the 1950s, sports broadcasting became a province of weekend afternoons, rather than prime time. Entire shows sponsored by one company became the economic model for both entertainment and sports. By the mid-1960s, the amount and costs of broadcasting sports increased to a point that individual advertisers found it increasingly difficult to pay for sponsorship of major events by themselves. The modern approach of "spot advertising" took over. Advertisers would pay for one or more placed advertisements during a sports event, with payment negotiated between the broadcaster and the advertisers based on ratings measurements. This system created a bonanza for both sports leagues and the broadcast networks (and local stations as well).

### Network Broadcast and Cable Television

The number of hours of sports on network television increased as the audiences grew and the multiplying ranks of spot-buying advertisers coveted these valuable minutes. This mutually beneficial situation persisted well into the 1980s. As technology improved, so did the quality and sophistication of the broadcast. Television networks and local stations began to pay ever-increasing rights fees, which increased the revenues of the rights holder, whether it was a league or an individual team. The experience of baseball is illustrative. In 1950, Major League Baseball earned $1.2 million from national broadcasts. By 1960, that amount had tripled, to $3.3 million. But note the exponential increase since then: over $16 million in 1970, $47.5 million in 1980, $365 million in 1990, and $570 million in 2000 (Schaaf, 2004). Since 2006, the rights fees have averaged $670 million per year (Sportsbusinessnews.com, 2006). The increasing revenue to team owners from television was one reason for the increased demands of the Major League Baseball Players' Association.

The experience of the NFL is even more striking. Baseball was "America's national pastime" well before the advent of television, but the NFL was largely made by television. Because the NFL had less public exposure than baseball, the league should have embraced television as a vehicle to gain exposure for the sport. Early attempts by the Los Angeles Rams and Philadelphia Eagles to televise home games met with resistance from the league, which imposed strict rules prohibiting the broadcast of NFL games in any city where there was a home game. A federal court concluded that these rules violated the antitrust laws (U.S. v. National Football League, 1953), resulting in a prohibition of league-wide contracts until the Sports Broadcasting Act of 1961 (15 USC, sec. 1291) created an antitrust exemption permitting such agreements.

The Sports Broadcasting Act protects teams in smaller television markets by pooling broadcasting rights with teams located in larger, more lucrative television markets in order to assure small-market teams equal shares of television revenues and coverage (15 USC, 2009, sec. 1291). It created the present environment for network television rights agreements with the leagues. Besides the NFL, the other major sports leagues signed on to this legislation, but the legislation exempted college sports (15 USC, 2009, sec. 1293). Therefore, the antitrust exemption does not apply to the National Collegiate Athletic Association (NCAA). This omission hurt the NCAA years later when the Supreme Court concluded that its football package was an unreasonable restraint on trade under the antitrust laws (NCAA v. Board of Regents of the University of Oklahoma, 1984).

After the passage of the Sports Broadcasting Act, the NFL teams agreed to sell their television rights as a single package and to share broadcast revenues equally among all franchises. This revenue-sharing idea originated from the new commissioner, Pete Rozelle, and a number of the venerable NFL owners. This turned out to be a brilliant move. Rozelle argued that the league's competitive balance on the field would eventually be destroyed if teams in major television markets continued to sell their broadcast rights individually. The inequity would diminish the overall attractiveness of the NFL's product. Another reason for the single rights arrangement was that the rival American Football League had signed a similar television package with ABC one year earlier.

## Types of Television Deals

For the NFL, NBA, and Major League Baseball, television agreements follow what has become known as a "traditional" model. The network pays a specified rights fee to exclusively broadcast the events, sells commercial airtime, and keeps the revenue derived from that airtime. Production costs are covered by the network. This approach also applies to national cable networks, such as ESPN.

Why do broadcast and (more recently) cable networks spend large sums of money on major sporting events? The first reason is to draw a large audience, to justify large advertiser fees. The Super Bowl is a prime example. In 1967 a thirty-second advertisement during the Super Bowl cost $42,000, whereas in 2010 the same ad would cost up to $3 million (Smith, 2010). Throughout much of the 1960s and 1970s, the networks earned profits on such deals. However, profitability sagged in later years, as ratings fell flat. CBS, ABC, and Fox networks made an estimated combined loss of $5.5 billion on NFL, NBA, Major League Baseball, and other major sports contracts between 2000 and 2006 (Fatsis, 2003). Yet the networks continue paying more for broadcasting rights. That leads to the second, and more likely, reason for the hefty fees: prestige. Broadcasting a product such as the NFL or Major League Baseball gains or maintains credibility for the broadcaster (especially if it is an up-and-coming network) and serves as a lead-in to other programming. In other words, it adds to the reputation of the broadcaster.

Fox's winning the rights to broadcast NFL games in 1994 serves as a case study. Fox's bid—an astounding $1.58 billion, well ahead of the previous contract price paid by CBS—resulted in great publicity for the then-fledgling operation. Although Fox wrote off $350 million in losses that year, the network as a whole showed an increase in profits of almost $100 million (Noland & Hoffarth, 1997). On the other hand, the loss cost CBS, the prior rightsholder for many years, considerable prestige and a few affiliated stations, which jumped to Fox upon the news that the upstart had won the broadcasting rights for National Football Conference (NFC) games.

In late 2004 and early 2005, the NFL reached new, more lucrative broadcast rights agreements. The league concluded six-year deals with CBS and Fox, totaling $8 billion, as well as a five-year, $3.5 billion extension of its deal with DirecTV, also starting in 2006, in which fans can buy a package of games through the satellite system. In addition, ESPN will pay $1.1 billion over the length of an eight-year contract to televise *Monday Night Football*—a program staple on ABC since 1970. In addition, after an eight-year hiatus, NBC returned as a licensee with a package of prime-time Sunday night games, while ABC became the only network not to televise NFL games (Shapiro & Maske, 2005). In 2009, the network agreements were extended two years, so that all broadcast rights agreements expire in 2013. The total payments the NFL receives from the three over-the-air networks and ESPN over the life of the present agreements amounts to about $17 billion. In addition, for those interested in games not broadcast in their markets, the NFL has a $4 billion agreement with DirecTV to broadcast games for the league's "Sunday Ticket" service until 2014. The NFL also has its in-house broadcast entity, the NFL Network, which provides coverage of events such as the draft, and eight Thursday night games per season.

Since 1973, the NFL has had a "blackout rule," which mandates that a game cannot be broadcast in a seventy-five-mile radius of its local market if it is not sold out within seventy-two hours of kickoff. For most of its tenure, the rule has been infrequently utilized as most NFLs games are sold out. However, with the economic downturn in 2008 and 2009, more blackouts have occurred owing to the lack of sellouts (Gregory, 2009).

Major League Baseball's present agreement, which expires in 2013, is divided into broadcast and cable segments. Fox retains the exclusive rights to broadcast selected Saturday games throughout the season: the All-Star Game, the World Series, and one League Championship series alternating yearly between the National and American League (the other airs on TBS).

Fox pays a total of $1.8 billion or $260 million per year for the seven-year term, For Fox, this was a decrease from $2.4 billion under the prior agreement. As noted earlier, that 2001 deal was not profitable for Fox (which took a $225 million writeoff on this contract) (Martzke, 2003).

On the cable side, in 2005, in-season cable television rights were secured by ESPN for $2.37 billion over eight years ($296 million annually) and by Turner Broadcasting ($700 million, seven-year deal through 2013). Under this arrangement, ESPN broadcasts up to eighty games per season, on Sunday, Wednesday, and Friday nights. Turner also broadcasts a Sunday afternoon game of the week and has exclusive rights to the post-season division series.

The NBA's present deal with ABC/ESPN and Turner Broadcasting dates from 2007 and expires in 2016. An integrated broadcast and cable package, Disney (the owner of the network and cablecaster) pays a rights fee of $4.6 billion over the life of the contract. With Turner's fee, the deal totals $7.4 billion, or $930 million per year, a 20 percent increase over the prior six-year agreement. Telecasts are divided among ABC, ESPN, and ESPN2. ABC broadcasts at least fifteen regular-season games and fifteen postseason games, including the NBA finals. ESPN and ESPN2 broadcast seventy-five regular-season games, mostly on Wednesdays and Friday nights, and can broadcast as many as twenty-nine playoff games, including the conference semifinals and one conference final (Gough, 2007). It also has the rights to simulcast full games live on ESPN360.com and ESPN Mobile TV.

Unlike the package of postseason college football bowl games, the NCAA controls the rights to postseason men's basketball games through its tournaments, whereas the various athletic conferences sell the regular season games. As noted in chapter 4, the NCAA lost control of top-level football after litigation in the 1980s. However, the Association adroitly kept its hands on the basketball tournament—and has reaped great financial rewards. In 2002, CBS renewed its NCAA contract for exclusive coverage of the men's basketball tournament for $6.2 billion. In 2010, the contract was amended, so, starting in 2011, CBS and Turner Broadcasting will broadcast the tournament under a fourteen-year, $10.8 billion agreement, whereby the annual fees paid to the NCAA average $771 million.

Significantly, the $10.8 billion figure represents just the TV rights fees. Other revenue from the corporate partners program is expected to push the value to more than $11 billion in total and close to $800 million annually (Ourand and Smith, 2010).

ESPN also entered into an eleven-year contract through the 2012–13 season, costing $200 million, which includes twenty-one championship games in women's basketball, and the men's and women's College World Series, World Cup, and indoor track and field (Clarke & Seltzer, 2003).

Rights to broadcast games from various conferences also command impressive sums. Presently, the following conferences have rights deals with ABC/ESPN:

- The Southeast Conference (SEC), fifteen years, $2.25 billion, expires 2023.
- The Big Ten football, ten years, $1 billion, expires 2017.
- Bowl Championship Series, four years, $495 million, expires 2014.
- Big 12, eight years, $480 million, expires 2014.
- Rose Bowl, eight years, $300 million, expires 2014.
- Atlantic Coast Conference football/basketball, twelve years, $1.86 billion, expires 2023.
- Pac-10 football, five years, $229 million, expires 2011.
- Big East football, six years, $200 million, expires 2012.

CBS has the right to broadcast SEC basketball and football under a fifteen-year $895 million deal, which expires in 2023, and Big Ten basketball under a ten-year deal for $200 million, expiring in 2016 (Ourand & Smith, 2008).

The Major League Baseball, NFL, NBA, NCAA, and Olympics agreements follow the traditional licensing method. However, alternative methods exist. One, known as the "revenue-sharing" model, involves the National Hockey League (NHL) and the former Arena Football League (AFL). These leagues sold their broadcast rights to NBC, but neither received rights fees from the network. As a consequence of the relative novelty of the AFL and the poor rating performance of the NHL in the United States, as compared with other sports, these agreements required the network to split the advertising revenue with the leagues after the network has paid the associated costs. NBC was able to obtain all of the broadcasting rights, yet avoid all financial risk associated with having to pay rights fees (Gross, 2004). On the cable side, in 2008 the NHL concluded a deal with Versus that is worth $210 million over three years.

A third method of securing broadcast rights is simply buying airtime. Certain events, notably Ladies Professional Golf Association (LPGA) events, follow this model. The rightsholder keeps advertising revenues generated from the event after paying the costs of buying the time and production. Although the Professional Golfers' Association (PGA) also has bought time, the PGA has more corporate sponsorship than the LPGA, so the LPGA has to use its own money to ensure broadcasts (Kazmierski, n.d.).

## The Olympics

The most lucrative single-event broadcasting contract involves the Olympic Games. Approximately 4.7 billion viewers globally saw at least some portion of the Beijing Summer Games in 2008. In the United States, it was the most-viewed event in television history (Associated Press, 2008). For the 2010 Winter Games in Vancouver, the corresponding estimates are 3.5 billion worldwide (Vancouver2010.com, 2010) and 190 million Americans (Reynolds, 2010). U.S. television networks have paid enormous sums of money for the rights to broadcast the games. The rights fees paid for exclusive rights to broadcast the Games in the United States account for the great majority of the money earned by the International Olympic Committee (IOC) for broadcast rights.

In 1960, the total rights fee to broadcast the summer games was merely $400,000. In 1996, the Atlanta Summer Games cost NBC $456 million, and in 1998 the Nagano (Japan) Winter Olympics cost CBS $375 million. NBC has since purchased the broadcasting rights for all the games, beginning with the Summer Olympics in 2000, up to and including the summer games of 2012. For the rights to all of the games, NBC has paid a staggering $5.57 billion. This breaks down as follows: summer 2000 (Sydney), $715 million; winter 2002 (Salt Lake City), $555 million; summer 2004 (Athens), $793 million; winter 2006 (Turin), $613 million; summer 2008 (Beijing), $894 million; winter 2010 (Vancouver), $820 million; and summer 2012 (London), $1.18 billion. Commenting on the 2004 Olympics in Athens, NBC noted that, in addition to profiting from advertising, carrying the Olympics served as a platform to publicize its fall schedule (Albiniak, 2004). As of this printing, the IOC has not decided on a U.S. rightsholder for the 2014 Sochi and the 2016 Rio Games.

Broadcasting the Olympics poses unique issues not found in other sports. Since the Games are often held in time zones well ahead of the U.S., many, if not the majority of, events may be on tape-delay in North America. Therefore, the results of the events would be known beforehand, diminishing audience interest. Because U.S. rightsholders have paid such high sums to broadcast the games, they must maximize the potential audience by delaying the marquee events for a prime-time broadcast.

In the age of broadband access and instantaneous results, this model has come into question. Although the IOC has considered splitting broadband rights from television rights, it has rejected this option, although the possibility of subdividing mobile and digital rights may exist sometime in the future (Mickle and Ourand, 2010).

## Cable Television and Carriage

Cable television has a distinct advantage over traditional broadcast television because it has two streams of revenue: advertisements and user fees. The program services found on cable negotiate a fee per subscriber with a local cable operator and the fees earned constitute a solid income base.

Almost every cable operator carries local over-the-air broadcast stations, yet the relationship between them is complicated. Under the 1996 Telecommunications Act, over-the-air broadcasters have two options with regard to carriage: the first, known as the "must-carry" rules, requires the cable operator to carry the station. If the broadcasters opts for must-carry, then it cannot charge the cable operator for the privilege of carrying the station (Signal carriage obligations, 2007). Traditionally, the majority of stations chose must-carry. However, the law provides a second option, known as "retransmission consent," whereby broadcasters seek fees from the cable provider for the inclusion of broadcast signal. This option has forced the operators and broadcasters to negotiate and has sometimes led to threats of a local station being pulled off the cable service (Retransmission consent, 2001).

That conflict is especially relevant for the rightsholders of sports programming. Without retransmission consent revenue, broadcasters would not be able to match ESPN's bids for most sports rights, when those rights expire in 2011 (NHL), 2013 (NFL and Major League Baseball), 2013 (NASCAR), and 2014 (MLS). More such disputes may occur in the future as broadcasters look to increase their revenues.

But sports programming puts also puts pressure on cable operators (and by extension on satellite and mobile telephone companies) because it is very expensive. Of the $29 billion in estimated fees paid by cable, satellite, and phone companies for TV channels in 2010 (excluding premium-movie services such as HBO), 40 percent goes to sports cable channels. These include ESPN and its spinoffs and Fox Sports Net. For example, ESPN charges more for its channels than any other cable service and some have questioned whether the rights are worth the cost. Although marquee events such as *Monday Night Football* draw large audiences for ESPN, other events draw smaller ratings that often fall below shows on USA Network and Nickelodeon (Gorman, 2010).

## Local Broadcast and Cable Television

Except for the NFL, local teams negotiate their own broadcast and cable agreements. The traditional method remains similar to the network arrangement, in which a station pays a rights fee to broadcast games, but retains advertising revenue. This is common in Major League Baseball, where each team negotiates a broadcasting and/or cable deal. However, in some arrangements—especially before cable television—the team simply bought time at the station. In the last two decades, however, cable sports networks have siphoned many of these games from their over-the-air rivals. Today, a typical agreement involves an over-the-air television station broadcasting a stipulated number of games, with the rest broadcast by a cable provider. For example, KCAL-TV will broadcast about fifty Los Angeles Dodgers games each year, from 2006 to 2013, while the rest are aired on Fox Sports Network, a cable programmer (Stewart, 2004).

### League-Owned Sports Networks

In the last decade, sports leagues have created their own cable networks, offering more programming under their ownership. Often these networks are subscriber based and carry events not under contract to a particular network or local service. Many have been successful. As of 2010, MLB Network has 54 million subscribers and has broadcast a modest number of games, but has nongame programming, such as awards shows, draft coverage, and fantasy sports. NBA TV, which broadcasts to 45 million homes, programs ninety-six live regular-season games per season. The 30-million-subscriber NHL Network broadcasts fifty-six games. The NFL Network has 50 million subscribers (Ourand, 2009).

### Regional Sports Networks (RSNs)

### Non-Team-Owned

Most local cable television rights center on non-team-owned regional sports networks (RSNs), notably those by Fox Sports, Cablevision and Comcast. Because of the value of their programming, RSNs have achieved market power and are a desired part of the programming package offered by cable system operators. In some cases, as with Cablevision and Comcast, the RSNs own or are owned by the local cable operator (Mabin, 2006). These RSNs can easily generate instant cash flow, most of which comes from advertisements as well as the fees paid to them by the cable operators.

### Team-Owned or Operated

A number of National Basketball Association (NBA), NHL, and Major League Baseball owners have started up their own sports networks, in an attempt to keep all the TV profit. Probably the best-known example of a team-operated network is YES, controlled by the New York Yankees. Since its launch in 2002, YES has brought increased revenues to the Yankees' empire. In 2004, it had an estimated value of $1 billion (Higgins & Becker, 2004), increasing three years later to an amount between $2.8 billion and $3.5 billion (Sandomir, 2007).

Theoretically, team-owned networks give the team more control to set prices and programming. Yet they have considerable risks. High startup cost and production fees mean a great deal of upfront expense. No guarantee exists that cable operators will accept the station. YES had to fight for a year to get carriage on Cablevision, a leading cable operator in the New York metropolitan area, and millions of viewers had no access to Yankees games during this dispute. Disputes usually center on the carriage fees paid by the cable operator for picking up the station (Johnston, 2010).

If the team does not do well, or viewers simply do not watch, the team's network may fold, which happened with the Minnesota Twins, Kansas City Royals, Portland Trail Blazers, and Houston Rockets. Ultimately, these teams signed with established sports networks (Grover and Lowry, 2004).

## Media Ownership of Teams

The purchase of a team by a media company presents issues of synergy between the team and the parent company. On the one hand, such an arrangement may serve two parties well. The team does not have to find a media outlet and the media parent has ready-made programming. Such arrangements have existed. The Los Angeles Dodgers (owned by Rupert Murdoch's News Corp. until the team's sale in 2004), the Chicago Cubs (owned by Tribune Co. until its bankruptcy in 2009), the Atlanta Hawks and Thrashers (owned by Time Warner until 2004), and the New York Knicks and Rangers (owned by Cablevision) serve as examples. Whether this has contributed to team success or hurt the quality of the team is a matter of debate. Some media owners lack knowledge about a sport, or their team is simply a small cog in a vast empire and does not merit major attention (Vilkomerson, 2006).

## New Technologies and Sports

Since the last edition of this book, the dizzying pace of change involving the application of new technologies in sports means that platforms that did not even exist a few years ago have taken an increasingly prominent place in the sports media landscape. The utilization of digital, broadband, mobile, and social networking may lead to a transformation of the way sports are disseminated to viewers in the next decade. While traditional broadcasting and cable still lead in revenue production, the monies generated by newer media have filled the coffers of the various leagues, and may be one reason why the traditional leagues have weathered the economic downturn of 2008 relatively well.

### Wireless Technology

Cellular telephones have achieved market penetration rapidly, to the point that over 80 percent of the U.S. population owns a cellphone (Stevens, 2007). Moreover, the technology has evolved into far more than a simple telephone without a cord. The newest models—so-called "smartphones"—display sports video capabilities that serve as a major media platform and a major new revenue stream.

The NFL took note, ending its association with Sprint and signing an exclusive four-year agreement with Verizon, starting with the 2010 season. Valued at $720 million, it gives fans access to live footage of every game, something previously available only through a satellite television package. The agreement allows live streaming of NBC's *Sunday Night Football* and NFL Network's *Thursday Night Football* and includes game highlights and an extensive collection of on-demand video featuring analysis, live radio broadcasts of every regular season and playoff game, access to fantasy sports information, customized NFL ringtones, draft day coverage, and profiles and blogs (nfl.com, 2010).

The other leagues and National Association for Stock Car Auto Racing (NASCAR) also have exclusive cellular deals. In March 2008, Sprint, the title sponsor of the Sprint Cup Series, announced the availability of NASCAR Sprint Cup Mobile on many Sprint phones. The features include Live Race Audio, Real-Time Data, Breaking News and Information, Video on Demand, and Instant Alerts about race results, qualifying, season statistics, breaking news, and analysis (NASCAR.com, 2008). In 2010, Major League Baseball began to provide live baseball so subscribers can watch live games on an iPhone or iPod touch. The features of the service include news, schedules and interactive rosters and player stats for every team, a video library searchable by player or team, and game videos (MLB.com, 2010). The NBA, through MobiTV, has made available its "League Pass" service to the iPhone via the League Pass Mobile. League Pass Mobile allows people to stream live NBA games onto their iPhone. There's also the ability to view stats from the current game, and look at scores from games across the league. Subscribers can also replay full games after the game has been played (NBA.com, 2010).

### The Internet

In recent years, Internet transmission of sporting events has blossomed with the ascent of broadband technology.

At a minimum, just about every amateur and professional team and league has its own website with information and articles and blogs about teams, players, and league issues. In addition, there are many independent websites and blogs that cover sports. Some are simply fans engaging (or ranting) about their teams, but others provide important and accurate information about aspects of the business of sports. Because websites and blogs come and go, a recitation of important sites probably is not as useful as utilizing search engines, bookmarks, and subscription services to find appropriate information. As always, one should note the source(s) of the information and confirm the information. Also the Internet contains important documents, including league collective bargaining agreements and/or governing information such as the NCAA manuals and the constitution and bylaws of such organizations as the International Olympic Committee.

Athletes often have their own websites and blogs. Although athletes' names are generally not trademarked, they do have a certain commercial value and the unauthorized use of their names could be a misappropriation resulting in liability. In the past, some have attempted to register domain names matching or similar to the names of particular athletes in an attempt to "cybersquat" or sell the name to the athlete. Such a practice is illegal under U.S. law, and a victim can sue for damages in a U.S. court (Anti-Cybersquatting Consumer Protection Act, 1999). In 2009, the Toronto Raptors' Chris Bosh won the right to own chrisbosh.com and was awarded damages of $120,000 for trademark infringement (Beck, 2009). Alternatively, the person may seek arbitration to get the domain name under the Uniform Domain-Name Dispute-Resolution Policy (UDRP) under the aegis of ICANN, the organization that assigns Internet domain names. The UDRP does not award money damages, but can cancel, suspend, or transfer the domain name (ICANN.org, 2009).

In 2009, NBC Universal Sports launched an online service whereby one could watch certain niche sports events through a PC. These events, such as the world track and field and ice hockey championships or certain cycling races such as the Giro d'Italia, are made available for a relatively small sum, giving access to those fans while earning some revenues for the web rightsholder (universalsports.com, 2010). With universal broadband a greater likelihood in the United States and abroad, this platform may become more prevalent in the next few years.

Although blogging has been utilized by millions, bloggers' goal is not necessarily a financial one. Bloggers have found an easy and often effective way to communicate their feelings and passions and have contributed to a "24/7" quality of sports commentary, placing greater strain on athletes, coaches, managers, teams, and leagues.

### Social Networking

Recently, the advent and ascension of social networking has provided exposure to players and coaches. A case in point involves the Kentucky head basketball coach John Calipari, who had over 1 million followers on Twitter and 138,000 fans on Facebook in 2010. The advantages of utilizing such networks in the Web 2.0 era means that he can connect and interact with fans more directly and personally. It also aided his philanthropic ventures, raising $1.3 million for the victims of the earthquake that ravaged Haiti in early 2010.

An example of the fund-raising potential was a promotion with a pizza chain in which customers entered a code so that $1 of each pizza purchase would go to Kentucky Children's Hospital, which received $63,000, said Dave Scott, who co-wrote Calipari's book, *Bounce Back: Overcoming Setbacks to Succeed in Business and in Life*. The promotion was used in every state; only 25 percent of the participants were from Kentucky (Evans, 2010).

However, professional leagues have attempted to control the time and content of tweets and other social website entries. In 2010, Major League Baseball banned MLB.com writers from tweeting about all non-baseball topics and criticized players for their Twitter usage in general (Gleeman, 2010). A year earlier, the NFL announced a policy to crack down on the use of Twitter by any players, coaches, and staff. However, less than one month later, it amended the policy to "allow players to use social media networks this season." It also announced that "players, coaches and football operations staff would be allowed to use social media up to 90 minutes prior to kickoff and after the game once traditional media interviews are complete" (MLD, 2009). On the collegiate level, in 2006 Kent State University banned Facebook after some students posted inappropriate pictures on it (Pollack, 2006). More recently, Texas Tech's head football coach, Mike Leach, banned the use of Twitter on the Texas Tech team.

---

### Ethical Issue: YouTube

YouTube is a service that permits easy uploading of user-generated content. Many YouTube videos are "home-made" and show individuals engaging in many activities. However, the ease of YouTube has resulted in claims of copyright infringement and litigation between media companies and Google (which bought YouTube in 2007). In the area of sports, much content—including highlights of major sports events—is available. Some of it comes from license agreements made between certain sports leagues, such as the NBA and NHL—but other content derives from individuals recording copyrighted events and uploading them for the world to see (Lynch, 2007). The issue of copyright infringement on YouTube was litigated before a federal trial court, which concluded that federal law immunizes the website from liability for infringing uploads (Viacom v. YouTube, 2010).

## The Future

Increasing the sources and types of revenue-enhancing deals will be a primary goal of the sports industry, and over the next five to ten years the maturity of what are now considered "new" avenues of distribution will likely have major effects on the dissemination of sports information. The evolution of mobile technology as an alternative programmer changes the way fans view their sports. Untethered from a computer or cable television, mobile users may become the primary audience in the next generation. In addition, the viewing public will utilize their PCs or Macs to watch what used to be called "television." Will this make broadcast television obsolete? Doubtful, but the days of millions sitting in front of a large-screen television at an appointed time may be in the past. Or may not.

The more traditional forms of program dissemination such as network television and traditional radio remain viable as they need marquee programming. For the networks, the NFL and Major League Baseball still bring a sizeable male demographic that few other broadcasts attract. And cable will remain a major player as well. The multiplicity of channels on cable continues to offer more exposure to niche sports such as cycling or lacrosse. The conversion of U.S. television receivers to digital receivers operating in a high-definition format, in the latter part of the first decade of this century, enhanced the experience of watching sports. With the advent of 3-D television, one wonders if that will be the next frontier of television. Of course, pitfalls exist. Not every promising technology becomes a commercial success. And format wars cause public confusion.

Finally, there is the sports viewing public. Will the day come when demand for sports information drops, resulting in decreases in rights fees among the networks, cable services, satellites, and Internet providers? Or will sports fans give up on sports and find other avenues of entertainment? Who knows?

### Information Check

When writing about media issues in sports, a journalist should determine:

1. Does a media, online, or mobile rights deal exist?
2. If so, how is it structured?
3. Is it a traditional rights-fee-oriented agreement?
4. If so, how and when is the compensation paid?
5. If the deal involves a sharing of profits, when and how are the profits to be shared?
6. Who controls the content?
7. When and how can these deals be terminated?
8. Do they have regional, national, or international application?

## A Short Summary of U.S. Media Rights Deals

(See Tables 13.1–13.7) (*Street and Smith's Sportsbusiness Journal*, 2009).

*Table 13.1* Major League Baseball

| | |
|---|---|
| Broadcast network television | Fox: $1.8 billion, seven-year deal through 2013 |
| Cable network television | ESPN: $2.37 billion, eight-year deal through 2013<br>TBS: $700 million, seven-year deal through 2013 |
| Satellite | DirecTV, Dish Network, iN Demand: seven-year deals through 2013 |
| In-house network | MLB Network (54 million subscribers as of 2010) |
| Radio (terrestrial) | ESPN Radio: $55 million, five-year deal through 2010 |
| Radio (satellite) | Sirius/XM: $650 million, eleven-year deal through 2015 |

*Table 13.2* NFL

| | |
|---|---|
| Broadcast network television | Fox: $5.76 billion, eight-year deal through 2013<br>CBS: $4.96 billion, eight-year deal through 2013<br>NBC: $4.82 billion, eight-year deal through 2013 |
| Cable network television | ESPN: $8.8 billion, eight-year deal through 2013 for *Monday Night Football* |
| Satellite | DirecTV: $4.0 billion, four-year deal through 2014 for exclusive *NFL Sunday Ticket* (offering out-of-market games) |
| In-house network | NFL Network (50 million subscribers, as of 2009) |
| Radio (terrestrial) | Westwood One: $30 million, two-year deal through 2010 |
| Radio (satellite) | Sirius/XM: $220 million, seven-year deal through 2010 |

Table 13.3 NBA

| | |
|---|---|
| Broadcast network television | ABC (part of a $7.44 billion, eight-year deal through 2015–16) |
| Cable network television | ESPN and TNT: $7.44 billion, eight-year deal through 2015–16 |
| Satellite | DirecTV |
| In-house network | NBA TV (45 million subscribers as of 2009) |
| Radio (terrestrial) | ESPN Radio (through 2015–16) |
| Radio (satellite) | Sirius/XM (through 2010) |

Table 13.4 NHL

| | |
|---|---|
| Broadcast network television | NBC (no rights fee—revenue share) through 2010–11 |
| Cable network television | Versus: $232.5 million deal through 2010–11 |
| Satellite | DirecTV |
| In-house network | NHL Network (30 million subscribers as of 2009) |
| Radio (terrestrial) | Westwood One |
| Radio (satellite) | Sirius/XM: $100 million, 10-year deal through 2015 |

Table 13.5 NASCAR

| | |
|---|---|
| Broadcast network television | Fox: $1.76 billion<br>ESPN/ABC: $2.16 billion<br>(Both part of an eight-year, $4.8 billion deal through 2014) |
| Cable network television | ESPN (see above)<br>TNT: $640–680 million, as part of an eight-year, $4.8 billion deal through 2014 |
| Satellite | TNT: Speed Channel through 2014 |
| In-house network | Speed Channel (74 million subscribers as of 2009) |
| Radio (terrestrial) | Through International Speedway Corporation |
| Radio (satellite) | Sirius/XM: five-year, $107.5 million deal through 2011 |

Table 13.6  NCAA

| | |
|---|---|
| Broadcast network television | Original deal—CBS: $6 billion deal through 2013 gives the network rights to sixty-six championships, including men's basketball. CBS can sublicense most rights to other carriers. Revised in 2010: CBS and Turner $10.8 billion (2011–2025) |
| Cable network television | ESPN: rights to twenty-two championships CBS College Sports: rights to a minimum of ten championships |
| Satellite | DirecTV |
| In-house network | None |
| Radio (terrestrial) | Westwood One (through sublease by CBS) |
| Radio (satellite) | None |

Table 13.7  Olympics

| | |
|---|---|
| Broadcast network television | NBC Universal: 2012 Games $1.18 billion. Includes all domestic media rights |
| Cable network television | NBC Universal |
| Satellite | None |
| Radio (terrestrial) | Westwood One (sublicensed by NBC) |
| Radio (satellite) | None |

# References

Albiniak, P. (2004, August 9). The name of Olympic promotion; NBC sets up gold-medal Olympics ad campaign to hype new season. *Broadcasting & Cable*, p. 4.

Anti-Cybersquatting Consumer Protection Act (ACPA) (1999), 15 USC 1125(d).

Associated Press (2008, September 5). Beijing TV coverage drew 4.7 billion viewers worldwide. Retrieved April 17, 2010, from http://sports.espn.go.com/oly/news/story?id=3571042

Beck, H. (2009, October 15). Bosh wins a legal ruling on case on domain names. *New York Times*. Retrieved May 2, 2010, from http://query.nytimes.com/gst/fullpage.html?res=9E07EFD6113EF936A25753C1A96F9C8B63

Clarke, M. M., & Seltzer, H. (2003, August 4). The big bucks behind the big leagues. *Broadcasting & Cable*, p. 10.

Evans, T. (2010, March 23). Facebook and Twitter keep Calipari ahead of the game. *New York Times*. Retrieved August 25, 2010, from http://www.nytimes.com/2010/03/24/sports/ncaabasketball/24calipari.html

Fatsis, S. (2003, January 31). NBC Sports maps a future without the big leagues. *Wall Street Journal*, sec. A, p. 1.

Gardyn, R. (2000, April). Putting the "World" in the World Series. *American Demographics*, p. 28.

Gleeman, A. (2010, April 27). Major League Baseball bans MLB.com writers from using Twitter for non-baseball topics. NBCSports.com. Retrieved May 10, 2010, from http://hardballtalk.nbcsports.com/2010/04/mlb-bans-all-beat-writers-from-using-twitter-for-non-baseball-topics.html.php

Gorman, B. (2010, May 18). Weekly cable primetime viewership. TV by the numbers. Retrieved August 25, 2010, from http://tvbythenumbers.com/2010/05/18/usa-leads-cable-primetime-viewership-tnt-skies-over-adults-18-49-ratings/51800

Gough, P. (2007, June 28). NBA's $7.4 billion TV deals boosted by new media. Reuters. Retrieved March 19, 2010, from http://www.reuters.com/article/idUSN2830146220070628

Gregory, S. (2009, September 10) With fewer sellouts, NFL's blackout rule under fire. Time.com. Retrieved March 18, 2010, from http://www.time.com/time/business/article/0,8599,1921401,00.html

Gross, A. (2004, May 23). TV deal a step back. *Journal News* (Westchester County, NY), p. 8C.

Grover, R. and Lowry, T. (2004, November 22). Rumble in regional sports. Businessweek.com. Retrieved May 7, 2010, from http://www.businessweek.com/magazine/content/04_47/b3909143_mz016.htm

Higgins, J. M., & Becker, A. (2004, November 1). Squeeze play; As pro teams launch their own sports networks, some hit it big, but many strike out. One loser: Fans. *Broadcasting and Cable*, p. 1.

ICANN.org (2009). Uniform Domain-Name Dispute-Resolution Policy. Retrieved May 2, 2010, from http://www.icann.org/en/udrp/udrp.htm

Johnston, T. (2010, Spring). Baseball doesn't strike out on the YES Network. *Stanford Business Review*. Retrieved May 16, 2010, from http://www.gsb.stanford.edu/news/bmag/sbsm2010/featureyestvbaseball.htm

Kazmierski, J. (n.d.). The truth about the LPGA and the PGA. Retrieved January 25, 2005, from http://www.langegolf.com/jkaz-article.html

Kumar, R. (2008) A project report on market research of color television. Retrieved May 16, 2010, from http://www.scribd.com/doc/12730665/-market-research-on-color-television.

Lynch, M. (2007, July 9). What's mine isn't yours: Sports, copyright and YouTube. *Medill Reports*. Retrieved May 5, 2010, from http://news.medill.northwestern.edu/chicago/news.aspx?id=40539

Mabin, C. (2006, January 11). Growing numbers of professional sports teams start own TV networks. *Kentucky New Era*. Retrieved April 20, 2010, from http://news.google.com/newspapers?nid=266&dat=20060111&id=vwUxAAAAIBAJ&sjid=l-AFAAAAIBAJ&pg=3346,811396

MacCambridge, M. (2004). *American's game* (pp. 67–70). New York: Random House.

Martzke, R. (2003, October 27). Fox has good, bad Series moments. *USA Today*. Retrieved May 11, 2010, from http://www.usatoday.com/sports/columnist/martzke/2003-10–26-martzke_x.htm

Mickle, T., & Ourand, J. (2010, March 1). IOC sets '14–16 media plan. *Street and Smith's Sportsbusiness Journal*, p. 01

MLB.com (2010). MLB.com "At Bat 2010." Retrieved May 1, 2010, from http://mlb.mlb.com/mobile/iphone/

MLD (2009, September 1). NFL's new Twitter policy: great for journalists, bad for players. Yahoo Sports. Retrieved May 10, 2010, from                http://sports.yahoo.com/nfl/blog/shutdown_corner/post/ NFL-s-new-Twitter-policy-great-for-journalists-?urn=nfl,186553

Mullen, L. (2004, July 19). Sirius aims for the stars, signing Brady, Madden and Hawk. *Street and Smith's Sportsbusiness Journal*. Retrieved April 26, 2010, from http://www.sportsbusinessjournal.com/article/39845

Mullin, B., Hardy, S., & Sutton, W. (2007). *Sports Marketing* (p. 371). Champaign, IL. Human Kinetics.

NASCAR.com (2008, March 4). Phone it in: Cup Series fits in your pocket. Retrieved May 1, 2010, from http://www.nascar.com/2008/news/headlines/official/03/04/sprint.mobile/

NBA.com (2007, June 27). NBA extends and expands partnerships. Retrieved April 25, 2010, from http://www.nba.com/news/nba_tv_extensions.html

NBA.com (2010). NBA game time. Retrieved May 1, 2010, from http://www.nba.com/mobile/

NCAA v. Board of Regents of the University of Oklahoma, 468 U.S. 85 (1984).

NFL.com (2010, April 1). NFL mobile kicks off with Verizon Wireless in April. Retrieved May 1, 2010, from http://www.nfl.com/draft/story?id=09000d5d8 1716d86&template=with-video&confirm=true

Noland, E., & Hoffarth, T. (1997, June 24). Murdoch plays to win; Fox sports; Major deals put Fox in forefront. *Los Angeles Daily News*, p. 1.

Ourand, J. (2009, November 9). What's ahead for league-owned networks. *Street and Smith's Sportsbusiness Journal*, p. 20.

Ourand, J., & Smith, M. (2008, August 18). CBS to pay SEC average of $55 million annually. *Street and Smith's Sportsbusiness Journal*, p. 4.

Ourand, J., & Smith, M. (2010, April 22). NCAA inks 14-year, $10.8 billion tournament rights deal with CBS/Turner. *Sportsbusiness Daily*. Retrieved, April 12, 2010, from http://www.sportsbusinessdaily.com/index.cfm?fuseaction=tdi.closingBell&tdiDate=2010-04-22

Pollack, P. (2006, June 26). Kent State bans student athletes from Facebook. *Ars Technica*. Retrieved May 10, 2010, from http://arstechnica.com/old/content/2006/06/7133.ars

Retransmission consent. 47 CFR 76.64 (2001).

Reynolds, M. (2010, March 1). NBC's final medal count: 190 million Olympic viewers. *Multichannel News*. Retrieved April 22, 2010, from http://www.multichannel.com/article/449441-NBC_s_Final_Medal_Count_190_Million_Olympic_Viewers.php

Sandomir, R. (2007, August 3). Yankees YES Network stake not for sale. *New York Times*. Retrieved May 4, 2010, from http://www.nytimes.com/2007/08/03/sports/baseball/03yes.html?_r=1

Schaaf, P. (2004). *Sports, Inc.: 100 years of sports business* (p. 13). Amherst, NY: Prometheus Books.

Shapiro, L., & Maske, M. (2005, April 19). "Monday Night Football" changes the channel; After 35 years on ABC, ESPN will take over in 2006. *Washington Post*, p. A01.

Signal carriage obligations. 47 CFR 76.56 (2007).

Smith, A. (2010, January 6). Super Bowl ads are going, going . . . Cnnmoney.com. Retrieved March 19, 2010, from http://money.cnn.com/2010/01/07/news/companies/super_bowl_ads/

Sports Broadcasting Act of 1961. 15 USC, sec. 1291, 1293 (2009).

Sportsbusinessnews.com (2006, July 13). Going inside MLB's latest $3 billion TV agreements. Retrieved April 29, 2010, from http://www.sportsbusinessnews.com/_news/news_347260.php

Stevens, T. (2007, Nov. 14). 82% of Americans own cell phones. Switched.com. Retrieved May 1, 2010, from http://www.switched.com/2007/11/14/82-of-americans-own-cell-phones/

Stewart, L. (2004, December 1). Dodgers headed to KCAL. *Los Angeles Times.* Retrieved April 15, 2010, from http://articles.latimes.com/2004/dec/01/sports/sp-nwbox1

*Street and Smith's Sportsbusiness Journal.* (2009, November 9). U.S. media rights deals, p. 18.

Universalsports.com (2010). NBC/Universal Sports Online. Retrieved May 6, 2010, from http://www.universalsports.com/index.html

U.S. v. National Football League, 116 F.Supp. 319 (D.C.Pa., 1953).

Vancouver2010.com (2010, February 28). The Vancouver 2010 Olympic Winter Games: By the numbers. Retrieved May 11, 2010, from http://www.vancouver2010.com/olympic-news/n/news/the-vancouver-2010-olympic-winter-games-by-the-numbers_297556Ko.html

Viacom v. YouTube 2010 U.S. Dist. LEXIS 62829 (SDNY, 2010).

Vilkomerson, S. (2006, November 19). Knickleheads. *New York Observer.* Retrieved August 26, 2010, from http://www.observer.com/node/36289

Ward, G. C. (2004). *Unforgivable blackness: The rise and fall of Jack Johnson* (p. 229). New York: Knopf.

# Glossary

**Agents**—See *Sports agents.*

**Amateur Athletic Union (AAU)**—Nonprofit organization dedicated exclusively to the promotion and development of amateur sports and physical fitness programs. At one time, it was the predominant amateur sports organization in the United States.

**Amateur Sports Act**—See *Ted Stevens Olympic and Amateur Sports Act.*

**American Arbitration Association (AAA)**—Founded in 1926, the AAA is the largest provider of alternative dispute resolution services in the United States. The organization offers mediation, arbitration, and other out-of-court settlement procedures. It often adjudicates and arbitrates sports disputes.

**American Basketball Association (ABA)**—A rival league to the NBA, which operated from 1967 to 1976. Four ABA teams—the San Antonio Spurs, New York Nets, Denver Nuggets, and Indiana Pacers—joined the NBA, along with the ABA's star players.

**American Football League (AFL)**—A professional league that operated from 1960 to 1969 as a rival to the NFL. The AFL successfully challenged the NFL's supremacy, prompting a merger of the NFL and the AFL in 1970. The AFL kept all of its teams and became the American Football Conference (AFC).

**Americans with Disabilities Act of 1990**—A 1990 law that prohibits discrimination against people with disabilities in employment, in public services, in public accommodations, and in telecommunications. In the area of sports, it has been utilized in primary and secondary school cases and in stadium design issues. The most famous ADA case involving sports is the Supreme Court's 2001 ruling permitting the golfer Casey Martin to use a cart while competing.

**Anabolic steroids**—Drugs that enhance muscle development, which allows athletes to train harder and recover more quickly from strenuous workouts. They are considered "performance-enhancing" substances.

**Appearance fee**—A payment made to an athlete to participate in an event. Allowed in certain individual sports, in an attempt to attract public interest to an event, organizers often pay notable athletes to participate in the event.

**Arbitration**—See *Salary arbitration* or *Grievance arbitration.*

**Assumption of risk**—An important defense to a negligence claim, in the sports context. It applies to a situation in which the defendant voluntarily exposed himself or herself to a known and appreciated danger. Getting hurt when tackled in a football game is an assumption of risk. Often this defense is part of a waiver of liability in a contract.

**ATP Tour**—The organization governing men's professional tennis.

**Bonds**—A debt security issued by a private corporation or a governmental subdivision. In sports, bonds are used as a means of financing new stadiums and arenas. Several important types of bonds exist:

*General obligation bonds:* Securities used for government financing, for which the debt is repaid from the government's general tax revenue.

*Lease revenue bonds:* Bonds issued by a governmental authority separate from the actual government. The bonds are issued as part of a lease agreement between the authority and the government, which leases the facility from the authority and then subleases it back to that very authority.

*Revenue bonds:* Securities used for government financing, for which the debt is repaid from special taxes that are passed or from the revenue of the stadium that the government financed with the bonds.

*Special tax bonds:* Securities used for government financing, for which the debt is repaid only from specific tax revenues.

*Stadium investment bonds:* When a team owner seeks private financing to build a stadium, in which the stadium itself is the backing for the loan; that is, the loan is secured by the stadium.

**Clayton Act of 1914**—Supplemental legislation to the better-known Sherman Antitrust Act of 1890. With regard to sports, the Clayton Act excludes labor unions from Sherman Act enforcement. Workers may form "combinations" (unions) that arguably may restrain trade by virtue of their labor agreements with management. The act legalized peaceful strikes, picketing, and boycotts by unions.

**Collective bargaining agreement (CBA)**—An agreement between a sports league and its players' association that governs the terms and conditions of the players' employment with the league.

**Comparative negligence**—A modern version of contributory negligence, whereby juries apportion liability among the parties, and a plaintiff's award is reduced by the percentage of fault that the plaintiff exhibited.

**Contributory negligence**—A traditional defense to negligence. If the plaintiff has contributed to his or her own injury, he or she is barred from recovering damages.

**Copyright**—A copyright involves the right of an author to control the communication of an "original work of authorship, fixed in a tangible medium." This definition imposes three requirements: the work must be original, an expression of an idea or thought, and presented in a fixed medium.

**Court of Arbitration for Sport (CAS)**—An independent institution created in 1983 to settle sports-related disputes. The CAS is under the administrative and financial authority of the International Council of Arbitration for Sport (ICAS) and is divided into two divisions, the Ordinary Arbitration Division (OAD) and the Appeals Arbitration Division (AAD). The OAD resolves disputes arising from all types of legal relations between parties, such as contracts for television rights or a simple sponsorship. The AAD resolves disputes arising from "last-instance decisions" taken by the tribunals of sports organizations, federations, or associations when the regulations or statutes of these bodies (or a private agreement) require the CAS to have jurisdiction.

**Defamation**—A false communication, either orally stated or in writing, that injures another's reputation or good name.

**Early bird exception**—An exception to the NBA salary cap allowing a team to re-sign its own free agent at a salary that is the larger of 175 percent of the player's salary in the prior season or, when the player has played for the team for some or all of each of the prior two consecutive seasons, the average of his salary. If this exception is utilized, the player must be signed for at least two more seasons.

**Eminent domain**—The right of a state or locality to seize private property for "public purposes." Accompanying that governmental seizure of property is the requirement that the prior owner of the property be fairly compensated. Many states have mechanisms to attempt to find the correct level of compensation. This is important, because the right to be compensated for an expropriation of property is guaranteed by the Fifth Amendment to the U.S. Constitution, as well as by many state constitutions. Eminent domain has been used in clearing land for building new stadiums and arenas, if public funds are used and some public benefit is found.

**Escalator clause**—A clause in a player's contract rewarding the player for extraordinary performance by automatically raising the value of the player's contract.

**Expansion franchise**—The addition of a new team within a sports league.

**Federation Internationale de Natation Amateur (FINA)**—The organization in charge of competitive swimming, water polo, diving, and synchronized swimming on the international level. The organization's members are the national governing bodies governing aquatic sports in each country.

**Fiduciary**—Relating to the circumstance in which, because of a special relationship, such as agency, one party must act with a high degree of loyalty and good faith, taking the interests of the client at all times. Sports agents and financial advisors must act in a fiduciary capacity for their clients.

**Free agency**—The ability of a professional athlete to freely negotiate a contract to play for any team.

**Grievance arbitration**—A process, usually prescribed in a labor agreement, stipulating that certain problems that arise out of a labor relationship emanating from an interpretation or misinterpretation of the player's contract be settled by an independent party. With a grievance arbitration clause in a contract, the claim must be handled through an independent arbitrator.

**Group licensing**—A standard licensing agreement that applies to all professional teams within a league for licensing the use of teams' names, logos, symbols, emblems, signs, uniforms, and identification of the member clubs. This type of licensing also can apply to players and is often controlled by the players' unions.

**Intentional torts**—A tort that is committed with the intent or desire to commit the act. In sports, an example would be an assault and battery.

**International athletic federations**—The chief governing bodies of particular sports that compete internationally. Responsibilities include conducting international competitions, detailing eligibility rules, choosing judges and referees, and resolving technical issues in their sports. These organizations are subject only to the limitations of the Olympic charter.

**International Olympic Committee (IOC)**—The organization responsible for organizing the Olympic Games. The IOC has the ultimate authority in deciding where each Games will be held and derives most of its funding from broadcast rights and the sale of Olympic memorabilia and merchandise.

**International Skating Union (ISU)**—The organization that governs international standards for skating. The organization is responsible for setting eligibility requirements for participants and for scoring systems.

**Ladies Professional Golf Association (LPGA)**—Founded in 1950, the LPGA is the organization governing women's professional golf. The not-for-profit organization sponsors thirty-three events under the LPGA Tour.

**Larry Bird Exception**—An exception to the NBA salary cap allowing a team to re-sign its own free agent for an amount not exceeding the league's maximum player salary as long as that player has played for the team for some or all of each of the prior three consecutive years.

**Licensing agreement**—A contract in which a *licensor* grants a *licensee* permission to use his/her property for a specific purpose. In sports, the term is usually applied to trademark license agreements involving property such as team and league logos.

**Liquidated damages**—A reasonable estimation of damages after one of the contracting parties breaches a contract.

**Lockout**—The employer counterpart of a strike. In a lockout, the employer prevents the players from working in an effort to gain a better bargaining position in labor negotiations. A lockout may occur upon the expiration of a collective bargaining agreement.

**Loyalty clause**—A clause in a player's contract which allows the team to withhold specified types of compensation if the player breaches his obligation of loyalty to the club.

**Luxury tax**—A tax imposed on portions of a team's payroll that exceeds set thresholds, with the excess funds being used for designated items, such as, in Major League Baseball, player benefits and an industry growth fund.

**Major League Baseball (MLB)**—The organization controlling elite professional baseball in the United States and Canada, created through the merger of the National League and the American League in 1903. For years, both leagues operated with considerable autonomy. Each had its own league president. In recent years, this power has been limited as the two leagues have lost some of their independence.

**Major League Baseball Players' Association (MLBPA)**—Players' union for Major League Baseball.

**Major League Baseball Properties (MLBP)**—The organization that holds the exclusive trademark and licensing rights for Major League Baseball and oversees the marketing and protection of individual trademarks and products.

**Major League Soccer (MLS)**—A league representing professional soccer in the United States. MLS's structure is closer to a "single-entity" league than the traditional model favored by the NFL, NBA, NHL, and Major League Baseball.

**Masking agents**—A substance that will cover or hide the presence of performance-enhancing substances in an athlete's system.

**Naming rights**—The right to name a stadium for a stipulated term and fee. Such rights are an important source of revenue for stadium owners.

**National Basketball Association (NBA)**—The predominant league for professional male basketball players in North America. Founded in 1947, it has thirty teams.

**National Basketball Players' Association (NBPA)**—Players' union for National Basketball Association.

**National Collegiate Athletic Association (NCAA)**—The governing body that regulates eligibility requirements, recruiting practices, and sports competitions of the over 1200 member institutions that offer collegiate sports.

**National Football League (NFL)**—The premium league of American professional football. Founded in 1920, its prestige increased in the 1960s. It merged with its rival, the AFL, in 1970, creating the present structure. Presently, thirty-two teams compete in the NFL.

**National Football League Players' Association (NFLPA)**—Players' union for the National Football League.

**National governing bodies (NGBs)**—Organizations in charge of running a particular sport in a given country. It is the responsibility of an NGB to set eligibility standards for participation in the sport. NGBs must abide by the rules of their international federations.

**National Hockey League (NHL)**—A North American league of professional hockey players. Founded in 1917, it expanded from six teams in the 1960s to thirty teams presently.

**National Hockey League Players' Association (NHLPA)**—Players' union for the National Hockey League.

**National Labor Relations Act (NLRA)**—Law that sets the structure of labor relations in the United States. It allows workers to form unions, engage in collective bargaining, and strike.

**National Labor Relations Board (NLRB)**—The federal agency that administers the National Labor Relations Act. This board is responsible for sanctioning those who participate in unfair labor practices.

**National Olympic committee (NOC)**—A committee in each Olympic participating country that is the sole authority responsible for the representation of that country at the Olympic Games, as well as at other events held under the patronage of the IOC.

**NBA Properties, Inc. (NBAP)**—The organization that holds the exclusive trademark and licensing rights for the NBA and oversees the marketing and protection of individual trademarks and products.

**Negligence**—A tort involving fault, not intention, defined as a standard of care that is less than what another reasonably prudent person would have exercised in a similar situation. In sports, negligence cases may be brought against supervisory personnel who failed to utilize safety procedures adequately.

**NFL Properties (NFLP)**—The organization that holds the exclusive trademark and licensing rights for the NFL and oversees the marketing and protection of individual trademarks and products.

**Nonstatutory labor exemption**—A legal doctrine that serves as an exemption to the antitrust laws. Essentially, any union–management agreement that was a product of good faith negotiation will receive protection from the antitrust laws. That means that the provisions of the agreement cannot be attacked as collusive or anticompetitive.

**Personal seating license**—A one-time fee paid for interested ticket holders to hold a permanent seat at a stadium, usually a newly constructed facility.

**PLAYERS, INC.**—A subsidiary of the NFLPA that handles the marketing and licensing of player names and images.

**Professional Golfers Association (PGA) Tour**—A tax-exempt group of professional golfers who play in more that 100 tournaments on three tours: the PGA Tour, Champions Tour, and Nationwide Tour.

**Recklessness**—Conduct that is not intentional, but does foresee the possibility of harm, and carried out even though the actor is aware of that risk of harm. If a hockey player high-sticks another player, who falls on the ice with a massive concussion, the act of high-sticking could be deemed "reckless."

**Reserve clause**—A clause in player contracts that generally allows the team to retain a player for the next season, provided a minimum salary is met, when the player and the team cannot agree on the terms of a new contract.

**Right of publicity**—A right that is grounded in one's right to privacy. It allows a person to protect and control the use of his or her identity for commercial purposes.

**Rights fees**—A fee associated with the right to broadcast a specific sporting event.

**"Rozelle rule"**—A requirement imposed in the NFL that requires a team signing a free agent to provide fair and equitable compensation to the team losing that player. The rule was included in the league's first collective bargaining agreement in 1968.

**Salary arbitration**—A settlement method to resolve salary disputes between a team and a player frequently included in collective bargaining agreements. A neutral arbitrator or group of arbitrators renders a decision as to the compensation of the player based on figures submitted by the owner and the player and accompanying evidence of a player's performance, ability, and leadership. The arbitrator's decision is usually binding.

**Salary cap**—An annual limit imposed on a professional sports team on the total salary it can pay its players. Salary caps vary and often have important exemptions, such as the Larry Bird Exemption in the NBA. Presently, the NBA and NHL utilize salary cap systems.

**Seating license**—See *Personal seating license*.

**Sherman Antitrust Act of 1890**—A law, based on Congress's power to regulate interstate commerce, making illegal every contract, combination, or conspiracy in restraint of interstate and foreign trade.

**Sports Agent and Responsibility Trust Act (SPARTA)**—A federal statute prohibiting sports agents from signing student-athletes into representational contracts with bribes or misleading information.

SPARTA provides a uniform standard for prosecuting agents who choose to ignore NCAA rules and state law.

**Sports agents (athlete agents)**—Professionals, often lawyers and accountants, who represent professional athletes in negotiating player contracts, endorsement deals, and sometimes in personal finance.

**Sports Broadcasting Act of 1961**—An act permitting certain joint broadcasting agreements among the major professional sports. It permits the sale of a television "package" to the network or networks, a procedure that is common today. The law has been interpreted to include the so-called "blackout rules" that protect a home team from competing games broadcast into its home territory on a day when it is playing a game at home.

**Standard Player Agent Contract**—A standard contract that players sign with their agents. It sets out the scope of the agent's responsibilities as well as the terms of compensation. The players' associations in most of the major sports often limit the fees charged by agents for their work in negotiated contracts with professional teams. Contracts with endorsement companies are not limited.

**Student-athlete**—Usually refers to an amateur high school or college athlete. Under NCAA rules, student-athletes are restricted in accepting payments for their athletic services and cannot sign professional contracts with teams or agents.

**Ted Stevens Olympic and Amateur Sports Act (Amateur Sports Act of 1978)**—A federal law mandating that the responsibility for coordinating all Olympic athletic activity is vested in the United States Olympic Committee. It also directs the United States Olympic Committee to encourage and provide assistance to amateur athletic programs and competition for handicapped individuals.

**Title VII of the Civil Rights Act of 1964**—A federal law prohibiting discrimination in employment based on race, color, religion, sex, or national origin.

**Title IX of the Education Amendments of 1972**—A federal law prohibiting discrimination on the basis of sex in any federally funded education program or activity. Title IX has led to a major increase in the number of women competing in collegiate sports over the last thirty years.

**Tort**—Any civil wrong, excluding a breach of contract, in which a plaintiff would be entitled to remedies, most commonly monetary damages. Examples of torts are assault, negligence, and product liability.

**Trademark**—Defined as "any word, name, symbol or device or any combination thereof adopted and used by a manufacturer to identify his goods and distinguish them from those manufactured or sold by others." A trademark may include the teams', leagues', and unions' names, logos, symbols, emblems, designs, uniforms, likenesses, and visual representations.

**Trademark infringement**—An unauthorized use of the trademark, defined as "the reproduction, counterfeiting, copying, or imitation, in commerce, of a registered mark in connection with the sale, offering for sale, distribution, or advertising of any goods or services on or in connection with which such use is likely to cause confusion among consumers as to the source or origin of the goods sold." The offender is subject to liability, by damages and/or injunctive relief.

**United States Anti-Doping Agency (USADA)**—The official antidoping agency governing Olympic sports in the United States. The organization's mission is to eliminate the practice of doping in sports.

**United States Football League (USFL)**—A rival football league to the NFL that functioned from 1983 to 1985. Claiming that the NFL engaged in anticompetitive practices to hurt the USFL, the new league instituted a lawsuit against the NFL. After a highly publicized trial, the USFL won a total award of $1 in damages. Facing $160 million in debt, it folded shortly afterward.

**United States Olympic Committee (USOC)**—The U.S. national Olympic committee, having exclusive jurisdiction over all matters pertaining to U.S. participation in the Olympic Games, and the ultimate authority with respect to United States representation in the Olympic Games.

**U.S. Figure Skating (USFS)**—The national governing body in the United States for figure skating. The USFS is responsible for creating rules and for organizing and sponsoring competitions for the purpose of increasing interest in the sport.

**US Speed Skating Association**—The national governing body in the United States for speed skating.

**Vicarious liability**—Liability of a supervisory party for the actions of its subordinate. Usually applied in an employer/employee relationship.

**Women's National Basketball Association (WNBA)**—A professional women's basketball league based in the United States. Founded in 1997, the league, originally a single-entity league, moved to an owner-based format in 2002. Presently, it has thirteen teams.

**World Anti-Doping Agency (WADA)**—An independent organization overseeing and monitoring compliance of the World Anti-Doping Code. Most international sports federations, as well as the International Olympic Committee, accept WADA's jurisdiction.

**World Hockey Association (WHA)**—A rival league to the NHL founded in 1972. In 1979 the NHL absorbed four of its teams: the Quebec Nordiques, Winnipeg Jets, Edmonton Oilers, and New England Whalers.

# Author Index

# Subject Index